Accession no.
36198970

KU-302-578

Body, Movement, and Culture

WITHDRAWN

University of Pennsylvania Press
SERIES IN CONTEMPORARY ETHNOGRAPHY

Dan Rose and Paul Stoller
General Editors

A complete listing of the books in this series appears at the back of this volume.

Body, Movement, and Culture

Kinesthetic and Visual Symbolism in a Philippine Community

Sally Ann Ness

LIS LIBRARY

Date	Fund
28.3.14	d-che

Order No
2uS368x

University of Chester

UNIVERSITY OF PENNSYLVANIA PRESS   Philadelphia

Copyright © 1992 by the University of Pennsylvania Press
All rights reserved

Printed in the United States of America

The author gratefully acknowledges Ablex Publishing Corporation for allowing portions of the article, "The Latent Meaning of a Dance: The Cebuano Sinulog as a Model of Social Interaction" (in *Communication and Culture: Language, Performance, Technology, and Media. Selected Proceedings from the Sixth International Conference on Culture and Communication, Temple University, 1986*, eds. Sari Thomas and William A. Evans, pp. 128–33 [Norwood, N.J.: Ablex Publishing Corporation, 1990]) to be reprinted in this volume.

Library of Congress Cataloging-in-Publication Data

Ness, Sally Ann.
    Body, movement, and culture: kinesthetic and visual symbolism in a Philippine community / Sally Ann Ness.
        p.   cm. — (University of Pennsylvania Press series in contemporary ethnography)
    Includes bibliographical references (p.   ) and index.
    ISBN 0-8122-3110-4 (cloth). — ISBN 0-8122-1383-1 (paper)
    1. Sinulog (Dance).   2. Folk dancing—Social aspects—Philippines—Cebu City—Case studies.   3. Choreography—Social aspects—Philippines—Cebu City—Case studies.   I. Title.   II. Series: Series in contemporary ethnography.
GV1796.S57N47   1992
793.3'19599—dc20   92-15310
                                                                        CIP

For Marc, who lived through it all,
and made it possible.

And for my parents and sisters,
for their trust and their love.

Contents

Illustrations   ix
Acknowledgments   xi
A Note about Pseudonyms   xiii

1. Ethnography and Choreography   1

2. Troubled Times   18

3. Views from the Swimming Pool   23

4. The Looks of the City   33

5. The Niño   58

6. The *Tindera Sinulog*   86

7. Customers and Performers   98

8. Latent Symbolism in the *Tindera Sinulog*   117

9. The Troupe *Sinulog*   132

10. Historical Development of the Troupe *Sinulog*   154

11. The Parade *Sinulog*   177

viii   **Contents**

12. The Symbolism of Desired Recognition   199

13. The Resilience of the *Sinulog*   219

Notes   235
References   273
Index   287

Illustrations

4.1. The Philippines.   34

4.2. Cebu Island.   35

4.3. Cebu City.   37

5.1. The Santo Niño.   61

6.1. *Tindera* performing *sinulog* in front of the basilica entrance.   88

7.1. *Tindera* offering candles for sale.   103

8.1. Two cadets at *sinulog* parade displaying typical contact behavior.   123

9.1. Diagram of column formation used in troupe *sinulog paso* choreography.   136

9.2. Diagram of stepping figure used in troupe *sinulog paso* choreography.   137

9.3. Diagram of curvilinear stepping figure used in troupe *sinulog sayaw* choreography.   142

9.4. Diagram of column interweaving figure used in troupe *sinulog sayaw* choreography.   143

9.5. *Tukod sa espada* (arch of swords) formation.   145

9.6. Diagram of troupe *sinulog estocada* stepping pathway
for *Pit Señor* sequence.   147

9.7. Diagram of spiraling *estocada* trio and column
formation.   148

9.8. Diagram of *estocada* rotation pattern for trio section.   149

9.9. *Estocada* trio demonstration.   150

11.1. Map of 1985 *sinulog* parade route.   178

11.2. A parade contingent dressed in "Visayan style" and
using authenticated gestures and props.   189

11.3. A parade contingent dressed in Mardi Gras or
"*Ati-atihan*" style.   195

12.1.–5. Floor patterns used in the parade *sinulog*.   201

12.6. A bas-relief of the Santo Niño located over the main
entrance of the basilica shows characteristic "incipient
baroque" curvilinear decorative designs.   206

12.7. Parade contingent dressed in "Muslim style" and
using "Muslim-style" gestures.   211

13.1. Parade dancer manipulating a Santo Niño image in
the "*itsaitsa*" style.   229

Acknowledgments

Many individuals and agencies have made valued contributions to this work. Special thanks are due to Resil B. Mojares and the staff of the Cebuano Studies Center at the University of San Carlos, Cebu City, Philippines, for their invaluable assistance during the fieldwork phase of the research project. Thanks are also due to the staff of the Institute of Philippine Culture at Ateneo de Manila University for their assistance and cooperation. It is not possible to mention all those in the Philippines who gave generously of their time and attention in support of the fieldwork process. Among the many who deserve acknowledgment, however, I would like to thank Carmen Baugbug, Mary Jane Calderon, Erlinda and René Alburo, Dolores Suzaro, Josephina Gonzaga, Lawrence Liao, Fe Susan Go, Delia Villacastin, Sydney Silliman, and Thavanh Svengsouk and the staff of the Cebu City U.S.I.S. for their assistance and support.

Acknowledgment is also due to Linda McMannis, who provided the English translations of *sinulog* lyrics. The maps and diagrams were drafted by Linda Bobbitt at the University of California, Riverside. All of the photographs used as illustrations were taken by Marc Ness.

I would also like to acknowledge my debt to Jean-Paul Dumont, Carol Eastman, John R. Atkins, Simon Ottenberg, E. V. Daniel, Michael Cullinane, Gayl Ness, and Peggy Hackney for their scholarly advice and guidance throughout the doctoral and postdoctoral writing phases of the research. My sincere thanks are also due to the members of the Music Department at St. Lawrence University, who listened to tapes of *sinulog* music and provided helpful commentary and analysis, and to Certified Movement Analysts Pamela Schick and Sandra Kurtz, who volunteered their time to act as consultants viewing videotapes of the *sinulog* performances. I am very grateful as well to Carol Bloodworth, Phil Huston, Veronica Kann, Kathleen Adams, and Susan Rose, all of whom were most helpful in reading drafts and making useful comments and suggestions. To Susan Leigh Foster, without whom this text would have been neither undertaken nor completed, I remain deeply grateful for her sincere and invaluable support. To editor Patricia Smith, whose patience and encouragement have also been essential in bringing this project to a successful conclusion, my most sincere thanks as well.

This research was made possible by a 1983 National Science Graduate Fellowship Award, a 1985 Charlotte Newcombe Fellowship, and a 1991 National Endowment for the Humanities Summer Stipend Award.

A Note about Pseudonyms

With the few exceptions listed below, pseudonyms have been used for all of the individuals mentioned specifically, either by nickname, by first name, or by full name, in the text. The well-known figures, "Cacoy" Cañete and "Pitang" Diola, whose views and life accomplishments already have been published elsewhere, have not been given pseudonyms. Neither have pseudonyms been used for individuals whose statements mentioned in the text were published elsewhere: historian Resil Mojares, columnist Manuel Satorre, mayors Ronald Duterte and Florentino Solon, and the basilica rector, Father Galinde.

Chapter 1
Ethnography and Choreography

Sinulog

Imagine gentle currents of energy, flowing freely through and beyond your body, forming warm pools of movement in the space just
around you. Your hands are brought to life in this softly pulsing current. They wave around in the watery space, leaving invisible traces
of their movement hanging in the air. The current spreads down into
your legs, which begin to bear your body's weight alternately, subtly
shifting your body from side to side through the liquid space in a
slight sway. Your knees become involved, bending alternately as they
adjust for the arrival and departure of your body's weight.

Unless its pulses are so gentle that they die away within your body's
center, the resilient current will eventually reach through to your feet,
which balance, each in turn, your swaying body. You step lightly, as
though you walk, or perhaps softly jog, upon a smooth surface of
silken pillows filled with sand. Your dance continues for a timeless
interval, until the current dies away.

This brief reverie recounts one impression of a practice called "*sinulog*," a ritual dance performed throughout the Central Philippines. In
Cebu City, the second largest city in the Philippines, and the site
where the observation that inspired the above description actually
took place, the face of a child beams down upon this performance. It
is the child's tender expression that is said to call forth the mild flood
of emotion from deep within the dancer's body and animate the
dance. This child is known as the Santo Niño de Cebu, an image of
Jesus as Boy King. The figure of the Santo Niño is venerated as the
Almighty and Most Merciful Defender of the Cebuano people.

The currents of movement inspired by the Santo Niño de Cebu had taken several forms in Cebu City when I encountered its *sinulog* dancing in 1984 and 1985. They had manifested as individualistic improvisations similar in appearance to the body movement process described above. They had also manifested as rehearsed group dances that presented theatrical narrative structures and abstract collective dance figures. In 1980 and 1981, they also became the focus of elaborate civic celebrations, which achieved national and international recognition for the city. These latter events generated large-scale competitive exhibition dances performed by thousands of volunteers from all over the region. Yet the various performances of the Cebu City *sinulog* all retained a certain choreographic common ground that created, to a limited extent, similar physical and mental experiences for their participants. Regardless of their differences, the performances all were viewed as generally "the same dance," as variants of a single phenomenon, "the" *sinulog*.

Why did this particular movement experience endure and even flourish in Cebu City's social context? What was the source of the dance's many levels of resilience? In sum, what ordinary and/or extraordinary meaning did the *sinulog* choreographic practices possess for their neocolonial culture bearers? These are the central questions of this study. Their answers lie in understanding Cebu City's "cultural predicament," and in understanding the forms of symbolism that can operate in choreographic phenomena.[1]

Beginning

To fully comprehend what the act of performing a choreographed movement can mean in an "other" culture—that is to say, in a society whose organizing principles, social institutions, and value systems are profoundly unfamiliar or exotic relative to one's own—a person must have some idea of what performing any choreographed movement can mean at all. There must be some appreciation of how getting oneself physically through a choreographic moment can affect a human being, and how it can affect one's own cultural understanding.

Dance is, for some powerful reasons, the most shallowly interpreted art form in the contemporary United States. It is a stigmatized art form, whose practitioners are given only a marginal economic, intellectual, and political place in U.S. society.[2] From the standpoint of political economy, choreographing human movement can be considered a radically "unproductive" activity—having no material result—and can be difficult to commodify and mass produce as a participatory experience. This makes the enterprise of choreography itself distinctly unsuitable for playing an integral role in a consumer-oriented society.[3] It should come as no surprise, therefore, that in contemporary U.S. society there is no widespread popular understanding of why the art of performing or designing choreographed movement might become the central focus of a normal person's life. There is no widespread appreciation of what the process of mastering a choreographic experience can mean to an ordinary culture bearer.

The following short essays that make up the rest of this introduction are drawn from experiences both in the United States and in the Philippines. They are intended to introduce the reader to the kind of meaning the performance of choreographed movement can acquire for a person whose life has always been centered around the art forms of "Western" theatrical dance. This is a kind of meaning different from that most historians, political scientists, economists, and other social scientists have studied and valued, for it is meaning that develops in relation to essentially creative or *originative* figures of thought and action. It is meaning that must emerge from personal and subjective reflection, and in an attuning to the moment-to-moment experience of being physically alive. Yet, this is a kind of meaning that also has a cultural basis and relevance. It is as a student of this kind of meaning that my ethnographic voice has developed—a voice that speaks from a specific, fairly exotic, subcultural margin within contemporary U.S. society, and from a marginal vantage point within the discipline of anthropology as well.[4]

In all of my ethnographic interactions with the inhabitants of Cebu City, I was initiating, responding, and interpreting information as would a performing student of choreographic phenomena. As a student of such movement experiences I came to know and to "bear" my own culture, having been involved more or less continuously in this pursuit since early childhood. It was as such a student that I also came to appreciate the culture bearers of Cebu City. My process of physical, subjective, and dynamic attunement to choreographic phenomena is what I seek to expose and illustrate, toward the end of creating a shared voice for readers who may wish to discover in the rest of this text something new, both about an "other" culture and about their own. In Paul Stoller's words, I invite the reader here to "dwell within" me as I walk along my solitary path in a foreign cultural field—a field of dances, both familiar and strange.[5]

The Choreographic Figure

In Seattle, in the late 1970s, I once learned a short section of a modern dance masterwork entitled "For Betty." Choreographed by Bill Evans, one of America's leading dance artists, "For Betty" consisted of a suite of non-narrative dances performed to music by Bach. The section I learned, taught to me in a repertory class by a member of the Bill Evans Dance Company then performing the work, explored two-dimensional, planal shapes and transitions. The section was about cycling, about changing from one kind of cycle into another, about becoming a curve.

In the first breath phrase of the section, I learned to scoop the air behind me with my right arm and bring that armful all the way over my head so as to release it and let it fall down in front of me. This scooping circle, I learned, had to be seen as the echo of a circling movement that began in the hip joints—a movement like those used to keep a Hula-Hoop in action. The horizontal pelvic cycle translated into the wheeling cycle of the arm, as though the arm was somehow the Hula-Hoop that was kept in motion. The challenge of this phrase lay in transforming a posture into a gesture with complete smoothness, without a single detectable "hitch" or moment of disconnection ever becoming visible in the transferring of energy between the torso and the limb. The class was to practice this movement for over an hour, three times a week for six weeks, perfecting its smoothness.

Who was this "I" that learned the dance? Initially, the person learning "For Betty" was the "I" of ordinary life, a being that rode the city buses daily up and down Seattle's steep hills and lived in a run-down college dormitory in its marginally safe Central District. This "I" performed such everyday actions as folding bathroom towels and straightening bed sheets, buying groceries at local health food coops, and drinking innumerable cups of Seattle's famous everyday coffee from the heavy mugs and cups of its many coffeehouses. This person who entered the studio of the repertory class was an "I" that had emerged from a certain habitual posture, a daily "Seattlite" posture so well practiced that it no longer needed to be mindful of the relationships between its major bodily members. This was an "I" that lived mainly in its visual and aural imagination and memory, up "inside" its head. It possessed an arm, which served "me" throughout the ordinary courses of the day, lifting mugs, holding books, clutching bags, and so forth. However, in the process of acquiring the choreography, this normal "I" that had started out to learn the movement turned out to be inappropriate for the task.

There is something essentially anthropological about choreographic phenomena. A dimension of human experience becomes more vividly accessible, more available to representation and study than in perhaps any other form of symbolic action. This dimension might be formally referred to as the dynamic mentality of one's neuromusculature. No one can acquire a choreographed movement skillfully, artfully, without keeping an open mind—literally, an "opening" mind. Nobody, "no-*body*," can learn an unfamiliar neuromuscular pattern without being willing to acquire a new and perhaps startling insight into who it is they actually are—that is to say, a truly plural being or figure. In Martha Graham's well-known terms, the physical organism must be *serviced* by its own intentions—by its Self—in order to execute a choreographed movement. The integrating of "I" emerges and becomes observable in this process of dancing, even in the mastery of one short breath phrase.

The choreography of this section of "For Betty" was designed so that the arm of the dancer had to re-attune itself continuously to the undulating shift of weight in the torso, and coordinate its own momentum with momentum generated at the hip joints. The initiation of the arm's action could not be visually cued or arbitrarily begun in response to the dancer's will alone. It had to be the result of an awareness of a whole system of relationships governed and inspired by the force of gravity acting on the arm and the body's weight center.

As the cyclical weight shifting became a familiar pattern to "me," "my arm" also became more sensitive to this kinetic chaining that had to occur for complete integration of the phrase. "I" began to close my eyes and let "my arm" perform. Over the weeks that passed, habit set in. The posture of everyday life disintegrated as the new patterning took over.

On one particularly good day, as this disintegration happened, a mental and verbal—that is to say, a symbolic and *cultural*—transformation simultaneously occurred within me as well, as "I" performed this dance. As "my arm" became a knowing source of action, something happened to "me." "Me" was "re-membered" by "my arm." The distinct sensations of memory, personality, and a socially constructed linguistic "voice" bodily relocated themselves. While the movement was occurring, the linguistic label "me" began to assert, with striking force and clarity, a redefinition for itself, a new cultural construct within the body of its subject, or bearer. Its first referent was no longer a vocal breath phrase, a voiced "me." Its first referent was no longer a face, a pair of eyes and ears, and a brain. "Me" or "I" now meant itself to be a limb, swinging and scooping freely through the air, "listening," as it went along, to the heavy rhythmic rocking of the pelvis to which it was connected. "Me" now meant "its self" to be of another mind. To the "me" of everyday life, it was a radically "other" mind, an exotic mind composed by a limb's neuromuscular intelligence, a mind exploring its environment through something other than its eyes and ears. In sum, what had been "my" arm became "me," and what had been "me" lost consciousness, and this transformation presented a microcosmic moment of liminality and "culture shock."

The new thoughtworld constructed by this choreography provided a number of insights. When "I-my-arm" had the full conceptual resources of my "self" at its command, the miracle of balance was suddenly effortlessly present throughout the entire skeletal structure of the new person, present and accessible in a way it never had been before. Gravity was apparent simply as a dynamic force, flowing down through the bones of what was now my mind into the floor, rooting the being of the whole person to what felt like the very center of the planet itself, without interference of any kind. "I" felt "my" ankles release a clutching sensation that they held habitually, and had held throughout everyday existence for as long as I could remember. "I-my-arm" flew through the air, beyond the control of the faint echoes of the "I" of my ordinary self. Attuned to the real force of gravity, balance was a certainty no matter how wild the cycling became.

It was a simple action, this choreographed movement of "For Betty." Yet the dance filled me, all the "me's" "I" knew, with a fierce joy. I was literally out of my head, and my head felt intensely relieved, for a while, to be nothing other than a weighted limb, a counterbalancing force whose nature was carefully understood by another knowing member of the organism.

These kinds of experiences, the "re-memberings" of "me," are part of what draws an individual to the serious study of choreographed movement in contemporary U.S. society. They are culturally challenging experiences, which test the limits of the normal constructions of the social self. U.S. culture bearers tend to think of themselves as individuals who "have bodies."[6] There is a general tendency to assume that the mind of a human being is the same thing as its brain, that human intelligence lives and flourishes only inside the area of the cerebral cortex, and that human learning is a process that must necessarily involve the sense of sight or the sense of hearing, and the echoes of those senses that we call "imagination," but preferably no others. Yet, in the mastery of choreographed experiences, there is no way to get around the fact that the human mind is a plastic figure. In this context, there is no master perspective on one's self, no single "I" that can tell "my body" what to do in every circumstance. In dance, the mind's "I" can become variable, and may inhabit the person in an infinite number of ways, investing the authority of the first person in different body parts, or in the whole body simultaneously in any number of spatio-temporal relationships.

When I think of dancers, I think of their bodies. I think about them because I am thinking of the way these people figure themselves out as culture bearers. Likewise, when I think of the dances of "other" cultures, I am curious about the collective motives that influence the generation and maintenance of a traditional choreographic form of self-conduct, about the way that a culture makes up its minds and its "I's" through a dance. This is one dimension of the intersection of ethnographic and choreographic inquiry: a common hermeneutic interest in understanding, exploring, explaining, and representing what it can mean to be a physical human "self."

The Choreographic Instrument

I watch a person run to catch a bus and then think about a dancer running and leaping across a stage. How would their body movements *feel* different?

I watch a person gesturing in conversation and then think about the gestures of an orchestra conductor. What exactly is the difference between these two physical experiences?

Sometimes, when I am performing ordinary daily tasks—folding up a bath towel, moving a potted plant from a table to the floor, or walking to the corner store—I feel almost as though I am doing someone's dance. It happens when the rhythm of the action is especially clear, clear enough to vocalize as a sound phrase. In the case of folding a towel, holding it by both corners, one in each hand, and pressing the center of the top edge to my sternum with my chin to hold it steady, the phrase might emerge as:

"a-*dee*, a-dah, a-deeeeee . . . dah"
(one fold, another fold, holding center/releasing chin and letting top half fall over bottom . . . folding finished).

There is always a sense of release. Through practice, the "task-ness" of the task becomes insignificant.

There is another realization I make in these dancelike moments that reminds me of the heart of what I know as the experience of performing choreographed movement. When I am performing the taskless task, I feel myself acting "better" than I actually need to. The rhythm of the arm movements is more articulately phrased than it needs to be, the sections of the towel come out more equally divided than they really need to be, the contact of my fingers with the fabric of the towels is more delicate than it needs to be, and so forth. No perceivable effort with better than adequate form. These characteristics begin to turn the ordinary action into choreography for me.

Here is where "dance" and "sport" have parted company in my

experience. The athlete achieves excellence in form because the task or the competition inspiring the game demands it. Outstanding form is compelled by a difficult objective, the desire to win against one or several other players. Form doesn't follow this function so closely in dance. Choreographed movement, as I have studied it in a variety of ballet, modern, and jazz dance studios throughout the United States, is somewhat more purely playful, although it can be a very serious kind of play. It is what it is, for the sake of something more like poetic amazement or amusement.

Charlie, a Filipino choreographer who lived in Cebu City, once taught me a short dance. Charlie was something of a genius in the local community. Commercial businesses would contact him to choreograph their advertisements. His sister had studied in Los Angeles and had danced on television there, evidence that talent of a certain kind ran in his family. Yet Charlie was more than a commercial artist, catering to the tastes of popular culture. His own dances, which he taught as a supplement to his aerobics classes, were original creations, unlike any others I saw anywhere else in Cebu City or in the Philippines in general.

Charlie never made a fuss over me, an *Americana* a good ten inches taller than himself and all his other students. It was a rare sort of acceptance in my field experience that he offered me. I had on occasion nearly caused traffic accidents in the city center as drivers would screech to a halt to get a better look at my extraordinarily tall build—nearly six feet tall. I never managed to make it through the public market without attracting a throng of children, who simply couldn't believe that a human being could be as tall as I was. A chorus of "Superwoman!" "Wife of the Giant Snake Monster!" or simply, "Hey, Brooke Shields!" continually followed me about in public life, as local men attempted to come to terms with my stature. Whenever I appeared in a new place, action invariably came to a halt as people stopped to take me in, a human spectacle, understandably something like a freak of nature in their world. I was thus always grateful for the moments of peaceful anonymity allowed me in Charlie's classes.

Charlie seemed to understand what it was to be extremely different from the rest of the people who inhabited his world. In his own way, he was as different from the people he lived with as I was. He never tried to manipulate me, never sought favors or sponsorship, as did so many hopeful, young would-be emigrants about town. Charlie was gifted, and he accepted his gift, even while it destined him to a life on the periphery of society. It was his very lack of artfulness that defined him as a person of real talent. He was his own source of meaning. He would walk lightly into the studio, say hello in a chatty, affectionate way to his regular students, and begin the class. During the class, he never scolded, or shouted, as some of the other aerobics teachers sometimes did, but he always corrected. In his own quiet, cheerful way, he knew precisely how he wanted us to behave.

Charlie's dance included a series of hand gestures: both hands began the gestures above and slightly in front of the right temple of the forehead, alternately making outward chopping movements, like those of a Swedish massage therapist, while traveling downward and in front of the torso, finishing the chops near the left hip bone.

The trace form of the gestural series had a classical sort of appeal. It was the pathway of a staircase, which the hands ran down, striking each step with an action just like that of a mallet striking a xylophone. The trace form left hanging in the air was a visual scale.

As I grew more and more familiar with this gestural series, my impression of it changed markedly. At first I thought of it as a task to master, a skill to acquire, a puzzle to solve. When the task was accomplished, however, and my hands could run quickly and fluidly down the scale, the series began to take on meaning in its resemblance to similar movements, like those of the masseur, or the baker kneading dough, or the karate chop of a martial artist. The posture of the hands resembled that of the all-purpose Filipino hand wave, all digits bound together to form a flat, paddle-like surface, easily flexed and extended. I would raise my hands to begin the dance phrase, and flashes of similar movements would pass through my mind. Glimpses of minibus hawkers hanging out of their vehicles to wave pedestrians on board, flocks of uniformed schoolchildren waving to each other on their way to classes, and an immense mass of devotees lining the streets of the city to wave at the image of the Santo Niño as it processed majestically throughout the city streets on fiesta day—all of these images came and went in the instant of preparation. The sense of the specific skill acquired by the hands was not replaced, only enriched by these memories. My hands grew better and better at the task, better than I had thought they could be.

As time passed, the web of meanings grew more general, expanding to include all of the activities in which my hands were instrumental, all the moments of holding, slapping, pushing, grabbing, twisting, clapping, pinching, tying, tapping, squeezing, snapping, and so on, that involved my hands. In that ultimate awareness, I found the movement to be a source of deep pleasure because of the amplitude of disparate images generated by it and because of the extraordinary skill acquired through practice that was never evaluated and constrained in terms of some functional norm. The "chopping hands" dance, as it came to be called, when its action was so ingrained in my memory that its performance sparked no new connections, became a reminder that my hands were inherently instrumental, fabulous with respect to the sheer diversity of their acquired skill. I would raise my hands to begin the movement, and, as in the moment of death, the life of my hands flashed before my mind. As they moved through the sequence, they realized a potential otherwise uncalled for in their ordinary life. They impressed me. They expressed me. I was moved by them.

When dancing, you are not an ordinary instrument, like a towel or a knife, but you are aware of being extraordinarily instrumental all the same. Your body becomes the key to relating a tremendous imaginary reservoir of purposeful instances of self-conduct, in the most ideal terms conceivable. The imagined reservoir itself, which is exposed and generated by this activity, is both a cultural and a choreographic construct. It is the reservoir of a human being's *habitus* or lifeway, a reservoir of memory, whose depth and surface may be grasped in its full significance perhaps only via extraordinary, "metafunctional" practices, such as dancing.

The Choreographic Ethnographer

I claim to write as would a performing student of choreography. However, in so doing, I do not leave the realm of ethnography. Granted, my orientation toward the study of "culture" has led me to focus on ordinary life, as well as extraordinary events, in a Philippine city in a way different from what the conventional ethnographer might have done. The identification with choreographic experience led me to look at the social life of the city almost as a deaf person would, noticing first what may seem to the average reader to be a silent world—a world without speech, vividly alive with visual forms.[7] The orientation led me to value the most minute and routine bodily actions, the everyday practices or "ways of operating" that generally are viewed only as an obscure background or transparent basis of social activity.[8] Likewise, the choreographic interest led me to interpret observations of social action in a more immediately physical—which is to say, subjective and figurative—manner than is typically expected of an ethnographer. And it led me to observe the public life of the city *first* as an ongoing stream of behavior, whose style or "form" of unfolding was as significant as the "content" of its various social dramas. However, my orientation, in spite of these various differences in emphasis and focus, did not alter the fact that my basic approach to fieldwork was anthropological. Indeed, it was precisely *because* I was engaged as a performing student of choreography would be, caught up in the struggle of mastering an unfamiliar way of moving through life, that I found myself to be engaged in an ethnographic process as well.

The performing artist, of which the student of choreography is one select type, and the ethnographer actually have a lot in common when it comes to the sort of self-discipline they must develop in their respective lines of work. The mastery of a choreographed movement is something very like an ethnographic act, if it is not precisely that, just as the mastery of a cultural role is fundamentally an act of performance. In both cases, there is a desire to become an integral part of a foreign realm—a stage or a world—and this serves as the motivation for undertaking the work. In both cases, having been a part of "the production" itself is the source of ultimate satisfaction, even if this might entail sacrificing the opportunity to know that lived world objectively, as a totality, the way an audience member would.

A dancer, when cast in a given work of choreography, often finds her- or himself facing the challenge of playing a part that may feel completely foreign. It may be a role unlike any he or she has ever played before, cast in a work whose basic structure and principles of action seem absolutely new. The style of action to which the performer must conform may seem not only unfamiliar, but distasteful, repugnant, absurd, or dangerous. Yet, his or her obligation, and the challenge that generally appeals to those who are drawn to the performing arts, is to overcome the initial shocks of an alien style of action and to adapt to it, to fully *assume* it. "If I am asked to walk bent double at the waist, with my arms reaching back and upwards until I think they are going to break, well, I must do it," says the dancer. The role of the performer is not to judge, but to learn and to execute, to trust the judgment implicit in the choreography.

A performing artist, when rehearsing a new work, must thus become immersed in the work's initially unfamiliar patterns. With practice, through trial and error, and with whatever help those who are working with the performer have to offer, he or she eventually learns to "get the best of" the work, and, ideally, to enjoy or even love performing it. The goal of the performing artist in rehearsal is a sort of atonement, or, even more literally, an "at-one-ment," an expert reconciliation of oneself with another style of doing and being.[9] The hope, generally speaking, is that the performer will learn, often in some surprising way, how the new work brings out the best from within. There is as well the excitement and responsibility of the performance itself, the fact that eventually the performer's efforts will come into public view and may come to be considered a valued addition, perhaps an inspiration, to the audience's social and personal lives.

The ethnographer stepping into a foreign culture is like the student of choreography learning to step into a dance. At first, there is the awkward encounter with new ways of doing things, which must be accepted, not altered. Like the dancer, the ethnographer must learn by participation, through repeated interaction, with the help of those around him or her, such as they have to contribute. Attempting to defer consistently to the designs of an initially alien way of living, the hope of the ethnographer is like that of a performing artist: eventually, some competence within or some mastery over a foreign way of acting will be gained; eventually, some audience or readership will benefit from and be inspired by whatever atonement the ethnographer has achieved within this culture through his or her trial-and-error experiences.

While many would take issue with the claim that ethnographic fieldwork is a performing art, few would argue with the notion that it is a performance-oriented discipline. The central importance of "participant observation," the distinctive method of fieldwork in cultural anthropology since the time of Franz Boas, is ample evidence of this consensus. In this respect, my approach to interpreting the "culture" of Cebu City, as I encountered it in 1984 and 1985, exploring it as a performing student of choreography, should not be considered a radical departure from the traditional ethnographic method. It is simply an extension of one of its more interpretive and humanistic veins.[10] I have viewed my findings in the same light as have most interpretive fieldworkers: as the set of impressions, observations, theories, and insights, formed from interaction, with the help of those around me, that enabled me to adjust my own habits of action so that I could begin to learn to participate in the social life of this lowland Philippine city in a way that would be welcomed and deemed familiar by its more experienced inhabitants. My approach is a departure only in that my particular inroad into this interactive learning process— choreographic experiences—has been a somewhat novel choice.

The Symbolism of Rapport

Pam Schick, a prominent Pacific Northwest choreographer, had an adroit reply to the often asked, somewhat discouragingly naive probe, "What does a choreographer do?"

"I make the invisible visible," she would answer.

"Making the invisible visible" involved the human body not as an object per se, but as a means, or *figure*, for revealing something else: the dynamics, present but otherwise invisible, of the world in which a person or several people moved. Choreography is not just something that is "set" on somebody's body. It is also something that occurs in "a space." It is something that happens in and to a certain area of the world.

One of the things made visible in any choreographed movement, whether it is the creation of an individual artist or the creation of an entire culture—a folk tradition—is the human capacity for establishing rapport. Revealing the tensions and fluencies, harmonious or discordant, that exist habitually or instantaneously between people or between humans and various elements or aspects of the world around them is one general kind of relation that choreographed movement invariably makes apparent.

There was an expert stick fighter living in Cebu City, a world class champion of that sport, known as *arnis*. He was known popularly as "Cacoy" Cañete and was something of a local celebrity. He was sixty-four years old when I met him, in his own backyard, where he had an open-air, shaded pavilion that served as an arena for his practices and matches. He was in the middle of giving a lesson to another martial arts master from the United States when I arrived. The pupil was a black belt karate champion, an American of Tagalog descent who liked to be called Manny.

Watching Cacoy spar with an opponent, or simply watching him run through his moves with his weapon, revealed the rapports he had spent his lifetime cultivating, rapports that had repeatedly won for him the title of grand national *arnis* champion. Every time he moved, he represented these relationships, which were the essential "products"—the "rendered visibilities"[11]—of his life's work, and which had found the highest acclaim in his local society as well as in a certain specialized global society.

While Cacoy would hardly have considered himself a dancer, he was a performing artist of a sort, a martial artist. He told me that he believed dance training was important for his students because it enhanced their body awareness and control. As he said this, he executed a brilliant little maneuver initiated from his hip bones, twisting on his axis a quarter turn and then shifting directly sideward from his right to his left foot, moving so accurately, so quickly, and with such a dramatic shift in quality, from a feeling of utter release at the outset to one of perfect control at the finish, that his own artistry and self-mastery were unmistakable, and unmistakably linked to one another, thus proving his point.

It was immediately obvious that Cacoy had a wild spirit. Without even looking at him, a person could sense it. He expressed it in his vocalizations, wailing when he attacked his opponent with a haunting high-pitched cry that reminded me of a wolf's howl. He had the capacity to move with a hysterical madness, a completely untamed ferociousness. The bursts of energy he manifested in the occasional surprise attacks he feigned were so powerful and sudden that by the time a person registered their impact, the movement was completely over and done with, and Cacoy would have changed his character entirely, lightly walking away from the exchange with a nonchalance that both belied and bespoke an absolute mastery. These were truly unbelievable moves he concocted, difficult to perceive because the visual and the kinesthetic reactions to them seemed incompatible. A strike *that* strong couldn't possibly be so quick; a blow that uncontrolled couldn't possibly be so accurate. Yet, somehow, they were.

Cacoy was also quite a clown. He interrupted himself frequently during the course of the lesson to tell a pun, doubling over in glee, pointing at me with his mouth wide open as he enjoyed my reaction to his humor. Manny remarked on how unusual this joking behavior was in a martial arts teacher. Such authoritative characters had tended to be much more grim and single-minded in his own quite extensive experience. It occurred to me that all of Cacoy's kidding around was somehow a balance to his warrior instincts. He jealously guarded all evidence of his fighting prowess. I saw just brief glimpses of his ability that evening. A step here, a blow there, a quick example of a training drill, these were the most that Cacoy allowed himself to exemplify while I was present. Only his humor was for free. He was something of a wizard masquerading as a jester.

Even though the moments when Cacoy really "did his stuff" were relatively few and far between, there was something so extraordinary about the manner in which he handled his weapon, a stick about three feet long and an inch thick, that they have remained vividly implanted in my memory even years later. The remarkable thing about them, particularly given the aggressive context of their appearance, was that they were profoundly gentle moments. They were moments of great understanding, between a man and an object. Granted, it was an object that had been his companion through many of the most rewarding and the most painful moments of his life. Nevertheless, every time Cacoy moved his weapon, a bond between them, between the man and his instrument, at once subtle and profound, became apparent; a trust implicit in the movement of the stick, an anticipation of its behavior that had become second nature over the years, compelled attention.

It was a bond made visible through absences. He didn't watch the stick closely enough to be able to attune his arm so accurately to its movement as it flashed through the air toward a seemingly undefinable goal. Yet somehow the timing was perfect, pinpointing targets within millimeters. He didn't have to use his eyes to know where the stick would be at any point or where it was going. His knowledge of its presence and its habits of action with respect to gravity was a part of his own character. He knew the weapon as he knew his own limbs. It was this intimacy that allowed him to make a strike with his eyes closed, absolutely calm, without hesitation, without concern, and, although with lightning speed, without urgency. A lifetime of practice made its presence known every time Cacoy and the weapon moved together. The spectacular aggressiveness of the actions Cacoy was able to produce was tempered by the poignancy of the relationship he maintained with his instrument. The respect he commanded from an observer, even an untrained newcomer like myself, was as much a result of this rapport as it was a result of his ability to perform as an exceptionally fearsome contestant.

What was made visible in this particularly well-seasoned relationship was a set of values relevant to the issue of manipulation, a social issue of central importance in any culture, but one that, I was to learn, had a particularly salient character in Cebu City and the Philippines in general. What Cacoy's masterful demonstrations made vividly clear was that manipulation could be a matter of life and death, of aggressive as well as defensive action, and that its most effective employment combined a surprising freedom with an agile capacity for reacting and reinitiating action. Aim and force, while essential, took second place to a finely tuned impulsiveness, so that the trace form revealed by the process of manipulation itself was a flurry of echoing, ribbon-like curves that reverberated with astonishing frequency all about the bodies of the fighters. The pattern evident in the performance, so highly crystallized as to form a caricature of social action, was one I was to encounter again and again in my interactions with the city's inhabitants. It took a genius like Cacoy, however, to present it with such clarity that even a passing stranger could not help but be struck by its distinctive design.

Observing and coming to terms with distinctive forms of rapport made visible and tangible in choreographic phenomena provides yet another avenue of inquiry for the ethnographer who studies choreography as a performer. The cultivation and masterly demonstration of choreographic rapports provides a certain type of challenge. It creates action that can take years to perfect. Through the manifestation of such rapports, even the simplest gesture can make visible a culture's most cherished and carefully shaped relationships.

Beginning Again

As the foregoing discussion has begun to exemplify, my strategy in developing this ethnographic account has been to write of Cebu City and its *sinulog* forms by moving among several perspectives, all of which were useful to an ethnographer studying choreographic phenomena with a performer's orientation. At times, I assumed the standpoint of a passing visitor, a role I played myself, and a character for whom the *sinulog* was, in every case, designed to have a specific appeal. In addition, I sometimes observed social action from the standpoint of a performer in the process of mastering symbolic movement. I also sought, in the traditional "interviewer" role of the more standard social scientist, the perspective of the participants: the performers, choreographers, and audience members who expressed their experiences to me. Finally, I have written from the standpoint of a temporary resident of the city, one immersed in the study of its dynamic culture.

The chapters that follow emphasize one or several of these perspectives with respect to each of the three *sinulog* variants performed in Cebu City in 1984 and 1985. The first variant, the individual, improvisational *sinulog*, is characterized in Chapter 6 as a bodily experience and as a ritual process. The dance is then described in Chapter 7 in terms of its participants and their life experiences. Finally, this improvisational *sinulog* is analyzed in Chapter 8 as a symbolic construct, multivocal in both latent and conventionally recognized signifying capacities. The second variant, the troupe ritual *sinulog*, is described in detail in Chapter 9 as a complex choreographic and ritual process. Its history and changing social relevance are recounted and analyzed in Chapter 10. Chapters 11 and 12 focus on the third variant, the secular and promotional *sinulog* form. Chapter 11 details the performance processes and the brief but complex history of this assertedly "cultural" *sinulog*. Chapter 12 recounts the various dimensions of symbolism made both visible and invisible in the varied but stylistically coherent choreography of this form. The concluding chapter (13) provides a more general discussion of the historical, contemporary, and ethnographic significance of the Cebu City *sinulog* practices, focusing on some of the complementary and problematic interrelationships that developed among the three variants in 1984 and 1985, interrelationships which allowed for a public recognition of all of the variants as belonging to a single *sinulog* tradition.

Before turning to the choreographic foci of the study, however, the text turns first to the world in which the *sinulog* dancing was situated—the world of Cebu City itself. The *sinulog* choreography, as

I came to understand it, was an expression of this urban world, a "pressing out" or a symbolic extraction of that world's dynamics: its climactic conditions, its patterning of time, space, and people, and its contemporary religious, socioeconomic, and sociopolitical situation. Chapters 2 through 5 deal with these aspects of the cultural "stage" on and against which the dancing was performed.

Cebu City has changed rapidly since my stay in 1984 and 1985, and it would misrepresent the contemporary character of the site to pretend that the realities of the mid-1980s have remained unchanged. The text proceeds, therefore, with a past-tense recollection of the ethnographic scene.

Chapter 2
Troubled Times

Human blood looked oddly ordinary, spilled on the crumbling pavement of the street. I was on my way through downtown Cebu City one afternoon, when I suddenly came upon a puddle of partially congealed human blood lying just off the sidewalk, spread like strawberry preserves over the battered surface of the road. I had nearly stepped right into it. The police had come and gone. The body had disappeared. Just the blood remained.

"This is bad," I thought, stupidly. It was a vague, obvious thought, but it seemed to resonate like an alarm siren from the street. "Bad" was the only word that fit. It was the only one basic enough. It didn't seem possible that a word could be so embedded in a visual scene, that it could attach itself so securely to a set of concrete, lifeless details that could be viewed—indeed, from a social scientist's perspective, *should* be viewed—as plain, cold facts. Hours later, the word was still droning on inside my head. Regardless of what I tried to think about what I had seen, how I tried to use its details to reconstruct what had happened on the street, how I tried to analyze its import as a fact about local social life, only "bad" came through, blocking any further interpretation.

The stabbing had occurred only minutes before I had arrived. Yet there were no actual sirens, no ambulances, no flashing lights on sawhorses, not even any tape around the area. There were hardly any onlookers. It was disturbingly banal. One minute I had been en route from an interview with a dance instructor. The next, I was staring at a pool of human blood. That was how violence appeared to me as a stranger in Cebu City. It intruded unexpectedly into otherwise ordinary moments.

No squeamish physical reaction accompanied my first encounter with human gore. Having grown used to picking my way through all kinds of decaying animal matter normally discarded in the city center streets, a puddle of blood was nothing unusual. Ignorance spared me. It was Rosa Gonzalez who actually identified it as human. Rosa nearly threw up on the spot. She dragged me away from the mess to the other side of the street and stopped there until she could take her hand away from her mouth.

Rosa was my interpreter. I had never meant her to have to translate her country's violence for me. However, the task had presented itself abruptly, and Rosa bravely addressed it. She had seen human bloodshed before. It was only after understanding her reaction that I looked over at the scene and thought, "This is bad."

Shifting almost immediately into "ethnographic mode," we tried to gather information from the store owner and the few hangers-on about the murder. Not much was forthcoming. There was speculation that it had been over drugs. There was speculation it had been a personal vendetta of some kind. There was speculation it had been a robbery attempt. That was the most we ever learned about the incident.

We thought of pressing further for details of the crime from more established sources, but decided against it. Neither one of us had much faith in our ability to elicit information from the newspapers. The police also seemed beyond our reach as a source of information. Rosa didn't even suggest going to them. It was common knowledge around the city that the resources of the police department couldn't be stretched far enough to cover the cost of fully investigating every crime. I was quite certain that they had no desire to be reminded of that by some ugly *americana* poking her long nose into what was definitely none of her business. This murder had involved no prominent local figures, at least not openly. It was destined to sink into oblivion quickly, as soon as somebody got around to mopping up the blood.

Murders like this one, in broad daylight, in the middle of town, were on the rise in Cebu City during my stay, which began in late 1984 and ended in mid-1985. Here and there, in a few spots along the sidewalks, small wreaths of flowers or candles and crosses would mark the spots of killings. It surprised me that such vulnerable offerings remained in these much-trampled places for many days, sometimes several weeks. The death symbols, however, were respected. They were a way for the whole community to recognize the violence.

Other responses were far more problematic. Revenge killings were rumored to be on the rise in the city, although it was impossible to say with certainty that this was in fact the case. The killings were viewed as one of the results of the Marcos regime's "peace and order" campaigns. "Peace and order," in local discourse, most often stood for "violence and chaos." Doublethink phrases of this sort frequently fell from the tongues of the citizenry, usually uttered heavily and with an edge of bitter sarcasm. No classic image of the Orwellian nightmare, however, would do justice to the state of the Philippines or Cebu City in particular at this time. There was certainly nothing as grandly organized or technically sophisticated as Big Brother brutalizing the populace, even though the government had become so centralized that a provincial driver's license had to be processed through Manila.

In fact, for the most part in Cebu City, specific acts of violence were not cast as institutionally orchestrated, in either their instigation or their control. Papers did not report, and local talk did not suggest, that any massive, government-backed purges or "salvaging" campaigns were being undertaken within the city by the army, the constabulary, or any other governmental force. Instead, papers would most frequently report cases of privately motivated violence. Two friends would go out one night, get drunk, and shoot each other. Their bodies would wind up splashed across the front page of the next morning's editions. Some residents believed that the press misrepresented these incidents, that the communist New People's Army was arranging the removal of key people under such guises, as well as through sniper killings that were later attributed to personal quarrels. There was no ultimate consensus on the causes of the increase in violent crimes. By all accounts, however, the control of violence was not a matter that could be left solely in the hands of the establishment. There was no widespread confidence in the collective "peacekeeping" forces of the day.

The extent of the escalating violence and its consequences for the safety of the average city resident could easily be overstated (which local papers seemed to relish doing). Its indicators were prone to misinterpretation by outsiders. For example, the sight of security guards bearing automatic rifles while stationed at such ordinary locations as department stores, beauty parlors, and restaurants was intensely frightening to me at first. It seemed an obvious sign of a world poised on the brink of mob warfare. However, I eventually learned that the weapons generally served a function little different than the metal badges I had grown up to respect as symbols of power and authority in my own hometowns. Moreover, violent acts did not typically erupt without reason, despite what my encounter with the blood shed on the street had suggested. The more I heard about killings, assaults, and other acts of violence, the more evident it became that violence nearly always arose in context, as the result of a feud, vendetta, rivalry, or power struggle of some kind between parties who knew each other well. Accounts did not tend to focus on violence generated by random hostility—the sort one worries about when left alone late at night on the streets of Manhattan, Los Angeles, Washington, D.C., or Chicago, for example.

The precise nature and extent of the violence that was manifesting in the city at this historical moment would be difficult, if not impossible, to establish, and fully comprehending it would require an extensive study of its own. Nevertheless, it is fair to say that, by any resident's account, I lived in Cebu City during troubled times. My husband Marc Ness and I arrived just weeks after one of the most devastating typhoons in recent history had wreaked havoc in the Visayas, taking many hundreds of lives in addition to ruining countless farms and reefs. It was also the eve of the government's acceptance of austerity measures (imposed in order to secure the crucial "rescue programme" of IMF loans), which were already generating strikes and demonstrations. Marcos's reputation at home and abroad appeared to be in the final stages of disintegration, as the international banking community and the U.S. government became more open in expressing their loss of confidence in his ability to maintain control and produce results. No viable alternative, however, was as yet in sight. Cory Aquino's bid for the presidency was still over a year away. People took note of the weakening administration and wondered, without really wanting to know, what would happen next.

However, the bleakness of this picture should not be overstated. Late 1984 through early 1985 was also a faintly hopeful period. The Agrava commission produced an official report on the Aquino assassination that, although a disappointment in some essential respects, did result in the temporary removal from office of the chief of the armed forces, General Fabian Ver, one of the main culprits in the tragedy. The temporary appointment of a professional soldier, General Fidel Ramos, in Ver's place generated widespread hope for the improvement of the military. Similarly, while the austerity measures had raised the inflation rate to over 60 percent, they had also momentarily put the country back in relatively good standing on the international economic scene. Even the strikes they had generated had inspired hope. A jeepney drivers' strike organized just days before our arrival had been celebrated for its effective nationwide stoppage of work—the first strike of its kind in local memory. A national consciousness of unified resistance to the government finally seemed to have been aroused.

People in the city knew big changes were in the making. The stream of relatively high-level U.S. officials beginning to flow through Manila, and, at long last, beginning to open up channels of communication with the country's organized opposition leaders, was sure evidence of that. Yet the future still seemed dark, ominous, and uncertain. Such was the day-to-day political context of the *sinulog* "field" site.

Chapter 3
Views from the Swimming Pool

On most days, barring unforeseen catastrophes of the sort recounted in the last chapter, the city did not appear to be such a grim place to live. From many vantage points, it was a genuinely pleasant locale. There was, for example, an outdoor swimming pool at my host institution, San Carlos University,[1] where I used to chat about the city and my fieldwork with Elisabeth Rosaldo, another cultural anthropologist. The pool was a lovely spot for reflective conversation—naturally cool, kept spotlessly clean, surrounded by beautiful ferns and palms. It was always deserted except for us and the spying eyes of a few curious students who wanted to see for themselves that American women did in fact dare to wear swimming suits in the water without T-shirts or skirts covering them. The pool was the perfect combination of developing world technology and tropical charm. It was a Westerner's haven, taboo for the majority of the far more modest locals, and a shelter from all else I identified as the "real world" of the city that existed outside the walls of the university.

I often felt that I cultivated a clearer image of the city while I was "off duty," relaxing in the pool. This "gaze," as Foucault would have called it,[2] remains one of the most vivid of my fieldwork. It was a selective perception of the local reality that appeared especially objective, generous, and self-contained. I found myself using this advantageous "view from the swimming pool" to begin to frame the central questions of my study.

Elisabeth had done her fieldwork in Japan—a somewhat controversial choice for a Filipina anthropologist, she informed me, since the nationalist sentiments widely felt among the intellectuals in the country supported ethnographic research only within the Philippine archipelago. She had two sisters living in Cebu, both of them, like

herself, belonging to the fortunate minority of self-reliant professionals (one in medicine, one in educational administration), who had
managed to maintain a fairly stable and prosperous, though not extravagant, existence in spite of the difficult times. They were all relatively permanent inhabitants of Cebu City. However, the family home
was to the south, in Dumaguete on Negros Island.

Elisabeth was neither a native Cebuana nor a Catholic, nor a practicing *sinulog* dancer. Her frame of reference was international. The
very fact that she would go swimming in the pool with me was clear
evidence of how different her worldview was from the local one we
both thought I was supposed to be studying. I placed her behind the
scenes of my urban fieldworking efforts, well outside the bounds of
"informant" status. It was only long after my departure from the city
that I recognized Elisabeth as a culture bearer whose identity, insights, and values were very much relevant to my ethnographic interests. At the time, however, we were simply two innocent social
scientists, temporarily surrounded by a local scene that neither one of
us really felt we could claim as fully our own.

One afternoon at the pool, in a mood of rueful skepticism, I complained to Elisabeth that it now seemed I'd come halfway around the
world to study a meaningless event. The *sinulog* dance was turning
out to have quite a reputation around town as a cheap and phony
tourist attraction that had been copied from another island's fiesta
celebration, the *Ati-atihan* of Panay. My bona fide "informants" were
telling me it was just a fake, another empty scheme employed to generate income for the city. The dancing that went on at the Santo Niño
church, they said, was a farce as well. Nobody but a half-wit, a sucker,
or some poor ignorant farmer who hadn't yet entered the twentieth
century could attach much significance to any of it. It was all *pala-
bas*—all for show—a contrived illusion based on an archaic practice
nobody really believed in anymore. My own interest in it was quickly
becoming a liability. People typed me as gullible, stupid, and worse:
a condescending Westerner who, true to form, was casting about in
vain for quaint practices that no longer appealed to anybody real.

These dark thoughts amused Elisabeth, who was always sympa-
thetic to my fieldwork anxiety attacks. The "meaningless event" label
seemed to strike a chord. She chuckled softly as she repeated the
term, and brought it up again in later conversations. For a little while
it became a kind of password, so that when I'd first see her after a few
days, I'd half expect to see her smile and ask, "So how's your study of
your meaningless event going?" Somehow we both knew that we were
playfully breaking a cardinal rule of the discipline in discussing my
research that way. We both knew that the things an anthropologist

studied could be revolting, absurd, esoteric, or taboo, but they could not, under any circumstances, be meaningless. "Cultural" phenomena, if they had nothing else in common, were always supposed to be meaningful. That was the one expectation to which they had to conform. No anthropologist worth his or her salt could study a meaningless event.

From the start of my fieldwork I was faced with a paradox. Here I'd found a dance that was enjoying tremendous popular success, forming the center of a celebration that was drawing crowds of spectators, which broke records for what had always been a massively popular occasion—the fiesta for the patron saint of the Philippines, the Santo Niño de Cebu. Here was a dance currently put forth as a key symbol of regional ethnic identity, possibly the province's most powerful instrument in its process of establishing for the city and its province an aura of regional autonomy. In sum, here was a dance that had become a central element in an ongoing campaign of "localization," which was drawing boundaries that differentiated a local "Cebuano" inside from a national or global outside.[3] Yet it was this very symbol that was being decried by residents themselves as a forged copy, that was plagued by persistent rumors of inauthenticity and meaninglessness.

What kind of a place or people could even be accused of stooping to such a trick? It was a question that haunted my research, a question I hoped I could avoid as a false question, if and when I did dig up some evidence of a widespread coherent meaningfulness for the dance. As my investigation progressed, however, it became clearer and clearer that the paradox would not go away. The *sinulog* was generating a multitude of contradictory interpretations within the city. It did not help to define a stable, continuous, homogeneous social entity, closed, coherent, and markedly different from my own, that would pass for "a culture." It was itself a fragmented tradition, that had splintered into a number of different performance styles, each influenced by different contextual factors.

The question of Cebu City's fitness as a locus of "authentic culture," however mythical that phenomenon itself might actually be, thus remained always in the back of my mind, casting doubt on my wisdom in selecting such a topic and such a location for an anthropological study. To put it bluntly, Cebu City, especially as it appeared from such privileged vantage points as the university pool, was unfortunately one of those places that people who care about "being cultured" tend to have in mind when they think of places with "no culture"—neither the "high" culture of dominant state societies, which can be measured in terms of museums and established schools of various classical arts, nor any "low" culture, which can be measured in terms of exotic rituals and customs. An American visitor in 1901 summed up the still prevailing attitude toward the city and its lack of "local color," writing: "It would be hard to imagine a more uninteresting, bedraggled down-at-the-heel place than this . . . not wild or barbaric enough to be interesting, nor yet civilized enough for comfort."[4]

As this dim view indicates, there were no traces in Cebu of any ancient, independent state center, which, as far as is known, never existed there in the first place. Equally disconcerting, there was no renowned and intricate conventional rule system for reckoning kin or prescribing marriage alliances or regulating complicated inheritance practices around town. Neither was there any outstanding native custom of dress or grooming—no colorful sarongs, turbans, hairdressings, or jewelry that distinguished other places in Southeast Asia. There were not even any deeply disgusting or shocking foods offered in the markets and restaurants, which were as often as not Chinese or "Western-style" anyway. Perhaps most "revealing," there was no common and exclusive language—a most trustworthy sign that, even if material circumstances had indicated otherwise, a distinctive and cohesive indigenous worldview did not exist. No one linguistic system, foreign or domestic, reigned supreme in Cebu. Everybody spoke variations of "mixmix," a blend of the vernacular, Cebuano Visayan, with English and Tagalog vocabulary and phrases.

To add to the "no culture" argument in demographic terms, the city was also infested with nonlocals—recent and often temporary arrivals, mainly from other regions of the nation, but also from other countries. They came from the other islands of the Central Philippines or Visayas and from Mindanao to the south, with a sprinkling of Tagalogs, Europeans, Americans, and Chinese thrown in. These new arrivals were not just passing strangers like myself; they often filled key positions in the city's most powerful institutions, as did Elisabeth and her siblings. While these individuals tended, in my observation, to be responsible professionals, committed to different aspects of the city's well-being, they made no claims to being authentic Cebuano "natives."

Native sons and daughters, if one defined them in terms of pure Malay ancestry, were something of a nonentity among the city's managing elite. Chinese mestizo families, who had been in residence and involved in the city's local economy since the sixteenth century, had dominated it since the nineteenth.[5] While the bulk of the city's Filipino population was ethnically homogeneous, although regionally diverse, a racial division, although impure, did separate the rich from the poor. The lines of power became more obviously influenced by foreign blood—mainly Chinese, but Spanish as well—the farther up them one climbed. Chinese names such as Gaw Trading, Lu Do and Lu Ym Corporation, Gaisano Merchandising, and Cathay Hardware figured prominently among the top merchandising and manufacturing corporations in the city, their assets totalling in the tens of millions of pesos.

This pattern of outsider inhabitation and control had been going on for centuries. Even the established insiders were only a few generations removed from a half-foreign ancestry.[6] Yet the city could hardly be called a plural society, for these incoming outsiders had always had a habit of "going local" (which was not at all the same thing as "going native"). While the mixed ethnic heritage of prominent citizens was carefully remembered and made note of, when they married into the local society they tended nevertheless to shed the bulk of whatever foreign language, religion, dress, and other cultural trappings they might be bearing and conform to the local "mixmix" within a generation.

There was one significant exception to this culturally problematic trend, a religious exception. For several hundred years, Cebu had actually been a "temple city" of a sort,[7] attracting pilgrims from all over the archipelago to its miraculous Santo Niño image. This genuinely distinctive cultural asset was housed in the Basilica Minore del Santo Niño, or Santo Niño Church, an eclectic but basically Romanesque eighteenth-century stone church and convent. The expression of temple city status, however, was limited largely to this building. It was not, in other words, symbolized by any cohesive geomantic architectural design that engulfed the entire urban location. Although the Santo Niño church was a relatively outstanding landmark within the city, and within the nation, for that matter, it could hardly have been compared to those of Indonesia's Prambanan valley, Cambodia's Angkor, or Mianmar's Pagan. Moreover, even this, the community's main source of cultural unity—its Roman Catholic religious devotion—was popularly recognized as being of foreign origin, borrowed from Spain. On the surface, at least, it also appeared to define its inhabitants in a mix of borrowed, not local, cultural terms.

In short, Cebu City had long ago joined the list of places that had been dispossessed of what a layman might consider "local culture." It lacked the "high culture" sought by the "cultured" socialite. It lacked the exotic culture sought by the adventurous tourist, or even—although disciplinary doctrine would forbid admitting this—the cultural anthropologist.[8] It even lacked any "pure" sort of local ethnic culture, in the sense that its local practices and customs were a blend of many different traditions.

Instead of appearing as a highly cultured place, from any of these perspectives, Cebu City appeared as a fragment of the Third World grappling for a toehold in the First. While the city could not claim the full status of a "primate city" such as Manila, Bangkok, Saigon, or Singapore, at a regional level it did bear a strong resemblance to those more cosmopolitan locations. Only a tenth the size of Metropolitan Manila (itself with a population of around six million in 1984), Cebu City nevertheless was many times larger than any other city in the province or region, particularly if its adjacent suburbs and municipalities were taken into account. It was growing roughly one-and-a-third times as fast as the rest of the province, showing a relative pattern of density increase roughly similar to that of Manila in relation to the nation as a whole.[9] Indeed, Cebu City in 1984 was itself a moving entity, in the process of an explosion, mushrooming out and condensing in simultaneously as its population increased by around 40 percent in a decade.[10]

These trends related to the perception that Cebu City, like Manila, was a center of opportunity, a place where a person might have a future. Cebu City was the capital of the province, the seat of the Augustinian Province of Santo Niño de Cebu, the educational, economic, and administrative center of its region. Migrants, who generally were coming from rural areas of the islands of Samar, Leyte, and northern Mindanao, imagined Cebu as a place for job-oriented, mobile, rational, metropolitan citizens of a nation-state to carry on their business, which concerned other Philippine urban centers such as Manila, Davao, Bacolod, Tacloban, along with those of the United States, Japan, Europe, and other foreign places. The Mactan Export Processing Zone, for example, which had been created in the 1970s in an effort to encourage foreign corporate investment, was located just a few miles from the city center on Mactan Island. In 1984, it housed the plants of multinational corporations of the United States, Hong Kong, and Japan. Names such as Lotus, Timex, and Fairchild had both a local and a global meaning for the city's residents.

As with Manila and with most other cities entering into similar relations of dependency all over the developing world, the image of potential was largely an illusion. In reality, 40 percent of the city's half million inhabitants lived in slum areas that had no drainage, sewer, or water supply, which had grown up near places of work (docks and factories), along rivers, and beside public markets.[11] Prime targets for government or corporate development projects, they were settled, most often illegally, largely by newcomers—migrant squatters. Unless a migrant was very lucky or arrived with connections to the city's enterprises already made, he or she was likely to end up living in a slum, in constant danger of eviction, working as a vendor, a fisherman, a helper or servant, or with no fixed job at all. Even for those who managed to avoid the slums, poverty was the rule. The vast majority of urban workers earned an average of around 700 pesos a month, while the government's estimated minimal income for a family hovered at around 2,000 pesos a month, increasing since 1982 with inflation at a rate of 15 percent a year.[12] Like Manila, Cebu City was a place of hopeful illusions and shattered hopes, a real center of commerce and industry, but also of hardship. Nearly half its inhabitants were not fully residents, still waiting for a legitimate place in the city and the society, living "on hold" in primitive quasi-rural conditions created in the cracks of the city's main design, cracking it further in the process.

Cebu, in sum, was a classic example of what Renato Rosaldo (1988) has termed a "postcultural" place. That is to say, it was yet another, rather tortured locus of advanced capitalism. It was a place whose cultural differences were becoming largely imperceptible to a Westerner like myself, because it was a place full of people, who appeared to be struggling, oftentimes desperately, to become just like me and my economically developed kind. While there might have been a lower rate of success in this attempt than I was used to, nevertheless, the goals being publicly set forth were ones I easily identified as those dominating my own culture. Moreover, the city was composed of what I'd learned to recognize as down-to-earth, practical, common-sense categories of institutions. The factories, jails, universities, movie houses, department stores, hotels, supermarkets, and office buildings of the city provided ample evidence of how extensively this lowland community had been participating in the developing world.

What made Cebu City unusual, however, was that, even before its entry into neocolonial "post-culture-hood," the city's cultural integrity (to return to the original question raised from the swimming pool) had been problematic. Cebu City was and always had been a cultural border zone, a half-baked "stop" located between more stable "cultured" places. In its earliest history, its between-ness was established mainly with respect to Greater Asia and its trading partners. Archaeological evidence indicated that a large settlement had existed at least as early as A.D. 1000 and that this settlement had extensive trade with China, perhaps initially and certainly by the 1400s, as well as with Indonesia and Indochina.[13] By the 1600s, European centers entered into the scene, with Spain dominating the city until the close of the nineteenth century. In the twentieth century, U.S. centers had taken precedence, although they were by no means the only ones involved.

The city, in other words, was not just a product of postmodern times. It was also, and equally, just a plain old port. Well, not just a port. It was the main port of entry for the region, the largest by far of twenty-two municipal ports in its province, with 5,000 meters of berthing space. It was arguably the finest port in the Philippines, with mountains to the west and Mactan Island to the east creating the best natural shelter to be had by any harbor in the archipelago. Cebu was the third-largest port city in the Philippines,[14] hosting over 15,000 seagoing vessels a year. It was a close rival of Davao City on Mindanao Island, which was itself second only (though a far second) to Manila.[15] In the year before my arrival, Cebu had done over U.S. $200 million in export/import trading, half of it in copper, which was the island's major mineral resource.[16] USAID and World Bank loans had recently funded an expansion and modernization of port facilities, so that, by 1984, mechanized equipment capable of handling container shipping as well as a variety of other cargo could reclaim for Cebu City its ancient status as an international port. Coconut oil, copra products, lumber, and dolomite made up the bulk of its exports, in addition to copper—all of them considered traditional products of the province. In recent years, new products such as shell craft, abaca fiber, a variety of garments and footwear, and, in particular, rattan and buri furniture could be found making their way onto ships in increasing volumes. There were also commercial crops (corn, sugar, mangos, bananas, grapes), along with an increasing trade in marine products (anchovies, sardines, herring, swordfish, and snappers, to mention only a few). While these last items played a relatively minor monetary role in the port's activity, their production employed well over half of the province's population.[17]

The financial profile of the port clearly revealed how strongly foreign agents and trends governed its development. It maintained vital links to local industry and manufacturing, but served mainly to draw wealth away from its hinterland, into its urban center, and beyond to more powerful centers. It was, in this respect, a pretty classic example of a neocolonial dependency.[18] Like any port, however, and not only the neocolonial varieties, it was polluted. Not a single aspect of its culture—its architecture, its language, its landscape, its religion, its government, its economy, its ethnic make-up, its society—none of these was of a pure, unmixed variety, nor had they ever been. Instead, they were—as has been said of the English language—"gloriously impure."

Cebu had thus been marked by borrowing and lending across its porous boundaries for as long as could be known. So it was that, long before the dawn of either the Spanish or the U.S. occupation, the city's inhabitants had developed the capacity to shed, grow, and graft cultural and postcultural skins. They were a people well-versed in creating cultural "just-like-nesses," whether it was a just-like-ness to the culture of the United States, or of Spain, or of some other "elsewhere." This had been their historical selective advantage, the trait that had allowed them to cope throughout their colonial history with the various forces of domination they had endured. It was not, however, a trait born of domination, but of necessity, of the trade that had, through times of relative freedom and through times of relative oppression, always served as the port's lifeline.

In this respect, Cebu City derived much of its cultural character from the tides that sustained it, always in flux, in a permanent state of improvisation with its new arrivals and departures. It was not surprising that, in 1984, the symbol the city had chosen to assert the steadfastness of its cultural integrity and that of its province was under attack. A transit point from earliest record, the place had no clear signs that it had ever had any stable or standardized "culture" of the type indicated. In a place like this, no symbol of "culture"—in any sense of that term—was safe, given the volatile and dynamic nature of the object that it claimed to represent. Such was the city's cultural predicament.

My questions, then (which may be of interest to those who frequent such developed spots as swimming pools), turned out to be these: How was Cebu City's essential status as a border zone, a regional port, masking its status as a genuinely cultured place? How could I do better than plea for attention to the "damaged" or "polluted" culture of the city, subjected, as it had been, to centuries of foreign influences? How could the tendency to blur boundaries between whatever "we's" and "they's" I might in vain try to define be understood in such a way as to expose and not deny the presence of a local culture? In sum, what kind of a culture could exist and endure in such a place as this?

A few partial answers were immediately obvious. It was going to have to be a culture born and reborn in rapid succession. It most likely would be a purely impure culture, a culture nourished by assimilation, sustained in acts of translation and improvisation, and visible in duplication. Irony and paradox would be its prevailing characters. It was going to have to be a culture borne (and born, as it turned out) by all sorts of recent arrivals and passers-through as well as by some longtime natives. The nature of a port as a sociocultural entity quite different from a rural scene had to be acknowledged if Cebu City and its people were to join the ranks of the ethnographically documentable.

The swimming pool was, of course, not the place to start investigating this local culture. As noted at the opening of the chapter, the swimming pool was all but lifeless most of the time. Its very emptiness, in fact, was a hopeful sign for me—I was still a fairly traditional culture seeker myself in 1984. The emptiness indicated that there were limits to the assimilation of foreign influences, that there was an "other" culture out there in the city resisting such modern Western appurtenances. So I began my discoveries by venturing out into the city's streets and looking.

Chapter 4
The Looks of the City

Any city gives form to the space and time it inhabits, as well as to the people who inhabit it. In so doing, it may reveal some of its residents' more basic attitudes toward public and social life, attitudes that also serve to form the basis of symbolic expressions. There were many ways to look at how these attitudes revealed themselves in Cebu, to look into the city's nature, and to look for its culture. There were views from the air, views from the sea, views from the pier, the market, the streets, and views from the homes, churches, and businesses. No one perspective told everything. One had to move among them.

An Overview

Cebu City, as it existed when I first laid eyes on it in 1984, would be impossible to represent in its empirical totality, so varied, so numerous, and, often, so minute were its material constructions, which were in many cases quite temporary or transient. As is typical of many towns and cities in Southeast Asia and throughout the developing world, an extreme variety of technologies coexisted in the city in somewhat startling juxtaposition to one another. Enormous luxury cruise ships steamed by the harbor, overtaking in their progress relatively tiny, twin-outrigged sailboats made of bamboo.[1] Buildings ranged from multistoried concrete structures to shacks made of scrap wood and woven rattan screens.

The missionary Alcina, who visited Cebu in the late 1600s, speculated that its original name, Sugbo, may have been given to it because it meant "to throw itself into the water." In spite of its enormous growth since Alcina made that observation, the city in 1984 still appeared as Alcina described it: "about to plunge into the waters of the

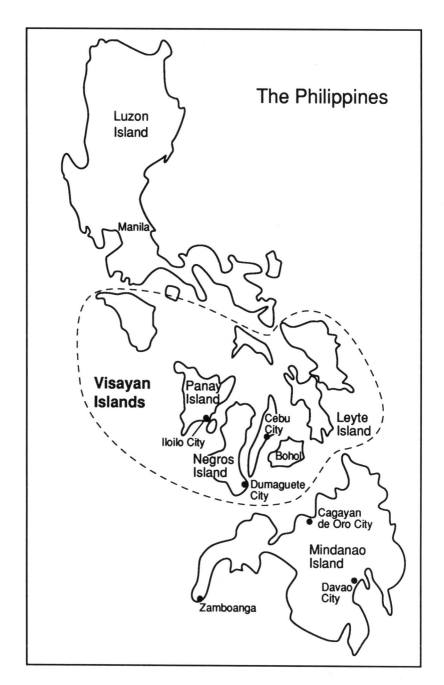

Figure 4.1. The Philippines.

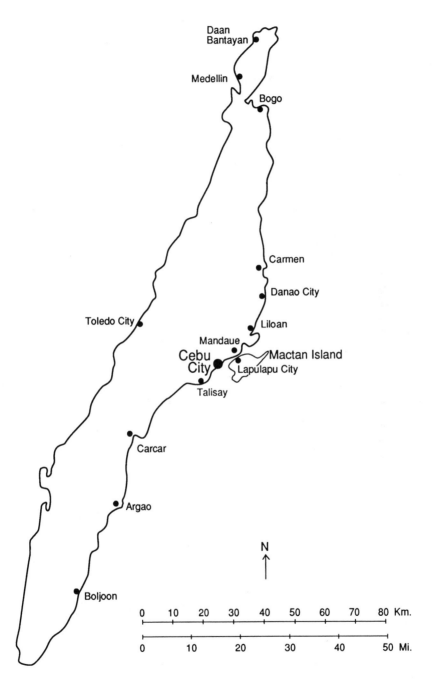

Figure 4.2. Cebu Island.

sea."[2] The relationship between Cebu City and the water was primary to its character.

Shaped like an enormous scallop shell, the metropolis fanned out from a point of land on which stood a triangular stone fortress, Fort San Pedro, which was built early on in the Spanish colonial era.[3] The landmark seemed to anchor the city, planted, as it was, at its hub, as if to insist that the foreign power that had engineered it was the original source of the community. That effect, however, was a lie. The fort had not given birth to a fortress city, partly because nothing worth encasing in battlements ever developed during the centuries of stagnation when the Manila-based galleon trade temporarily strangled Cebu's commercial life.[4] Moreover, Cebu was not, in fact, a creation of the Spanish regime. It had existed as an amorphous but thickly populated coastal settlement sprawling back into the hills long before Spanish forces impressed their gridmarks, landmarks, and plazas upon it.[5] Nevertheless, the city center, its model *ciudad*, flanked to the north and south by nuclear communities, did represent Spain's first attempt at urban planning in Southeast Asia, though it remained only half-realized for centuries for lack of investment. For four short years, 1565–69, the port of Cebu was the single keystone of Spanish territorial occupancy, economic exploitation, regional administration, and religious conversion in the Orient.[6]

Initially, the colonial city had had a racist plan. San Nicolas, the southern locus, was intended for the native *indios*, while Parian, the northern locus, housed the Chinese, already in residence by the end of the sixteenth century. Only the *ciudad* itself, the central segment of the settlement, had been intended for the Spanish *europeos*. However, while much of the original street plan and some plazas of each settlement survived into the twentieth century, racial distinctions in residential areas had long ago been blurred by 1984.[7]

The entire city now sprawled out to cover a land area of over 280 square kilometers—a little less than half the size of Metropolitan Manila. Seen as a whole, it looked like a giant catacomb, whose major arterials, fanning out in relatively straight paths, sometimes gave an illusion of linear organization that was not supported—one might even say it was contradicted—by the winding lanes and narrow side streets that connected them (Figure 4.3). The abrupt fluctuations in planning style expressed highly varied experiences of public and private existence. The broad and straight arterials were the traces of political movements, the showpieces of politicians since the American era, who used them to demonstrate their progressive public-spiritedness.[8] The narrow and crooked lanes that filled in the territory between these more imposing arterials, on the other hand, had

Figure 4.3. Cebu City.

no such rhetorical significance, and presented an entirely different set of possibilities for managing movement in more private, residential locations.

The street plans spread back into steep hills—a central range that reached elevations of 3,400 feet in some places and ran the entire length of Cebu Island (approximately 231 kilometers/139 miles long). Metropolitan Cebu extended the full width of the island, about 35 kilometers (20 miles) at its widest point. The urban area stretched 47 kilometers (30 miles) up and down the coast. However, the heart of the city was still clustered in the first few blocks around its waterfront, the core modeled on the Spanish plan, radiating inland from the fort.

The streets of Cebu did not typically run along flat surfaces, just as they did not run along straight paths. Instead, their forms, even those of many major streets, were irregular. Normally, a body was always on a slant in the city, with the degree of slant constantly changing. It became much more noticeable in the hills, where the homes of the very wealthy had been relocated in the elite urban flight from the inner city after World War II. It was much more subtle in the districts of the city immediately bordering on the city center. These newer sections, themselves the creations of multinational agencies, did have pancake-flat, grid-like road plans, particularly the Cebu Reclamation Project, which lay less than a mile north of the main harbor (see Figure 4.3). However, the flat areas proved to be the exception rather than the rule. There was almost always a tilt of some kind, a tilt that led down to the harbor. Whenever a person followed the path of least resistance, he or she always came back to the waterfront. It was the same with the *sinulog* movement style, the same with historical accounts of local ritual: allowing the forces of the natural environment to govern one's action meant ending up eventually with a host of gentle waves.

Natural Elements

The environmental outlook of the city, the view that made visible its geographical situation, was obviously one I sought to attain, given its fundamental importance for the local "culture." Yet I found this to be a blinding perspective, on the whole. Geography raised questions, questions that reasserted themselves hourly during every day spent in the city. They were largely unanswerable questions, concerning awarenesses so basic to the existence of the city's inhabitants that to even know how to articulate an answer would have required a kind of objectivity that resident status itself made virtually impossible. Yet they were questions that could not be dismissed. In my often recurring fantasy, that I could somehow wake up one day a native-born *Cebuana*, thus solving all my ethnographic puzzles at a single stroke, the first questions I dreamt of answering for myself concerned the meaning of natural elements: What was it like to take living on the ragged edge of a long, narrow, limestone rock, roughly the size of Long Island,[9] for granted? What was it like to experience the sun's progress through the tropical sky as an ordinary day, and to have that progression change only subtly throughout the year? And, most pressing, what was it like to live with intense heat as a normal circumstance of life?

Coming from the temperate, arid environments of the U.S. Northwest, the relationships between sun, water, air, and land that were normal for Cebu, sitting, as it was, in the humid tropics, seemed extraordinary. Here there were no long, wide rivers orienting the landscape. There were no seasons as I knew them. The temperature hovered at around 80 degrees Fahrenheit all year round, with high humidity. Only the rain patterns of the monsoon climate varied throughout the year, light from March through May and heavy from July through October. Even those seasonal cycles tended to vary erratically from year to year.[10]

Cebu, in addition, did not fit the stereotypical image of a tropical island paradise. Sheltered from the full effects of the dominant airstreams by islands on all sides, it did not see as much rain as most places in the archipelago.[11] The rain that did come caused one of the worst erosion problems in the Philippines. Ninety percent of the topsoil on the island suffered from some kind of erosion, and over a third of the island's topsoil had been removed through the devastating combination of rain, deforestation, overcultivation, and a generally steeply sloping terrain. It was actually something of nightmare, as island paradises went, with only the hardy cogon grass growing where tropical forests ought to have been.[12] The soil could not support wet rice cultivation to any significant degree. Corn sufficed instead.[13]

My preoccupation with the heat was typically American. Schoolteachers working in the Philippines in the early part of the century were as struck by the heat as I was two generations later. It claimed top priority in their diaries and letters home, outranking both insects and domestic service relations in importance.[14] My experience was no different. I was constantly struggling to cope with the heat of the city, always overpowered by its furnacelike pressure, exhausted by its relentless strength, overcome by the smells it produced—the smell of hot pavement, hot coconut oil, hot fruit, hot stone, hot metal, hot wood, hot people, hot water—and I was helpless against its ability to make my own flesh swell, blister, burn, and break out in rashes. Cebu City always seemed to be baking in an invisible kiln. It was a place where the rawest materials cooked simply by being exposed to the day. The sun and its movements had gone crazy. It leapt with astonishing speed into the sky around six o'clock in the morning, traveled a breathtaking course, much too long, as it seemed to me, across the sky, and then crashed behind the horizon shortly after six in the "evening." The dynamics of its movement, and the sort of day it defined, produced a jarringly strange, exotic sense of what "daytime" was for a newcomer to the tropics.

While it seemed clear that these prejudices against the climate were not shared by the city's inhabitants, there appeared no clues as to how, in local terms, the weather and its heat were understood. The special

significance of surfaces in the city, the importance of sleep and stillness in the pacing of activity (with peak activity periods occurring
around sunrise and sunset) and the observance of the noon siesta, all
these I interpreted as consequences of the sun's influence. However,
they were only tacit signs of understanding. The most overt "traditional" reference to the local understanding of the sun's influence
I came upon was the proverb, "Ang kalibutan mohunong sa iyang
pagtuyok kon wala nay init ug ulan," or "The world will stop turning
when there is no more heat or rain."[15] Named as one of two key conditions for the functioning of life-as-usual, the influence of the sun
was matched only by that of water.

Water was a more popular topic. Characters of liquid and solid in
local mythology, in fact, assumed the opposite roles of those they assumed in American and European mythology. The essential substance of bodies, and of the earth itself, was portrayed as liquid,
composed of water, not solid. Solids were characterized as a kind of
precipitation, the by-product of fluid interaction. For example, a creation myth told all over the archipelago described how land was first
produced when the sky and the earth engaged in a fight with one
another. Land was the result—the trace—of a conflicting relationship
between earth, understood to be a body of water, and sky, understood
not as a space devoid of material but as a realm filled with currents
of wind.[16]

The understanding of liquid substances as primary, and also the
sensitivity to the properties of fluids, was apparent in rituals of healing, protection, and thanksgiving performed in Cebu City at the time
of first contact with Spain.[17] Alcina, in the seventeenth century, recorded the Cebuano aphorism, "For one who has hope of life, water
is a medicine."[18] Currents of water were described as the equivalent
of altars of sacrifice. Offerings placed on the surface of the current
ensured safe journeys, good harvests, and protection from predators.
Water was seen as the source of life and the agent of health, as well as
the realm of death, which was characterized in terms of drowning,
with corpses being transformed into water during the night.[19] As the
ancient name of Cebu, Sugbo, attests, life in Cebu City originally
arose from and returned to the water. Water governed the rhythms
and the processes of the city's life.

Echoes of the ebb and flow of the settlement's ancient life-style were
still visible in the social movements of the city in the 1980s. Sources
from which activity tended to develop and into which activity dis-
solved still appeared to be fluent, not solid, mobile, not stable. Solidity
and stability did, of course, play vital roles in public life, but they were
not the background that made visible its central elements. Instead,

the "ground" of the world was constructed as liquid and flowing. Fluency of all kinds, as opposed to strength or single-minded determination, for example, was tacitly recognized as of primary importance for coping with the environment in a variety of ways.

Language habits, once again, most aptly represented the depth and pervasiveness of this mobile orientation. The customary greeting used around town was generally nothing like the English, "How are you?" with its assumption of a steady state of being. Instead, people greeted each other with, "Asa man ka?," "Where are you going?"—to which the customary reply was "D'yan lang," or "Just there," meaning nowhere in particular. The greeting was used even when people were not visibly en route to any place. Likewise, when people did *mosakay* or take a ride, they did not speak of their journey as a temporary movement that would end with a return to more normal stasis at a fixed or stable point, place, goal, or "stop." Instead, in local terms, their ride would "pass by" various possible drop-off stretches. This "pass by" phrase was used in English as well as in Cebuano, in place of "going to." Transporting oneself was thus represented as an unceasing, not temporary condition. This essentially fluid patterning manifested itself outside the language in a multitude of habits of social action as well.

Public Movements

The array of daily activities, the public patterning of space, time, and people—all of the public goings-on that served as the vibrant backdrop for the *sinulog* performances—these visible yet intangible and fleeting processes revealed shared attitudes toward the basic fluidity of social life and the world around it. I discovered these patterns by walking. When seen from the streets, Cebu's less tangible characteristics, its more subtle patterning of ongoing behavior, became visible. It was only from such a pedestrian perspective that the "movement world," as I came to think of it, could be seen to emerge within the city. At the same time, the nature of the built environment emerged in detail as well, often in a vivid contrast of some kind vis-à-vis the stream of behavior, creating for the strolling visitor a scene of contradictions and ironies wherever one happened to look.

The city's monuments and architecture were modeled largely on European or American designs. There were several modern monuments, of López de Legaspi (an early colonizer), the beloved former President Ramón Magsaysay, who died in a plane crash leaving Cebu, and the heroic figure José Rizal, martyr for the cause of independence at the turn of the century. These served initially to help define the terrain for a newcomer. In addition to the landmark of Fort San Pedro, there was a small, octahedral sanctuary housing Magellan's Cross, the world-famous artifact planted in 1521 upon Magellan's arrival in "the East," which served as another point of orientation. A number of eighteenth- and nineteenth-century stone churches, convents, and schools completed an array of Spanish-era constructions, built by the Augustinians, the Jesuits, and the Recollects, among others. The elaborate Taoist Temple up in the hills gave monumental form to the wealth and faith of the Chinese element. The public works from the American era, aside from the construction of much of the city's street plan,[20] also included the Provincial Capitol Building, the Customs Building, and the City Hall/Municipio, which had all been built between 1910 and 1940. Over a dozen parks and plazas, designated as symbols of freedom and independence, dotted the terrain as well. All of these constructions were planned, permanent, and map-worthy. They made the city "legible" as a geographic entity. They also, when viewed in isolation from the life that engulfed them, could make for a somewhat misleading impression of the city's character.

On my first walk through the city, I noticed that it appeared to have been constructed quite recently. In the case of the main arterial, Colon Street, which ran in an arc around the city center, there was not a single material object observable on the street that was more than one hundred and fifty years old, and most were less than forty. Yet Colon was widely recognized as "the oldest street in the Philippines."[21] My impression of it, gained from observing its material aspects, was fundamentally mistaken. It was the pathway traced by Colon, its curving route, which intersected several of the main roads running down to the waterfront, that dated back to López de Legaspi's time at least (1565). The street's "trace form," the spatial form left by its traffic, not its substance, was a widely recognized sign of antiquity and continuity.

There were thus at least two worlds present in Cebu City. There was a material world, a planned, highly visible world so dominated by foreign and contemporary products that it was often difficult to believe when viewing it that it wasn't a part of "the West." There was also a transitory world of activity, a vital world of human movement constructed through and on this plan that struck me, quite forcefully, as exotic—that is, different from my homeland. Cebu City was a place where "things" were likely to seem new and borrowed, but "ways," in the literal sense of the term, were likely to be old and locally distinctive. Intangible, though not invisible, patterns of movement—densely packed streams of traffic, individual footpaths, horse-drawn buggy trails, and jeepney movement—daily retraced the steps of local ways, sometimes those of antiquity, while the material constructs made reference mainly to contemporary foreign contact. The ritual *sinulog* dances, which were popularly believed to be indigenous forms of pre-Hispanic origin, were no exception to this rule. They symbolized an ancient way of moving amidst the many modern influences now present in the city.

The two socially constructed worlds were, of course, interrelated, continually acting on each other, and it was in the rapport established between them that the distinctive character of the city enunciated itself. The two most distinctive aspects of this interaction, as I observed it at close range, were (1) the patterning and manipulation of surfaces and (2) the expression of plurality, or duplication in both spatial and temporal organizations of activity and material. Both general features of public pedestrian life expressed the fundamentally fluid style of local social behavior, and they became important sources of insight into the choreography of the *sinulog*.

Surfaces

Surfaces of all kinds—edges, facades, borders, roofs, floors, skins, faces, and linings—were objects of much concern in Cebu, making it a typically Philippine city in this respect. They were built of galvanized iron, concrete, tile, brick, stone, asbestos, nipa, cogon, or makeshift materials. The materials emerged as a vast collage of opened walls, nets and webs, grilles, slats, canings, friezes, shingles, thatches, screens, and laces. They were remarkable in their permissiveness, allowing air, though not light, to penetrate easily. Whether I was looking at a *terno* (a fancy blouse made of *piña*, pineapple fibers), a rattan screen used for shade at the market, or the hardwood balcony of a nineteenth-century stone and tile mansion, the idea was basically the same. A breath of wind could pass through them. However, there was no view of what was behind them.

Structures facilitating circulation are healthy architecture in the tropics—there is nothing negative about "drafty" houses there, as there can be in colder climates. Cebu City's traditional surfaces allowed more comfortable temperatures to be maintained. The uninterrupted flow of movement from outside to inside and from inside to outside proved an effective way of coping with the environment. Permissive surfaces were associated, not with a lack of solidity, or with weakness, or potential illness, but with wisdom and well-being.[22] Given the tropical climate, solid surfaces would have been dysfunctional—until the arrival of air-conditioning. In this regard, the solid barriers and airtight structures of the more modern buildings in the city revealed dramatic changes in attitudes toward construction. The massive shopping centers and office buildings that lined most of the main streets switched the emphasis in design from surface to content, redefining survival in terms of a certain kind of inner environment, as opposed to an ingenious intermediary between inner and outer environments. The two contrasting styles of construction coexisted uneasily. To pass from one sort of structure to the other was stressful, and unhealthy. People often complained of catching colds and chills when obliged to move between an "air-con" environment and a non-air-conditioned building.

Regardless of their design, however, nearly all of the surfaces of Cebu City were considered holy ground. Their adornment often had a religious character, a fitting tribute, it appeared, to their ecological significance. Pictures of saints or of Jesus hung on interior walls in nearly every dwelling. Miniature shrines were fixed on the dashboards of buses and cars. Quantity appeared to be as important as quality—the more religious references apparent on a given surface, the better. Icons of various patron saints, for example, were both numerous and ubiquitous.

Like so many visitors, I was first struck by the concern for surfaces as it was evidenced on the jeepneys, the main form of public transportation in Cebu City. They were covered, both on their interior surfaces and on their exterior surfaces, with a wide assortment of decorations: tassels hanging from mirrors, paintings or fringe lining the interior ceilings, statues, miniature furniture or liquor bottles on the dashboard, and painted stripes of different colors and widths on the sides and hood of the exterior. The jeepney was a symbol of the local movement style as well as its agent. It expressed the values of the world it transported, which seemed "centered" on its surfaces.

The most striking example of the special regard for surfaces was apparent with respect to the surface of the human body itself, the skin and its clothing. Skin was spoken of as an indicator of a person's emotional character, something like the opposite of the American concept of a person's "guts." This outer boundary of a person was seen as vulnerable and delicate—easily injured—but it was also precious as a source of intelligence and beauty. One of the first characteristics women would mention, when they would speak to me about the beauty of some child or young woman they had seen, was the condition of their skin, whether it was fair or dark, smooth or rough.

The standards for human surface coverage also resonated with religious authority. Rosa, an ardent Catholic, recounted an incident at the basilica where a priest had denied her communion because she had appeared at the altar in a sleeveless dress. The priest had slapped her bare shoulders and said, "This is a church, this is not your house," and bid her go away. Likewise, in the women's dress code of San Carlos University, the rules for proper clothing were stated in terms of how much of the arm and shoulder were covered, and whether or not skirts must cover the knees. Modesty prohibited the display of bare skin—of uncovered surface area. When students spoke of the "immodest" costumes worn by various *sinulog* parade dance groups, they expressed their disapproval, not in terms of how tightly the costumes fit, but in terms of how much skin was exposed by the costume.

The value on surfaces was so "deeply" held that it appeared to work even in a sort of symbolic reversal. That is, while surfaces were adorned with precious objects of all kinds, likewise, objects found on surfaces, by their very location, gained value as well. At least this was in part how I explained the exceptional indulgence shown to visitors to the city—those social beings who arrived and temporarily remained situated on the edges or surfaces of the local society, who were not identified as being a part of its centers of power and control. Custom dictated that these guests be treated with special tolerance and generosity. Locals recounted with enthusiasm, for example, fiestas of years gone by when everyone had opened their houses to visitors and exhausted the resources of the household in an effort to make sure that whatever desire a visitor might have could be satisfied on the spot. This indulgence was not simply something reserved for honored and expected guests. In the fiesta context, the perfect stranger was the ideal guest, a complete outsider who was to be overwhelmed with the local good will. Guests, strangers, visitors—in sum, peripheral figures of all kinds—were meant to be treated as precious objects, carefully handled. Their location on the edge of society reinforced more functional ideological reasons for such favored treatment.[23] The indulgence shown to visitors was another example of how surfaces tended to bring out the best in their substances.

In my more unreflective, impressionistic moments, I sometimes perceived Cebu City as a collection of surfaces upon which human life draped itself. People seemed at home in an environment that allowed them to wade in it, or float upon its surface—to leave the constraints of a "pure" upright stance and adjust to more three-dimensional conditions. Even when walking, an activity that required a basically vertical orientation, people did not depend on an imagined vertical axis in order to maintain their balance, as is typical in the more "uptight" urban worlds of the United States. Much less habitual tension was carried in the skeletal-muscular systems of the walkers in this city than I was used to seeing in public walking behaviors. Another U.S. movement analyst, who later watched videotapes of people walking to and

LIBRARY, UNIVERSITY OF CHESTER

from the Basilica del Santo Niño, picked up on the marked difference in collective postural style immediately. In a casual viewing session, she took one look at the throngs of bodies passing by the main portal of the church and remarked with her first breath, "Wow, they really let it all hang out, don't they?" Her response was not intended to contain any negative evaluation whatsoever. On the contrary, the words were uttered in a serious, positively impressed tone. The analyst was appreciative of the ease of the walking style constructed by these urbanites and its marked difference from U.S. tendencies in analogous contexts.

Rosa, who was noted by her friends and teachers for her "get up and go," provided numerous examples of this tendency as well. She had a habit of literally lying down on the job at every available opportunity, and with the most productive results. Discussions would begin with the two of us sitting upright, and, before I knew it, she would be curled up on her side, her head resting with a cheek against her palm, avidly expressing some opinion. Whenever she "got into" the exchange of ideas, she tended to move to such an off-vertical orientation. She was the most adaptable companion I've ever known, in this respect. She could conform the shape of her person to whatever the available surfaces in her immediate environment might happen to be. The statements she made from these seemingly casual physical attitudes clearly indicated that she was not bored or fatigued. On the contrary, she was usually more engaged in the interaction after assuming them than before.

The collective public behavior of the city's inhabitants, on the whole, appeared to manifest a striking lack of interest in stressing the uprightness of the human condition, in the most literal sense of that phrase. This initially led me, with my foreigner's biases, to the mistaken impression that the city was inhabited by figuratively "spineless" creatures—an impression that carried with it several unfortunate associations, and a mistake many foreigners had made before me. Filipinos in general, I later discovered, were anxiously aware of their reputation for spinelessness.[24] The rapport established with surfaces carried with it a host of problematic associations outside the local context. The reactions, I realized, reflected my own biases, which ran very "deep." The value of surfaces indicated that, to understand local symbolic form, I would have to make some fairly radical adjustments in my own worldview. "Superficial," it was already clear, had a different meaning in the local context—something more like the meaning the concepts "fundamental" or "basic" had acquired in my own. States such as "edginess" or "being on edge" I needed to redefine in positive or at least neutral terms. Metaphors for worth no longer worked in terms of "shallow versus deep." Shallowness, particularly "thin-skinned" shallowness, could be a precious asset in this environment. The "icing on the cake" could more essential than the cake itself. The cover of the book would have to be judged as carefully as the book's interior. Still waters might not run deep, but that would make them no less interesting. A "well-grounded" argument (which, in this context, could as easily mean a free-floating one as a heavily anchored one) need not necessarily "stand firm" when tested.

The different patterning of surface/realm relations evident in the city's many material and movement constructions represented a very different, very positive valuing of surfaces, edges, and borders. My initial negative reactions to them revealed how deeply ingrained the biases against tropical border zones—as well as other sorts—were in my own value system. They shaped an epistemology of shelter and informed the organizing metaphors of a discourse of understanding.

Plurality

The other distinctive aspect of Cebu City's make-up was related to, and intensified by, its rapid growth. The city was extremely crowded. Spaces that seemed suitable for twelve people, such as the space inside a jeepney wagon, were used to accommodate twenty or twenty-five. Businesses that, I would have assumed, required their own lots of land sprang up in the area between the edge of a sidewalk and the traffic of the street. The sidewalks themselves were regular communities in miniature, something I found close to magical in its strangeness. If there was room for a weed to poke through on the sidewalk, there was room for a new business to be set up, be it watch repair, fruit selling, candy vending, or shoe repair.

This is not to say that the inhabitants of Cebu considered urban living conditions optimal or even normal. The available space of Cebu was considered cramped and overcrowded by all, and becoming more so. The city had, like nearly all the cities in the country, been growing more and more densely populated. Its density was somewhere around 1,800 persons per square kilometer in 1984.[25] Although its average density was nowhere near that of Manila proper (it was, indeed, around twenty times less), or even that of other regional cities, such as Iloilo on Panay Island, it was, nevertheless, changing at a rate around twice that of either of these other locations or of anywhere else in the region. Its density was increasing at about 20 percent a year.[26] High concrete walls, edged with broken glass, framed the homes of the wealthy for blocks upon blocks in various districts of the city and stood as symbols of the struggle to possess and control space, among other scarce resources. Battles over government resettlement projects that threatened to dismantle slum squatter areas were a well-known theme in the city's recent history.[27] Spatial conditions created tensions that put an edge of discomfort on all activities.

Yet, in spite of these shared perceptions, I found that my values for patterning space differed markedly from local ones. The first time I made a purchase in a local department store (a moderately expensive place to shop), a salesgirl, an immaculately dressed young woman sporting a polyester uniform complete with name tag and an air of assured competence, calmly took the skirt I had purchased and started folding it to put it into a bag for me. She folded . . . and folded and continued to fold, while I stood by in amazement, my eyes growing larger and larger, as I restrained the impulse to reach out and snatch my new purchase from her hands. She folded the skirt up into a ball only a few inches in diameter, stuffed it into a plastic bag small enough to hold a postcard snugly, and, as if that weren't enough, scotch-taped the bag shut. I half-wondered if she were afraid the skirt was going to somehow try to make a break for it. How could she possibly have seen fit to push the entire skirt into such a little place, I thought to myself? And yet there was something practiced about her manner, some pronounced consideration and care in her hand-eye coordination, that gave me the distinct impression that she felt she was doing her job well, making my purchase fit for a journey home. In the routine practices of everyday life, it became clear to me that packing things tightly into places had a general aesthetic appeal, as well as a practical value. Even in situations where conditions were perceived as uncrowded by others, the space appeared overloaded to me.

A common understanding of the use of space pervaded most public areas. Shop windows, carts, billboards—display areas of all kinds—filled their given spaces with as many objects as possible, arranging them in neat, often intricate patterns. Businesses seldom displayed single objects as examples of their stock. Instead, the standard strategy was to devote space to displaying number—or numerousness—to indicate, by means of resemblance, the volume of goods available for sale. The representation of valuable objects was thus constructed as a celebration of multiplicity, not uniqueness. The number of objects presented in a given display was usually too large to allow for a count of individual items to be taken easily. Instead, it was large enough to generate the perception of a *pool*.

Given this interest in displaying plurality, Cebu City appeared remarkable in terms of its sheer quantity of detail. My eye was continually drawn, as I walked through the city streets, to pools of different shapes and substances: lines of chewing gum pieces, neatly arranged with each piece tilting at exactly the the same angle in a line displayed on the old wooden boxes of the poorer street vendors; spirals made of handkerchiefs set out for sale on the sidewalks, and carefully stacked pyramids of corn, star apples, green mangoes, or *pomelos*—enormous grapefruits. Millions of duplicates presented themselves in thoughtful terms along the streets.

The interest in duplication and multiplicity did not negate personal touches. Names of small businesses often referred in familiar and informal terms to their owners. Julie's Bakery and Pete's Kitchen were two such enterprises in downtown Cebu. The names advertised a friendly casualness, giving the city the look of one huge neighborhood of long-time friends. The collective effect was an atmosphere, in many respects a false atmosphere, of relaxed familiarity.

Much of the duplication evident in Cebu City was of American objects. "America" saturated the materials of the city with its most commercial messages. Advertising of American brand names such as Coke and Colgate was everywhere; American popular music, mainly love ballads, filled the air; American-style clothing was displayed in the stores; American movies—family shows, such as *Splash*, *The Natural*, and *The Karate Kid*—were almost always being shown in one or several of the city's main theaters. Any American in Cebu would have felt flooded by the quantity of these secular and commercial references. I never outgrew a faint sense of disappointment over the distortion of what I automatically, but quite incorrectly, interpreted as the representation of American life, pulled out of its original context and imposed onto these foreign streets. In this respect, as well, the city was typically Philippine in its affect, for nowhere else in Southeast Asia does such overwhelming evidence of American contact appear.

Temporal patterns echoed spatial ones in Cebu. Time made its presence felt in the city through the movements that engulfed its noisy streets, surging and fading in a perpetual series of waves that were for the most part constructed with the aid of machinery of various kinds. Again, the patterning expressed a positive value for intensified multiplicity. Radio music was, perhaps, the most obvious example, since it was always and everywhere in evidence. Music from businesses spilled over into the streets outside, making it virtually impossible to escape their sound, which mixed with the constant roar of unmuffled engines but somehow overcame it. Whatever the current handful of hit songs happened to be, they were played on radio stations frequently. A big hit might be played as often as every twenty minutes all day long for weeks on end. Nobody seemed to mind the redundancy, although I found that at times it nearly drove me to distraction. In time, I came to accept it as it blended in with all the other seemingly shortened cycles of activity.

Rides of all kinds manifested the patterning as well. Public vehicles stopped and started with such frequency along roadways that they never really seemed to get going. There were no freeways, and not even main arterials were free from congestion. The organization of public transport thus intensified the pattern. Moreover, aside from general "pausing" areas in the city's center, I never located designated "stops" for any vehicle's route. When someone wanted to get off of a vehicle, they would call out or bang on a surface, the vehicle would slow down, and off they'd go. Catching rides was a similar process. The sustained effect of traveling for a rider was one of short phrases of slowing down and speeding up. Even on long rides throughout the island, local buses would pause to accommodate the needs of individual riders so frequently that I felt an urge, when I first started using these services, to just get out and walk, purely out of a need to feel a sense of "really" getting somewhere.

The rides also revealed the way beginnings and endings of temporal forms were constructed and reconstructed amidst the flux of action in the city. With most activities, regardless of the actual spans of time needed to perform them, there was an interest in and an appreciation of the quality of time's movement, particularly the quality of time as it quickened. Cebu City was constantly filled with representations of time's fleeting quality: with thousands of sudden movements of body parts, with countless moments of urgency. These occurred among the crowds of people on the streets whenever they needed to make contact with one another. "Timey" actions executed in a fluent manner— sudden nods, accelerating statements, quick hand gestures—were used to organize the most fundamental social processes: greetings and farewells, inclusion and exclusion, consensus and disagreement. Manifesting the rush of a feeling—intensifying the sense of immediacy that is the essence of an impulse—had an expressive function roughly equivalent to the role of firmness in American culture. Where I would firmly agree, with a nod, a handshake, a vocal phrase, or some other gesture, my local counterpart would quickly agree. It happened constantly in every kind of communicative context.

Conversely, individuals in busy public places of Cebu seemed, to U.S. eyes, strangely disconnected from, or at least unconcerned with, the forces of gravity. Person-to-person interaction appeared at once exotically syncopated and strangely impersonal, or "cold"—that is to say, without a marked stress or emphasis on the inherent power, volume, or force of the action. Even in the most subtle and fleeting actions, the value on quickening was apparent instead. For example, I watched countless chess games going on on the sidewalks and in the restaurants of Cebu, and my eye was always caught by the style in which the pieces on the game board were typically moved from place to place. Players would study the board as their turn came about and then suddenly whisk a piece of their choosing into the air so quickly that I would feel my neck jerk back slightly in a startled reaction as my eyes struggled to keep up with the sight of the gesture. The players' action of grasping these pieces was performed without caution, without carefulness, but rather in a release of tension, as if a moment of decision had passed and the consequences of following out that decision were no cause for alarm or hesitation (the *bahala na*, "come what may" attitude sometimes described in the literature on Philippine values).[28] At the same time, however, the initial action of the grasp was performed with precision, and the elevation of the piece into the air usually traced a finely gradated curving pathway through the space. The initiation, while "careless" or releasing, was deft all the same. When I watched local chess games, I found myself admiring the nerve of the players as well as their skill, and this reaction was due in part to their agile yet unrestrained style of initiating a move on the board. The poignancy of time's passing was keenly understood in Cebu City. Even the smallest facts spoke to this large issue.

Temporal spans also ended in what were to me exotic ways. What I came to recognize as typically "ending-like" initially seemed completely "endless"—what I might have thought of as a "middle" sort of moment. Again, I first noticed the patterning in radio music. The "fade out" was far and away the most common mode of "ending" recorded tunes. Social gatherings of many kinds, as well, tended to assume a similar form. Fiestas, for example, did not end in a wild finale. Instead, they died gradually, in the week following their main ceremonies. Departures on almost any social or public occasion exhibited a similar character: they faded, as opposed to stopping abruptly. Whether the occasion was a church service, a student meeting, or a birthday party, the fluidly gradated pattern of departure held true.

Endings, however, could also close on a quickened note. It took me a while to catch onto the fact that I was continually creating mild chaos in my interviews with residents by my style of ending them, which did not involve this quality. My own cues for the idea that "now our conversation is over" consisted of statements of affirmation and emphasis—for example, "Thank you very much for all your help!" These expressions somehow confused the issue, for often the person being interviewed would start off on a new thought, or would simply cringe and return to an idea already discussed. I eventually noticed that endings were constructed differently. They were not affirmed or emphasized, they were not pressed in any way. Instead, conversations more often ended with abrupt, hurried phrases that, to me, appeared to evaporate into thin air. Most commonly the phrase used for me was, "Okay Sally . . . ," said quickly and with the attention that had until then been focused on me melting away in a blur. I often felt as though I were slinking away from these conversations, as though I were ending them stealthily or somehow dishonestly. Or else it seemed I was being "dismissed" with a "curt" nod of the head or some such quickened gesture. With time, I realized that this style of ending had nothing to do with honesty or dishonesty. It was simply a way of breaking the flow of time to mark an interval. Quickness opened and closed interactions as effectively and humanely as emphasis could.

The value on quickening seemed to lie behind the preference for intensified duplication, which served to make possible a greater number of experiences of this temporal quality. Manifestations of quickening in time tended to characterize the initiation of all kinds of repetitive activities, from the most casual, such as the nod of a head in agreement, to the most important, such as the implementation of a new government program.

Games, dances, and other collective social acts also employed intensely repetitious patterning as the normal mode of organizing action in time. Religious services, for example, at the many large Catholic churches in Cebu were tightly scheduled. Services followed one another continuously throughout religious days, with crowds swelling and shrinking as worshippers arrived and departed continually. The cumulative sensation was one of an endless repetition of short activity sequences—a pattern of echoes.

Arnis, the martial art of stick-fighting noted in Chapter 1, was another activity that organized energy through highly intensified repetition. The form was, in fact, designed around the principle that duplication could be a deadly force. As Cacoy's demonstrations and those of other fighters I witnessed later illustrated, the goal was not to overpower one's opponent with a single blow of great force, or to pierce one's opponent with one mortal stroke, but rather to develop the ability to deliver a number of blows in rapid succession over the largest surface area possible. Training of the fighting arm emphasized a repetitious movement, that, when perfected, looked like the fluttering of a butterfly's wing, so rapid and fluent were its actions.

Brief and repetitious phrasing of action was also recognized locally as being capable of carrying a certain irony, particularly when it manifested in patterns of law enforcement. During my stay, it was the traffic laws that were gaining most comment as a typical example of the sporadic nature by which rules were tightened and relaxed in a seemingly endless fashion. A foreign expert had been imported to strictly enforce traffic regulations pertaining to the city's major intersection. His presence was greeted with general amusement. The effort, though seemingly designed to bring about a permanent change, was only temporary, I was told, again and again. People predicted that it would last a couple of months and would then be abandoned, only to be taken up in a year or so, at which time it would be abandoned again. Another case in point was the enforcement of the dress code at my host institution. Students and faculty members alike noted that the enforcement of the women's uniform dress code was generally strict at the beginning of a term but was bound to fade in a few weeks' time, only to be revived again after some undefined interval of time had passed. The pattern of rule enforcement was described in terms of a repetitive tensing and releasing that appeared to continue endlessly and was characterized as short-lived. What struck me as peculiar about these episodes was not their actuality—oscillation in the enforcement of social rules is typical of communities everywhere. What was striking was the way in which people reconstructed action scenarios by focusing on the short-lived, impulsive repetitiveness of a pattern of action, and by claiming that style as distinctive of their own local world. Intensive duplication was the frame people in the city used to tell stories about themselves. They tended to explain it as a "Filipino" trait.

Duplication, however, was also a feature of the city's life that could be constructed in a particularly local manner. Voice phrasing in communication of many kinds revealed it. Drivers, for example, called out their routes about the city in a hawking style that was unlike any I heard elsewhere in the Philippines. It had a peculiar two-syllable, swelling/fading lilt. Calls swelled into full voice as the destination's two-syllable code word, *Lapu* or *Opon* or *lisay* was repeated in a rush. "Lapu, lapu, lapu, lapuuu . . . . " Eventually they died away. The collective effect of the hawking, while it obviously was not consciously orchestrated, was a percussive, musical quality that pervaded the atmosphere of the city's center, where many drivers and conductors were continually advertising their services. It was not simply repetitive, this temporal duplication. This local mode of phrasing created short, elastic, two-phasic patterns, patterns that "bounced" repeatedly through otherwise unmarked temporal intervals. It was a type of intensely repetitive patterning that could best be described as "resilient."[29]

Resilient phrasing was basic to the local accent. Whenever anybody made a list of ideas for me, whether it was in English or Cebuano or a mix, a bouncy, singsong patterning, quite distinct from the lilts of other islands, would come through. Elastic phrases also figured prominently as rhetorical devices for delivering key responses or arguments at public speaking occasions. I encountered the pattern whenever I attended public lectures and discussions, which were held sometimes within the modern, air-conditioned rooms of the U.S. Information Agency and other times in the classrooms and lecture halls of the city's many colleges and universities. Speakers did not typically deliver "punch" lines; they did not drive home their main points. Instead, they would repeat a line judged to be particularly important a number of times, letting it echo resiliently, usually in an abbreviated phrase that had two accents, so that its meaning could sink in before continuing their argument. Humor, also, was modeled along resilient lines. There was a marked preference for puns (although this was by no means unique to Cebu) that conveyed humor, again, not through clinchers or punch lines, but instead through a duplication or slightly distorted echoing.

The particular dynamics of this resilient phrasing style set the Cebu City scene apart from other places in the Philippines. Its importance as a marker of Cebuano ethnic identity was brought home to me on an occasion when I asked a resident expert on Cebuano dance why it was that the *sinulog* could be recognized as distinctively Cebuano. The question had been bothering me, since, even though the dance was being promoted by the city as its own unique ritual act, it was common knowledge that lots of other towns and cities on other islands also had *sinulog* dancing, and had for as long as anyone could remember.

The question presented no problem for my informant. She answered without hesitation that the *sinulog* of Cebu City was indeed uniquely "Cebuano" because it was bouncy—a distinctive quality, she said, of all Cebuano folk dance. She began to demonstrate for me, using steps that were organized in terms of the same two-phasic, delicately elastic patterning that I'd heard employed in the hawkers' calls.

Resilient phrasing did indeed appear in most forms of Cebuano dancing I observed. It did not serve any special expressive purpose, but was simply the accepted baseline for movement. "Free-style" social dancing that was done in discos and at parties, a form modeled on contemporary American social dance, was also typically performed using a uniform, resilient baseline. Even aerobics classes maintained activity using two-phasic resilient patterns. The phrasing was a pervasive feature of all kinds of local dance movement, both "traditional" and nontraditional.

The extent to which resilient phrasing influenced Cebuano life over the centuries could perhaps best be measured by its incorporation into the vernacular language itself, where it served a role on the borderlines among the language's systems of syntax, semantics, and phonology. It was used to represent a certain verbal mood, a pattern described in the linguistic literature as "reduplication," which occurred whenever a verb root was repeated. *Sayawsayaw*, for example, was the reduplicated form of the verb root *sayaw*, which meant "to dance." The reduplicated or resilient form indicated an ordinary or low-key manner of performance. It included a sense of generality or indeterminacy. *Sayawsayaw*, for instance, meant that over a period of time, during a party, perhaps, a person danced, not intensively, but now and again, more or less continuously throughout the party. Reduplicated or resilient verbs conveyed an easygoing attitude, whereby the actor referred to in the conversation does not invest an extraordinary amount of energy in the act performed, but performed in an ongoing, normal progression of acts. It represented a general mode of performance, one in which the habitual repetition of action acquired a "non-intense" and relaxed or free-flowing character.

Reduplication occurred with two-syllable verb roots in Cebuano (unlike Tagalog, for example, which uses single syllables as well as dual-syllable verb roots). It was the two-syllable root, that, when reduplicated, produced the singsong quality that was the basis of the local accent. The structure of the vernacular language indicated that the source of this local phrasing style was a relatively ancient one.

Highly duplicatable, quickened patterning was thus a mode of organizing social energy, both mental and physical, in time and in space. It was an especially salient feature of local life and a recognized element of Cebuano ethnic identity. In the *sinulog* performances, this phrasing style was perhaps the most powerful polysemic or multivocal sign evident in the performance process. It represented a calm but liquid energy state, animated only slightly by minor sources of disturbance.

Summary

The city, like a giant seashell, was perched at an end of the earth—on the edge of a body of water. Clusters of structures crowded together. Their surfaces displayed meticulously ordered arrays of duplicates— many times with an American subject, but just as often with a religious theme. Baking in the tropical heat, people went about their business in these troubled times beneath a powerful sun, some of them inside the air-conditioned wombs of the modern era, and some of them be-

hind the permeable surfaces that had served the place for centuries.
If there was always the heat, there was also always the water, whose
movements provided the metaphors that people constructed so as to
manage their community, flowing along on the surface currents of its
fluctuating circumstances.

Such is the portrait I have painted.

It would be an injustice to the inhabitants of Cebu City were I to
give the impression that the above generalizations fully account for
the vast array of behavior and symbolism I observed in their community. There were, of course, numerous opportunities to observe objects and individuals who did not conform to the patterns given
above. For every preference I have noted, exceptions were apparent.
For example, one of the most compelling instances I have ever seen
of "backbone"—postural verticality—I observed on Cebu Island. It
was manifest in the torso of a young woman plaintiff stating her case
in an informal arbitration process that took place in quiet tones inside
the small, cement-block meeting hall of a *barrio* several miles south
of the city. The woman sat all by herself on a rough wooden bench,
clutching an old black umbrella as she faced the man she accused
of cheating her out of her share of lottery winnings. She took her
place on the bench, neatly assumed a posture that would have satisfied the strictest nineteenth-century American schoolmarm, and
told her story, without ever changing anything about herself along
the way. She "stuck to her guns" mentally and physically, and she won
her case.

The diversity of behavior apparent in Cebu City was no less extensive than that observable among any human community. A full range
of phrasing patterns, spatial forms, and bodily attitudes was present.
The characteristics mentioned above, resiliency, surface values, off-
verticality, were remarkable to me, not by their mere appearance, but
because they appeared in an array of contexts that were surprising to
me, and because they appeared as frequently and as regularly as they
did. They all contributed to the notion of what a "self" was in this
community and how it was likely to behave, and with what it was likely
to interact, all things being equal. It is in relation to these habitual
modes of conduct, situated as they were both historically and contem-
porarily in the distinctively built environment of the city, that the
movement style of the *sinulog* can be interpreted.

Having described in some detail how Cebu City lived in space and
time in 1984 and 1985, and how it coped with its tropical, neocolonial
island environment, and having given some information concerning

the beings that inhabited this world and molded its character, there remains one other symbol that must be introduced before focusing directly on the *sinulog* performances that were staged by these human "selves": the Santo Niño de Cebu, the local source of inspiration for the *sinulog* and for much of what it represented.

Chapter 5
The Niño

Symbols, particularly those caught up in sacred processes, are often analyzed in weighty terms, with a focus on their power, force, or potency. Victor Turner went so far in his early work as to characterize a symbol simply as "a positive force in an activity field" (1967:20, 26). "Dominant symbols"—a culture's most forceful and meaningful symbols—were described by Turner (1967:27–30) as possessing three empirical properties: condensation, unification, and polarization. Dominant symbols, in other words, bear a striking resemblance to magnets.

Magnetism can be understood essentially as a particular sort of movement. It is movement that is literally nothing, if not attractive. It is movement that can't be offensive, by definition. Magnetism is interest in motion. It is the movement of collection, of crowd-forming, and of city-making.

It would be hard to imagine a symbol whose magnetism surpassed that of the Santo Niño de Cebu. This figure, by all popular account, appeared to have charmed the populace—not only that of Cebu City, but of the entire region and most of the rest of the nation as well. Social scientist Douglas Elwood formed a hypothesis in the early 1970s that there were only two dominant Christ images in the Philippines: that of the Santo Niño, the Holy Child King, and that of the Tragic Victim. There was certainly no evidence in Cebu City in 1984 to indicate otherwise. Such was the power of the Santo Niño that it was believed to share the mental stage of the archipelago's Christ imagery only with the figure of Christ crucified.[1] It was a classic example of a Turnerian dominant symbol.

The ubiquity of the Niño's presence in the various spaces of the city suggested a kind of public acceptance and acknowledgment of its miraculous power that seemed to have no limits. So potent, apparently, were the Niño's powers of goodness that its purity could never be endangered, no matter what its environment. Virtually no place in Cebu was unsuitable to serve as a location for a replica of the Santo Niño image. Every desktop, every altar, every shelf and corner, whether that of a luxurious "air-con" office or that of a lean-to rattan shack, was a potential shrine. No home or office or vehicle seemed complete without a Santo Niño image, or several. There was no service or prayer from which the Santo Niño image was necessarily excluded. The candle sellers at the basilica, who made a business of saying prayers for their customers, regularly reported that, even when a customer had asked them to pray to the Virgin Mary or to one of the saints, they always included the Santo Niño in the prayer as well. As one candle seller laughingly remarked, "Bisag unsang adlawa 'starring' g'yud na ang Santo Niño" ("Everyday, without a doubt, the Santo Niño is the star of the show"). To be sure, the magnetism of the Santo Niño was not all-pervasive or omnipotent. Undoubtedly, areas and individuals escaped, resisted, rejected, and resented its influence. However, the available evidence from public life clearly indicated that the Santo Niño's following included an overwhelming majority of the city's population.

Part of the attractiveness of the Santo Niño de Cebu was unmistakably innate. There were aspects of the image's physical appearance that compelled attention and admiration even from relatively undevoted, disinterested, and dispassionate observers like myself. Not unlike the *wayang kulit* shadow puppet figures of Java and Bali, the actual image of the Santo Niño de Cebu, the wooden figure that served as the model for all the replicas found throughout the city, was itself a highly complicated miniature. It had the inherent and immediate allure typical of all miniatures. That is to say, it condensed and enriched the values of the world from which it was drawn.

The Santo Niño de Cebu was less than twelve inches tall. It stood atop an ornate nineteenth-century, double-tiered bronze pedestal that was gilded with floral motifs. Even with this additional stand, however, the little statue did not approach the height of a normal child of the age it represented, which was about four years old. The face of the Niño was only a few inches in diameter, its hands and feet equally tiny.

The dwarflike nature of the Niño, however, was not in the least belittling. Indeed, as scholars who have studied the image most closely have repeatedly observed, littleness was its weapon, not its weakness.[2] Its minuscule scale effected a magnification of the space around it, creating an almost tangible aura of greatness in its chapel. It was at

once a tiny and an immense presence, and it was its very tininess that
intensified its immensity. To approach the Santo Niño was to confront
and grasp enormity in a profoundly intimate way.[3] One didn't need
to be a devotee to appreciate this dynamism.

The complexity of the miniature's appearance resulted largely
from its embodiment of highly contrasting figures (Figure 5.1). The
face, with its dark curly hair and soft, childish features, was clearly
that of a very young boy—not an infant in a cradle, but a child more
independent of its mother's care. It personified the Divine Christ
Child, an image of Jesus as a boy. However, the body, which was
posed in a sophisticated asymmetrical position, had been given more
adult proportions and attitudes. The legs rotated outward, the right
leg bent in the sort of stance with which Louis XIV of France has
become associated. The right arm was bent from the elbow, with the
hand raised to the shoulder in the conventional two-fingered gesture
of a supreme pontiff's blessing.[4] The left arm, also bent at the elbow,
but only to a right angle perpendicular to the torso, presented an
open palm supporting a globe. The acclaimed Filipino author Nick
Juaquin once remarked that the Santo Niño de Cebu carried in hand
what Magellan had in mind—a global consciousness. The image's posture and gestures expressed the figures of mature authority.[5]

The Niño's aura of adult magnificence was enhanced greatly by its
attire. Boots, gloves, and crown were all made of gold, as were the
globe, the staff, and the scepter that it carried. All were literally drip-
ping with diamonds and pearls. The body was clothed in so many
layers of silk, linen, lace, and velvet that the courtier's figure, save for
the hands and feet, was virtually indiscernable. Its inner vestments
resembled priests' smocks or albs.[6] A velvet cape, embroidered with
gold and silver threads, fell from its shoulders to the foot of the pedestal. Sashes and pendants of gold coins, emeralds, garnets, rubies,
and more diamonds were draped over the front of the outermost
tunic, a bishop's dalmatic.

Given all this glorious finery, the image appeared, not as a person,
but as a fabulously adorned surface, a surface that obviously had been
the object of an entire culture's unflagging attention, so cleverly integrated were its minute but priceless ornamental details. Over each
and every available square centimeter of the figure there appeared
the signs of a grand devotion.[7] So elaborate was the symbolism of the
image's surface ornamentation that its movement was a momentous
occasion in its own right. The changing of the Niño's clothes, called
the *hubo* ceremony, was a ritual of major importance that marked the
beginning and the ending of his fiesta. Only the highest ranks of

Figure 5.1. The Santo Niño.

the city's longtime elite women, the *camarera*, or ladies-in-waiting to the Niño, were allowed to orchestrate this transformation. Maintenance of its surface finery was thus one way in which the image was involved in the reinforcement of established class differences.

The surface decorations of the Santo Niño de Cebu all worked in opposition. That is to say, they served to enhance and highlight by their very contrast to it the one undecorated feature of the idol: its tiny, smiling face. The face was the naturalized nucleus of the image, its dynamism evidently so intense that no modification could improve upon it. The face, pure and simple, was the ultimate and miraculous expression of the miniature's majestic largess. Yet it was the face of a child, while all other aspects of the statue, its costume as well as its pose, represented a full-fledged king.

The propagation of a casting of Jesus as both boy and king had been a Spanish undertaking, conceived in the sixteenth century, and promoted most avidly and successfully by the reformed order of Discalced Carmelite Nuns led by Saint Teresa of Avila.[8] The complex figure of the Holy Child King, brought back to Prague with the Carmelites, inspired a spectacular resurgence of cult worship in Western Europe during the Counter-Reformation movement of the seventeenth century.[9] The devotion to what then became known as the Holy Child of Prague eventually spread all over the world, captivating Christians in such remote areas as South Africa, Ceylon, China, the Bahamas Islands, Australia, Thailand, and the Philippines.[10]

In the Philippines, the emergence of this devotion to the Holy Child was somewhat complicated. The Infant King actually arrived on Philippine shores on more than one occasion, in more than one guise, over the course of the centuries. The arrival of the image of the Santo Niño de Cebu was the first and most remarkable appearance. It occurred with Ferdinand Magellan's arrival in 1521, when, according to Magellan's chronicler Pigafetta, a wooden image of the child Jesus was presented to the queen of Cebu, the wife of Rajah Humabon, on the occasion of her baptism.[11] After Magellan's death on Mactan Island during a skirmish with the local chief Lapulapu, and after the hasty exit of Magellan's expedition shortly thereafter, the Niño evidently remained in the queen's possession. Over forty years later, when the next Spanish fleet arrived under the command of Miguel López de Legaspi, a crew member, Juan Camus, while inspecting the charred ruins of Cebu City, discovered an image of the Holy Child Jesus in a pine box obviously brought from Spain.[12] The finding of the Santo Niño was treated as a miraculous omen of good will by the colonizers. López de Legaspi ordered that the image be enthroned in the very first church built, in a chapel for the image on the spot where it was discovered. He also ordered that a feast be held annually to celebrate the finding of the relic.[13]

From this fortuitous beginning, the Santo Niño de Cebu proceeded to inspire its own cult worship independent of the Carmelite Infant of Prague devotion and was entrusted to the care of the Augustinian

Order, the founders and first missionaries of Catholicism in the Philippines.[14] Eventually, the Carmelite devotion, along with duplicate images of the Infant of Prague, also arrived in the archipelago, and the devotion to these images was fostered by the Redemptorist Fathers as well as the Carmelites in the Philippines.[15] While the Infant of Prague and the Santo Niño sprang from the same original European source, the worship of the two in the Philippines was nevertheless distinguishable.[16] The Infant of Prague devotion in Europe began over a century later than the Santo Niño de Cebu and became a worldwide cult. The Holy Child of Cebu, in contrast, had a uniquely Philippine history that predated the European devotion to the Holy Child of Prague, while later incorporating certain aspects of it once it had been brought to the archipelago.

Cebu's Santo Niño, as Holy Child images go in the archipelago, had thus had a highly "original" history in the Philippines. The first baptism of the whole archipelago, the first Christian procession and festival in the Philippines, the first Christian church erected in the archipelago, and the first Spanish settlement established in the archipelago, all these originated in the name of the Santo Niño.[17] While it embodied this original and layered history, the miniature Niño of Cebu was at the same time a sculptural metaphor. It represented the juxtaposition of the dissimilar elements acquired over the course of its history, as well as their ultimate merger. Within the figure, the seasoned *patron* played off against the pristine *enfante*, the courtly guardian-defender played against the untamed, yet vulnerable juvenile ward, the august omniscient played against the eternal innocent. The image was irreducibly multivalent, its complex of personalities melded into a single figure, while still remaining somehow mutually dissociate. One could say, as Jacques Derrida has said of a linguistic sign, that the image differed from itself. Whatever character might be immediately recognized within the figure was just as quickly checked by the perception of another facet, itself subject to the same upstaging by a rival persona.

The play of dissimilar characters inhering in the little image presented an impossible combination, a presence that defied or preceded reason, a presence that could not conceivably be present, and yet, undeniably, was. Logically speaking, the idol was an empirical error, a theme not meant to become an entity. One of its two major opposing characters, the boy or the priest-king, should have deferred to the other, but neither did. Both clamored for identity at once in a synchrony that should have been discordant, given their radically different characters, but somehow was not. The Niño image, in sum, was a distinctively Philippine trace of an enigma, a particularly darling and endearing little trace, perhaps, but a baffling, perplexing, and difficult mark of implicit "othering" (both characters continuously emerging as the Other to each other), nonetheless. Representing an essentially mysterious being, mysterious because its identity could never be fully resolved, the symbol's appearance went beyond ordinary forms of reality—or before them.

Ultimately, the Santo Niño image represented nothing other than a movement. It was an expansive movement: the restless but indulgent movement of conflicting identities asserted in unexplainable harmony by its differing characters. It inspired reflection in any observer familiar with its symbolism, devotee or no, on the universal miracles of possibility, of which it was itself an example. Like all religious images, the Santo Niño de Cebu effected a sense of identity with a believable though mysterious source of all being. In this particular manifestation, however, that source was unmistakably acknowledged as an origin of a highly complicated kind. Moreover, in a more pragmatic and historical vein, the image invited contemplation about local miracles and mysterious truths, most centrally about the tensions and contradictions within the society that most clearly reflected those of its own constitution. While its royal bearing and adornment clearly conveyed messages about the hierarchies and power structures that it was frequently employed to reinforce in the society at large, the image nevertheless also represented the hope and the destiny of meek and vulnerable social figures to belong as well, during a moment of miraculous reflection, to the highest ranks of the Philippine omnipotent.[18]

The worship of the Santo Niño reached out, although in different ways, to all sectors of the city's society. The church in which it was housed, the Basilica Minore del Santo Niño, drew such an eclectic congregation that it achieved a reputation as a kind of haven for anonymity. As one longtime observer and historian of the local culture once remarked, there was a kind of freedom associated with frequenting the Santo Niño's church that was unavailable at other churches in the city. In smaller churches, one was likely to be more under the thumb of the rector. Other large churches tended to have certain emphases. The Sacred Heart church catered to the upper class, the Redemptorist church had a political orientation. Joining a certain church could label a member as a progressive or a radical or a conservative, or as some other sort of Roman Catholic. At the Santo Niño's church, however, no such labels were applied.

The appeal of the image, at least as it was conceived in popular discourse, transcended factionalism. It was publicly acknowledged as

a source of integrative energies, which had the capacity to speak, albeit in different ways, to all. The human diversity of the scene at the
Niño's chapel that the prominent Manilan journalist, Kerima Polotan,
described in 1974 was still accurate ten years later:

The school girls come in on their way to school; the housewives, before going
shopping; the dowagers, heavy with diamonds; office workers, barrio folk,
some afflicted souls prostrating their infirmities before the Child; an occasional sophisticate, a pregnant mother, a pair of sweethearts, humanity bur-
dened with the business of living. There are beggars, too . . . they don't enter
as beggars, but as worshippers. (1974:55)[19]

The Basilica del Santo Niño's congregation, like that of the city as a
whole, was a mixed bag, with no pure strains predominating. The
fiesta practices, which over the centuries had included such activities
as bullfighting, Chinese fireworks, beauty contests, basketball games,
and disco dances, illustrated how every ethnic influence in the community had become caught up—engaged, though not erased—in the
devotion.[20] All economic strata were involved as well. Longtime elite
residents took charge of the Niño's clothing and surface maintenance.
They also joined the ranks of the Cofradia del Santo Niño, the service
organization formed by López de Legaspi in 1565 to lead and maintain
the worship and feast day of the image.[21] Middle-class members from
all occupations, like Cacoy, the martial arts instructor, and Rosa, my
interpreter, were faithful attendees of the weekly prayer services at
the basilica as well. The bulk of the Niño's following, however, like
the bulk of the city's population, was poor.[22]

The Niño image was, in this respect, a symbol that claimed to unite
people, a symbol that tended to bring people together despite all that
normally kept them apart. While it by no means eliminated, and, in
fact, through rituals like the *hubo* and the elaborately organized fiesta
procession, actually reinforced the divisions of class and ethnicity that
existed within the city's society, nevertheless, the image also inspired
a mythology of faith and devotion that attenuated these divisions to a
larger extent than could be accomplished by virtually any other force
within the culture. The tens of thousands of diverse devotees that
appeared en masse daily, weekly, and yearly before its chapel and in
its courtyard, the thousands of duplicate images located throughout
the city, and the innumerable references to the Santo Niño de Cebu
in place names, business titles and imagery, and other forms of public
discourse all bore witness to the overwhelming influence of the image
as one element of relatively common ground in the city's complex
social life. In sum, the image was a positive though deeply compro-

mised symbol of what has been called "anti-structure," the sense of community that transcends the differences created by a culture's social structure.[23] Over the centuries it had become enmeshed in an array of devotional practices that effected for its devotees what Turner (1977:46) has termed "normative *communitas*"—a shared experience of the human condition constructed and constrained by the sanctions and conventions of the existing social order.

The Niño's Impact on the City

For hundreds of years, the Santo Niño de Cebu had inspired a gigantic yearly cycle of collection and dispersal, a pattern of pilgrimage to and from its shrine, which, since 1965, had been granted the eminent title Basilica del Santo Niño de Cebu, but was still known to many simply as St. Augustin's, or the Santo Niño church.[24] In this regard, the image of the Santo Niño had given Cebu City something akin to a cultural pulse rate. It quickened once a year in January during its fiesta celebration, when tens of thousands of devotees from all over the archipelago journeyed to the basilica to pay their respects and fulfill their vows of pilgrimage.[25] Pilgrims would say their prayers over the nine-day or "novena" prayer progression leading up to the procession of the image, which was regarded as the symbolic reenactment of its original carriage to its original chapel. They might also bring along their own replicas of the Holy Child, to set inside the basilica and thereby "participate" in the occasion.[26] As a gesture of reverence, the pilgrims would approach the image to give the foot of the idol's votive stand a kiss or a loving touch, satisfying the ultimate aim of their journey: to draw ever nearer to the Santo Niño de Cebu.

Into the city's already highly heterogeneous composition, the fiesta brought an even more colorful admixture. The majority of the temporary influx was from rural areas. In this respect, the celebration amounted to a brief but huge infusion of "rurality" into the urban center. When pilgrims arrived from the outlying regions at fiesta time, many had nowhere to sleep except the sidewalks or the wharves. They brought to the city's devotional celebration a variety of non-orthodox peasant traditions. Among them was the practice of the *sinulog* dance ritual, which was defined within the city, in the more charitable references, as an alternative form of prayer.

Since the 1950s, this yearly devotional pattern had come to be echoed in a more purely urban vein throughout the year. Every Friday afternoon the basilica courtyard (the basilica's interior had proved too small for the crowds) filled and emptied successively with local devotees, who gathered to join in "perpetual novena" prayer services to the Niño, held in both English and Visayan.[27] The perpetual novenas, like the yearly fiesta novena, consisted of hymns of praise, sung in Latin and in English or Visayan, and set prayers acknowledging the Santo Niño as Patron of Cebu and the Philippines and as the source of self-discipline, charity, and all forms of right conduct. The prayers also sought the assistance of the Niño with all doubts, temptations, trials of loneliness and weariness, failure, troubles, sorrows, illnesses, weaknesses, and shortcomings of every kind.[28] Every week, year in, year out, hundreds upon hundreds arrived in the courtyard, followed the novena service, and then departed until the following Friday.

These forms of worship, the novena, and the fiesta prayers, processions, and feast, established Cebu City as a center for religious practice relating to the Santo Niño. The practices had much in common with those of other religious centers in the Philippines, such as those for the Santo Entierro, or Black Nazarene, of Quiapo Church in Manila, the Santo Niño of Kalibo, on Panay Island, or the Virgen sa Regle of Opon on nearby Mactan. Some centers of pilgrimage, such as Tacloban City on Leyte Island, which also had a miraculous Santo Niño image, openly imitated on a smaller scale the worship practices of Cebu, making themselves into miniature devotional duplicates of Cebu City.[29] Despite the similarities, however, the worship of the Santo Niño de Cebu had both a temporal and a spiritual magnitude, an immense gravity all its own, which gave the city unique religious standing throughout the archipelago.

The port of Cebu City was, by the action described above, defined to a considerable extent as the Santo Niño's dwelling place. Somewhat like the *tautau* ancestral idols of highland Sulawesi, the Niño served as the permanent protector of the port and its domain.[30] He was regarded as a legendary Supreme Defender, who inspired movement in his devotees, gathering them in and allowing them to scatter. Yet the Niño himself remained relatively immobile, serene in his basilica. Only on the yearly occasion of the image's procession through the streets of the city center—a ponderous, rigidly structured movement process involving swarms of honor guards and military that was staged with utmost solemnity and decorum—did mobility become a theme in its existence.

This extraordinarily stable character of the Niño exhibited in orthodox ritual practice profoundly complicated the identity of Cebu City, contradicting the city's identity as a marginal outpost of civilization. Since the arrival of the Niño, the city was no longer simply a transit point in a circulatory system. With the Niño, it became the heart, or one heart, of it as well.

Shaky Claims to Centerhood

The gift of "centerhood" bequeathed upon the city by the Niño was, however, somewhat fragile. It was, in reality, always in danger of disintegration should the image and its symbolic forces become involved in the cycles of arrival and departure that governed so many aspects of the city's social life. As journalist Jaime Falar noted in a local newspaper in 1975, on the day commemorating López de Legaspi's discovery of the image, "Today . . . is thanksgiving day for the thousands of [the Santo Niño's] devotees. For the image could have been lost from our ancestors and us but it has been willed to stay" (*The Freeman*, April 28, 1975).

Unlike most other objects that had passed through the port, the Niño had not come and gone. It had persisted, and had become a permanent fixture in a place where "temporariness" otherwise seemed to reign supreme.[31] While there had been periods when the little idol had been "held prisoner" in its own convent, guarded in a strong room accessible only to the convent prior himself,[32] after centuries of precarious residence, the Santo Niño had come to be recognized throughout the nation as having a rightful home in Cebu City. Local myths, however, still tended to express the cultural anxiety generated over the image's potential instability.

In many of the legends told about the Holy Child of Cebu, the main tension in the plot concerned the conflict between the Niño's childish delight in mobility and his attachment to his chapel, altar, and pedestal, all of which were often represented as confining, not comforting structures. He was typically characterized as a wanderer (*hinlakawa*), an epithet many of the vendors at the basilica used to describe him to Rosa and me. One of the more respected members of the basilica vendor community, for example, when asked to describe the Santo Niño's character, cited the Niño's habit of leaving his chapel to roam about the countryside disguised in a *buri* straw hat. On one occasion, she remarked, the Niño had paused to cure a child's sickness, but otherwise he wandered for no express purpose. Another vendor recounted the often-cited legend of the caretaker who every morning had to pick *amor seco* burrs out of the Niño's dress, evidence of the image's nocturnal wandering.[33] There was also the story of the sacristan, or chapel caretaker, who repeatedly found the dress of the Niño wet and having the distinct tang of the sea each morning—clear evidence of the Niño's nocturnal meandering along the seashore.[34] Try as the locals might to keep him safe and secure inside their premises, the Niño in these myths could never be completely settled in, much less pinned down. He was represented as a free spirit, capable of departure and desertion of his home base at any moment, in spite of his record of perfect loyalty to the city. Restlessness was an integral part of the Niño's local personality, which was described with amusement, but clearly dominated by accounts of his faithful adherence to his dwelling place.

Sometimes the legends focused more on the Niño's escapades when he strayed from his chapel. These tales provided rationalizations for the disturbing mobility of the Niño, casting his absences in a justifiable and even commendable light, making the best of their inevitability. Vendors around the basilica, for example, recounted the well-known story of the smiling, curly-haired boy who bought fish in the morning from the peddler outside the Santo Niño church, but who deferred payment until the afternoon, when the peddler would find no one but the Augustinian priests to settle the bill, themselves puzzled by a string of fish lying at the foot of the Niño's altar. Variants of the myth substituted necklaces or rings, or religious paraphernalia for the fish, but in every case, the plot was the same. A boy would buy on credit, disappear, and the priests would be left with the goods on their altar and the bill to pay.[35]

Some stories showed more charitable, milder forms of mischief. For example, there was the legend of the Spanish sailor passing through Cebu who was left by his ship when he disembarked to take communion at the Santo Niño church. A small boy suddenly appeared who offered, in remarkably fluent Spanish, to take the sailor to his ship by *barco* (native dugout). After an unbelievably quick journey, when the *barco* had reached the sailor's ship, the sailor asked the boy's identity. The boy replied, "I am Jesus of Cebu," and vanished into thin air.[36] In the same vein is the legend of the couple who forgot to fulfill their promise to bring back to a sick friend a sliver of the Cross of Magellan,[37] which they were to obtain while celebrating the Santo Niño's fiesta in Cebu. On their return, however, they were amazed to learn that a chubby boy with curly hair wearing a red suit had delivered the relic for them, saying that he had been sent by them.[38] Again, the Niño's surprise journey served to confuse, amuse, and rescue the devotees, who became aware of his capacity for movement only after he was safely back on his pedestal.

The combination of mobility and heroism could be even more pronounced, as in the legend of the kidnapping by Muslim slave traders of a dozen children, which was supposed to have taken place at the 1888 fiesta in Cebu. The children were delivered back to Cebu by a "thirteenth child," who had cleverly rerouted their ship back to the city without the captain's knowledge. The child savior vanished, however, after returning the victims.[39] On a somewhat more political note, the same combination of mobility and bravery is suggested in the story of the attempted human sacrifice of a young boy during the time of King Humabon. The boy chosen was a mysterious but beloved figure in the community, one who had no home of his own but roamed from house to house, living off the charity and good will of his friends. The capture and imprisonment of this intended victim caused miraculous healing and unification of the people, who rose together to protest the human sacrifice. When the boy was eventually freed he suddenly vanished, and in that moment the people knew he had been their Santo Niño.[40]

The mobility theme could also be combined with even more classic examples of protector myths. For example, there was the legend of the time when mad dogs ruled the kingdom of King Humabon, until a boy appeared—the Holy Child—who miraculously tamed them all, and then vanished.[41] Another told of the time the bathing of the image delivered the region from drought. The bathing was occasioned by the Santo Niño's having left his altar in order to play games with a local peasant boy who had happened by chance upon the chapel.[42] A more modern variation on the theme described the appearance of the curly-haired boy at the U.S. Army headquarters in 1942, wanting to enlist in colonial forces in order to defend Cebu.[43]

In all of these legends, the saving power of the Santo Niño was combined with a mobile nature. However, his movements always ended with utmost abruptness once his mission was fulfilled, returning him to his altar. The legends thus included reminders that control over the image's location was anything but absolute.

Other popular legends addressed the vulnerability of the Niño's residence more directly. One basilica candle seller, for example, recounted the well-known story of the first attempted transfer of the Niño by the Spaniards to Manila, when they first shifted their base of operations there. As the story goes, when the crate in which the image was packed was opened in Manila, it was found empty. Meanwhile, the Santo Niño reappeared to everyone's surprise back in its chapel in Cebu. Seven similar attempts were made to transfer the image, each time encasing it in yet an additional packing crate. All failed. Finally, one of the Manila priests had one of the image's legs cut off to prevent its escaping, but even that proved ineffective. The Santo Niño always returned to Cebu. The asymmetrical stance of the image's legs, however, was still believed by many to be the result of that ill-conceived amputation.

An alternate version of this legend substituted the pope and Rome for the Spaniards in Manila, but the plot was basically the same. When the crate arrived in Rome, it was found empty. Meanwhile, bad times fell on Cebu—crop failures, epidemics, and famine—until it was discovered that the Santo Niño had returned to his pedestal. In yet another variation, the image was sent to Charles V in Spain. This story depicts the Santo Niño image changing from gold, which was said to be its original substance, into wood. The transformation was taken as a sign of the Niño's displeasure at his being transferred away from Cebu.[44]

In all of these stories, the threat of a forced departure at the hands of outsiders was overcome by the Niño's miraculous powers of locomotion, which were channeled this time in one direction only: toward Cebu City. In this respect, the myths, as Lévi-Strauss might have expected,[45] represented an ideal resolution of a critical problem. What they resolved over and over in different scenarios was the lack of an assured residency for the Santo Niño in Cebu City. The depiction of repeated and eventually violent attempts to remove the main source of the city's stable magnetism indicated how high the level of cultural anxiety could rise over the potential impermanence of the Niño's enduring presence in his provincial home, and the loss of "centerhood" his absence would entail.

The Localization of the Niño

As the myths related above indicate, the magnetism popularly attributed to the Santo Niño de Cebu resulted from more than its physical appearance or its venerable orthodox rituals. The image's appeal was also, in large part, a function of its having been made to serve as an interpretive instrument for the heterogeneous and unstable local culture. No more immune to localization than any other arrival to Cebu, the Santo Niño image not only represented the forced entry of Spanish Catholicism, and of Christianity in general, into the archipelago, but it also represented the penetration of local beliefs and practices into localized Spanish culture and Christianity. Its symbolic influence had been made to move in two directions by the various factions invoking its miraculous authority, and it was precisely this cultural flexibility that gave the Santo Niño de Cebu an extremely forceful political significance in addition to its religious importance. Over the course of its residency in Cebu, it had been employed to set up as well as repress a variety of ideological claims about the nature of social life in its catchment region.

Foremost among the image's ideological powers was its capacity to make readable and tangible a mythic argument for the archipelago's conversion to Roman Catholicism. The Santo Niño had a largely unchallenged and much celebrated reputation as the original common

ground of Christian religious worship in the Philippines.[46] One imagined scenario by J. Bulatao, for example, created for the *Catholic Digest* in 1965, presented a widely cited interpretation of the Niño as
having had a critically important evangelical role at the time of its
rediscovery by López de Legaspi. This account was also slanted to pay
tribute to the Catholic missionary effort:

> There was no doubt about the popularity of the Santo Niño among the
> islanders, and when Legaspi had a shrine built for it and they saw the white
> men kneel in prayer before it, the natives were favorably impressed.
> The pagan homage paid to a Christian symbol which the natives consid-
> ered their own gave the Augustinian Father Andres de Urdaneta and his
> small band of missionaries something to start with in their heroic work of
> planting the seeds of Christianity in the Philippines. (1965:36)

Enhancing its capacity to frame this mythic religiocultural "common ground" was the convenient fact of the Niño's initial abandonment by its Spanish carriers, a fact that was also put to use effectively
in popular discourse. No historical account of the image's arrival to
the archipelago failed to highlight the forty-year hiatus, from 1521,
when Magellan's expedition departed, to 1565, when López de
Legaspi's expedition arrived. During this period, the Santo Niño de
Cebu was characterized as having been absorbed absolutely into the
local island scene. Although records of López de Legaspi's discovery
of the Niño indicate that the image might well have been completely
uninvolved in local religious practices, and stored away simply as another item of the chief's treasure,[47] the accounts of the early history
of the Niño image in Cebu that appeared in fiesta programs, newspaper articles, and other popular literature overwhelmingly focused
on and supported legends of its temporary adoption as a pagan idol.
The 1985 fiesta program, for example, contained a section entitled
"Origin of the Holy Image" that focused entirely on the forty-four-
year hiatus, claiming:

> In those unaccounted years, the Image became part of Cebuano life. And
> this is probably why, when asked about the Image as it was found in 1565 by
> the Legazpi expedition in one of the village houses, the natives refused to
> relate it to the gift of Magellan. . . . Thus the unaccounted 44 years of stay of
> the Image in the hands of the natives is part of Philippine history. The Santo
> Niño, as writer Joaquin put it, "connected, he linked, he joined together our
> pagan and our Christian culture; he belonging to both." (1985:9, 11)

A wide array of legends also focused precisely on this "purely" local
period of the Niño's history, recounting various miraculous acts of

protection and defense performed by the image when it was believed to have been worshipped as a local deity in King Humabon's court.[48]

A variety of motives for cultivating and asserting this myth of totally local identity for the Santo Niño de Cebu were apparent in Cebu. For the Roman Catholic Church, asserting a more familiar identity for the Niño could only encourage widespread local acceptance and consumption of what was unquestionably, regardless of historical disjunctures, a symbol of the Church's own design. For the devotee population at large, different benefits were apparent. By claiming a native identity for the Santo Niño, followers also enhanced their own symbolic capital vis-à-vis the rest of Christendom. In this regard, the veneration and the folklore of the Niño revealed in high relief a two-way process of cultural translation with respect to opposing claims to legitimacy—the legitimacy of a history of forced intervention and domination in the case of the Roman Catholic Church and its supportive elite, and the legitimacy of full membership and participation in the world religion of Roman Catholicism in the case of the heterogeneous Santo Niño devotee community.

In addition to its asserted character as the Philippines' original divine intermediary, representing and interlinking indigenous and Hispanic belief systems and their respective legitimacy claims, the Santo Niño de Cebu also had been put to use throughout its history in framing and translating questions and answers about the nature of political interaction. Another popular legend, for example, which was based on an actual historical event, told the tale of Juan Dyong, who, after proving himself a brave defender against the Muslim raiders from the southern islands, in the first half of the nineteenth century became a leader of the peasants and amassed an armed and angry throng of followers to resist the Spanish aristocracy's plan to convert local farmlands into grazing grounds for fighting bulls. The night before Juan Dyong was to confront the Spaniards in Cebu City, a small boy about five years old awakened him from his sleep, telling him the Bishop of Cebu wished to have a meeting. The bishop, for his part, was intercepted the next morning by the boy as well, who told him that Juan Dyong wished to have a meeting, and that the bishop should treat the brave man with respect. The conference between the two ended with a peaceful resolution in Juan Dyong's favor, both sides in the end wondering whether the small boy had been no other than the Santo Niño.[49]

The Niño, in this myth, made visible the possibilities of the go-between in local political interaction, as well as tacitly assigning to that diplomatic role an unquestionable moral ground through its own identification with it. Only the Niño could create and traverse a no-man's-land between local and foreign factions. The legend's narrative created a disjuncture between opposed factions, effectively removing agency from the subordinate faction by asserting that the Niño alone could make claims on both foreign and local authorities necessary for moving them into a relationship enabling them to resolve the conflict. Ultimately, however, the Niño's interests were represented in the legend as being aligned with those of the more vulnerable faction of Juan Dyong. Thus, while the folktale employed the Niño to replace the voice of the subordinate local group at a critical moment in the conflict, it nevertheless asserted that the Niño's priorities were those of that group as well.

In short, the Niño image was construed in folklore to represent a deity who had, like so many incoming outsiders, "gone local," and had done so for motives that established foreign sources could not impugn. That is to say, the Niño was characterized as an orphaned saint, voluntarily delivered by colonial powers into local care. An erasure of foreign affiliations and the implantation of local roots into the image's character allowed the Niño to stand in opposition to the Spanish culture that had first delivered it into the Philippine scene, and over whom it was still considered to maintain a most powerful influence. As myths and legends repeatedly observed, the Niño still spoke fluent Spanish, and was cast as a most understandable figure to Spanish Christians, even though he was also cast as a local deity.

This pattern of aligning Christian images with local interests was not, of course, unique to the Santo Niño. In the Philippines, a widespread tendency to localize European images in terms of both belief and practice had been evident from first contact, often to the chagrin of incoming missionaries.[50] The Christian conversion of the archipelago was largely a result of such "saint-centered" religious activity.[51] Christian images of Jesus, Mary, and various saints fit easily into hierarchical pre-Hispanic beliefs about the importance of minor deities of the skyworld who could act as intermediaries between humans and the most powerful, though absolutely inaccessible, supreme being, *Laon*.[52] The physical images themselves constructed and fulfilled roles as mediators virtually identical to those filled by the wooden, bone, or golden images of pre-Hispanic *diwata, anito,* or *nono* spirits, who had moved between devotees and whatever actual spirit the image represented, and who in the Visayas were believed to have special powers of curing and preventing illness.[53] Christian images all over the archipelago, as in most areas where Iberian colonial traditions had predominated,[54] were typically translated into familiar figures whose spiritual counterparts then functioned as co-opted patrons. Many different images of the Virgin Mary, such as the Mother of Perpetual Help, the Virgin of Immaculate Conception, the Virgen sa Regle, and the Virgin of Guadalupe, among others, had been caught up in similar processes of adoption and translation into the local culture. So had numerous images of Jesus as the Tragic Victim.

However, the Santo Niño was uniquely suited to being made over in such a local fashion, regardless of what ideological purposes might be served in so doing and for whom. Again, there was the fact of the image's independent survival on local shores, and the Santo Niño de Cebu was the only such case of a Christian symbol left so utterly free of foreign control, even for this relatively brief span of time. Moreover, from a biblical perspective, the Santo Niño was something of a blank slate. There were no critical passages of scripture to constrain the characterization of Jesus as a boy of four or five. There were no famous parables from this period of his life. Had there been, the whole notion of the Boy King probably would have been out of the question. Instead, there were only a few vague references, in Isaiah in the Old Testament and in the revelations of Saint John in the New Testament, that prophesied the coming of "a little child" who would "lead the world."[55] Otherwise, the Santo Niño, as a distinct personification of Jesus, was wide open to interpretation. He was a most malleable and unfettered subject, a prime candidate for conversion and enculturation so as to serve a number of competing local interests simultaneously.

The childlike aspects of the Niño described previously were also amenable to the localizing tendencies of the Niño's various devotees. As a child deity, the Santo Niño de Cebu had a strong affinity with indigenous Malay cosmology. The impish, trickster-like character that legends so often attributed to the Santo Niño of Cebu resembled closely those of folklore figures such as the boy Juan Pusong and the young adult trickster Pilandok.[56] Trickster figures appeared in stories and plays found from Batanes to Sulu,[57] and under different names throughout insular Southeast Asia.[58] In some Malay traditions, particularly in Balinese society,[59] divinities were often conceived of as children to be taken care of and indulged, rather than as authorities whose wisdom and leadership were to be respected. The personality attributed to the Niño fit remarkably with this ancient Malay perspective, and this convenient resemblance was made the most of in its process of localization.

The unique potential of the Santo Niño de Cebu to assert the possibility of untainted "localness" inspired attempts at even more complete erasures of its Spanish origins, which occurred in both orthodox and folk contexts. The most popular origin myth, for example, which was often cited by the basilica *sinulog* dancers, told of the arrival of the Niño in Cebu as a lump of burnt wood, an *agipo*, that persistently turned up in the net of a poor fisherman every time he cast it. The fisherman finally brought the *agipo* to his home, where it transformed during the night into the figure of a little child.[60]

In this myth and its variants, all traces of foreign cultural origin are deleted. The Niño is depicted as having emerged from the surface of the sea in a crude, quasi-organic state, "cooked" wood that only upon exposure to local life refined itself into a human figure. The location of the discovery of the *agipo* conformed closely to pre-Hispanic indigenous concepts of divine arrival, in which the skyworld, a world more primeval than the earthworld, contributed to the creation of the earthworld by casting both animate and inanimate objects out of its own domain down onto the seas, where they eventually reached or became part of the landscape. Folk Catholic beliefs, building on this concept of arrival, classified *ingkantos*—spirit beings of the earth world—as fallen angels who dropped out of heaven into the trees or fields or waters of the earthworld to live and most likely cause trouble among humans.[61] Like the Niño, *ingkantos* were noted for their fascinating beauty, their foreign physical features (curly hair, blue eyes, light skin, and so on), their fabulous wealth, their extraordinary power, and their unpredictable tendency to appear anywhere at any time and play jokes on people.[62]

The popular *agipo* origin myth of the Santo Niño served to claim an alignment for him with indigenous spirits.[63] The motivations of devotees for performing such ritual actions as the *sinulog* dance or simply the lighting of candles, which will be discussed in detail in the chapter that follows, closely paralleled what is known about motivations for making similar deferential offerings to pre-Hispanic spirits. They were inspired by a need to appease a capricious deity who could turn dangerous or beneficent according to the most subtle and unpredictable of influences.[64]

The mythology of the Niño thus served to frame notions of "localness" and "otherness"—notions of cultural integrity—for its devotee population. The extent to which the folklore surrounding the image could detail these claims seemed to have no limits. One addition to the *agipo* origin myth, for example, highlighted and then resolved the problem of the image's Western features by recounting the temporary theft of the Niño by Spaniards from the palace of King Tupas, the chief of Cebu during López de Legaspi's time. According to this version, the Spaniards changed the features of the image from native to European, giving it a high nose instead of a flat one and curly hair instead of straight, and placing a globe in the child's left hand, replacing what were said to be its original contents, a pearl set in an open shell.[65] In this myth, where it is the Spaniards, not Cebuanos, who must answer to the charges of cultural theft, the desire expressed for a role reversal in terms of which culture could claim the nativity of the image reflected a more general desire for the reversal of other cultural relations—political, economic, and social—as well.

Even in the basilica's novena services for the Santo Niño, where the purely foreign origins of the image were most likely to be set forth and celebrated, the influence of the erasure process was apparent. The "Señor Santo Niño Hymn," for example, which was sung either in English or in Visayan at every novena service just before the closing prayer, dwelt at length on the nature of the Niño's arrival in the Philippines, characterizing it as follows:

Dinhi ning pulo
ta gisaad gigasa
Pinadala sa Dios
O pinanggang bata
Karon ug Kaniadto
banwag ka's kalag
Among gabayan
siga ning dughan

Ang sakayan nila
Midunggo dinhi
Aron magmando
Ni-ining yuta namo
Apan nagbu-ot ka
Tipon kanila
Aron ka maghari
Imong pinili

One day to these Islands
As gift and in pledge
God sent You to us
O beloved Child
And always you have been
The light of our souls
The guide of our people
The flame in our hearts.

The ship You were sailing
Arrived at our shores
To conquer this land
The pearl of the seas;
But You had decided
To stay in this soil
To conquer our people
And give us a name.[66]

No mention of Magellan or Spain or any human foreign agent was included in these texts. The arrival of the image was conceived of in terms of "God," who more or less literally replaced Spain as the sender of the Niño. There is also a vague reference to a ship, sailed only by the Niño, as opposed to Magellan or any of his fleet. (In the Visayan version, a vague reference is made to the possessors of the ship as *kanila* or, simply, "them.") The ship only, as opposed to any specific foreign power, was represented as having an intent to conquer. An extended metonymic figure of speech thus replaced both Spanish individuals and Spanish colonial forces as the instrument and instigator of the Niño's voyage. As with the *agipo* origin myth, Spain was effectively erased in the hymn's text in favor of a discourse that included only the local scene, God, and the Santo Niño.

Given the high degree of fluency in the translation of the Niño back and forth into both foreign and local cultural terms, as well as its remarkably permanent residential status in the provincial city of Cebu, the Niño image emerged as an ideal symbol of Cebuano regional ethnic identity and, on certain occasions, as a symbol of Philippine national identity. So influential was the mythology of identification that linked the Niño with the local culture that, during the revolutionary period, it was even invoked in direct opposition to Spanish authority. The Cebuano journalist and revolutionary, Felix Sales, for example, recounted in his memoirs of the late nineteenth century how Cebuano members of the Katipunan independence movement used "Long live the Katipunan! Viva Santo Niño!" as their rallying cry, in answer to the Spanish soldiers' "Viva España!"[67] The identification of the Niño image with "localness" served the various and conflicting agendas of both dominant and subordinate interests emerging from its devotee community.[68] In this respect, the localization of the Santo Niño de Cebu resembled that of the Virgin of Guadalupe in Mexico, another case of the translation of a religious figure whose acceptance into the local culture exceeded the limits colonial powers had sought to set for it, even while their power over its orthodox worship remained largely in force.[69]

In the Philippine context, the two-way translation process of the Niño also resembled that of the *sinakulo* passion plays performed on Luzon Island, which had, in a much more elaborately defined manner, served the same dual functions of inculcating the colonial value of loyalty to Spain while at the same time providing the native peasantry with a means of articulating their own political values, ideals, and hopes.[70] The selection of the Santo Niño de Cebu as the dominant symbol of the city's secular or "cultural" fiesta promotion campaign in 1981 was simply the most recent attempt to frame, through the symbol of the Niño, a discourse of identity and to assert within that contentious and argumentative discourse an autonomous and distinctive status of Cebu City vis-à-vis other locations in the nation and around the world.

The Niño's Symbolic Force: Personal Experiences

The public evidence of preoccupation with the veneration of the Santo Niño de Cebu might seem to indicate that a fairly extreme form of iconolatry was the predominant sort of religious experience in the city. To be sure, such an arrangement would have fit neatly with the striking preference for duplication and its highly positive value on the creation of likenesses, replicas, images, and icons that were so prevalent in other aspects of the city's public life. But the reality of the devotion was more complicated. Local religious practice was undeniably "saint-centered," but the understanding of divine presences went far beyond a fixation on icons.

I began to be convinced of this after a conversation one day with a candle-selling *sinulog* dancer named Consuelo Benitez. Consuelo worked by the octahedral shrine adjacent to the basilica grounds in which Magellan's Cross was kept. If anyone should have been caught up in an obsession with the image of the Niño, it was a person like Consuelo. She had been raised in the local Catholic tradition, with its heightened emphasis on the Santo Niño de Cebu. She also made her living directly off the worship of the image, since most of the candles she sold were lit specifically for the Santo Niño. Her customers typically asked her to say prayers and do *sinulog* dance rituals for the Santo Niño, so that, to ply her trade, Consuelo was obliged to fill her working hours with acts of devotion to the image. Consuelo's dependence on the little idol was thus more intimate and essential than many devotees. Her rational defenses (assuming she might have needed or wanted any) against a fixation on the Niño were unaided by the benefits of any secondary or higher education. She was a prime candidate for idolatry. Yet she clearly was not following that path.

Twenty-nine years old when I met her, Consuelo had been born less than twenty miles south of the city in the town of San Isedro. Her occupation as a vendor was not a fall from better times. Her mother and grandmother had been vendors at the basilica before her, as her sister-in-law and mother-in-law were now. It was what the women of her family did when the child-bearing years came to a close. Consuelo had started even earlier, when she was still single, at the age of twenty-two. The trade, she remarked, came as a welcome change from being a maidservant in Manila. Consuelo was one of the teeming masses who had been drawn to the nation's capital with hopes of a better future there, only to be disappointed. However, she was fortunate enough to have been able to return to the provinces and to have work and family waiting for her. Unlike many, she could go back home to what she viewed as a better life after all.

Consuelo was exceptional in some respects, most obviously because she was physically handicapped. A polio victim at the age of one, her legs were of different lengths. She walked with a severe limp, and could not endure standing for long periods of time. This was a decided advantage in her trade. The Santo Niño, like any saint, was believed to show partiality for those who suffered from permanent disabilities. A cripple's prayers were bound to carry special influence. Consuelo sold an average of one hundred candles a day, clearing twenty-five pesos. This was twice the average volume of the other candle sellers. On a Friday—the novena day—she could double her sales. Working from six in the morning until six at night every day she could manage, she supported her husband, who had so far been unable to secure permanent employment, and two children on the typical income of the city's poor families: 600 to 800 pesos a month. Most of her business came from passing jeepney drivers, many of whom were regular customers.

I met Consuelo when I was making the rounds with Rosa. Rosa would handle questioning and tape recording of the verbal responses of vendors while I made notes of their behavior. Most of the vendors tended to ignore me, assuming that I couldn't speak Cebuano. Consuelo, however, was different, partly because I'd spoken with her by myself on a previous occasion. She quickly assessed my interest in her as a representative of some larger reality than the candle-selling trade. Her conversation ranged beyond the immediate preoccupations of her work, something very few other vendors of the many that I met achieved. She was given to reflections on the nature of her people and their society. This was not, as far as I could tell, out of arrogance or narcissism or some frustrated desire for authority. She simply tended to think in those terms.

When we asked her about the recent changes brought about by the *sinulog* promotion, Consuelo reported differences in the selling scene. Before 1980, she said, only very few requested the *sinulog* dance when they bought candles. They only wanted the vendors to be sure to light the candles bought and say prayers. After 1980, however, people started to ask for the *sinulog*, and now all the passersby wanted it. Having answered the question, Consuelo could have stopped there, but she did not. She ended with a broader argument, saying, "Kita mga Pilipino day, hilig man g'yud mosakay" ("We Filipinos, Miss, definitely have a tendency to ride along"). The comment inspired Rosa to quote a local proverb in assent: "Ang langaw nga motuntung sa bukobuko sa karabaw magpakakabaw nasad" ("A fly on the back of a carabao acts like a carabao too").

Consuelo was somewhat skeptical about the *sinulog*, alert to the inherent hypocrisy of surrogate praying. She remarked that she sometimes suggested to her customers that they pray and dance for themselves, since she was not really convinced that her prayers on their behalf would be heard or judged as sincere. She made no attempt to rationalize her business in terms of some special personal gift, and did not try to pass herself off as a medium or a person with unusual spiritual power. She had doubts about the inherent worth of the *sinulog* dance ritual and wondered why the candle simply could not be set in a proper place and lit. Consuelo found herself caught up in a somewhat thoughtless cycle of impure ritual action. She participated, doing whatever the customer wanted, so as not to lose her business, and was grimly aware of the moral shortcoming that proceeded from that economic imperative. She saw her customers participating out of a shallow need to follow the current trend.

When Consuelo spoke of the Santo Niño, however, her skepticism vanished. The Santo Niño, she said, was Jesus Christ when He was young, the Son of Our Father. Every prayer she uttered, whether for herself or for her customers, called on Him. It was she who had summed up her devotion with the "star of the show" analogy mentioned earlier. She was familiar with a number of the legends surrounding the Niño's origin and action, and described his mischievous childish character. She cited the case of a woman driven mad by having failed to keep a promise to Him and knew of recent apparitions and miracles for which she believed He was responsible.

After Rosa had finished with the standard interview questions, Consuelo and I began to talk in a version of "mixmix" more heavily laden with English about the act of prayer. I explained that I, too, had been raised as a devout Christian and that the Episcopalian faith I had practiced bore many resemblances to Roman Catholic ritual.

When Consuelo realized that we did share some religious common ground, she immediately encouraged me to buy a Santo Niño image to have with me whenever I felt the need to pray. That would have been, I guessed at the time, the first step closer to her experience of prayer. The strategy was one I recognized. Several published accounts of other devotees existed that recounted how a special relationship with the Santo Niño had begun when someone had given them a duplicate image for their very own.[71] When Consuelo made this suggestion, however, it seemed like a non sequitur to me. I was surprised that Consuelo, whose skepticism regarding the superficial adoption of popular customs had already been firmly established, could believe that a statue of a figure that had never been a presence in my life might inspire my praying. I admitted this to her, explaining that in my experience it had always been enough to simply focus on the words and feelings of a prayer itself. I told her I could not figure out why some external object, like a statue, could do anything but detract from this process in my case, given my background.

Consuelo understood both my confusion and the depth of the question I was asking her. When I had finished my "mixmix" speech, she paused before replying and gave me a penetrating look of a kind I hadn't seen her use before, as if to let me know that she recognized the conversation had shifted to a more challenging plateau. Her face bore the slightly amused expression of a person who knows a game between experts is in the works. However, the exegesis on local idolatry I was hoping to receive was not forthcoming. Instead, Consuelo smiled and, in English, said, "Yes, God is everywhere." I knew from her tone that the discussion had been closed. I could not ask her to elaborate.

In spite of its brevity, however, the reply did settle the issue we had confronted, the issue of the character of divine presence. What Consuelo was telling me in that final phrase was that she and I were not as far apart in our views as I might have been thinking. The Niño image was to her by no means the ultimate expression of divinity in her religious practice, however important it was as a means to some religious ends, particularly those requiring a divine intercessor of some kind. Neither was it a messenger for a distant supreme being located only in a heaven far beyond earth. God was everywhere in Consuelo's human world. The here and now was still a place, and a significant place, for an all-pervasive, transcendent being.

Keeping Consuelo's insight in mind, I began to interpret comments about the role of the Santo Niño image and its immense pool of duplicates somewhat differently after our conversation. It made more sense to think of the image and its innumerable replicas as a kind of architectural phenomenon, not as figurative decoration or as iconic ornamentation, but as essentially building-like. What the stone walls, wooden floors, frescoed domes, and stained glass windows of churches did for me, the Santo Niño images of Cebu City could also do. The objects animated and gave dynamic form to constructive intentions.

There was the case of my Cebuano language teacher, Eloisa Vargas, for example, who existed at the opposite end of the social and educational spectrum from Consuelo, but whose rapport with the Santo Niño and its duplicates was in some respects similar. A genteel, middle-aged woman with a well-weathered sense of humor, Eloisa Vargas lived with her husband and children in a large suburb of the city. I studied with her intensively for several months, joining a crash course in Cebuano Visayan she was leading for three incoming missionaries, two from Indonesia and one from Eastern Europe. We five made an odd assembly, using the resources of an array of highly different languages, of which only English was common to all, to try to make sense of the local vernacular.

No one can teach a language to others without revealing something essential about his or her own character. Eloisa Vargas felt somewhat at a loss in structuring the lessons, since she had no scholarly expertise in Cebuano and had no reliable written guide. Nevertheless, she persevered, bravely appearing day after day to present her lessons. She faced the sharp questions of her pupils in session after session with a strained tranquility, never losing her temper no matter how strongly provoked by the impatient missionaries, always trying to find a new angle that would bring order to the chaotic grammatical system she herself was only beginning to study objectively.

I noticed one day that on Eloisa Vargas's desk there sat a tiny replica of the Santo Niño. I asked her why she had it. She told me that it cheered her up when she felt depressed. She remarked that she didn't get to church very often these days. The demands of the new language class on top of an already full schedule left her little spare time. She said it helped to be able to see the image instead. "I have a real spiritual connection with the Santo Niño," she told me. When her children used to be sick, she recalled, she would go and look into the face of the Niño, and she would feel comforted.

In Eloisa Vargas's account, the Niño images could serve as a kind of substitute for a visit to a church. They imposed a sense of peace and tranquility upon the troubled surface of a person's world, creating an atmosphere in which it was possible to move toward a posture of repose for worship. Religious architecture, in my experience, was designed for the same purpose, to locate comfort in orderliness so as to inspire serenity.

In this respect, the Niños of Cebu had a structural significance as well as an iconic one. They not only presented a human likeness of divinity, but also created a self-reflective threshold in their devotees where chaotic and negative emotional states were transformed into positive and composed ones. As one devotee reported to a journalist after he had acquired a Niño image for his couturier shop, "There were less difficulties that came my way and *I began to see clearer.*"[72]

The images served a purifying function in this respect. They appeared wherever there might be a need to clean up the emotional messes people worked themselves into during the course of their social lives. As the preeminent Cebuano historian, Resil B. Mojares, once noted, "In the image . . . is focused . . . the popular yearning for a more livable present and a better human order" (1981:44). Likewise, a priest who was in fact critical of the lavishly materialistic aspects of the Niño devotion also asserted that one of its main benefits was that it "uncoils our many tensions, and converts our over-serious attitude to our problems into a trusting, relaxed, and smiling outlook."[73] To be sure, this was only one way in which the images could be engaged by the local population in their acts of worship, and the images' function was by no means identical for all residents. However, this purifying effect was most often cited as a way in which devotees related to the images on a day-to-day basis.

As the fabric of Cebu City's society and that of the nation in general was seen to be in a long-term process of unraveling, a process that spanned several decades, the potential for emotionally "messy" situations in the city was increasing in proportion with the peace and order problems. The need to have an available means of coping with foul-ups, as the effectiveness of established secular sanctions continued to decline, was ever present. The Niño images provided one such means of coping, serving as an emotional "mopping up operation" for the turmoil that complicated the lives of the city's residents.

In sum, observations and accounts indicated that the Santo Niño de Cebu image and its duplicates did not necessarily represent or function only as iconic messengers to God Almighty, as survivals of an idol-oriented pre-Hispanic way of relating to divine power. The practice of prayer that they inspired was not wholly defined in terms of message transportation, but in terms of emotional transformation. The Niño imagery in Cebu City constructed chapel-like dynamics for its devotees wherever it appeared, making room for intangible sanctuaries within which it was possible to find and resonate with the balanced rhythms of tranquility regardless of how often they were upset by the unexpected shocks of daily life.[74]

The Santo Niño de Cebu had collected the miracles of many centuries, for which it had invariably been given credit, and condensed them along with the countless ritual acts, the innumerable prayers of thanksgiving and petition offered by its immense congregation of devotees, into a single, intensely potent symbol of hope. It also framed a flexible and unstable discourse of unity for the overwhelmingly Roman Catholic local populace, who, regardless of class, age, sex, politics, or ethnic heritage, recognized the Santo Niño as their patron saint. While its orthodox rituals and practices tended to provide opportunities for the established powers in the society to reinforce the class and ethnic distinctions that had maintained their dominant positions, the folkloric discourse articulated for the Niño also provided scenarios for envisioning a subversion of those distinctions, achieved via the alignment of the image with pre-Hispanic, natural, and childlike characteristics.

The appeal of the Santo Niño image was thus derived not only from the innate attractiveness of its gorgeous miniature form, or from its physical antiquity, or from its global renown alone. It was also derived from its capacity to define and stabilize a local identity for its heterogeneous and hierarchical society. The intersection of these various dimensions of attraction produced a magnetism unequaled by any other religious object in the nation. Orthodox Spanish Catholic doctrine concerning Jesus, savior of his sinful flock, along with ancient native concepts of both infantile divinity and locally exclusive protective loyalty, met and became infused with the intense emotions of desire, promise, fear, faith, joy, and grief. Through this complex fusion, the Santo Niño de Cebu emerged as a dominant symbol—*the* dominant symbol—of Cebu City's local culture.

Chapter 6
The *Tindera Sinulog*

Images of the Performance

A pool of life continually stirred around the basilica. Parishioners and visiting worshippers passed in and out of the large stone portals; occasional tourists searched for spots to take photos of the church's impressive eighteenth-century facade; vendors stood with multicolored balloons by the main entrances to the courtyard near the stations of security guards, and children selling raffle tickets roamed around the courtyard looking for customers with spare change.

Amidst this array of activity, tiny eruptions occasionally burst forth upon the ebb and flow of movement created by the courtyard traffic. Every once in a while, a noticeable bobbing up and down became apparent just outside the basilica's main portals. Hands holding candles would appear, engaged in a miniature dance of rhythmic pulses that made them easily visible amidst the flux of pedestrian motion. The candles moved gently. They appeared to be floating, as though upon a mantle made of softness itself.

The gentle outbursts flared up and faded away quickly. They broke upon the surface of the scene as if from nowhere and disappeared quietly after only seconds, or perhaps a few minutes, had elapsed. Once the floating hands appeared, there was time only for a passing observer to identify them as belonging to a woman and to begin to distinguish her person from the rest of the scene before the dance was over.

As a rule, she would be an old woman, wearing a faded dress and rubber thongs (what in the Philippines are generally referred to as "slippers"—sandals that are not worn in public if more substantial shoes are owned). She typically would be quite obviously poor, judging from her attire. Despite her fortuneless appearance, however, this dancer, by virtue of her movement alone, would become a kind of beacon in the courtyard crowd while caught up in the ritual process. She would gaze steadily beyond the life of the courtyard into the dim interior of the basilica, waving her candles at the image of the Santo Niño. Her whole figure would sway in rhythmic pulses, displaying a kind of resiliency that resembled the movement of small waves of water as they traveled across the surface of a calm sea—a particularly mild version of the aforementioned "Cebuano style" of resiliency.

The *sinulog* dancer typically presented in these performances a rather curious combination of levity and seriousness. This was curious to me and to local observers as well. One newspaper report, for example, described the dance as a "queer quaint sway balance."[1] The movement was not forceful; yet neither was it undignified. The action was gentle, but the manner was restrained. The steps were tiny, the sway of the hips diminished. The upper body of the dancer typically remained erect and unchanging during the performance, and the facial expression revealed no trace of any emotions that I ever saw easily evoked in casual interaction. The gaze, though muted, was not withdrawn. The face of the dancer bore the absorbed, motionless expression of a person enraptured by a distant, beloved source—which was how the dancers themselves described the experience (Figure 6.1).

Despite the air of solemnity created by some features, the quality of the diminished gesturing used in the ritual was nonetheless outflowing and generous. It was a fundamentally fluid style of gesturing, even though the arms were seldom extended to their fullest capacity. The arms of a dancer, in this regard, never unfolded completely the emotions and intentions they expressed in movement. The gestures might even have appeared coy were it not that the untempered, outpouring quality of the action seemed incapable of withholding feeling and so provided no opportunity for teasing or coquettishness. There was also an extremely fragile, aged character evident in the movement that interfered with any perception of it as flirtatious. The level of energy invested in the dancing was so low it barely animated the body. The center of weight hardly shifted, the hands barely flexed, the arms were held up as though they were on the verge of collapsing limply to their hanging resting places. The liquid flow of movement through the body was disconnected, animating some areas and leaving others relatively lifeless. It was a ghostly performance. Its motivating spirit appeared to be fading rapidly from the present time.

As the dancer would appear from nowhere, so would she vanish, blending back into the courtyard scene after no more than a minute

Figure 6.1. *Tindera* candle seller performing *sinulog* in front of the basilica entrance.

or two, becoming once again a body in no way easily distinguishable from the others present. Her dance had involved no climax, but had instead revealed a rhythmically marked interval, potentially though not actually eternal in its continuous, buoyant pattern.[2]

So the *sinulog* dance appeared to a passing visitor: minimal, impromptu, and pedestrian. Various American scholars unfamiliar with the performance and its context, who in recent years have watched tapes of the performances I observed in 1984 and 1985, have at times even questioned whether or not the behavior really merited the label of "dance." The *sinulog* required no special costume or musical accompaniment. No feature of personal appearance was altered for the performance: no special hair-dressing, no make-up, no particular type of preparation. Nor was an acrobatic or otherwise technical skill demonstrated in the dancing. The body movement process was definitely not aerobic. There was nothing to distinguish the performer from an ordinary passerby except the possession of a bundle or bag full of candles and the fact of the performance itself. I as well, upon first viewing the *sinulog*, found it hard to believe that this was the ritual that was once said to have been the climax of the yearly Santo Niño fiesta celebration, when pilgrims would perform it en masse inside the basilica on procession day. It was equally difficult to understand why this dance had become the inspiration for the city's Santo Niño festival promotion and a central symbol of Cebuano regional pride.

My initial exposure to *sinulog* dancing was to the form just presented, which I came to call the "*tindera*" *sinulog* in recognition of its performers, the vendors who sold candles on the basilica grounds.[3] As Consuelo's critical account in the previous chapter illustrates, the *tindera sinulog* was definitely a commercialized form of the ritual. It was an artifact of business for the vendors who practiced it. Yet, despite its contemporary commercialization, nobody I ever spoke to about this dancing ever questioned its authenticity. In fact, the *tinderas'* dance practice was described by some city residents as the only "real" version of the *sinulog* dance. Its realness was a key feature of its public image, which placed it in a somewhat curious and ironic contrast to the more recently commercialized *sinulogs* that had been developed for the yearly civic festivals.

The authenticity of the *tinderas'* ritual dance was not seen as problematic for two main reasons. First, it was considered anything but an import. This *sinulog* was recognized within the city as the dance form that bore the genuine marks of ancient local custom. There was no "localized" aspect of it. It was simply seen as local. Its style was not typecast as Hispanic, or American, but unquestionably "indigenous." Local dance experts had picked up on its resilient phrasing, among other characteristics, and identified that patterning as distinctively Cebuano. Second, the *tindera sinulog* was still danced as a ritual, which was assumed to be its original context, although the contemporary religious setting in which it was performed was, of course, no longer "purely" indigenous.

Given these sources of stylistic and functional authenticity, the *tindera sinulog* was referred to by many as the most "original" *sinulog* form. It was certainly the form that provoked the most reflection about local sources of antiquity. To the Cebu City community as a whole, at least insofar as that community's attitudes were expressed in public statements, the *tindera sinulog* had its most widely recognized meaning as a dance of ancient origins. In the 1985 fiesta program, for example, the section given over to describing the ritual *sinulog* performance focused entirely on describing the possible pre-Hispanic origins of the dance. The text reviewed references to dancing made by Magellan's and López de Legaspi's chroniclers, as well as oral traditions relating dance practices of the earliest Cebuano chiefs, emphasizing the "centuries-old" character of the *sinulog*.[4] Press material on the dance prepared by the Ministry of Public Information also focused on the pre-Hispanic origins, speculating on the pre-Christian functions of the dancing in male circumcision ceremonies.[5] The *sinulog* was publicized as an ancient practice, a status that was claimed mainly by default and intuition in combination with the inconclusive evidence gleaned from the vague observations of early Spanish missionaries.[6]

There was, of course, no way to prove the actual age of this choreographic form, and I had no intention of spending any time on the topic, since I was well aware that origin searching had been deemed something of a lost cause in cultural anthropology. However, in spite of my own reticence over the issue of origin, with the *tindera sinulog*, antiquity intruded upon me, or at least its ghost did. The dance definitely had the look of a process that had been molded by an ancient source. Watching the body movement and the spatial trace forms it made visible, I felt I was looking upon a tattered remnant of a garment made of fabric so old it was about to disintegrate. Antiquity inhered in the dance's symbolism, lending it a magnetism of its own that could not be ignored. Ancient sources, whether "real" or not, lurked within this cultural symbol, influencing its character and appreciation, and forming an essential aspect of both its meaning and its being.

Because it presented and represented authenticity, originality, antiquity, and pure "local-ness," the *tindera sinulog* was not an altogether typical symbol for Cebu City, a place where the bulk of social life was so frequently awash with incoming, short-lived influences. While the dance had been appropriated by a group of traders to serve their economic needs, it also had acquired many of the earmarks of a non-marginal tradition. The *tinderas* were, after all, local devotees, who saw themselves as continuing a practice that they assumed had probably been performed in a like manner by Santo Niño devotees over the centuries. Once again, the stabilizing influence of the Niño was apparent. It had spawned a relatively "pure" local form of symbolic action, which further messed up the otherwise predominant character of the city as a highly permeable area, a place through which things passed, going to and from distant destinations.

The dance, in this regard, was a rather rare find, and was understandably valuable as such, despite its unremarkable contemporary appearance. To interpret the *tindera sinulog* choreography, there was no need to look very far afield. There were no apparent distant influences, at least not spatially distant. Instead, it was necessary to look within and around the city itself, into the lives of the performers and their more immediate surroundings.

I came to understand this *tindera sinulog* form as a manifestation of local habits, of what Pierre Bourdieu has termed *habitus*. That is to say, it was one of those durable and reasonable but largely unreasoned practices, collectively orchestrated, yet largely unruled and subjectively perceived, always improvised but nevertheless systematically regular in appearance, function, and interpretation. It was, in sum, a kind of outgrowth or by-product of some of the city's most abiding and prevalent "dispositions" or structural tendencies.[7] Moreover, I found no evidence to indicate that the choreographic form of the *tindera sinulog* was not of the ancient local origin of which it was promoted to be.

The movement symbols appearing in the dance spoke to a variety of everyday contexts and acquired meaning as a condensed expression of extremely familiar patterns of individual and collective conduct.[8] This form of *sinulog* expressed the values of the subculture that kept its practice alive in modern and postmodern times, the group of women candle sellers at the basilica and their customers. While it was undeniably a symbol of the culture bearers of a transit zone, it most articulately constructed and represented an *insider's* identity for that locus—an identity whose frames of references were locally derived in some essentially, and relatively exclusive, ways. This *tindera sinulog* clearly illustrated the fact that even a border land can have an interior design.

The Ritual Process

As the previous description of the dance indicates, the *tindera sinulog* was not primarily concerned with making a visual impact on some pedestrian spectator clientele. It was a dance meant to be felt, not observed. Its symbolism was internally oriented, concerned with the dynamics of an interior landscape only vaguely manifest. It was not about making the invisible visible. Its choreography was designed to transform an existing life situation from the inside out.

Yet, while the *tindera sinulog* was not a spectacle, it was nevertheless a social dance, a ritual service with ritual functions. The general effect of the *sinulog* was one of two kinds, depending on whether it was done before or after the fact of some miraculous intervention attributed by the devotee to the Santo Niño. In the latter case, the *sinulog* was classed as a *pagpasalamat*, an act of thanksgiving. In the former case, it was described as a *gihangyo*, an act of request or petition. In either case, however, the ritual was deemed the visual expression of a *panaad*, an act of promise, and was considered a *halad*, or sacrificial offering.

As was mentioned in the previous chapter, the most common idea associated with the performance was *pagampo*, an act of prayer. The dancing was not viewed as an accompaniment to prayer, or as a trance transcending prayer and producing a possession state. It was thought of as a form of praying, whose physical aspects were as essential to the construction and conveyance of the sacred message as is the physical act of kneeling commonly employed in the prayer practices of numerous Christian denominations.

In spite of its brevity, the *sinulog* contained three distinct ritual acts. The introductory rite was begun as the dancer, the *tindera*, took an erect stance, generally with a slightly more vertical orientation up and through her spine than was otherwise adopted, and displayed whatever candles the customer had bought out in front of her upper torso or face toward the Santo Niño image. The dancer created a moment of stillness using this pose, during which she said prayers (either aloud or unspoken) to the Santo Niño. These communicated the specific needs and requests or thanks of her customer. The name of the person for whom the prayer was offered was announced at this time, as well as the reason for which the *sinulog* was being performed. During this phase, dancers withdrew their attention from the activity taking place around them in the courtyard and focused intently on the image of the Santo Niño, or on the principal entrance to the basilica's nave, if a focus on the image could not be arranged.

Although the prayers for the customer's requests were improvised by the *tinderas*, they nevertheless achieved something of a standard form. For example, one *tindera* used the following prayer for any customer coming from outside of Cebu City:

Señor Santo Niño, Kang [name of customer] kini. Mituman siya sa panaad Nimo gikan pa siya sa lain lugar aron pagatuman sa iyang saad. Hatagi siya [request is specified].

Señor Santo Niño, this is for [name of customer]. He has fulfilled his promise to You and has come from a far away place in order to fulfill that promise. Grant him [request is specified].

A typical prayer requesting good health proceeded as follows:

Señor Santo Niño. Imong kaluoyan intawon [name] nga modagkot. Hatagi siya sa kabaskog sa lawas. Hatagi siya sa iyang gihangyo.

Señor Santo Niño. Please show mercy to [name] who is lighting a candle. Give her vitality in her body and give her what she asks.

A standard prayer for long life proceeded as follows:

Señor Santo Niño, a nia intawon si [name]. Nagpasalamat nga Imo siya gidangat sa lain katuigan. Imo unta siyang hatagan ug dugan pang mga katuigan.

Señor Santo Niño, this is for [name]. He thanks you for your having given him many years and asks that you give him many more still.

Some prayers, as the following example illustrates, combined several requests:

Señor Santo Niño, a nia ako Imo kaloy-an naa nia siya atubangan nga muyo ug nagampo na Imo siyang [request is specified]. Na ang iyang gipamayo intawon Santo Niño Imo pagahatagan ug pagatumanon sa kanunay maka-ampo siya Kanimo ug taga-an siya sa kanunay Nimo nga grasya. Pa-abton siya Nimo sa lain katuigan ug taga-an Nimo siya ug maayong lawas.

Señor Santo Niño, this I beg of you for that one who is in front of you begging and praying to you for [request is specified]. Please give to him Santo Niño what he asks of You and fulfill his request for which he is always praying to You and give him always Your grace. Let him reach another year and give him good health.

As these examples illustrate, the *tindera sinulog* was a personal and focused ritual, verbally articulated in an unelaborate, straightforward style. It was generally performed with respect to the specific needs of a single designated individual. Two kinds of *panaad*, or individual promise-making, were possible through the ritual: a perpetual vow or promise, and a single, event-related prayer. Consuelo, for example, related that a number of her customers were actual pilgrims who came regularly from other areas of Cebu Island and had the *sinulog* performed every Friday as a *panaad* in which they prayed most often for good health. They were desirable customers, in her view, who generally bought several candles at a time in order to emphasize the importance of their journey and their perpetual vow fulfillment. Consuelo, as well as several of the other vendors, associated perpetual vows with rural practices and pilgrimages. Event-related vows, in contrast, covered a variety of good and bad occurrences and were more commonly the motivation for urban residents.

While prayers for good health were by far the most commonly invoked and were believed to be the original and ancient inspiration for the *sinulog* ritual, requests tended to vary with age and gender. For example, Consuelo's male customers typically asked for protection from evil and disgrace (*panalipdan sa kadaotan*). Young couples requested prayers for marriage and everlasting romance (*magdayon*). Mothers asked for the healing of their children and for them to be assisted in passing examinations at school. Wives frequently asked for the resolution of marital problems, such as infidelity or domestic violence.

In general, however, requests related to the problems encountered by an individual during the course of his or her transitory life. The *sinulog* ritual was never performed in order to give thanks for long lives that had ended painlessly, or to ask for the eternal rest or pleasant afterlife of ancestors or friends who had died. The dance was a rite for the living, a means of coping with day-to-day events and circumstances.[9]

During the phase of the ritual that followed the verbalization of the request, the gentle, bouncing *sinulog* movement was performed. The juncture between the opening and central phases of the ritual was absolute. A different movement realm was entered in this phase of the *sinulog*, one that made little reference to the relatively static one just left behind. Regardless of the specific nature of the request or the sort of person for whom it was intended, the choreography remained the same. The dancing was not meant to be a pantomime of the customer's current difficulties or a specific solution to their problems. Its symbolism was more abstract, more idealistic, and expressed not the customers' needs, but his or her emotional connection with the Santo Niño at the moment of the performance.

Tinderas reported that they were bound in the performance to take on the feelings of their clients in order to communicate their prayers adequately. They did not need to depict the event that was to be transformed, only the customer's emotional reaction to it. If clients were distressed over the poor health of their children, for example, the *tindera* would be obliged to empathize and find ways in her performance to express their distress, making it her own in the process. Facial expression, tempo changes, and sometimes the energy quality or spatial intent of the gestures were all means by which the emotional state of the customer was represented by the *tindera* in the dancing. A "sad" (*kasubo*) dance would generally have a slowed tempo, and the movements tended to have a downward emphasis. A "joyful" (*kasaya*) rendition, in contrast, tended to have quickened, upwardly oriented actions.

The *tindera's* movement process in this phase of the ritual also transformed the candle, making it a blessed and vibrant object. This intermediary danced phase of the ritual was thus often referred to as the "dedication" (*pahinongdan*) or "endorsement" (*magendorsar*) phase. During this phase, the candle became symbolic of the specific individual determined by the customer. When the *tindera* performed a *sinulog* for the healing of a child or infant who was present at the time, she sometimes danced holding the infant instead of or along with candles, either cradling the infant in her arms or holding its hands as it stood in front of her. These performances were relatively rare. However, they underscored the close symbolic relationship between the candle as it was manipulated in the dancing and the person for whom it would be lit. The treatment of the candle, its introduction into the pulsing energy field set up by the *tindera's* body movements, resembled the treatment an individual ideally would also have undergone. It depicted a dynamic state of personal grace, or what could be regarded as a miraculous movement realm.

One of the major contrasts between the middle segment of the ritual and its opening and closing phases was the improvisational and idiosyncratic character of this dancing. Unlike the relatively standard verbal prayers employed, the *sinulog* dance was thought of by the *tinderas* as a spontaneous process. It could not be rehearsed. To do so would have undermined the authenticity of the dancer's intent. While the opening and closing actions derived their spiritual power and sanctity from their identification with conventional standardized forms, the logic was reversed within the central segment of the ritual. The more personal, the more immediate, and the more internal the inspiration and the act, the more genuine and spiritually potent it was believed to be. The mental processes required by the different phases of the ritual were both complicated and oppositional, requiring the dancers to shift back and forth between roles that were by turns largely conformist and individualist. Every *tindera* orchestrated this shifting differently. The initial movements into the central phase of the dancing, as well as the way a closure to the intermediate phase was created, became moments where the distinctive movement preferences of each *tindera* tended to manifest themselves.

In the final phase, the *tindera* resumed a position of prayer (standing, candles displayed). She then spoke more prayers to the Santo Niño, repeating the prayers offered earlier or slightly varying the wording. In addition, *tinderas* occasionally offered such standard prayers as the Lord's Prayer or rosary prayers. For the most part, however, the closing phase mirrored the opening one, giving the *sinulog* ritual a symmetrical "ABA" compositional form. The initial and final acts created an entrance and an exit to a sacred interval, which became animate in the central phase of the ritual. In this respect, the ritual process was organized from the inside out in a temporal as well as in a kinesthetic or physical sense. At its core was the "indigenous" practice, which was bounded at both ends, opening and closing, by orthodox Roman Catholic symbolic action. As a performance experience, the *tindera sinulog* was "centrally" a ritual of fluent physical activity, framed by relatively motionless verbalization and posturing.

To conclude the ritual, a conventional bow was made toward the Niño to mark the *tindera's* act of leaving His focused presence. This involved the lowering of the dancer's center of weight, usually accomplished by flexion and shifting of the lower limbs, as well as a down and forward tilting of the upper torso and head. The standard Christian movement symbol, the sign of the cross, was also performed during this postural shift, making this closing action the most technically complicated one in the ritual process. Again, the organization of the transition into this relatively complicated movement was another moment in which the individual styles of the *tinderas* tended to differ markedly.

After the conclusion of the ritual prayers, the candle was taken to one of the *tinderas's* iron grates, which were the size of large frying pans and were located just outside the grounds of the basilica. The candle was lit there as an offering, completing the ritual act. At no point did the candle actually move into the church, for this act was forbidden by the basilica clergy, who, according to the *tinderas*, had ruled that only votive candles of the type sold inside their own store could be burned inside the church.

One summary observation on the performance process of the *tindera sinulog* bears comment in particular. As should be evident from the descriptions given so far, the movements of the ritual in all of its phases were movements taking place in the closest proximity possible to the facade—the external surface—of the basilica itself. Unlike older versions of the *sinulog* ritual, which will be discussed in detail in Chapter 10, this *tindera* ritual *sinulog* existed literally on an edge, a condition that greatly influenced its choreographic design. The symbolism of the dancing expressed on many levels the activities of interiority placed in marginal or border zone circumstances.

Chapter 7
Customers and Performers

The participants involved in the practices of the Cebu City *tindera sinulog* adopted one of two roles: that of customers (passive but commanding sponsors) or that of performers (active but subordinate stand-ins). Neither of these two roles formed a complete ritual persona. The roles were the fragments of a single former social self, a complete devotional persona that had become fractured as the devotion to the Niño had modernized.

The Customers

The *tinderas* dealt with the entire spectrum of the Niño's urban, suburban, and rural followings. Customers ranged from teenagers to the elderly, and the people for whom the dances were performed were of all ages as well. Both men and women became customers. More often the customers were women, but male customers, as Consuelo's account illustrates, were by no means uncommon. The devotees were both educated and uneducated, rich and poor, professionals and laborers. They were not, however, foreigners. Tourists and Westerners did not employ the *tinderas* (except for one case of a passing Japanese, and that was considered extremely odd by the *tinderas* who had observed it). The *sinulog* trade was strictly a local and regional operation, catered to and by the inhabitants of the region.

In a very literal sense, the *tinderas* had their fingers on the pulse of the city. They learned about the problems and good fortunes of those who turned to them in times of both personal need and thanksgiving. The variety of reasons that brought people to the *tinderas* to request a *sinulog* gave indications of some of the main sources of tension in the urban community, and how they affected different sectors of the population differently.

The case of a university student, a young woman who went by the nickname "Pina," provides a good example of the complex motivations of *sinulog* clients. Pina was a native Cebuana whose family lived in San Nicolas, the district the Spanish had set up as the original ghetto for *indios* in the sixteenth century. She was a relatively "pure" product of the local culture, never having lived or traveled abroad for any extended period of time. Her values revealed a characteristic blend of local and global orientations.

Pina was an energetic character, who was both earnest and successful in her attempts to embody the image of the Westernized modern woman of the 1980s. Well under five feet tall, with a stylish pixy haircut, she took and taught aerobics classes in her free time and was fond of listening to the latest pop tunes on her Walkman tape player. On the days when she didn't have to wear the school uniform, she would appear impeccably dressed in casual clothes, jeans, and oversized T-shirts resembling those in the latest issues of teen magazines. In many ways, Pina was more in touch than I was with U.S. popular culture, a fact that created a mildly embarrassing tension between us. I often had the feeling that I was a disappointment as a representative of America for most of the city residents I encountered. Pina seemed particularly nonplussed by the limits of my knowledge on the topic of U.S. popular culture. Her knowledge of American popular music was far more extensive and timely than mine. She could rattle off a list of popular American rock bands, names that meant little to me, and name their hit songs just as easily. It was Pina, in fact, who first introduced me to the music of the new teen sensation, Madonna, whose hit song, "Like a Virgin," had been playing constantly for weeks in the university cafeteria.

In speaking of her religious life, however, Pina saw herself as a wholehearted follower of local "folk Catholic" religious tradition. She described enthusiastically her own family's participation in the ritual dancing that accompanied the yearly fiesta procession of the Santo Niño image in their district of San Nicolas.[1] Her experience of this devotee *sinulog* dancing was an extraordinary emotional release. She characterized herself a "real believer" in the miraculous power of the dancing and its effect on the Santo Niño.

Pina's identity was thus divided between secular pursuits, which she recognized as foreign, and her religious beliefs, which were classed as "native." The division was one I was to encounter in a number of other local culture bearers as well. Religious practices considered unorthodox by the Roman Catholic Church could be employed as badges of local identity.

When we were strolling along one of the beaches of Mactan Island one afternoon during a picnic outing of the Anthropology Club of Pina's university, Pina gave me a specific example of her *sinulog* worship habits. She said she was a regular customer of one of the *tinderas* at the basilica, whom she would visit whenever she had a specific reason for wanting a *sinulog*. These *sinulogs*, like her own procession dancing, had mental and emotional, as well as miraculous, effects in Pina's view. She focused on the case of preparing for school examinations. In preparing, she recounted, she would grow fatigued from studying and would become, as she put it, "so tense." As she uttered this phrase during our conversation, she prolonged the stress on the final word. Her brow knit, and the muscles of her face constricted into a frozen frown. The expression aptly represented a behavior pattern that culminated in rigid stasis, from which there appeared to be "no way out." When this happened Pina would meet with her *tindera* (whom she referred to as her *manang*—a deferential term used for senior women). The *tindera*'s performance of the ritual cleared her mind, she said, and made her feel confident going into the examination. "You feel so . . . calm," she explained, as a result of the *sinulog* performance. As she paused in the middle of this sentence, she exhaled quickly and shook her head as her eyes traced out a gaze pathway like a halo a couple of feet above her head. The behavior resembled the movement of a fresh breeze circulating around through her brain. The achievement of this tranquil attitude was meaningful to Pina, whether or not the ritual actually brought about a high grade on the examination.

While faith in the immediate efficacy of the ritual ran high among the participants, the dance had meaning not only as a miraculous solution for problems, or as one means of maintaining the standard form of deferential rapport devotees felt obliged to establish with the Santo Niño. It also had meaning as way of effecting a mental and subjective change, of achieving a certain desired attitude toward life and its good and bad events. The dancing could be used, and inevitably was used, as a kind of offering in thanksgiving for the Niño's charity, as an expression of the debt devotees felt they owed to the Holy Child King and to God as well.[2] However, it could also and at the same time be used as Pina described it, as a way to "clear one's mind." From the customer's standpoint, the ritual was both a way of acting toward a divine Other and a way of knowing oneself anew. It was one means of exercising the purifying potential of the Santo Niño image.

The Performers

Although the *tindera sinulog* ritual and the ancient form it represented would not have existed in the contemporary scene without its diverse clientele, the individual characters the ritual serviced had little impact or connection to the symbolism of the ritual process. They were relatively invisible participants as far as the choreography was concerned. Even though their emotions over the event inspiring the ritual were translated into the performance by the *tinderas,* no more than a very general representation, filtered through the *tindera's* own movement style, was included in the dancing. Neither the customers nor their specific requests were represented by distinctive movement. Nor did the customers select *tinderas* on the basis of their dance style, influencing the choreography by patronizing whichever *tinderas* they deemed to be the best dancers. On the contrary, customers tended to ignore the formal aspects of the ritual completely in making their choices. If they became selective at all, as some did, they based their judgments on their personal rapport with *tinderas* whose religious commitment they respected.

On the other hand, the *tinderas* themselves, who, in the contemporary context, served primarily as stand-ins or substitutes for their customers, represented their own interests symbolically in the movement style on several levels, both individual and collective. In this respect, the *tindera sinulog* showed a kind of historical time lag apparent in its formal design. The relatively new status of the ritual as a service that could be performed indirectly, by way of paid stand-ins, was having an impact on the choreography only in a very general stylistic sense, in the *tinderas'* embodiment of "hostess" personae. For the most part, however, the movement symbolism expressed a blend of the *tinderas'* own personal and social values and attitudes regarding not only religious beliefs, but economic and political life situations as well. The ritual was surviving as an individualistic, nonhierarchical tradition, even though it currently was structured by patron-client relations. The time lag proved to be of central importance in the secular promotion of the ritual, for a visible representation of patrons and clients was precisely what the promoters sought to avoid. In any case, the story told in the *sinulog* choreography was largely the story of its performers, the *tinderas* themselves.

The *tinderas* formed a relatively homogeneous community, a fledgling subculture within the city that was itself a small facet of the more complex social scene revolving around the basilica. In some ways, the basilica *tinderas* and the social world they created in their work could be seen as an archetype for the whole city, which could also be described as a loosely structured, mobile collection of traders whose status as cultured persons was open to question by culture bearers from less marginal locations. The *tindera* "community" was a community that was predisposed, by virtue of its marginal socioeconomic status, to develop in its membership individuals adept at seizing short-lived opportunities. It was bound to be a community of impulsive tacticians who could not afford the luxury of rationally calculating every move they made in terms of some long-established strategy for conduct. This collective nature was represented in the choreographic form the dancers had cultivated, as well as in their more practical activities (Figure 7.1).

The *tinderas* were first and foremost a commercial community. They considered themselves to be practical people, engaged in a trade. Selling candles was their primary occupation, not being devotees. They found themselves at the lower end of Cebu City's economic spectrum, the end where the majority of the population found itself in 1984 and 1985.

The "community" of the *tinderas*, such as it was, like that of Cebu City, was a fragile one, with diverse loyalties. Its members arrived from and departed to a variety of home bases, sharing with each other during their working hours only a vaguely defined and limited sense of collective identity. Whatever cohesiveness the *tinderas* achieved as a group was for the most part imposed upon the group by the policies of external authorities, both civic and religious, by whose tolerance it was allowed to survive. The same might also have been argued for Cebu City as a whole.

In many respects, however, the *tindera* community was unusual. It was virtually an all-female community, a fact that was closely tied to the traditional role of women as religious authorities and as the most prayerful members in any given household.[3] It was also a relatively autonomous, though insecure, work force. Moreover, the trade sustaining the community had a long-term stable demand side that operated somewhat independently of other large-scale trading patterns in the city. These unique conditions were due to a combination of factors.

First, the *tinderas* were by and large an elderly community. While exceptions such as Consuelo were apparent and were increasing as the candle-selling community grew, the majority of the women were widowed grandmothers. They enjoyed the deference all elderly Filipinos are generally paid, regardless of sex or class. They were not subject to the authority of a husband or father. Nor were they hampered by the responsibilities of childbearing.

Figure 7.1. *Tindera* offering candles for sale.

Second, the *tinderas* were a hypermobile community; many of them traveled, not only from home to the basilica and back, but also to other churches on other fiesta days. While on foot at the basilica, they were highly mobile as well, although the mobility of any particular *tindera* was limited by the fact that senior members tended to stake out certain areas of the basilica courtyard as their private territory.

The *tinderas'* mobility was a sign of the very small amount of capital investment required for their trade. While it meant that their profit margin remained small—smaller than those, for example, of the stall owners who competed with them for business—it also meant that they were less easily exploited by church and city officials. If confronted, they could simply disappear for a while, until their presence was no longer noticed, and then resume selling again. Their trade carried little indebtedness, since most paid for only the candles that had already been sold at a profit. Those who made their own, which they recycled from candles burnt in their grates, didn't even have this expense. They paid no rents or taxes as *tinderas*. Their profits, small though they were, were their own. The *tinderas'* trade was like a preindustrial "undeveloped" form of commercial exchange, existing on the fringes of the developing urban economy.

Finally, the religious aspects of the trade had a distinctive effect on the trading community. The *tinderas* were, in a sense, professional devotees. The religious nature of the work ensured some permanence. As one Cebuano journalist once told me with regard to the support big businesses gave to the fiesta celebration, "When the economy is good, you have to advertise. When the economy is bad, you have to advertise even more." The same might well be said for the relationship devotees maintained with the Santo Niño: in good times they felt compelled to offer prayers of thanks; in bad times they felt even more compelled to pray for help. Regardless of the society's upswings and downturns, or of personal hardship or good fortune, the *tinderas* could be assured a steady stream of customers.

However, the *tinderas* were not a harmonious community, on the whole. About forty *tinderas* competed regularly for customers at the basilica in 1984 and 1985, although the ranks could swell to several hundred on fiesta days and other holidays. They sold candles from sunrise to sunset, twelve hours a day, with the bulk of their trading occurring between the hours of seven and ten in the morning and four and six in the afternoon. They sold anywhere from zero to one hundred and fifty candles a day. Every sale was important. Every customer lost represented a noticeable drop in the day's earnings. Fights between *tinderas* commonly and understandably occurred over the loss or gain of a single customer.

Aside from being small in size, the *tinderas'* income was also highly unstable. The selling situation at the basilica was loosely organized. Luck and timing were largely responsible for determining whether a *tindera* would sell eight or eighty candles in a given day.[4] A small amount of security did result from the practice of forming *suki* relationships (longstanding trading relationships between specific *tinderas* and specific customers), as was the case with Pina and her *manang*. *Tinderas* could be reasonably certain that these customers would patronize them on a regular basis. The *suki* trade, however, was seldom enough to guarantee a *tindera* a full day's income on any given day. Competition for new customers was always important.

The *tinderas* faced a challenging economic environment, to say the least. They competed for sales with the vendors who operated small, makeshift stalls adjacent to the basilica's walls, and also with the shop inside the basilica. They were at a particular disadvantage in competing with the basilica shop, whose short, flat votive candles could be lit inside the church itself, in special racks designed for that purpose. Since lighting a candle inside the church was obviously a more effective offering, the *tinderas'* only advantage over the shop was dancing the *sinulog* in addition to the sale. Nearly all the customers who bought candles from the *tinderas* asked them to perform a *sinulog*, which clearly indicated how vital the ritual was, in an indirect way, to the *tinderas'* business.

The economic benefit gained from the *sinulog*, however, was only indirect. This was because the dance itself was performed for no payment (*wa'y bayad*), as a religious service. It was a form of *indulgencia*, an indulgence shown by the *tindera* to the customer. The basilica *tinderas* believed that in order for the ritual to be effective, they had to perform it without charge. Otherwise the Santo Niño would not take the performance seriously and would not grant the request.

The status of the dance as a charitable service was a key factor in its overall social significance within the community. It transformed the *tinderas* as a work force from one that was essentially domestic in its orientation, each working simply for the benefit of her own household, to one that was essentially public in its orientation, working for the benefit of others' households as a form of charity. The *sinulog* was ostensibly a public service, a sacrifice of the *tindera's* labor for the good fortune and spiritual well-being of other community members. Its meaning as a form of labor was then necessarily ambiguous, for its appeal to customers depended on the condition that its economic significance be overtly denied. The *tindera* community thus was neither a purely domestic nor a purely public work force, but was paradoxically both of these.

A vaguely ambiguous identity resulted from this mixed condition, an ambiguity that was an essential characteristic of the community's social makeup. It was also a central stylistic element in the basilica *tinderas'* choreographic tradition. In the erratic and for the most part "unreadable" nature of the spatial forms created by the *tinderas'* gestures in the course of their dancing, the lack of a single, clearly determined structuring agency was aptly represented.

The quasi-commercial status of the *tinderas* was not the community's only source of ambiguity. The community's relationship to its own locus of trade was ambiguous as well. The relationship between the *tinderas* and the official basilica personnel, whom the *tinderas* referred to as "the Fathers," was a mildly strained and inconstant one.

The reaction of the basilica clergy to the *tinderas* and their dancing had varied over the years. The *sinulog* fell into the the subset of folk activities officially classified as "tolerated" by the Roman Catholic Church in the Philippines, as opposed to those folk practices that were disapproved of or condemned. Tolerated practices were not accepted as orthodox. However, they were not openly rejected, either.[5] They existed in a kind of theological limbo. In the *tinderas'* memory, most of the Fathers had been neutral or supportive of the dancing. However, the *tinderas* had also been expelled from the grounds at various times by different Fathers and lived in daily fear of being chased back into the streets by security guards. They understood that they might be construed as a colorful ethnic addition to the basilica courtyard one moment and as downgrading rabble the next.

In sum, the mental and emotional climate of the social world of the *tindera* community was one in which a struggle for short-term economic survival was being waged. Uncertainty and ambiguity characterized the working environment, even while thoughts of faith, tolerance, charity, and miraculous well-being were the focus of ritual performances. In many city dwellers' eyes, the semitransient *tindera* subculture was nothing other than a cultural backwash, a stagnant collection of impoverished peasants clinging to an outworn practice as a source of income. Yet these marginal characters, themselves only borderline members of a border-zone culture, were among the last remaining culture bearers of what was to become by 1985 the city's most famous form of symbolic action.

The contradictory qualities that formed the social environment in which the *tinderas* moved were aptly symbolized in their dancing. The *sinulog* body movement process revealed an undefined, disengaged attitude toward exterior space, while simultaneously presenting bodily forms that, as I was to learn in my discussions with these women, expressed shared notions of internal piety, deference, and devotion.

This ritual *sinulog* was a dance in which the practitioners could find clear, deeply held values even while a passing observer was left puzzled and unmoved by an outwardly vague and apparently nearly lifeless form.

Personalities

In spite of the difficult circumstances the *tinderas* shared, the life experiences that had led each one to such a marginal existence on the steps of the basilica were varied. They were a diverse group of individuals who played a variety of roles throughout the course of their work. The part of the spirit medium, the benign counselor, the friend, the grandmother, the servant, the withdrawn laborer—all of these were roles that I observed various *tinderas* assume with their customers. Each role attracted its own sort of clientele, and every *tindera* worked with one or several of these roles.

Each *tindera* was obliged to express aspects of her own character in the ritual's performance, while at the same time working within a shared stylistic tradition. In order for the ritual to be effective, it could not be interpreted as an empty duplicate of another's or of a standard ritual process. It had to have the genuine mark of the performer's individual expressive style. Every dance was thus believed to be a work of both ancient origin and originality, a combination that was later to be extended with spectacularly imaginative results to the government-sponsored secular version of the tradition. Every *tindera* managed this combined effect a little differently.

One of the more memorable characters among the *tinderas*, and one of the most convincing role players I was to encounter, was a woman named Sinafrosa. Sixty-two years old, mother of nine, she came from a farm near Danao City, a large town around twenty miles north of Cebu City. She slept on the sidewalk near the basilica six nights out of seven and went home only on Saturday mornings, which was when she would purchase her candles.

Sinafrosa's principal role-playing character was that of the wretched beggar. She was one of the *tinderas* whose working methods had helped most to sustain the reputation of the *tindera* community as a group of annoying vagrants preying on the sympathies of more well-to-do devotees. While she may not have been a financial wizard, as some of the *tinderas* were, she was a far cry from being an actual beggar. Sinafrosa worked on a credit arrangement with her candle supplier, a woman she referred to only as "Ascuncion." She would buy her candles on credit for thirty centavos each, leave for a week, and return on Saturdays with payment for all candles sold. Many of the *tinderas* operated on similar credit arrangements with independent suppliers. The alternative of making one's own candles was only open to the more established *tinderas* who had somehow obtained an iron grate of their own with which to collect and recycle wax. Sinafrosa was not one of these more industrious members. However, she was, in fact, the final link in a chain of small-scale manufacturing, a vendor who had been able to hold up her end of the bargain for three years as a full-time seller and on and off for several more years before that.

In practice, however, Sinafrosa was anything but the image of a self-reliant trader. She first approached me one afternoon in the basilica courtyard, asking for a *pinaskohan*. From the root term "*pasko*," derived from "Pascal," a *pinaskohan* is a gift of money given during a holiday season, usually Christmas, something like a Christmas bonus. Sinafrosa asked for this handout in a soft, pleading voice that matched the doleful facial expression she wore. Rosa and I had finished our interviewing for the day and were on our way home when Sinafrosa appeared, but we promised her we would return and interview her the following afternoon and pay her for her time. When we returned the next day, however, Sinafrosa was nowhere in sight. Apparently she had either not understood the agreement or, more likely, had interpreted the postponement as a refusal. Our interviewee of the day before went and found her for us.

She did not appear enthusiastic about talking. We made her uncomfortable. She wanted to be rewarded and let go as quickly as possible. However, just as we began, it started to rain heavily. Rosa and I sought the nearest shelter available, inside the basilica, along a cloister adjacent to the nave of the church, crouching beside a bishop's chair. Sinafrosa followed us hesitantly inside.

I became nervous about our situation when a crowd of curious passersby gathered around us after just a few minutes. It occurred to me that we might draw the attention of the basilica clergy, whose permission I had not gained for such a use of their space, and who might easily grow annoyed at the sight of a street person such as Sinafrosa being interviewed in their domain.

Fearing a confrontation, I abandoned the impromptu interview site and asked Sinafrosa to accompany me to another area of the basilica that was less open to the mainstream of traffic entering and leaving the nave. She agreed, but as we left the cloister and walked around the back of the nave toward the wing of the church that housed the basilica store and the entrance to the church offices (an even less wise choice of location, as it happened), Sinafrosa chose not to walk with Rosa and me. She trailed along at a distance of several yards, walking hunched over, her gaze fixed downward. She had hidden her candles in her bag as she began to move, careful not to appear to be soliciting inside the walls of the church. We sat on a bench and finished the interview, Sinafrosa eyeing the corridors furtively, as did I.

What Sinafrosa expressed in her behavior throughout this episode was her sense that she did not belong either inside the church or in a conversation with Rosa and me. She portrayed herself as a woman too unfortunate to merit such treatment. Again and again, throughout the conversation, she emphasized the severe limitations of her life and her own lack of authority. She said she had no feelings about her work. She stressed that there were days when she earned nothing. She didn't know the names of the priests. She didn't know where the term *sinulog* came from. She had no idea why the *sinulog* dance movements were performed the way were, except to say the Santo Niño called for these movements. She did everything she could to convince us she was helpless and ignorant, that her survival depended on our understanding and generosity.

For Sinafrosa, the communication of dependence and ignorance were vital elements of stock and trade. Although I was to become firmly convinced that, if there were one characteristic all of the *tinderas* shared in common, it was an intrepid will to survive, I also learned from Sinafrosa and those like her that the portrayal of ineptness and failure could become a valuable asset to their enterprise. They expressed this characteristic not only in their verbal interactions with potential customers, but in their dance styles as well. The low energy investment in the body movement process and the lack of interest in relating the body's form to any element in the environment save the Santo Niño in the *tindera sinulog* choreography could aptly represent such "weapons of the weak."[6]

Individual personalities could also stand out and overwhelm role playing. For example, there was the case of another *tindera*, named Generosa. Generosa was sixty-five years old. A tall woman, by local standards (around five feet, four inches), she wore her long, gray hair back in a bun and often appeared in brightly colored polyester print dresses. She enjoyed a certain prestige among the candle sellers at the basilica because of her seniority. Although she had been selling there for only a few months when I first met her, she had sold candles at the basilica eighteen years before, and there were several of the old-timers still around who remembered her from those days. Then she had not only sold on foot, but had owned outright three entire stalls for selling candles.

Seniority was the single source of authority in the basilica tindera community. A well-known pecking order that structured interaction was defined simply in terms of who had been there the longest. Generosa, however, possessed in addition a kind of confidence that was a rare quality among the vendors, an unusual sense of security that was derived from several sources, her seniority being only one among them.

Her outstanding characteristic was her worldliness. Like nearly all of the city's inhabitants, Generosa had the ability to move among cultures. The magnitude of her movements, however, placed her in a relatively elite category. Most of the *tinderas* moved only between one suburb and another, or from a satellite town to the city and back. Generosa, however, moved between entire nations, between the East and the West, and that ability meant a great deal to her. It distinguished her in a critical way from the rest of the sellers and gave her a different status as a mover.

She carried a passport, which she showed to me at the earliest opportunity. I was indeed impressed; I hadn't expected to see any candle seller pull a passport out of her plastic purse. She was correct in sensing that the document would create a bond between us, a bond that even Rosa and I did not share. I was one of the few people Generosa knew who had a passport, and one of the few who could appreciate how unusual she was for having one. The passport was a symbol of equality, evidence that she was, like me, someone who could travel globally. In stark contrast to Sinafrosa, Generosa didn't see herself as needing me in the slightest to better her life. She was, however, happy for my company.

She came originally from Bogo, a town on the northern end of Cebu about sixty miles from the city. Her parents had owned a small sugar cane processing business, but had sold it when they grew older, relocating in Misamis Oriental on Mindanao Island. Generosa herself had four children, now all grown, only one of whom, a son, was living in Cebu, working at one of the piers. She was proud of the fact that two of her daughters had managed to marry foreigners. One had married an Englishman and lived in London. Generosa had acquired the Philippine passport in order to visit them.

Another daughter had married an American and lived in Manila. Where the daughters had met their respective husbands was a subject Generosa avoided discussing, but the implication was that they had been what Rosa euphemistically referred to as "hospitality girls," a term used generally to refer to prostitutes in the Philippines.

Generosa's family, scattered throughout the archipelago, was the troubling focus of her life. She sold candles, she said, as a hobby, in order to keep her mind off problems with her children. She was unique among the candle sellers in this respect. She viewed her work at the basilica as an option, not a necessity. She could have lived with her parents on Mindanao Island. She even owned a plot of land there. She could have lived in Manila, with the daughter who had married the American. But she refused to live there because the husband would not allow her entire family (most significantly her son, I gathered) to move into his home. She had been invited to stay on alone in their house, but had moved out, disappointed. Generosa preferred street life in Cebu, she said, even though it meant sleeping on the sidewalks every night, bathing in the public washing areas, and eating always at open-air stalls, to life with a son-in-law who was so cruelly exclusive.

Although she was the only truly homeless *tindera* I encountered, she was also the only one who appeared to be in no financial trouble. She even had a grandchild living with her, whom she was supporting. This was not due to her candle sales, which she admitted were lower than average (she would make only fifteen pesos on a busy Friday, when others, who did more chasing after customers, could make double that or more). Her children sent her money regularly. When I met her, she was in the process of getting five thousand pesos' worth of jewelry out of hock. She claimed that, between the contributions of her son in Cebu and her daughter in London (who had just sent her fifty English pounds) and her own recent winnings at *jai alai*,[7] she was going to have no trouble coming up with the three thousand peso down payment. This was a remarkable sum for a *tindera* to muster, and would have taken the average *tindera* fifteen months or more to earn, let alone save. Generosa spoke of it matter-of-factly. She was well connected in a financial support network that involved a most precious resource: foreign currency. This gave her an economic stability of which the other *tinderas* could only dream.

As she distinguished herself financially and socially, Generosa also distinguished herself as a dancer. Her movement signature, exemplified in her *sinulog* gesturing style, was among the more technically complicated of the individual *tindera* styles. She held the candles in both hands at nearly full arm's length, well above her head. Using a continually alternating canon sequence, she traced dinner-plate-size circles with each handful. The movement started at her fingertips, but sequentially incorporated all of her arms and even her scapular region in the creation of sweeping curvilinear forms. She was one of the more highly integrated movers, one of the few to develop an action that brought the core muscle groups along the backside of the rib cage into the play of the gesture. Generosa's style was more sophisticated—and sophisticated in a way that allowed it to be more expansive—than those of most of the other *tinderas*. Her gestures were also more clearly drawn in space and more clearly sculpted than were the others. Her performance represented quite aptly her more cosmopolitan orientation. She physically articulated the notion that she not only knew where she was, but she knew both how to describe an "elsewhere" carefully and how to develop an integral connection between herself and that distant location.

I asked her how she had learned this dance. She replied that she had danced before she had ever started selling candles, that she had started as a child. Her parents used to dance *sinulogs* in Bogo as devotees of Señor San Vincente. They did it somewhat differently, using a grinding, stepping style that traveled sideways as the legs rotated in and out from the hip sockets, with the feet kept parallel to each other, never leaving the ground. It was meant to give the illusion that the person was floating, as if on a river (*panodpanod* was the term she used). That sort of stepping, Generosa said, was too tiring for her to perform all day, so she followed the other *tinderas* in the tradition of the tiny, flat-footed, meandering step style used at the basilica. Her arm gestures, however, retained the style of her mother's in Bogo. She noted that the traditional dancing had had a men's and a women's style (something that other *tinderas* had remarked upon as well). The man's style was like a warrior's fencing style, an *escrima* or *arnis* style of *sinulog*. The woman's style that she herself performed she described as slow and gentle.

Generosa's performance was inspired by a combination of influences: the traditions of her parents, the current standards of the local context, and her own individual preferences. The uniqueness of her personal situation as well as the things she held in common with the other *tinderas* were all represented in her dancing.

A third figure, who typified the more devout members of the *tindera* community, was a woman named Vincenta. Vincenta was a sixty-three-year-old widow, mother of seven, grandmother of four. She came from Tabogon, a town about fifty miles north of the city that was home for over a dozen of the basilica *tinderas*. Vincenta also spent four or five nights a week sleeping on the sidewalks near the basilica. She would stay for the busiest days—Thursday through Sunday—and then return to her family. The *tindera* trade paid her expenses, although her children also gave her a monthly allowance.

Vincenta had been a *tindera* for six years when I met her. For five years before that time, since the death of her husband, she had worked leading novenas and rosaries, a skill she had learned in her youth from a *tiya* (literally translated as "aunt" but a term used to describe a variety of female kin relations outside the immediate family). Vincenta switched to candle selling when she realized it would be more profitable. She said she could make twenty pesos on a good day, when she sold a hundred candles.

The special religious abilities Vincenta possessed when she started selling at the basilica caused tensions initially within the community. Her willingness to say a rosary or novena for a customer began to attract business for her, and the other *tinderas* took offense at what was deemed an unfair advantage. She recounted a confrontation with several of them, when they called her an "evil one" (*impaktuhak*—literally, one who "pecked away" at others). A senior member of the group, a character who went simply by the name of Francis, demanded that she charge extra for her additional services. Vincenta felt she had no choice but to agree. She had just had her first encounter with the social organization of the basilica *tindera* community. Although loosely knit and informally articulated, the community could respond quickly and effectively to new conditions, particularly ones perceived to be a threat.

Given her longtime commitment to religious worship, Vincenta, not surprisingly, had a relatively elaborate set of standards for the performance of the *sinulog*. She viewed the ritual as a difficult and dangerous responsibility, a burden (*kargo*) that was double-sided. On the one hand, she saw herself as responsible to her buyers and suppliers for delivering services, conveying prayers, and selling candles. The sad nature of many of the prayers, particularly those for the healing of sick children, weighed heavily on her. On the other hand, she was responsible for "facing God," as she described the act of prayer, and making sure that her actions would not be judged insincere or impious. Balancing these burdens, Vincenta said, had created enough anxiety to bring her to the point of tears in her dance on several occasions.

Tinderas agreed that sincerity in the *sinulog* ritual was communicated only through intense effort. They described it as a tightening of their hearts. In watching them dance, there was indeed apparent a tension in their upper torsos that served to hold rigid and isolate the upper body from the swaying hips, giving the dance a Polynesian appearance. Only when the tension permeated to the core of the dancer's insides, to the center of her heart, would a clarity of imagination result, achieving genuine prayer and a "loosened" frame of mind. One *tindera* described this effect as *hayahay ang pangahuna*, a refreshed kind of thinking, similar to that which Pina had demonstrated in her characterization of the calmness the ritual brought about for her. The

ideal mental and physical processes of the performance were conceived of as opposites of release and tension that sustained a balance
with each other out of which sincere praying developed.

For Vincenta, a mixture of characteristics combined to make the
sinulog a presentable form of devotion. In particular, she mentioned
two key attributes. In order for the dancing to be "fitting for God," it
had to be *natural* and *formal*. These were the Spanish-derived terms
she used herself. I was puzzled by this combination, which seemed
contradictory to me. Yet the terms were to come up again and again
in my conversations with other *tinderas*. How could a dance be simultaneously natural and formal? As it turned out, these two characteristics were each associated with specific elements of the dancing, and
both were related to what I learned was its single most essential element: the manner in which the shifting of the body's weight center
from one supporting limb to the other was repeatedly accomplished.

Vincenta connected the term *natural* with the distinctive style of
bounciness uniformly evident in the *tindera* dances. *Natural* dancing,
in her view, was individualistic and improvised—God did not dictate
the movement, she emphasized. However, the dancing was not by any
means supposed to be "wild" or completely open to personal choice.
Even within the relatively narrow category of "bouncy" movement,
there were desirable and undesirable styles—many ways to bounce.
Different sorts of bounce had different meanings, with different aesthetic, moral, and spiritual characteristics. *Natural* bouncing, although
it was thought of as unplanned and genuine in its very spontaneity,
was nevertheless a carefully constructed experience of a certain style
of weight shifting.

Vincenta contrasted the *sinulog natural* bouncing style with pelvic
bounces that were flirtatious in nature, what she called a *kiatkiat* style.
Kiat bouncing, as demonstrated, involved pelvic shifts that were oriented on steeply sloping vertical pathways. The movement was initiated from the outer side surfaces of the pelvis in such a manner as to
draw attention to its bony mass and musculature. *Kiat* pelvic bouncing was also linked to the batting of the eye lashes (*kipatkipat*). Vincenta echoed the general consensus of the *tinderas* in deeming it
completely inappropriate and even scandalous when used in *sinulog*
ritual dancing.

Also inappropriate, though less morally problematic, were the *un-
toluntol, atrasatras, iktiniktin, ibutitbut,* and *sibugsibug* styles of bouncing.
Iktin and *untol* both translate as "bounce." However, *iktin* bounces
were said to emphasize downward movement, like a basketball or
volleyball player's bouncing jumps. *Untol* bounces, in contrast, were
seen to have a strong rebounding quality, like the bounce of a ball

thrown hard against a wall. Both styles were considered objectionable, because they failed to manifest a key quality of prayer: its softness (*piano*).

Sibug, atras, and *ibut* styles all described forms of bouncing that moved backward with both *sibug* and *kibut* being associated with the waddling of ducks. These bouncing styles were simply considered ugly (*barut*)—visually unappealing.

Vincenta's contrasts, which were echoed by those of other *tinderas*, revealed several key attributes of the *natural sinulog* style. Its bounciness had to be initiated deep within the internal recesses of the pelvis. The bounce itself should not exhibit power, and its pathway should move not up and down or forward and back, but side to side. The bouncing style of the *sinulog* was, as another *tindera* put it, a sway (*kiaykiay*) of the sort a boat would make as it bobbed atop gentle waves. It was this sort of body movement that best expressed the concept of natural vitality in the body. The *tinderas* described the internal experience of the bounce as a feeling of "lightness in the body" ("*gaan sa lawas*"). It was this physical state that brought about healing and happiness, and mercy from the Santo Niño.

The *formal* quality of this *natural* movement style was related in Vincenta's mind, as in the minds of others, to its restrained range of movement and its slow pace. Prayer was a slow thing, a quiet, even silent thing. "If you shout," she cautioned, "God might become deaf." "Even if you whisper, God can hear you."[8] Perhaps this belief was related to the one Consuelo voiced, that God was everywhere. In any case, in Vincenta's view, movements as well as words could be evaluated in such terms of absolute proximity.

The diminished use of the pelvic bounce, the tiny step reach, the subdued gesturing, all of these features of the body movement process created a *formal* though *natural* appearance. This combination was the kind of behavior that was fit to be performed in God's direct sight. The notion of being in front of God, face to face, inspired this seemingly paradoxical mixture, a sort of spontaneous decorum.

Vincenta's standards of conduct revealed that a certain distinctive, articulately understood physical experience was essential to the expression of healing prayer. Devotion and constrained resiliency were one and the same notion, mutually defining each other in Vincenta's dance. The act of devotion manifest in the *sinulog* was not merely referred to, supported, or represented by resiliency, it was resiliency personified.

While this small array of profiles cannot do justice to the richness and variety of individuals who composed the *tindera* community, certain major themes do emerge from this array that to some extent defined the loosely knit group of vendors as a dancing subculture of a certain sort. For all of the performers that I came in contact with, the *sinulog* was thought of as a duty and a privilege, a source of income and an emotional ritual experience. While the *tinderas* did tend to vary in their assessment of the dancing—with the newer, younger *tinderas*, such as Consuelo, having more doubts about its ritual value than the older ones, such as Vincenta—nevertheless, for all concerned, the *sinulog* still remained, as Geertz (1973: 449) has said of the Balinese cockfight, a "sentimental education." It taught its practitioners about the aesthetic values governing the physical and emotional experience of prayer and divine healing. In the basilica context, the dance style was a sign of exchange, of age, of womanhood, of individual character, of poverty, and of time-honored values concerning faith, prayer, and devotion. These were its conventional meanings, and among them the most significant for recent history was the dance's representation of an apparently ancient and indigenous form of sacred conduct.

Chapter 8
Latent Symbolism in the *Tindera Sinulog*

The *tinderas* and their customers were never at a loss for words when speaking of the religious causes and effects inspiring the *sinulog* ritual, particularly when they involved stories and descriptions of the Santo Niño. When I asked about specific details of the *sinulog* dance style and their origin and meaning, however, they generally tended to come back at me with blank looks. "It is just the dance," the *tinderas* would respond ("Sayaw lang"), or "It is our custom" ("Ang naandan nga paagi"). The only explanation offered for the body movement style was that it pleased the Santo Niño because he was a child, and children loved dances. Why this particular kind of movement should be particularly pleasant for him, however, was left unstated. The waving hands, bouncing body, and "pointed" (*puntolpuntol*) stepping of the feet (the execution accenting the elevation of the foot off the ground) were not viewed as conveying any particular messages of their own. They were not described as an alphabet or vocabulary for encoding the prayers of the customers. There was evidently nothing like syntax or grammar in the performance process that was being consciously employed by the performers.

Certain elements of the style, however, did eventually emerge as being related to specific concerns and issues of the ritual. Vincenta's focus on the bouncy phrasing of the weight center, for example, illustrated that at least one characteristic of the performance had a specific meaning of its own, even though it was not a typical topic of conversation. Another example of this specificity of meaning was apparent with respect to the use of the eyes. I had observed that a uniform feature of the *tindera sinulog* style was that the eyes were active throughout the dance, maintaining a visual channel with the Santo Niño. Their steadfast focus upon the image appeared to me to be a statement of unwavering commitment, an expression of faith that seemed almost disembodied, because it was produced by muscles well hidden beneath the surface of the face.

The eyes, it turned out, were considered to be not only an expressive channel but a passageway for the entrance of spirits, both good and evil. One of the *tinderas*, for example, reported that evil spirits (*satanes*) sometimes possessed her during her *sinulogs* and made her body heavy and her prayers incoherent. Her way of dealing with this was to close her eyes when she felt it happening. When the feelings had stopped, she could open her eyes again and focus on the Santo Niño. In this discussion of the performance, the *tindera* indirectly made it clear that the eyes did have a specific function. They were a vulnerable channel through which saints and demons alike might pass inside the body.

As my discussions with the *tinderas* about the dancing developed, I began to realize that my first impression of their assessment of the style's components (that they had no specific meanings) was not entirely accurate. It was not that there was no meaning to the various elements of the body movement style, but that the meanings evident were so fundamental and obvious that they went without saying. As Bourdieu has noted with respect to the *habitus* of other cultures, it was precisely *because* the practitioners of the ritual did not recognize that meaning was being rendered by their choreographic designs that the designs themselves actually had more meaning than they knew.[1] The body movement process revealed some of the more deeply ingrained habitual ways of evaluating human conduct that were held in common by all the participants of the ritual.

Eliciting contrasts in pelvic bouncing patterns, for example, always drew humorous reactions from the *tinderas*. They saw the "flirtatious" and "ugly" alternatives as so obviously inappropriate, their meanings so transparent, that it seemed silly to have to bother with rejecting them. However, it was through these ludicrous question and answer sessions that I, as a foreign observer, began to understand a means of interpreting human body movement that was common to these performers but in some ways very different from my own. Although we did share an understanding of some aspects of the style and their expressive content, other features of the dancing related to altogether separate sets of images, activities, and values. There was indeed a practitioner's logic to the performance, which observations of the local scene convinced me was born of exposure to local movement practices. An "insider" orientation to the dancing began to emerge as this logic became visible.

In sum, there was more to the improvisational ritual *sinulog* of Cebu

City than a representation of the *tinderas'* social world, as described in the previous chapter. The dance practice acquired a broader significance as well. Its movement symbols had layers of latent meaning— meanings that were not conventionally recognized by its performers but nevertheless further enriched the dance's expressivity. The habits of action embodied by the *tinderas* presented ways of patterning action that were distinctive for the city's local *habitus* and that showed connections with broader areal patterning of social body movement as well.

In spite of the diversity of individual performance styles, a few movement characteristics, such as the resilient style of bounce Vincenta identified and the maintained gaze pathway of the eyes, did stand out as uniformly present in the ritual performances. These standard features came to define for me a coherent dance style of *tindera sinulog*. Aside from the two mentioned above, three other common characteristics stood out: the initiation patterning, a certain style of manipulation, and a spatial constellation, or tension, employed to integrate the gestural and postural statements of the performance.

As a stylized choreographic process, the dance appeared as more than a one-dimensional symbolic act, a ritual with its own causes and effects. From this style-oriented perspective, the dancing presented a small array of movement symbols simultaneously manifest, a collection of features: body parts used, phrasing patterns, spatial tension modes, each speaking in its own voice to separate issues. As I observed the everyday actions of the inhabitants of the city to see if and how these features of the ritual represented the border zone culture as well as the *tinderas* and their customers, it became clear that each of these regular features of the dance style connected with a different set of activities, all emblematic to varying degrees of the physical lifestyle of the city. The connections of the dance's resilient phrasing with the many aspects of daily life noted in Chapter 4 were perhaps the most striking and widespread. However, resiliency was not the only polysemic symbol apparent in the *sinulog*. The other collective aspects of the performance style carried latent symbolism as well, resonating with a variety of local activity patterns. Some of the symbols, like the style of gazing, were relatively limited and straightforward in their meaning. Some of them, however, like the resilient bouncing, called forth a variety of associations, relating to much more general and abstract contexts of activity.

Initiation

One of the more resonant polysemic symbols presented in the *tindera sinulog* style was the manner in which movement sequences were typically initiated or introduced. Initiations and reinitiations occurred continuously in the performance process, at the start of every resilient movement phrase and gesture. The patterning, as with those of other kinds of initiation events that have been analyzed in other cultures,[2] latently symbolized sociopolitical values concerning leadership, loyalty, cooperation, and chain of command.

The *tinderas* tended to employ at least two and often several different parts of their bodies to initiate and reinitiate movements. Multiple sources of inspiration were simultaneously apparent in their bodies, although not equally apparent. The *tinderas* located two general sources of initiation: a core source and a variety of distal sources.

"Core" initiation began in the center of the body, in the internal recesses of the pelvic area. These initiations were carried out subtly, the *tinderas* not wanting to draw attention to the movement of the hips *per se*, since that would have been considered flirtatious (the *kiat* style mentioned earlier).

"Distal" initiations, in contrast, began at the ends of the body: the fingers, the hands, and the feet. In the case of the hands, the *tinderas'* initiation practices were more specifically defined. It was not the bony masses of the hand itself, but the distal joint, the wrist, that most often led the action, which could engage the entire arm in some performances. A marionette-like quality resulted from this style of gesturing, as otherwise inert limb areas were brought to life by movements originating at points of articulation. The step initiation patterning was different, since the whole foot, a complex bony mass, did, in fact, start the movement process of the step. Again, however, the step was begun at the end of the limb, not by the knee, the thigh, or the calf. The initiation process of the step style was also handled in a subdued manner, to give the dance its respectfully pious, restrained, *formal* appearance.

In sum, the only movement process in which the *tinderas* typically chose to make initiation a salient theme was the movement process of the upper limbs, in which the wrists regularly took action first. The *sinulog* initiation style thus had both covert and overt characters. The overt, highlighted means of introducing a new course of action was to appoint the relatively vulnerable go-betweens (joint areas) that were most closely connected to manipulative members of the system (the hands) to do the most noticeable work. Meanwhile, the center of power worked covertly on more subtle transitions of its own design.

Observing this patterning, I realized that I had seen it before. It was a characteristic approach to initiating many movements of everyday life. Moreover, it was not unique to the culture of either the *tinderas* or the city as a whole. The initiation style was a trait that had swept through Cebu, marking it as a part of a much broader cultural sphere. Women's classical dances all over Southeast Asia, as well as in South Asia and East Asia, displayed similar patterning, highlighting the distally initiated movements of the upper limbs while constraining the movements of the weight center and feet. In this respect, the *tinderas'* distally initiated gestures marked their dancing as belonging to a certain broad cultural area.[3]

The initiation style of the *tindera* dancing related to many daily activities seen in the city's public life as well: the paddle-like hand-flapping used in standard gestures of greeting and approach; the initiation style of *arnis* stick-fighting, which emphasized a similar combination of understated pelvic and foot initiations supporting more spectacular actions led by the wrists and hands. As Cacoy, the local expert on the sport, once noted, *arnis* involved a combination of "body language" and "wrist language." A master could be distinguished from a novice quite literally by the flick of a wrist. Like the candle, which appeared to inspire the movement of the *tinderas'* wrists, the stick of an *arnis* fighter began the action of any blow.

The local running and walking style also utilized an initiation pattern similar to that of the *tinderas'* step style, even though pedestrian stepping habits were not as a rule foreshortened. People running across busy intersections, chasing after children wandering out into the street, or running after a jeepney, demonstrated a manner of human locomotion initially quite unfamiliar to me. I found myself laughing in reaction to seeing it without meaning to or knowing why. In analogous contexts in the United States, locomotion was typically initiated from the pelvis or from the thighs. People in Cebu City, in contrast, looked to me like little paddle boats, with their lower legs and feet working furiously while the pelvis remained relatively uninvolved. The feet led the rest of the body into motion, just as they did in the *tinderas'* dance. There were advantages to this distal locomotive style, which engaged fewer major muscle groups in the lower body, generating less bodily heat, and allowed for more nimble movement in crowded spaces, as well as facilitating quicker responses to sudden, unforeseen changes in the immediate environment. All of these effects were much needed assets in the city context.

The preference for highlighted distally initiated movement, supported by understated core initiations seen in the *tinderas' sinulog*, thus resonated with a number of different activities—martial art form, ordinary locomotor style, and conventional communicative gesturing, to mention only a few. It was also a general indicator of an "Asian" aesthetic movement style. In this respect, the initiation patterning was a resonant, though latent, polysemic symbol.

Manipulation: The *Sigue* Principle

The *tinderas'* style of candle manipulation also carried polysemic symbolism. Manipulation, in the most literal sense of the term, was a key theme in the *tindera sinulog*, as it was in social life in general. People tended to "have life in hand" in some form almost constantly while going about in public. I rarely saw an individual moving from one location to another without a bag or a basket in hand. If they were not holding a thing, then they were holding onto someone. Cebu City appeared to be a place where friends typically stayed in touch with one another while they were together in public (Figure 8.1).

Manual contact, while a pervasive feature of public life, was achieved and maintained in specific ways in Cebu. Hands were not clasped firmly, shoulders and waists were not hugged closely, arms were not taken tightly. In all forms of friendly manual contact between acquaintances, the touch was light, the placement of the contacting agent was somewhat vague, and, above all, the grasp used was loose. Clutching and grabbing were rarely seen in public. A person in Cebu faced more contact but less pressure than a person in the United States.

My most spontaneous personal experience with this local grasp style happened when my husband, Marc Ness, and I went out on a double date to an expensive discotheque with another American and his Filipina companion, Susan. Susan was not unlike most of the young women I had met in the city. She was a recent and temporary arrival, who worked as a receptionist at our apartment building. She was about twenty years old. Although Susan was a newcomer to the city like myself, she'd been invited there by the owner of the apartment building, who was a friend of her family's, and who had given her the job to help pay her expenses while she went to school. Susan was well-versed in the traditional deferential practices of the islands and had always kept her words to me, a married patron of the apartment building and five years her senior, to a minimum around the apartment building. She always greeted me instead with a silent smile when I would pass by her desk.

On the evening of this date, Susan's manner was slightly agitated. The generally serene smile was more tense than usual when she looked at me, even though she was clearly more comfortable with me than she was with the American in the driver's seat. When we got out of our car and walked toward the disco, Susan took hold of my elbow and continued to hold it loosely until we reached the door of the discotheque. I didn't judge her action to be one of extraordinary nervousness or fear, just mild caution.

Figure 8.1. Two cadets at *sinulog* parade displaying typical contact behavior.

She was walking beside me on my right side when she touched me, partially encircling my right elbow with her left hand. An impulse of surprise shot through my whole body, which I attempted to muffle immediately. I was flattered by the move. I recognized it as an appeal for support and wanted to respond in as ordinary a way as possible. I consciously exhaled, imagined water flowing down inside my arm along the bone, and felt the limb drop slightly, and begin to swing again of its own accord in synchrony with my step. In an instant, I felt her fingers change, relaxing also. We remained in touch in this way for many steps, adjusting our pace to one another to allow the contact to continue until we reached the steps of the disco.

Never had I felt such a grasp from a person I considered to be, generally speaking, a friend. There was contact but no pressure. The hand didn't feel friendly to me—it hardly even felt alive. However, it didn't feel "dead" either. It was just limp, not heavy, but passive in a refined way. It puzzled me. The grasp was so loose it practically begged to be broken. I might have attributed the limpness to our own unusual bonding, a Filipina choosing an American as a recipient for this kind of action. However, what I felt in her touch I recognized kinesthetically as the same quality I had seen in the contacting moves of young people all over the city, men and women alike. Feeling the grasp for myself, I was struck by its "unclinginess," and its delicacy. It was an unassuming presence, this hand around my elbow, yet it was tenacious; undemanding, yet persistent.

My experience with Susan confirmed observations that two key features of the local style of manipulation, which were also evident in the *tinderas'* grasp, were looseness and limpness. Possessive relationships established with things or with people through handling were more loosely organized than I expected them to be, though they were nonetheless clearly determined and ably defended. What was controlled was allowed greater freedom of movement, without being allowed independence. Serious interest in an object was not expressed by holding it tightly. It was expressed by holding it loosely and going along with the movement inherent in that object to a great degree. Looseness in this respect seemed to provide a recuperative means of coping with the city's typically densely packed spaces.

The extreme popularity of basketball in Cebu City became more understandable in light of this handling style. Basketball was easily the most popular participatory sport in the city, and in the province as well.[4] Not a school was without a court and a team. Usually there were several teams for different ages and grades of players as well as innumerable informal games going on. Fiesta programs included basketball games as one highlight of the social activities.

Everywhere it is played, basketball is a game about possession and control. However, its most important object, the ball itself, cannot be clutched firmly. It has to be released continuously from any possessor's grasp. It is kept under control, not through the strength of an individual's grip, but by adept dribbling, loosened manipulation, and by a pattern of rapid redistribution among players. The loose hold is the norm that gives collective action meaning. The structure of the game thus reinforced a widespread habit of social life in Cebu City.

Other, more routine functional activities revealed that the grasp style was related to more than casual public person-to-person contact. Manual rapports with "otherness" of many ordinary kinds demonstrated the same handling style. The loosened grasp was used when handling bottles, glasses, forks and spoons, and food of most kinds. The typical "grip" on a soft drink bottle—an item that would pass through the hands of the populace on many occasions during an ordinary day—resembled W. C. Field's manner of holding a cigar. Only the last tactile pad of the thumb and the index finger were typically used to manipulate the bottle.

When I first arrived in Cebu, the style struck me, with my foreigner's biases, as faintly humorous in certain contexts, particularly when I observed it among adult men, who used this "hyper-distal" grasp technique as frequently and habitually as did women and children. I had a conversation one afternoon with a professor of literature, for example, while he was drinking a soda pop in his office. I could hardly take my eyes off his bottle. He sat, leaning back in his chair, dangling his half-full pop bottle with a careless touch so refined it would have been the envy of any member of my mother's lady's bridge club. Forks and spoons were also used quite gingerly, and with limp wrists, by the population at large. They always seemed to me about to fall out of everybody's hands. I used to have to stifle the impulse, whenever entering a restaurant in the city, to rush around and save everybody's utensils from crashing to the floor in one big clatter. No one, of course, was really in danger of dropping anything, and, with time, I came to realize that much less actual pressure was needed to control utensils than I had ever suspected. My own biases had given me an unrealistic view of these manipulation processes.

These habitual expressions of a collective attitude toward object control and manipulation, which were seen in the varied activities of eating, game playing, and the interaction rituals of both impersonal service transactions and friendship, were the physical manifestations of what I came to call the "*sigue* principle" of Cebu City's public life. *Sigue* (pronounced somewhere between "seekay" and "seegay") was used interchangeably with "okay" in Cebu City and expressed general assent. *Sigue* also could be used as a substitute or accompanying term for expressions of departure. It could mean "yes," "good," and "I understand, continue," and also "good-bye" or "our exchange is completed." The expression generally conveyed the idea, "Yes, I will go along with what you have said." *Sigue* meant both acceptance and release. To say, "Oh *sigue*" was to open a mental gate, or at least to abstain from closing one. The willingness to make it possible for the movement of another's thought or action to flow on unobstructed, even when it was ultimately employed for one's own service, was the essential spirit of the *sigue* principle.

Sigue arguably was the most important word of the Cebuano language, the word that most dialogue was designed to produce in the end. It was the word I heard and overheard most often during my stay in the city.

The *sigue* principle was pervasive in Cebuano life, not only in nonverbal behavior, as illustrated above, but in verbal interaction as well. It was an integral part of the style of argument that was typical of public speaking in Cebu. While residents of the city had as much difficulty establishing consensus at public meetings as might any human group, they rarely took positions directly opposing each other when arguing. Instead, reactions and counter-arguments nearly always began with statements of limited accord, such statements as, "You want a more secure international policy, *sigue*, I agree." Then a counter-assertion was stated, often in terms of its being an overlooked possibility (for conceptual space, like actual space, was always packed with numerous possibilities). The reply usually took off in a different direction from the speaker's main argument without obstructing it.

In both verbal and nonverbal activity, various applications of this *sigue* principle appeared, which was symbolized in the *tindera sinulog* performances in the loose and gentle manipulation of their candles. The grasp of the *tinderas* thus symbolized a widespread strategy for handling social processes. The *tinderas* literally had a hold on social life as they performed.

Peripheral Spatial Tension

The last widely uniform feature of the *tindera sinulog* that was recognizable as a resonant movement symbol of the local culture was somewhat different in kind from those noted above. It was not a single feature of the performance, like a gaze path, a phrasing pattern, or an initiation mode. This final stylistic characteristic could only be described as a whole system of features that together made visible a spatial figure or form.

Between their gesturing body parts and their posturing body parts, the *tinderas* made visible a spatial constellation of sorts that was in essence negative. That is to say, what became apparent in this interrelating of bodily areas was a void, a distance, or a vacant area between the moving candles and the dancer's torso—specifically, the area of the more rigidly held chest and head. Even though the hand gestures were performed differently by every *tindera*, some gesturing close to the torso while others gestured at nearly a full arm's reach from it, a distance between the gesturing end of the body and the center of the upper torso, the region around the heart, was always made visible. The object offered, as well as the process of offering, appeared at a marked distance from the central core of the body. The pattern that connected all the features of the style was thus a spatial constellation that revealed a seemingly self-motivated object moving freely on an edge, which operated at a distance from a more tensely held central area of the body.

It was a puzzling pattern, hardly the sort of movement to be expected in a dance performed for a magnet of such strength as the Santo Niño de Cebu. The *tindera's* movement gave no recognition whatsoever to the tremendously influential pattern of collection and dispersal inspired by the image. Their dance was in no way a miniature depiction of the pilgrim's journey approaching and retreating from the shrine. Bridging or joining actions were not a central theme in the performances. The gestures of offering did not move directly outward from the heart. Instead, the expression created, and celebrated, yet another instance of surface making, defining a border zone from which the torso was held apart. It was the special value of surfaces that was depicted in the choreography, not the Santo Niño's miraculous powers of attractive radiation.

The appearance of a distance between the freely flowing candle and the bound torso was what might be called an "orchestrated" movement symbol, since it was formed not by a single feature of movement, or even simply by a collection of features, but by the interrelationships that allowed movements and the body to work together as an ensemble. The symbol revealed the body movement process as a microcosm, as an integrated, complex whole. In this kind of symbolic patterning, an individual performer was capable of representing the interworkings of a social action *system*, not just one element of action, and indeed this was the case with this orchestrated symbolic separation made apparent in the *tinderas'* dancing.

I interpreted this latent symbolism as the embodiment of the guest-host relationship mentioned in Chapter 4.[5] When the *tindera* took a candle into a performance, she was taking up an object she had just sold to a stranger, an object that symbolized an "other." The *tinderas* became hostesses in their dancing, and the treatment extended to the candle by the *tindera's* body represented the treatment visitors or guests were ideally accorded in Cebuano society. It was here, in the orchestrated symbolism of the performance, that the new status of the dance as a patron-client activity was expressed in the choreography.

As was mentioned in Chapter 4, a guest was ideally characterized as a relatively free spirit who was to be accommodated, treated with generous delicacy, and indulged in whatever way possible. The organization of hosting networks, however, was characterized in very different terms in the city. Being a part of the city's exclusively local or "host" structure, being on the "inside" of a group, inasmuch as such networks could exist in this highly mobile society, was generally spoken of in terms of restriction and obligation. This was typical not only of the city's interpersonal relationships, but of interpersonal relationships in general throughout the Philippines. The idea of "the debt" (*utang* in Cebuano and Tagalog) has been recognized as a widespread dynamic of Filipino social structure.[6]

This form of bonding was reported in the oldest descriptions of Cebuano social life.[7] Whenever a person entered into the "heart" of a social network and was acknowledged as a member, he or she became indebted to someone and was owed favors by someone else. Students and teachers, teachers and administrators, employees and employers, parents and children, all kinds of individuals on familiar terms with one another used the models of the debtor and the debtee or the master and the servant, which were roughly equivalent to the roles of the elder and the younger, to organize their interaction. This relationship of debt or "bound-ness" itself constructed the "inner" or relatively exclusive workings of the local society. "Insiders" were distinguishable from "outsiders" not by their geographical location within or beyond given social perimeters, but by the restricting tensions they created among themselves.

The hosting operations of the city's residents, in short, exhibited the same quality of "beholden-ness," of being a mass of constricting tension, that was exhibited in the core of the dancing *tindera*. Likewise, the behavior of the ideal visitor in social interaction resembled the behavior of the candle, buoyantly animated by its own impulses to action. Finally, the spatial constellation—that of isolated edge and center—in *sinulog* dancing was also present in the local guest-host relationship. That is to say, guests were also set apart, both socially and physically. They were housed and otherwise placed in special quarters in social gatherings, maintaining their privileged superficial status in the local scene. The deference to guests could even supersede that accorded to elders, as I learned when I was, on more than one occasion, made to sit in a chair while elderly insiders were obliged to stand for lack of seats. I found the custom painful and would leave these events with headaches, having had to fight continuously against the impulse to offer the chair to someone I viewed, with my outsider's logic, as a more deserving participant. To have vacated my seat, however, would have been an insult to the host, so I remained in place, trying to act like a proper guest.

Guests were indulged, but they were also distanced from the heartfelt relationships existing within the hosting group. As another American anthropologist once told me, in tones of long-endured frustration, Cebuano society was "designed to exclude." Although friendliness and good will were obvious in the treatment accorded visitors, isolation was nevertheless typically an accompaniment to this accommodating treatment in his experience as well.

The combined elements of the *tindera sinulog* dance style thus symbolized the general principles of conduct relevant to the important social activity of managing relative outsiders. In the *sinulog* case, the outsider was represented by the candle, which symbolized a customer, most likely a customer the *tindera* did not know and would not see again. In the end, the current socioeconomic significance of the dancing as a manifestation of patron-client ties was symbolized more systematically in the *tinderas'* dance than was the devotional pilgrimesque experience of attraction to the Santo Niño image. The orchestrated symbolism was the only aspect of the choreography that represented this relatively recent change in the ritual's social status, from a completely sacred nonhierarchical rite to a quasi-commercial patron-client interaction.

It was no accident that the latent symbolism of the *sinulog* dance form represented in a stylized way both widespread and systematic habits of social action. Dance practices all over the world are riddled with this kind of latent meaning. The attitudes and values embodied in them are those of the human beings that generate them. Gregory Bateson (1972:125) analyzed this phenomenon in Balinese dance, observing that the Balinese dancer embodied a central principle of balance evident in many contexts of Balinese public life. Mary Douglas (1979:114–22) made a similar, more sweeping argument, claiming that pollution rituals often use the body and its movement processes as a symbol of society, a microcosm of the social macrocosm, especially in contexts where a ritual expresses collective concerns over the definition and maintenance or defense of a society's outermost margins. Other scholars on dance and bodily symbolism have reached similar conclusions.[8]

The symbols embodied in the *sinulog* movement style revealed some of the distinctive "inner" workings of the city's local public culture. The latent symbols provided a rich array of references, each expressing a repertoire of meanings. The features of the performance process constructed a web of reference to many levels and layers of public life, emanating from an interior source of inspiration.

For the city and its authority figures, the *tindera* dance represented a living past, a somewhat fragmented but nevertheless "authentic" version of "pure" Cebuano culture. The dance was one of the few visible signs of what might possibly go uncontested as "indigenous regional culture." It was one of a handful of customs that had somehow survived recognition as a product of colonization and development. It was seen, in other words, as a sign of continuity in a world where nearly everything tended to change abruptly. The dance had the capacity to celebrate "Cebuano-ness" for a community that, as far as its leadership was concerned, was searching enthusiastically for memories. It was this perception of the *tindera sinulog* as an icon of a golden age that led to its revitalization and spectacular metamorphosis.

To the customers of the *tindera sinulog*, however, the dancing was mainly an investment not in their past, but in their future well-being. Likewise, in the *tinderas'* practical view, the *sinulog* was a symbol not of past, but of present concerns. It meant more rice and a trip home, as well as an opportunity to face the Santo Niño and to acquire grace (*maayong grasya*) in His presence. The body movement of the dance expressed how this grace was actually conceptualized in terms of physical experience, and how its image was conceived of by these performers. Grace was a matter of both physical restraint and mental freedom. Grace, at least for this loosely knit sector of the local scene, swayed. It gently bounced. Although the *sinulog* dancers led complicated lives filled with a variety of individual challenges, they were also one subculture while they worked within the city. They used what was basic to their common life-style on the margins of a transit point— their sensitivity to the currents of life's energy—to attempt to face and move their collective Savior, the Santo Niño.

The meaning of the performance process of the *tindera sinulog* thus stemmed from the interrelationships in which it participated, which connected many aspects of local life to the fulfillment of one particular and personal religious function. The dancing influenced the meaning of such general concepts as beauty, formality, sincerity, gratitude, and mercifulness, all of which were symbolized by different movement features. Feelings acquired articulate nonverbal forms in this crystallization of a particularly city-bound local subculture.[9]

While the specific features of the *tindera sinulog* performance gave a variety of information about certain emotions and contextual circumstances, as a totality the *tindera sinulog* performance provided a physical experience for what Santo Niño devotees referred to when they spoke of a *halad* (sacrifice, offering), or of *pagampo* (prayer). These more complicated devotional concepts were in part constituted by the qualities of resilience and manipulation, which were the essence of the *tindera sinulog* performance process.

Regardless of the actual antiquity of the *tindera* form, it was the undeniable fact that the dance necessarily originated with not simply a local resident, but a genuine insider—that is to say, a devotee perpetually bound to the Santo Niño—that made an authenticity of a pure and unquestionable sort possible for the *sinulog* practice. Yet the cost of this "insider-ly" character was considerable, since, being made of nothing other than local and not localized material, the *tindera sinulog* dance form was also associated with poverty and low prestige. The situation was reversed in another type of ritual *sinulog*, which forms the subject of the following two chapters. The striking differences in the choreography of this opposing "troupe" form of *sinulog* from that of the *tindera* form showed in fact how, like the Santo Niño, the *sinulog* could symbolize the practice of both a locally constructed insider and a localized outsider. The *sinulog* dance, like the Santo Niño, was also, on more than one level, a highly fluent symbol of the city's border zone culture.

Chapter 9
The Troupe *Sinulog*

Images of the Performance

The ritual may happen in the basilica's courtyard, or perhaps in a fragrant, walled garden on a shaded patio, or even on the polished hardwood floors of the *sala*, or entrance hall, of a stone and tile home. Or it may happen at an intersection of a *barrio* neighborhood's dirt roads. Wherever the stage may be, a Santo Niño image with candles lit around it is set up on an altar of some sort.

Drums sound as a company of brightly dressed characters enters the scene. Some are cast as victorious Christian heroes, some as Muslim infidels. Some are rulers, some are subjects. All are male, ideally. Before the Niño shrine, the dancers assemble, create a world of action for their Creator, and depart. Grave, somber marches, gracious ceremonies, lively sword play, and a duel to the death—all of these movements transpire in a ritual space that may exist for only a few minutes in some cases or for several hours in others.

The beating of drums, the twirl of swords, and the movement of a small army of colorful costumes were among the images evoked by the theatrical or "troupe" version of Cebu City's *sinulog* dance. Arches and grids were made visible in the choreography, while songs and calls emerged above the drum's accompaniment from time to time. The dancing was set to specific drum rhythms that served as a cue system for the dancers to begin and end different segments.

There was nothing about the staging of this theatrical *sinulog* that could have been considered "natural," in contrast to the ritual of the *tinderas*. It was anything but spontaneous; its rehearsal process ran for many weeks. It was anything but individualistic; the dancers (anywhere from ten to sixty could participate) acted as one body, their slightest movement determined by the choreography. Not a turn of the head, not a flick of the wrist was left to individual choice. The troupe *sinulog* was anything but pedestrian. It had all the elements necessary for a spectacle: costumes, highly orchestrated choreography, musical accompaniment, and a large cast of performers.

The total effect of this performance was complicated and organized. Its mood was alternately one of high-spirited play or serious reverence, not one of subtle humility or gentle simplicity. The ritual was diametrically opposed in many respects to that of the *tinderas*, which was a work of instinct and impulse, appealing to the more mysterious aspects of its folk–Roman Catholic society. The theatrical *sinulog*, in contrast, was a work of human genius. It was a sign of creative mastery as well as religious devotion.

The motives for the *tindera* and the troupe forms of *sinulog* in Cebu City were identical: both were interpreted as acts of veneration for Santo Niño images. However, the sources of inspiration, and the resulting choreographic forms each version took, could not have been more different. The troupe *sinulog* celebrated a masculine form of the original ritual, which historically had dominated its standard and collectively organized form.[1] It was also the "family-style" *sinulog*, organized by, for, and in terms of entire households, not single individuals. It was as well the Hispanicized version of the performance, in many respects a product of late-nineteenth-century values and influences. The dancing represented the final stages of the Spanish colonial era and, to a lesser extent, the American colonial era as well. It was a complicated symbol of past conflicts and contrasts. In addition, the troupe *sinulog* had also collected, and by 1984 was showcasing, contemporary symbols of nationalism.

While the *tindera* dancing in most respects presented a diminished but harmonious and internally oriented confluence of foreign and local religious symbolism, the troupe *sinulog* made visible the confrontational and contradictory oppositions that resulted from the meeting of the more antithetical aspects of foreign and local cultures. Its layers of meaning intentionally reached farther afield and were designed to address a more powerful and more worldly audience than did those of the *tindera* ritual. It was intended to make an impression on outsiders as well as insiders, and this circumstance created a clash of symbols within the design of its ritual process.

The Ritual Process

In its complete form, the performance of the theatrical *sinulog* happened something like the pronunciation of a word. The dance presented a set of segments that were like characters or letters. Each segment had a different theme and corresponding set of actions. The variety of symbols presented in the performance were thus not only layered but also sequenced, appearing, disappearing, and reappearing throughout the ritual as would the fragments of a kaleidoscope.

How the segments were arranged to form the composition of any given performance was left to the discretion of the drummer, who was both accompanist and conductor for the performance. In this respect, the performance style, rigorously prescribed though it was, also bore the mark of an individual mastermind. It could be adjusted from context to context, so that every ritual could be tailored to its various sponsors.

There were seven segments in all, although they did not all appear in every performance. The *elevación* (opening prayer) and *paso* (entrance march), however, always began the ritual. The *sayaw* (dance), *pagtukod sa espada* (arch of swords), *tinampilan* (pounding dance), *estocada* (sword play), and tumbling segments made up the rest of the spectacle. As the eclectic collection of descriptive labels, drawn from Spanish, Visayan, and English indicate, the separate segments of the ritual varied in terms of what sort of ethnic symbolism predominated throughout them.

Paso and Elevación

Although simple in design, the march of the *paso* and the prayer of the *elevación* segments had very detailed rules of performance and presented the main symbolic contrasts of the ritual.

Paso, in Spanish, means "step." The main activity of the introductory segment of the *sinulog* was simply that, stepping or marching into and around the cleared space, in effect claiming whatever area had been set up to become the "stage" area for the ritual. While this opening segment was indeed focused on stepping, it was also concerned with carriage, with what happened or did not happen to the rest of the body as the legs carried it about the space. It was in relation to these two features, the step style and the manner of self-carriage, that symbols of contrast developed.

The dancers were directed to walk looking straight ahead at all times, with their shields held in their left hands at waist level, the elbow bent at ninety degrees, and their swords held in their right hands so that the sword tips touched their right shoulders. The asymmetrical but highly specific and unmoving placement of the arms in the *paso* segment created a close association between the pose of the dancers' bodies and that of the Santo Niño image, whose arms, as noted previously (see Chapter 5), also remained frozen in an asymmetry related to the performance of the two separate tasks of pronouncing blessing and supporting the globe representing the world of Christendom. The relationship between the dancers and the image was not a simple relationship of imitation or identity alone. Instead, the resemblance was constructed more subtly by the application of principles of composition inherent in the Niño's form to the dancers' representation of an armed soldier's carriage.[2]

One message was made clear from the start with this rigidly defined marching pose: strict self-discipline was intended to prevail throughout the ritual. The main dynamic quality apparent in the *paso* was one of subtle but consistent control, control of the posture and control over the shape of the group figures presented. This tension was not great, but it endured throughout the opening ceremony. Along with the musical accompaniment, which consisted of a simple, slow drum beat struck with every footfall, the rigid posture created an atmosphere that both locals and outsiders such as myself identified as "solemn." The manifestation of this solemnity marked the beginning of this theatrical *sinulog* form.

Contrasting styles of performance were immediately apparent in the marching process. In spite of the rigid posture, the stepping of the *paso* typically was not performed with a solemn or disciplined gait, but instead employed a cushioning, flat-footed stepping that was similar to, although less diminished and "pointed" than, the *tinderas'* stepping. The step style of the *paso* looked curious because it did not reinforce the emphatic drum notes that sounded every time the dancers' feet made contact with the ground. The *paso* steps were not the steps a foot soldier, whether he might be plodding along or charging forcefully ahead. On the contrary, the spirit of the step style, in contrast to that of the upper body, was one of freedom, not control, one of buoyant levity, not plummeting gravity. The segment's overall quality of discipline was compromised by the step style, which, regardless of the drumming, made the most of the moment when the feet were released from the ground. To a passing observer, it looked as though the feet of the dancers, even while co-operating obediently in doing their part of the dancing, were playing a joke upon the solemn activity that was the main statement of the ceremony.

This mildly humorous effect was not intentional. The marching step style was not a focus of conscious training, and it was not mentioned in my conversations with troupe teachers. It was an unmarked

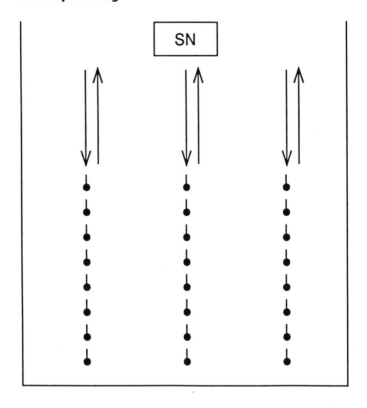

Individual dancers

SN   Santo Nino

——▷   Movements of the entire column (unless otherwise indicated)

Figure 9.1. Diagram of column formation used in troupe *sinu-log paso* choreography. (The Santo Niño altar appears at top.)

form of movement that simply occurred without instruction. Nevertheless, it was mixed into the otherwise "solemn" choreography. Its contrasting style expressed the meeting of two antithetical traditions: the Spanish-derived religious processional style, which governed the posture and the drumming of the dance, and a local unspecified or "natural" manner of locomotion.

Another symbol of contrast presented in the opening segments was apparent in the style of presentation used in the formation of group

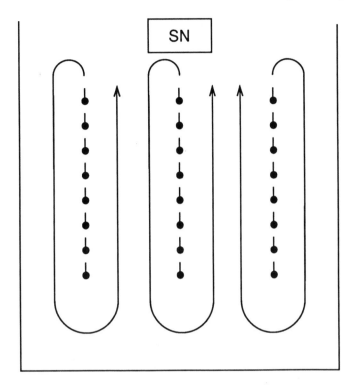

Figure 9.2. Diagram of stepping figure used in troupe *sinulog* *paso* choreography.

designs constructed by the corps of dancers as a whole. The distinctive spatial symbol of the troupe *sinulog* was a three-column formation, which proceeded through a number of transfigurations— braidings and column refilings—during the ritual's different segments (Figures 9.1 and 9.2).

Teachers of the troupe *sinulog* reported that one of the most difficult things to teach young dancers was to maintain these lines. Even when this was achieved, the dancers I observed never displayed any enthusiasm for or especial interest in the process of creating the unified spatial forms themselves, something that one of the current organizers of the ritual reported as the ideal experience of the dancing. Instead, a "one foot in front of the other" style or approach generally prevailed in performance. Gaze habits were kept to a downward and near-range area. Actions were accomplished in a body-oriented fashion. That is, actions were not clearly aimed at external locations or performed in a way that demonstrated a shared intent to link the movements of individuals into a single systematic shape or form visible in the space. As with the *tinderas'* dance style, the movements of the individuals in the troupe *sinulog* did not appear to be about making the invisible visible. Yet, unlike the *tindera* form, the choreography in this case clearly called for this kind of approach. The collective structure presented in the dancing was merely adhered to by its members, but they demonstrated no animated physical interest in it, preoccupied instead with their own individual body movements.

The lack of a clear collective attitude toward constructing the predominant spatial forms of the choreography gave another mixed message to an observer of the ritual. A strong feeling that the formations were somehow arbitrary was conveyed. Everyone dancing followed the ways established in the choreographic pattern, caught up all the while in the process of "doing his own thing," flexing his own limb, holding his own sword still, monitoring his own stepping rhythm.

The detached movement style underscored the fact that the use of the three-column formation, and the linear figures performed in the dancing, constituted the acceptance of a spatial design that was not only different from but even at odds with more pervasive local habits of movement. A wealth of evidence from contemporary life revealed this contrast. Somewhat like the Balinese, who believe that only demons run in straight lines,[3] people in Cebu City tended not to employ one-dimensional linear patterning, in most ordinary contexts as well as in symbolic action. That is to say, in everyday life in Cebu City, people did not use straight lines to organize themselves in space. When I would find myself waiting for service—to buy stamps or a ferry ticket, or to get on a local bus—I usually found that there was no line to organize the social process of "taking a turn."[4] Voluminous shapes, "clumps" of people that had the capacity to grow and shrink, were the forms people created to manage their turn-taking. These movement constructs were concerned much more literally with "takings" and with "turnings" than was the case with corresponding Western-style linear organizations. In situations where lines were considered unavoidable, an object would be substituted and used as a go-between for individual bodies, so that people would not have to make a line of themselves. The avoidance of collective linear action was thus supported by the *sigue* principle of loosened manipulation. Moreover, linear forms and figures were not typical of coastal central Philippine aesthetic traditions, which had been given such labels as "incipient baroque" in reference to the intricate curvilinear style of their floral motifs.[5]

The preference for curvilinear trace forms in individual movement patterning came out spontaneously in a conversation I had with a dance instructor from one of the leading universities in the city. Given that this was a person who had made a career out of developing a mastery of the local movement style, I tended to give extra weight to her opinions and preferences, and so I was quite struck one afternoon by the way in which curvilinear patterning unconsciously overcame and replaced linear designs when we were in the process of discussing the *tinderas' sinulog* movement style. She was demonstrating the "Cebuano way" of bouncing resiliently when it happened. As she started demonstrating the Cebuano-style bouncing, she began moving backward into a counter-clockwise spiral. This was a rather odd pathway, since the basic *sinulog* step pattern she had associated with this bouncing only moments earlier consisted of stepping straight forward and backward. When she focused her attention on the energy quality of that step, however, a curving spatial path was adopted instead, for no expressed purpose. As with so many scenes from daily life that I observed, linear forms did not come as "second nature" in many contexts. Spirals, diagonal slants, and voluminous figures were more likely to appear.

Two symbolic contradictions were thus made visible in the opening segment of the troupe *sinulog*. The local step style was opposed to the Spanish-derived processional carriage style, and the individual disengagement from the collective spatial expression was opposed to the predominantly spatial statement of the choreography—its three-column formation.

The end and climax of this opening section, as it was performed in 1984 and 1985, was marked by three things: the drum roll, the advance of three principal characters representing Magellan, King Humabon (Magellan's Cebuano host), and Lapulapu (Magellan's slayer), along with the youngest boy of the corps, to the altar, and the sinking of the corps to its knees for the opening prayer.

Breaking the stillness constructed by the kneeling corps, the boy would recite, sometimes along with the character of Magellan, a Visayan prayer in verse that would last about a minute. The segment was named *elevación*, in reference to the boy's action, because the prayer was "offered up" in a manner resembling that of a priest's elevation of the Host in the sacrament of communion. The child and Magellan spoke together in normal voices, all but inaudible to the dancers and the observers:

Matam-is Bathala nga pinangga
Maanindot maanyag nga bata,
Makabihag sa huna-huna.
Bilihon nga labi sa mutya,
Among dungog ug himaya,
Kalipay niay among yuta,
Kalipay nga dili mapana.
Ang Imong mahal nga larawan,
Amo nga ginalarawan,
Mao'g mahimong tuburan sa among mga kapalaran
Kadaut, katalagman, ii-way ning kapupud-an.
Ikaw ang among gila-umon ning among gikinahanglan.
Busa, walay sukud sa pagla-um,
Ning imong mga ulipon,
Nga sa gihapon imong pagapuminawon.

Sweet, Lord, most beloved,
Pretty, beautiful child,
Enchanting to imagine.
Most precious pearl,
Our honor and glory,
Happiness is in our land,
Everlasting happiness.
Your dear image,
We make an offering to your image,
The abundant source of our bliss and good fortune
Protect this place from evil and misfortune.
You, who are our hope for these needs.
So it is, with a hope that has no limit,
These your servants,
Trust that you will always hear them.

All, except the boy and the single column of dancers who represented Muslim warriors, rested on their right knee as this prayer was
pronounced (the Muslim or *moro* warriors bowed from the waist).
Again, at this point in the ritual, the pose and gestures of the upper
body were rigidly defined, down to the minute detail of exactly where
and how the tip of each dancer's sword must touch the ground. During this period the drum fell silent. The dancers remained frozen in
their collective deferential pose. The *elevación* choreography allowed
no possibility of contradicting the Spanish-derived processional style
of carriage. In the stillness, the world created by the dancers for the

Santo Niño was vividly defined as a world of straight lines and controlled postures.

Contrast, however, was not absent, even in this relatively static moment of the dance. While the silent corps represented nothing other than a nonlocal design in both its individual and collective structure, the verbal statement was made in fluent Visayan and represented, right down to its designation of the Niño as *Bathala* or God, an indigenous form of deferential rapport with the patron deity. Verbal and nonverbal channels revealed in stark contrast the confrontation of cultural symbolic traditions in the climactic moment of the opening ceremony.

When the prayers were finished, the characters of Magellan, Humabon, Lapulapu, and the smallest boy returned to their places in the columns. A drum roll brought the group to its feet, marking the end of the opening ceremony. The stage was now set, marked out by the opening marches and sanctified by the prayer, both of which presented the contentious interaction of contrasting symbolic traditions and styles that would be played out in the segments to come.

Sayaw

Sayaw, meaning "dance," set forth an array of possibilities different and more compliant from those presented in the opening segments, although the world constructed by the dancers was basically of the same design. The three columns proceeded through a two-part routine that allowed the separate lines to interweave and circulate (Figures 9.3 and 9.4). While the effect of the *paso* ceremony was to focus the dancer's concentration inward and create an attitude of prayer, the *sayaw* section effected the opposite. Its gestures brought the dancers out into the space around their respective stations in line as they proceeded through their figures.

The *sayaw* was performed to a moderate, waltzing drum cadence. It was the only step of the *sinulog* that used a three-quarter rhythm and so gave a subtle jolt to the performance sequence, switching its gears to a different way of measuring time and effort. The *sayaw*, in effect, demonstrated that there was more than one way to animate a spatial form and make it move.

The *sayaw* was the only segment of the ritual to come close to paralleling the aesthetic values seen in the *tindera* style of *sinulog*. The waltz step alternated from side to side, like a balancé. It involved a scattering arm gesture that swept outward, away from the body. Ideally, the gesture opened up the space around the dancers' torsos. The forearm was always kept at a distance from the torso, the arm remain-

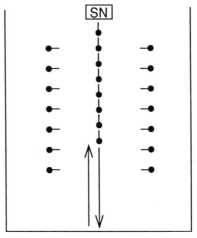

Figure 9.3a

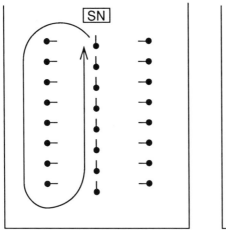

Figure 9.3b 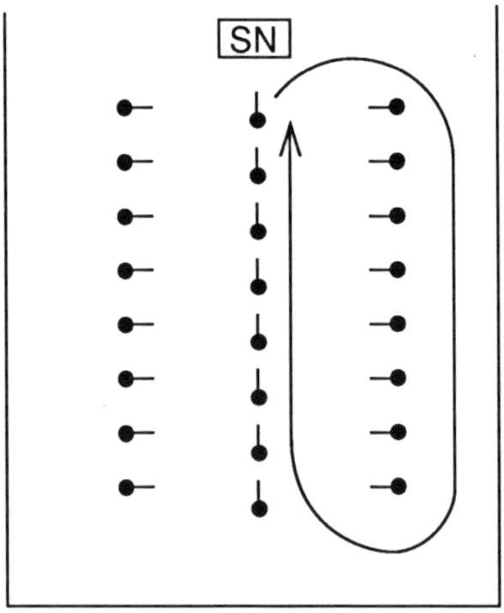   Figure 9.3c

Figure 9.3 a–c. Diagram of a curvilinear stepping figure used in troupe *sinu-log sayaw* choreography. (See the key to Figure 9.1 for an explanation of the diagrammatic symbols.) The dancers enter and form three columns. The out-side columns face in toward each other while the central column advances and retreats toward and away from the altar (Figure 9.3a). Next, the central column winds around the column to its left, circling it entirely (Figure 9.3b), and then winds around the column to its right to complete a figure-eight pathway (Figure 9.3c).

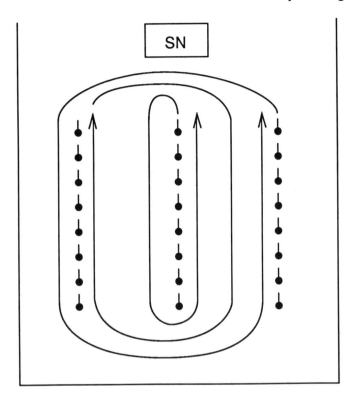

Figure 9.4. Diagram of a column interweaving figure used in troupe *sinulog sayaw* choreography. (See the key to Figure 9.1 for an explanation of the diagrammatic symbols.)

ing bent throughout the movement so that it nudged the space, as opposed to sweeping it away. When performed correctly, the gestures looked as though they were gently scooping out hollows or making pockets in the air, working carefully through a space that could easily have been filled with clouds that needed to be gently and carefully moved aside. These were "portly" actions. That is to say, they lacked grandeur but maintained a restrained cordiality. They expressed the same concept of "formality" that was articulated in the *tindera* ritual. Likewise, the *sayaw* steps were also supposed to be performed delicately, so that they exhibited the same careful *puntolpuntol* ("pointed") placement of the *tinderas'* dance style.

Stylistic contrasts were muted in this segment. The three lines of the corps, though not abandoned, were softened and rounded by the curvilinear group figures performed. The buoyant movements of the individuals were no longer set in contrast to any overall mood of severity and discipline. The different styles of posture and gesture in effect found common ground in this courtly waltz of gracious welcoming.

Pagtukod sa Espada

The *pagtukod sa espada* (arch of swords) segment returned to the initial standards set in the opening segments, with a few embellishments. It was performed to a steady, even drum beat. It sometimes followed the *sayaw* as a concluding figure to the whole ritual. The arch was made by the two outside columns, which faced inward (Figure 9.5). Meanwhile, the center column proceeded to circulate beneath the archway.

As with the *paso*, the main activity in this segment was marching in a highly regulated manner. However, the symbolism of the *pagtukod sa espada* section was more complicated in one respect: it presented a world in which the division of movement roles revealed a social hierarchy. The central column became the locus of privilege, for whose benefit the archway was made.

In previous generations, as recently as 1965, this figure portrayed the central column as Spanish kings, who passed under the swords of their loyal soldiers on the one side, and the offending *moros* on the other. By 1984, however, the dancers in the central line represented the main characters of a historical dramatization of the death of Magellan, a plot that held appeal for both its nationalist and its internationalist sponsors. By 1984, there were no longer any kings represented in the ritual. As one troupe leader put it, the Santo Niño was now the only king. In this respect, the symbolism inherent in the arch of swords segment choreography was multilayered. It expressed a fragment of imperial Spanish court etiquette that had come to be employed as Philippine nationalist imagery.

Tinampilan

As the Cebuano-derived name indicates, the *tinampilan* (pounding) segment introduced a distinctive and salient symbol of the local movement habits: resilient quickness. The group formations of the *sayaw* were repeated in this segment, so that the muted opposition noted earlier reappeared. The step itself, however, for which the segment was named, gave the group figures a different energy.

The *tinampilan* step sequence featured a moderately difficult pattern of weight shift, a series of three steps, the first of which crossed

Figure 9.5. *Tukod sa espada* (arch of swords) formation.

behind and the second and third of which stepped in place. The step demonstrated agility as well as accuracy. It was not the step of a soldier marching off to battle, but more similar to that of a sailor dancing a jig. The diminished but rapid pattern of weight shift, as well as the maintained pose of the upper body, resembled those of Philippine war dances performed in connection with the sea-to-land raiding that occurred well into the 1800s.[6]

The *tinampilan* was used either as a preparation or a continuation of the main ritual event: the *estocada* sword play. The spirited stepping picked up the pace and enlivened the dancing, lifting the performance out of its solemn mood. The segment as a whole stood in marked contrast to the opening ceremonies of the *paso* and *elevación*.

Estocada

The *estocada* or sword play segment of the *sinulog* was the section in which the climax of the ritual took place: the duel or improvised solo fight that, in 1984, represented Magellan's death at the hands of Chief Lapulapu. *Estocada*, a Spanish-derived term, in Cebuano meant "stab." The segment had four main sections: in-place demonstrations of a stepping/turning/jumping sequence, which the corps performed in unison; group figures that retraced the column formations; improvised sword play performed by trios, and, finally, the duel scene between Magellan and Chief Lapulapu, which on occasion was also performed as a solo.

The world constructed by the choreography and presented to the Santo Niño became more complicated in this section of the *sinulog*. The corps assembled not one, but two collective shapes before the altar. A spiraling form was constructed in addition to the corps' three-column formation. The splitting of the corps into these two separate figures made visible two discrete and contained spatial forms, each built on fundamentally different dynamic principles. The dancers took turns inhabiting both spatial figures, so that the main statement made in the choreography of the *estocada* segment focused on the facility with which individuals could traffic between the two markedly dissimilar realms. At this point, the ritual became a dance about translation, a dance in which the dancers demonstrated their spatial fluency.

The initial sequence of the *estocada* started with a jump and a shout, performed in unison by the corps. The two acts were integrated into a single symbol, which was itself yet another symbol of contrast. The jump initiated a unison four-count phrase—three jogging steps and a step in place with a half turn, to be repeated facing the opposite direction (Figure 9.6). Every fourth cycle was performed in a circular as opposed to a reversible pathway and began the next sequence with the same jump, accompanied by a twirl of the sword and what had become a famous cry throughout the city, "*Pit Señor!*"

"*Pit Señor!*"—probably a contraction of the verb *hangpit*, meaning "to call forth"—had become a popular symbol of the *sinulog* by 1984, a cliché used in newspaper headlines, advertisements, and theme songs to represent the inspirational and expressive force of the traditional devotion. In the aggressive versions of older forms of the ritual, the phrase had been called out repeatedly, at random intervals. "*Pit Señor!*" appeared in the theatrical *sinulog*, however, only at the point where the choreography called for a jump.

The contrastive nature of this combined vocal/aerial symbol became apparent in comparison with the act of prayer and offering performed during the *elevación*. Like the prayer of the opening segment, the words *hangpit Señor* were also offered up to the Santo Niño. They were literally "elevated," said in synchrony with the dancer's springing off of the ground. The inclusion of the *hangpit* call and its coordination with the jumping sequence achieved in the opening movements of the *estocada* what could be interpreted as an alternative restatement of the *paso* and *elevación* segments. The *estocada* offering style, however,

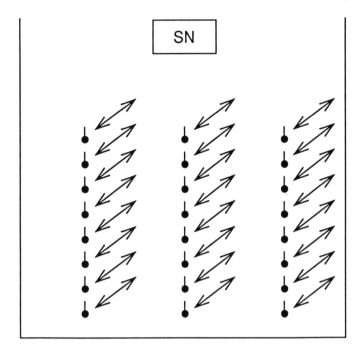

Figure 9.6. Diagram of troupe *sinulog estocada* stepping path-way for *Pit Señor* sequence. (See the key to Figure 9.1 for an explanation of the diagrammatic symbols.)

stood in high contrast to the Hispanic *elevación*. The *estocada* elevacion was postural, dramatically involving the whole body in an action of release. The Hispanic style of elevation of the prayer in the ritual's opening segment was a rigid gestural pose (only the arms expressed release and offering).

The insertion of this contrasting vocal/postural symbol of non-Hispanic devotional style into the ritual occurred at a critical juncture in the performance, the movement just prior to the climactic duel scene. The jumping *hangpit* phrases of the *estocada* segment in effect reinitiated the theatrical *sinulog* ritual in terms of folk-Catholic, non-orthodox devotional practice, bringing non-Hispanic symbolism—both verbal and nonverbal—back into the dancing as it prepared for its climax.

It was only after the initial *hangpit* symbol that the splitting of the corps into two spatial figures occurred. At this point the ritual became something like a "two-ring circus" in its basic visual impact, with the

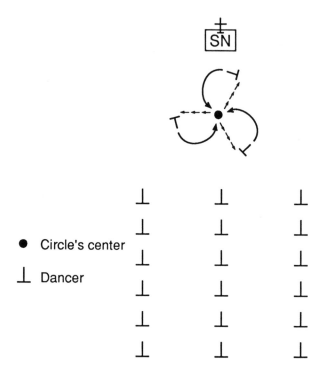

● Circle's center

⊥ Dancer

Figure 9.7. Diagram of spiraling *estocada* trio and column formation. (See the key to Figure 9.1 for an explanation of the diagrammatic symbols.)

front member from each of the three columns separating from his line to work together as a trio improvising sword play while the columns marked time behind them. Each trio had only a minute or two to display its virtuosity before it disbanded. The members retreated to the rear of their respective columns as a new trio was formed by the new front members (Figures 9.7 and 9.8). The rotating figure gave all the dancers a turn to play in the spiraling trio formation before returning to their ranks. The main characters, Magellan and Lapulapu, were positioned at the rear of the columns so that their duel took place at the conclusion of the segment.

The *estocada* segment, like the *tinampilan,* had a resilient baseline rhythm. The sword movements were fast and loose, whipping through looping trace forms that magnified the figure-eight actions of the controlling wrists. The sense of play and freedom were also

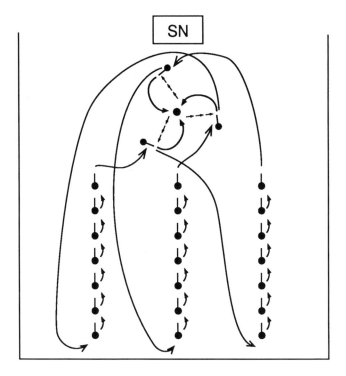

Figure 9.8. Diagram of *estocada* rotation pattern for trio section. (See the key to Figure 9.1 for an explanation of the diagrammatic symbols.)

increased by the loosening of the structure of the dancing. When joining in the swordplay of the spiraling trios, the dancers could improvise (Figure 9.9).

The trio formation presented another striking contrast of symbolic forms, this time with respect to the representation of a space of conflict. While the Hispanic style of organization of these soldierly characters was linear, emphasizing the sagittal, forward and backward dimension, the improvised pattern created by the dancers in trios presented a spiraling shape that had a three-dimensional character. The dancers did not move along the edge of some planal circular construct. Nor did they move directly inward and outward from some collective central point. Their movement, and the spatial figure they made visible, continually alternated between two forms: spiraling and shrinking as it moved inward, forward, and downward, then growing

Figure 9.9. *Estocada* trio demonstration.

and rising as it retreated outward. The dancers were drawn into the circle's most dense central point as their actions became more aggressive and intense. In recuperative moments, the circle enlarged itself as the collective energy dispersed.

This form depicted a miniature path to battle, a narrow, crooked, and curving path. At the end of this path was the center of the fighter's world, a center of conflict. The spiraling form symbolized a movement to do battle that located a home base at the structure's edge and an "away" place or hostile destination at its center. It represented a version of conflict dramatically different from that represented in the Hispanic columnar designs, which depicted fields or planes of bodies reachable in battle by a force of straight lines.

The spiraling formation used in the *sinulog* was not unique to this dance practice. It was one manifestation of a widespread choreographic pattern that also had appeared in other dances symbolic of warfare that were practiced in both southern and northern regions of the archipelago. The pattern represented a world in which to find and defeat the enemy one had to move, not abreast of one's comrades, but following in their footsteps—not a simple matter when the path they had trod was changing in three dimensions simultaneously.[7]

Two worldviews were thus constructed simultaneously in this segment of the *sinulog* ritual: the linear column formations, which were clearly of Hispanic design, and the swordplay circular forms, which presented a relatively indigenous vision of the shape of war. At the moment when the major dramatic statement of the ritual was made, the corps' energies were divided between these two fundamentally dissimilar cultural realms.

The climax of the dance erupted when the two principal characters, Magellan and Lapulapu, improvised a duel to the death, a scene in which several brief but intense encounters occurred in rapid succession, accompanied by the most spirited and powerful beating of the drum. This mock fight scene appeared as something like a human imitation of a cockfight, the two fighters bursting upon each other with extremely quick flurries of strokes.

During the duel between these two virtuosos, the action reached its peak. At the end of the duel, the mood changed abruptly. When Magellan finally lay still on the ground for a brief moment, calm settled over all the participants. After this, several things could happen. The initial phase of the *estocada* segment could be repeated, or the *sayaw* segment could be repeated, or the whole ritual could end abruptly. If the performance included the duel scene, however, it would often include the tumbling segment as well, which could also follow the *estocada*.

Tumbling

The tumbling was a relatively new feature of the *sinulog*, added after the end of World War II. This section presented a more "modern" interpretation of the ritual's spirit, using simple acrobatics to express a lively, fun-loving quality in the dance.

The tumbling segment, like the *estocada*, highlighted technical skill. A whole line of boys would simultaneously run toward another row squatting in front of them and roll across their backs, breaking over the front row as one long wave breaks upon a beach. While this new section was the most simplistic and vaguely defined in terms of group form and stylistic rules for postures and gestures, it was in other ways the most compelling to watch because it presented the performers with their most challenging physical tasks.

As the English label indicates, it was the one segment of the ritual that bore the mark of U.S. influence, incorporating gymnastic actions resembling those of physical education classes introduced during the American colonial era, when public education was first instituted on a massive scale.[8] The tumbling segment was also a symbol of contrast, bringing in the actions of yet another cultural tradition to complicate the ritual's choreography.

Kantas

Songs, or *kantas* (from the Spanish *cánta*), as they were called, were interspersed between segments at various points during the performance. Although one of these songs had Cebuano lyrics, most were in Spanish. They were not completely intelligible. The words had been handed down through several generations without translation, and enunciation patterns were gradually drifting away from the original, grammatically comprehensible expressions. The melodic forms dated back to nineteenth-century European popular religious traditions, with some mariachi, flamenco, and maleguéñan influences apparent in different tunes. The underlying pentatonic structure of several of the songs, however, was reminiscent of much older traditions. It was vaguely similar, for example, to the Spanish *cántigas* of the Middle Ages.[9]

The *kantas* were sung *a cappella*, at a normal speaking voice level, with the drum marking time. When a song was performed, the dancers stood in place or marked time as they sang. Unlike the moment when the cry *"Pit Señor!"* was uttered and the dancers leapt into the air, *kantas* and dance movements were kept separate during the ritual process, and the singing as well as the content of the lyrics played a markedly understated, secondary role in the performance. The *kantas* served mainly as links between different segments of the ritual.

These vocal links, however, were nevertheless themselves striking symbols of Spanish influence, perhaps the most "purely" Spanish aspect of the performance. While they were not perfectly accurate renditions of the original verses, they were nevertheless fairly precise copies of the original Spanish music, still sung accurately enough to be understood by a Spanish speaker. Their presence in the *sinulog* ritual symbolized its connection with the elite members of Cebuano society, since Spanish had, since its arrival on the island, been spoken only by the elite classes in Cebu. For the performers of the ritual, who came from the poorer *barrios*, or neighborhoods, where Spanish was not taught or spoken on a daily basis, the Spanish songs were among the more alien symbols of Spanish tradition, in contrast to the opening Visayan prayer and the *"Pit Señor!"* shouting.

Finale

The troupe *sinulog* ended without ceremony, at the will of the drummer. Silence was the only signal of the abrupt conclusion of the performance.

The length of the ritual depended upon who was sponsoring it and the occasion. In this respect, the troupe *sinulog* was somewhat like a lengthy, elaborate version of the *tindera* ritual. When the group performed at the basilica, for example, they generally took an hour or more, unless the priests set a time limit for them. The longest performances were given when special audiences were arranged and could last two hours or even an entire afternoon. The performance given yearly at the Casa Gorordo,[10] for example, where the dancing was sponsored by the Gorordo family in fulfillment of a perpetual vow of devotion, lasted well over an hour. Other performances, however, done in sequence at a series of homes in a given neighborhood on fiesta days, could be as short as fifteen minutes.

Regardless of the length and variety of the performance, the overall impact of the theatrical *sinulog* was one of a series of contrasting scenes that had the capacity for infinite reduplication, depending on how often the drummer decided to cue their performance. A common sequence began with the *paso* and *elevación*, then proceeded with a *kanta*, a *sayaw*, another *kanta*, and finally a *sayaw*. Other sequences might show more variety, proceeding with the *paso*, a *kanta*, a *sayaw* and *pagtukod sa espada, tinampilan, kanta, sayaw,* tumbling, and a final *kanta*. The *estocada* segment, while it was the most dramatic, was not necessarily included in every performance. It was reserved for occasions when the most elaborate renditions were presented. What was most basic to the theatrical version of the ritual was not its climax or any single segment, but its segmenting structure, which formed a chain of movements, all built upon the action of the three columns of the corps.

Chapter 10
Historical Development of the Troupe *Sinulog*

The development of the highly formalized theatrical ritual *sinulog* occurred over the course of many decades. It was, as said before, a work of genius: of the collective genius of Cebu City society, which supported, influenced, and fostered the ritual, and of the genius of the individuals who created and recreated the ritual, some of whose individual talent was still manifest in the choreography of 1984 and 1985.

Always a public spectacle, the troupe *sinulog* adapted its elaborate performance process to changes occurring in the society at large: to the changing motivations of its performers and the changing needs of its sponsors. The contextual meaning of its movements, and its movements within movements, developed both from its precommercialized context, in which it was remembered as originating from a characteristically masculine stylistic variant of the ritual tradition, and from the colonial structures and contemporary conditions with which it had interfaced more recently. These influences provided numerous dimensions of meaning to the ritual's choreographic symbolism. The ritual spoke of both Cebu City's religious and social transformations and one particular family's innovative and resilient tradition of religious devotion.

Originative Impulses: Masculine Devotional Dancing

While the theatrical version of the *sinulog* ritual reflected external influences, its roots were nevertheless as deeply embedded in indigenous traditions as were those of the *tindera* ritual. Though its choreographic form made reference to nineteenth- and twentieth-century contexts, its inspiration, like that of the *tindera* ritual, was believed to be far more ancient.

Many of the *tinderas* noted that the traditional devotional *sinulog* ritual practiced by previous generations had masculine and feminine styles. These alternative forms were described as having been composed of "natural" body movements. In both masculine and feminine ritual forms, authenticity of intent was associated with unrehearsed, spontaneous action. Body movements considered natural for men, however, were quite different from those considered natural for women.

Various *tinderas* reported that the masculine style of *sinulog* that was the precursor of the troupe form was more convulsive and energetic than the feminine style. It featured jumping and arm gestures that resembled fighting movements, either sword fighting, *arnis* stick fighting, or spear throwing. It also called for drum accompaniment. Judging from these comments, it appeared that the Santo Niño de Cebu, in times past, had attracted at least two very different indigenous practices to its devotion: a healing dance that still served as a referent of the *tindera* practice, and a war dance, which also fell under the label of "*sinulog*."[1]

At fiesta time, in the days when the *sinulog* constituted the religious climax of the fiesta celebration for the majority of the pilgrims arriving from surrounding areas, the masculine style was performed inside the Santo Niño church. The following account, written by Irving A. Leonard, a visitor passing through the city sometime in the 1920s, gives some idea of the traditional fiesta *sinulog's* more aggressive character.

The ponderous doors at the extremity of the chapel resounded with the occasional thumping and jostling of the impatient worshippers outside eager to demonstrate their devotion to the tiny Child. When the proper moment had arrived the priest at the altar gave a signal and the huge portals swung inwards with a mighty crash. Immediately the great nave of the ancient church was filled with a mass of howling, gesticulating humanity which rushed headlong into the chapel giving vent to piercing shrieks and unnatural cries. The violence of the scene did not abate when the mob—the word is used advisedly—surged into the presence of the imperturbable image but rather increased. Men and women, many with infants in their arms, began to dance and caper, holding up the bewildered babies towards the impassive little figure, and never ceasing for a moment to utter unearthly howls. Many of the women wore white handkerchiefs upon their heads which, while hopping about grotesquely, they snatched off, waved wildly in the air, and tore them to shreds in the Bacchanalian fury which seemed to rend them. It seemed, indeed, as if a Filipino Bedlam had broken loose in the venerable old church and had worked itself into a frenzy of ungovernable proportions. The comparative silence which but a few moments ago had reigned in the dim interior was transformed into an uproar of unintelligible sounds. The vivid hues of native costumes, mingling and intermingling as the worshippers spun about in a dizzy whirl, became a veritable kaleidoscope.

At length the ecstasy or frenzy—it is difficult to say which—wore off through sheer fatigue. The turbulent gathering, panting and perspiring, dropped back to the walls of the church and gradually resolved itself into a long line where it waited patiently and quietly, a marked contrast to the pandemonium which had so recently prevailed. Although the general excitement had subsided the air was pregnant with eager anticipation. The line began to stir into motion. As each individual passed before the Santo Nino, he or she bent and reverently placed a kiss upon the diminutive foot. This was the supreme manifestation of the devotion of the simple native who had, perhaps, journeyed far and spent his savings that he might, in this one occasion of the year, when the image was brought to light, pay his homage to the generous Giver of All Things. And with this gentle act performed the women may return to their homes happy in the assurance that they will be blessed with beautiful and healthy children.[2]

Leonard's description reflects his own cultural biases. His choice to contrast the "patient" and "quiet" line with the "bedlam" of the non-linear segments reveals the movement preferences of his own background. In any case, however, the account indicates that the "natural" movements of this devotional ritual were more akin to the style described by the _tinderas_ as being the masculine style than they were to the slow, quiet, restrained style "natural" to the _tinderas'_ ritual. The collective _sinulog_ ritual was not purely a war dance. As Leonard's account of the babies' presences and their manipulation indicates, the Cebu City Santo Niño fiesta _sinulog_ once combined elements of both masculine and feminine stylistic traditions. Individual variation was also exercised in the improvisational process of the dancing. Like the _tindera_ ritual, the fiesta _sinulog_ of former times was an individualistic, improvised event. However, it had a collective significance as the simultaneous, unrehearsed act of a huge congregation that the present-day _tindera_ improvisations lacked.

By 1984, little remained of the collective, more aggressive _sinulog_ form. The spontaneous and volatile, drum-accompanied dancing, which presented many of the characteristics the _tinderas_ recognized as "masculine," had all but vanished from the scene. Brief allusions to the masculine style were seen only infrequently, when pilgrims arrived, usually during fiesta time, and performed it individually. Drummers no longer came to play on the basilica steps to accompany the ritual at random, and the collective significance of what remained of the style at the basilica disappeared. Unlike the "female" style, which survived relatively unmodified in the practices of the _tinderas_, this more aggressive _sinulog_ ritual was gradually discontinued and replaced by an alternate drum-accompanied dance that became a theatrical troupe form.

Development of the Troupe

The first step in the development of what was by 1984 a small local network of seasoned public performers began with a single religious act: a peasant farmer's perpetual vow. The farmer was remembered by his descendants only as "Iklot." He lived near what by 1984 was a district in the northwestern sector of Cebu City called Banilad. Iklot was skilled in drumming and had accompanied the aggressive style of *sinulog* at the Santo Niño church. In taking the vow, Iklot promised that he and his descendents would train young boys to dance the *sinulog* to the beating of their drums before the Santo Niño every fiesta. This vow was made sometime around the turn of the century, possibly as early as the 1860s, but most likely closer to 1900.[3]

Why Iklot chose to cast the dancing as a children's form and thus create an infanticized version of the adult ritual was unknown. His specific motivation for the institution of the dramatic narrative sequence that began with this new form was also lost to memory. Iklot probably followed the classic pattern of the border-zone culture and began by duplicating. Children's dances performed in celebration of religious occasions were popular practices all over the archipelago. Moreover, the similarities of the battle scene depicted in his *sinulog* to other dance dramas of the area indicated that Iklot had been exposed to or involved in such performances elsewhere before making his vow and to some extent had drawn inspiration from them. The troupe *sinulog* of Cebu City most likely began as a compilation of borrowings from the practices of neighboring areas.[4]

Whatever the actual inspiration for Iklot's choreography, two facts stood out with relative certainty about the performance he instituted in Cebu City. First, Iklot's restaging of the ritual introduced Hispanic symbolism into the indigenous ritual style. Second, the creative choices he made in designing the new *sinulog* form struck a supportive chord within the Cebu City community.

The introduction of Hispanic symbolism was not a simple affair. The recasting of the dance as children's movement and the dramatization of the ritual brought different kinds of Hispanic influences into the choreography. It was the particular blend of Spanish-derived symbolism, in fact, that gave Cebu City's troupe *sinulog* a distinctive choreographic form, unlike any other reported to exist throughout the archipelago.

The introduction of a narrative segment and role-playing into the ritual forged a link between Cebu City's _sinulog_ and a Spanish-derived war dance/drama form, the _comedia_, which was practiced widely throughout the central and southern regions of the archipelago during the late nineteenth century.[5] The _comedia_, or _moromoro_, staged a battle scene between two groups, victorious locals (Christians, who were depicted as allied with Spanish colonial forces) and enemy foreigners (Muslim invaders, who could be either from Africa, if the _comedia_ depicted a Spanish scene, or from the southern areas of the archipelago, if the drama depicted a Philippine scene). The _estocada_ section of the theatrical _sinulog_ originally closely followed this format and, even with its more recent change of plot, was still within the genre of the _comedia_ tradition.

However, while the _comedia_ was one source of Hispanic symbolism for Cebu City's _sinulog_ ritual, it was not the only one. It was one highlight among a series of movements. Other segments of the choreography, not reported to be found in other _comedia_ forms, represented other influences. In fact, the carefully defined dance figures that preceded and followed the _estocada_ dance drama scene appeared to be quite unique in their design. No other reports of devotional dancing performed in other parts of the Visayas and Mindanao included descriptions of column formations or _kantas_ or anything like the _paso_, _elevación_, and _sayaw_ segments of the Cebu City form.[6]

However, these segments of the Cebu City _sinulog_ did bear a marked resemblance to dancing performed in some areas of Spain by boy choristers, specifically dancing practiced in Seville since the fifteenth century by a well known, highly esteemed group called _Los Seizes_ (The Sixteen). In the opening ceremony of the Seville practice, boy dancers stood in formation before an altar, dropped to their knees to pray, then rose and sang a song, after which they put on their hats and began to dance—a sequence almost identical to that followed by the theatrical _sinulog_ troupe. After this ceremony, the Seville dancers performed group figures before the altar that resembled those of a minuet or pavane, accompanying themselves either with castanets or with hand-clapping. Again, this choreographic form was basically similar in design to the _sayaw_, _tinampilan_, and _tukod sa espada_ segments of the theatrical _sinulog_, even in the detail of clapping hands to mark rhythm in the _sayaw_ segment.[7]

Chorister dances were an unusual feature of European religious practice and one that was characteristic of Spanish Catholicism in particular. Dancing in churches was outlawed in most European countries by the end of the seventeenth century. In Spain, however, some forms of it were preserved, under the control of the church, until the twentieth century.[8] The chorister dancing was one of these.[9] It was a popular and important practice, as evidenced by the fact that in 1642, when a royal decree outlawed the dancing, the people of Seville sent the troupe to the pope, who deemed their performance acceptable and reinstated it.[10]

While the dance of the Seville choristers had originally been performed as a healing ritual, to bring relief from pain or epidemic, its function eventually came to be defined more vaguely as "a reverence due to the saints,"[11] also Iklot's original inspiration for his dance. The Spanish chorister dance was also performed only on special occasions: to honor the Virgin Mary, in honor of Corpus Christi, or to mark the end of Carnival, which paralleled Iklot's intention to create a special fiesta performance.[12] The role played by the Seville choristers in religious processions was also virtually identical to that of the *sinulog* troupe in Cebu City. The Seville boys moved along with the procession—usually one of the processions bearing relics of saints and martyrs from their original graves to some newly prepared repository—and performed dances at positions along the route,[13] just as Iklot's groups and those of the drummers he trained came to do in Cebu City in the procession of the Santo Niño de Cebu.

Given this background, Iklot's *sinulog* in some respects appeared to have been a duplicate, both in form and function, of the Seville chorister dancing. It forged a link to an unusual and distinctive orthodox Spanish tradition. Given the similarity of some of the minute details of the choreography, it was even possible that someone involved in Iklot's organizing of the theatrical *sinulog* in Cebu may have had direct exposure to the Seville dance form, perhaps a friar or parish priest.

In any case, Iklot's original production was more than a copy of the other *comedia* dramas already being practiced in the region. Its Hispanic sources of inspiration were varied, articulate, and unique. They carved a social niche for the *sinulog*, identifying it more closely with orthodox Spanish Catholic worship as it related to children and with a specific devotional practice associated with Seville in particular.[14]

In this respect, the local culture of Cebu City distinguished itself from its surroundings in terms of what it had collected in this dance ritual, from whom, and from where. Borrowing had been a means to a unique creation. What historian Vincent Rafael has said of the influence of the Spanish language on Tagalog culture might well be said for the influence of Hispanic dance practices on the *sinulog*, that the practice of borrowing helped Cebu City's local culture to set itself off from, yet bind itself to, what came from the outside.[15]

Iklot's efforts found widespread acceptance and support within the city's turn-of-the-century society. The latter half of the nineteenth century had been a time of tremendous change for the city, change that had greatly increased the colonial and international significance of Cebu City for the world at large and, by the same token, had increased the significance of foreign relations for the residents within the city. Signs of the outside world took on a new meaning and value for the city's inhabitants during this period of growth and prosperity.

When Manila was officially opened to foreign trade in 1834, Cebu's importance as a regional port increased as widespread cultivation of commercial crops ensued.[16] In 1860, however, a more dramatic change occurred, when, after centuries of isolation from global trading networks, Cebu City itself was once again declared an open port.[17] This reopening was directed not toward other Malay ports in the region, but toward the markets of Europe and North America.[18] Between 1860 and 1900, a wealth of new opportunities were created for all sectors of the city's society, as British, U.S., Swiss, German, and Spanish foreign houses stationed representatives in the city, with substantial credit facilities.[19] Suddenly, the city's primary export products moved directly to foreign markets around the world. Wage laborers, skilled craftsmen, market gardeners, domestic servants, petty traders, and middlemen of all kinds poured into the city in increasing numbers, as large hacienda estates cultivating cash crops such as sugar and abaca were expanded in the provinces. The increasing population complicated the social structure of the city, creating more niches in its expanding status hierarchy. Urban society took on a more complex character as a new class of middle sector professionals began to share the social stage with the established wealthy provincial elite.[20]

Along with incoming human resources, an increasing amount of imported goods replaced local items in the city's material culture as trade increased in volume and diversity. Nails replaced rattan binding, cotton replaced local fibers, and European medicines replaced local remedies.[21] These signs of foreign life were welcomed by the residents, as their local economy boomed.

One of the ways members of the Cebu elite expressed their enthusiasm for their newfound cosmopolitan status was by "Europeanizing" as many aspects of their lives as possible. This trend had a political as well as a socioeconomic significance. From the mid-nineteenth century on, bureaucratic offices and political opportunities of all kinds had more and more educational prerequisites, and university studies were designed on European models.[22] The cultivation of a European educated lifestyle was a means to more prestigious community standing, as well as a sign of commercial success.

Not only Europe in general, but Spanish colonial society in particular was held up as an ideal for the urban elite of Cebu in the late nineteenth century. The Spanish community increased after 1860,

with more priests, administrators, soldiers, merchants, and professionals settling in the city.[23] They became a small but highly visible
and increasingly influential community whose most prestigious members, to quote historian Michael Cullinane, "took a place at the apex
of Cebu's society and . . . began to set the cultural tone for the elite"
(1982:282).[24]

The preference for a Spanish colonial lifestyle was maintained by
the Cebu elite throughout the Philippine Rebellion and the early decades of the American era—the time during which the troupe *sinulog*
originated. Again, to quote Cullinane:

> The urban elite of Cebu became intricately linked to the Spanish colonial
> society of the late 19th century. Its wealth, life style and high status in that
> society had been attained under Spanish sovereignty; few of its members had
> much cause for discontent. As long as their economic advantages could be
> maintained, the aristocrats of Cebu seemed to have no serious objections to
> the colonial condition. Their search for reforms was solely within economic
> matters, jointly with local Spaniards. (1982:280)

Material culture proved to be an important avenue for the expression of Europeanization, and of Hispanization in particular. In
the newly built stone and tile mansions of the era, elite families purchased English fabrics and European furniture for their interior de-
cor.[25] Religious imagery, always important in local religious practice,
became caught up in the Europeanization of interiors as well. Wealthy
families counted among their most precious heirlooms European
figurines and statues of religious figures, including Santo Niños,
which were set up on altars inside their homes.[26]

The imported Hispanic symbolism of Iklot's ritual *sinulog* not surprisingly found a warm reception in this social climate, which lasted
from the 1860s into the early decades of the American era. Iklot's
development of a fiesta *sinulog* ritual for the Santo Niño provided the
elite with a more spectacular and cosmopolitan form of veneration
for their newly imported, highly valued images.

During the early period of the troupe *sinulog*'s history, the audience
it cultivated was an audience intent upon staying in touch with distant
centers of culture. As one longtime witness to the *sinulog* commented,
in the old days, families would never have been interested in a drama
about Magellan and Lapulapu, or any other local event. They supported the performance because it was a way to celebrate their ties
with Spain, and viewed the troupe *sinulog* as a ritual that the priests
had developed that was enjoyable precisely because it accurately duplicated a Spanish tradition. The values of the city's border-zone society during this era openly asserted that "culture" arrived from afar.

The troupe ritual was one means of demonstrating that that culture had indeed arrived.

Iklot's children's dance became an institution in Cebu City. He was skilled in drumming and trained at least three subsequent drummers who became _sinulog_ troupe leaders during his lifetime. One started a _sinulog_ troupe in Guadalupe, a district located on the western edge of Cebu City. Another started a troupe in Mabolo, a nearby suburb, and a third started a troupe in Medellin, a town 109 kilometers north of Cebu City near the northwestern tip of the island.

The dance that began as one man's religious obligation had, by the end of his life, developed into a widespread performance event on Cebu Island. Each troupe developed its own traditions and preserved different elements of Iklot's original teachings, as well as modifying the choreography for its own purposes, so that the troupe tradition in 1984 and 1985 had a variety of performance styles.[27] In every case, however, the original collective _sinulog_ tradition was recast in the form of a children's dance that was designed to be visually appealing and that carried a combination of Hispanic influences. Iklot's personal act of devotion resulted in the _sinulog_'s acquiring a new array of meanings in Cebu City. The dance became a sign of childhood, of narrative dramatic form, and of the formal religious dancing of Spain.

The Following Generations: _Arnis_ Influences

While Iklot's creative orchestration of the different Spanish influences contributed greatly to the formalization of the original masculine variant of the _sinulog_ ritual, the process of refining the dance did not stop there. In subsequent generations, new influences appeared that to some extent reinvested the ritual with symbols of non-Hispanic design.

At the turn of the century, Iklot's son,[28] Buenaventura "Turang" Diola, took over the maintenance of the ritual from Iklot's star pupil, who is remembered only by the name of "Juancho." Juancho was the last of the skilled drummers to go regularly to the basilica and play for devotees wanting to dance the masculine style of "natural" _sinulog_. With his death, the link between the original spontaneous masculine style of ritual _sinulog_ and the formal children's spectacle was severed. While Turang, like his father, was remembered as a gifted musician and an ardent devotee, he played only for the children's ritual.

During the time of Turang, in the 1920s and 1930s, the dancers were instructed in the stick-fighting martial art exercises of _arnis_, which were incorporated into the dancing. Turang was reportedly an _arnis_ expert. His pupils remembered his using the same method of teaching *arnis* formal exercises that was used by the *arnis* master, Cacoy Cañete, in 1984. It was a method that assigned numbers to different moves, with the instructor calling out numbers in sequences to which dancers had to respond as quickly as possible. These formal *arnis* movements were performed during the *estocada* segment of the *sinulog* dance, when trios of dancers would demonstrate the set moves while traveling in a spiral. This form of training taught the dancers to move with both precision and agility in executing the longer training exercises of the martial art form. Cacoy, in fact, noted that there was still a formal exercise named *sinulog*, which he said was a reference to the use of *arnis* movements in the *sinulog* ritual.[29]

In this regard, it is fairly certain that, at least since Turang's time, the mock battle of the *sinulog* of Cebu City was never a loosely organized free-for-all, as was the case with other dance dramas of the region,[30] but rather a structured demonstration of formal skills, with limited room for personal innovation. The dancing became a fully improvised battle only during the high point in the drama when the leading personalities engaged in a duel.

The influence of *arnis* was another distinguishing factor separating the Cebu City *sinulog* from other dance rituals of the region. The dancing was not simply a product of interregional borrowing, but highlighted an original application of this relatively local practice. The inclusion of *arnis* forms into the *sinulog* ritual not only further formalized and elaborated the fighting movements of the dancing, it brought a locally derived fighting form back into the Hispanicized choreography. With Turang's innovations, the *sinulog* presented a formalized expression of warrior conduct that was not only Hispanic, but distinctively Visayan in design.

Recent Adaptations

The foregoing history was pieced together for me by several of Iklot's descendants, among them Espilita "Pitang" Diola, who had carried on the devotion that had passed from Turang, her father, to his star drummer, Macario Buntilao, and finally to Pitang herself shortly after World War II. The family tradition begun by Iklot had by 1984 lasted through the leadership of five different drummers.

Pitang was a woman of intense vitality, easily the most charismatic Cebuana I was to meet during my stay in the city. To me, she represented the ideal culture bearer, that extraordinary character renowned in her community as a "keeper of tradition." She was the one who could remember details, the one who would venture to discriminate between true and false, the one who could enjoy my esoteric interests in her world. She was a sort of social anchor, a comforting figure amidst the flux of characters inhabiting the city.

In spite of holding something of a celebrity status within the community, Pitang was no temperamental prima donna. When she was asked a question, she would listen carefully, and, although she was never at a loss for a reply, would generally defer to another's answer if one were offered in her place. As I came to know her over the course of our repeated conversations about the history and staging of her troupe's *sinulog* ritual, I began to get a sense of the sort of character it took, and had taken over the years, to keep the practice of the ritual alive.

Like her ancestors, Pitang was a person of very modest material circumstances. In 1984 she was in her fifties, living in a raised wooden cottage with her sister, "Andring," in the middle of a crowded, run-down *barrio* in the western sector of the city, the district called Mabolo. Their small home was furnished with makeshift wooden benches and cupboards. It was decorated mainly with a collection of large trophies that had been awarded to Pitang during several of the previous Sinu-log Project celebrations. These shining, beribboned sculptures stood out in stark contrast to the rest of the darkened wooden interior, the surfaces of which had been worn smooth with age and use. Pitang's life was full of such contrasts. In this she was probably no different from Turang and Iklot. Her assets, though of notable value, were almost completely intangible.

Pitang had lived with her sister all her life. They had survived with the help of their extended family by pooling their earnings and had worked at various forms of wage labor. During the Japanese occupation, a difficult time that stood out in their memories, they had been recruited to work in a cotton factory for a few years. Their current income, however, was earned at home, separating factory-made paper doilies and repackaging them for retail sale. The piecework paid five to ten pesos a day, less than the earnings of a *tindera*. Pitang and Andring were children of a poor farmer who had eked out a meager living on the fringes of the developing industrialized sector of the economy. Pitang was the first "modernized" member of her family line of drummer/choreographers.

Like her predecessors, Pitang possessed a broad range of skills. As a drummer, she had developed a stroke technique of clarity and strength on the *tambol*—her marching snare drum. She had a clear, uncolored voice and was capable of accurately singing *a capella* Spanish hymns composed of relatively difficult tonal intervals.[31] Her vocal range was only about an octave. However, in her singing of the *kantas*, she typically remained true to the traditional melodies, even when they went beyond her own vocal register. She did not modify the tunes for the sake of making her own rendition sound better. Her preservation of the original *kanta* forms was one example of the reverence for tradition she expressed in her life's work with the *sinulog* ritual, a reaffirmation of the positive social value of imitation, which ultimately involved self-sacrifice.

Pitang was also an innovative choreographer who had contributed original work of her own to the *sinulog* tradition, which had earned her her civic awards. She was as well a demanding teacher, with a critical eye for the subtle details of body placement and movement style that reminded me of the many ballet mistresses I had encountered in my own past. When I took her to watch a videotape of one of her troupe's performances from a previous year, she made no secret of her disappointment with the children's performance. It had involved too much *lingilingi*, or random turning of heads, she said, and the arm gestures of the *sayaw* had been tossed away, not carefully sculpted in the gentle *formal* style. Pitang had high expectations for all of her members, even the very youngest. She was also intent upon providing for her dancers an experience of the spirit of unity and faith that was at the center of her own worship. She was, in her own mind, a deeply committed devotee of the Santo Niño, and in her life the joy of that devotion had been won through discipline and close attention to detail.

Pitang's talents, however, involved more than a mastery of performing skills. An energetic community organizer, she functioned, albeit in a narrowly defined capacity, as a liaison between her own neighborhood and some of the most powerful factions in the city's society: the Augustinian order, the city government, and many of the city's wealthiest families. It was Pitang who bore the main responsibility for making sure that the troupe's rehearsals and performances went ahead on schedule, and that new dancers and drummers continued to be recruited into the group.

Pitang's era of leadership had once again seen new influences on the *sinulog* dance practice brought into play. She had been in charge of the troupe from the time of Philippine independence through Martial Law, a period in which nationalism and internationalism had been the abiding central themes in public life, both secular and religious. The first major instance of change happened abruptly, in 1965, when the festivities for the fourth centennial of Christianity in the Philippines caused the meaning of the performance to be reinterpreted by the leadership within the city's religious community. Celebrations held throughout the nation in 1965 highlighted distinctively Philippine Catholic traditions that had developed over the centuries.

In Cebu City, the troupe *sinulog* was selected as a key symbol for the city's own quadracentennial festival program.

Always considered an enhancement to the fiesta, in 1965 the performance was construed as an impressive gift, offered by some of the city's most powerful religious leaders to national and foreign dignitaries alike. To prepare for the celebration, a contest was instituted by the basilica (then, still St. Augustine's Church), offering a prize of five hundred pesos to the group in Cebu City who could stage the best *sinulog* dance drama. This competitive context, not surprisingly, inspired many alterations in the troupe *sinulog* performances, not only in the choreography, but in the membership of the troupes as well.

The major change was a reinstitution of adult male participation in the ritual dancing, marking the end of the infanticization of the form. This recasting of the dancing to its original adult status, however, was hardly a return to the past practices of traditional devotees, for the adult members now had nonreligious and competitive motivations for joining the performances. Until 1965, the typical form of payment offered for *sinulog* performances was a *merienda*, or small meal. The announcement of a cash prize prompted adult men who had been *sinulog* dancers in their childhood and adolescence to rejoin the *sinulog* troupes of their youth. Both the Guadalupe and Mabolo offshoot troupes, which now had longstanding performance histories of their own, formed adult *sinulog* troupes at this time that performed in the competition beside the children's troupes.

Pitang also accepted adult males back into her troupe on this occasion. When the troupe won first prize in the competition, some of these new members collected the prize money, leaving Pitang and the children's troupe with nothing. The presence of adult male members resulted in similar financial strains on Pitang and the troupe on several other occasions. In this respect, the 1965 celebrations generated a long-term strain on the troupe organization by increasing its economic value for the adult segment of the *barrio* community.

Major changes in the choreography occurred at this time, as well as in the casting of the ritual. Pitang added the tumbling segment of the ritual to the children's version in order to make it more spectacular and competitive. In addition, a rescripting of the *estocada* drama took place. Prior to 1965 the *sinulog* had presented a battle scene in which Spanish kings and Visayan Christians teamed up against *moro* natives. For the contest, however, a more specific story line, the death of Magellan at the hands of Lapulapu, was substituted for the original theme. This popular narrative was in keeping with the fourth centennial's theme—the arrival of Christianity in the Philippines.

With the institution of this change of plot, the message of the ritual became somewhat ambiguous. The character of Lapulapu was conflated with the original *moro* villains of the southern islands. The political significance of the plot could now be read in two contradictory ways by the audience. On the one hand, the ritual could be interpreted as venerating Magellan, who was portrayed sacrificing his life at the hands of the evil Lapulapu in order to bring Christ to the Philippines. This reading held appeal for the powerful conservative elements in the religious sector of the community. On the other hand, the play could also be interpreted as venerating Lapulapu, victorious in his violent rejection of Spanish imperialism brought by the evil Magellan. This reading held appeal for the powerful nationalist propagandists in the government sector. While these interpretations were contradictory, both served to make the script appealing to different types of audiences, who read into the drama the meaning they preferred.

The fourth centennial celebration thus served to complicate the cast, plot, and design of the *sinulog* performance, in addition to bringing it considerable notoriety. After the celebration, the troupe maintained the changes that had been made for the special occasion. However, the event did little to alter the role of the *sinulog* troupe in the fiesta celebration. The troupe still joined in the procession, still performed on the basilica steps, and still staged private showings in addition to their public demonstration at the church.[32]

Down through the generations, the performers and choreographers continued to modify and redesign the troupe *sinulog* process in order to keep the ritual alive. The layers of symbolism that met and combined in the performance process by 1985 represented local, regional, national, and international interests even while the performance remained essentially what it had always been: an expression of familial and collective devotion to the Santo Niño.

Obviously, the efforts of the Diola family did not tell the whole story of the troupe *sinulog*. The dancing had never operated in a vacuum. The survival of the ritual had always been a community affair. It involved not only relatively poor *barrio* families who supplied the performers. It involved more than the Roman Catholic Church community, which encouraged and fostered its production. The troupe *sinulog* also depended upon the more powerful families within Cebu City society. These were the families that supported the troupe production by inviting the dancers into their residences and rewarding them for their efforts. By 1984, families would pay as much as five hundred pesos to have a private performance staged. The troupe *sinulog* was a vehicle of meaning on several levels for the elite families of Cebu, and they remained a faithful and supportive audience who left their mark on the performance as well.

The Sponsors

Although there were no remaining witnesses to Iklot's original *sinulog* troupe, there were still some local residents around in 1984 and 1985 who remembered the performances of the small *barrio* boys of fifty and sixty years ago who danced the *sinulog* under the instruction of Turang Diola. According to Pitang, immediately after the performance on the basilica patio, the boys would go from house to house in local neighborhoods giving private performances of the *sinulog*. They visited all kinds of houses. They would stop in the unpaved roadway in front of homes in their own *barrios*, if any family there had a Santo Niño image of its own that could be put in a front window as a focus for the children's performance. They would also make stops in more well-to-do neighborhoods, in front of the homes of middle-class families that also had images they wished to venerate. The most memorable performances, however, were given for the city's most notable mestizo families—the Osmeñas, the Borromeos, the Guantu-angcos, and the Gorordos, among others. The troupe would go out of its way to stage a *sinulog* at the invitation of one of these powerful families. This practice continued through to Pitang's time.[33]

Staging a private performance involved only a few minor changes from the church ritual. Candles would be placed upon some sort of altar, along with the family's own Santo Niño image, in effect re-creating in the family's home the setting of the basilica. No changes were made in the performance, except that when the moment came to jump and cry "*Pit Señor!*" the boys might also cry out, "This is for . . . ," filling in the names of all the children in the specific family for whom they were performing. After a performance staged outside the home *barrio*, the troupe was generally given a small meal in return for their performance. The entire visit might last an hour or more. Then the troupe would depart for the next home.

The private staging of the *sinulog* performance reinforced several key values held by prominent families. Some of these values, like the Europeanization mentioned earlier in connection with the late-nineteenth-century context of the troupe's beginnings, were on the wane by 1984. Europeanization in particular had been replaced by a value on nationalism, which was represented as a symbolic overlay in the current casting and dramatic plot. Other values and their corresponding symbols, however, had been maintained from the time of Iklot through to the present era.

The most essential, long-lasting value reaffirmed by the troupe ritual was a value on family loyalty. This was especially prominent in the case of families that had made perpetual vows to sponsor the *sinulog* every year. Hosting the *sinulog* was an opportunity to honor the wishes of one's parents and grandparents, as well as an opportunity to confer the Santo Niño's blessing upon one's children.

The importance of asserting elite family loyalty had increased greatly in Cebu during the closing years of the nineteenth century, when the troupe ritual first appeared. Prominent families in increasing numbers had begun to disperse and resettle members on large haciendas throughout the island and on other nearby islands.[34] Given this trend, fiesta celebrations became significant moments when the entire family could collect in its original urban residence and reassert its solidarity through various symbolic actions. In 1984 and 1985, the assertion of family loyalty was still a vital function served by the troupe *sinulog* ritual.

The staging of the performance on the family's grounds also reaffirmed the idea that the family home and the church's temple ideally could be of one and the same status. The *sinulog* was one of several devotional practices, like the matins, angelus, and novena prayer services that were observed morning and evening in the mansions of the city's wealthy.[35] These had been practiced over the course of the century, and their combined effect was to elevate the status of a family residence into that of a de facto temple. Mojares (1983:104) has reported that the houses of the wealthy in the late nineteenth and early twentieth centuries had "a distinct monastic quality" that was conveyed by their religious symbols and the rituals that celebrated them. In 1984 and 1985, prominent homes still maintained private altars that displayed costly religious imagery around which the household could gather for prayer.

This identification of the home with temple status, which occurred not only in the homes of the wealthy but throughout all sectors of the city's society, was more than a result of nineteenth-century circumstances. It was a habit of thinking that had relatively ancient roots. Early accounts of local life indicated that religious worship, typically involving images, occurred not in temples but in the homes of community leaders.[36] In 1984 and 1985, the troupe *sinulog* was one means available to reaffirm this still deeply held value that home and sanctuary could be one and the same. Every time the troupe replicated its Santo Niño ritual in front of, or on the grounds of, a private household, it reinforced this idea.

In hosting the *sinulog* performances, families also demonstrated their solidarity with the Augustinian community itself. The Augustinians were the most powerful religious order in Cebu at the turn of the century, when the troupe *sinulog* was forming, owning much of the best agricultural land on the island as well as a large amount of land inside the city limits. In 1984 and 1985, the Augustinians remained a most prestigious and influential force in the urban society.[37]

The relationship the Cebu elite had maintained with the Augustinian order over the centuries was complicated. There had been a long and bitter rivalry between the Augustinian order and the largest faction of "elites" in the community, the Chinese mestizo families. These families had established a church in the Parian district of the city—the district north of the city center that, by the early nineteenth century, dominated the local society. This conflict eventually led in the 1870s to the dismantling of the Parian parish, which had been run by secular mestizo priests from the beginning of the nineteenth century.[38] The incident caused a major rift between the Augustinians and the Chinese mestizo elite community.

By the 1890s, however, this dispute had been settled for over a decade. The city's mestizo elite, in its efforts to make the most of the rising value of urban property and the boom in cash crop cultivation, had been obliged to enter into business in cooperation with the Augustinians, forming lease or purchase arrangements for the prized Augustinian land holdings.[39] As their interest in owning land, both urban and rural, grew throughout the 1880s,[40] so did their interest in maintaining a cordial rapport with the Augustinian community. In addition, during the early years of the American era, the Augustinian order and the city's elite held a joint interest in conserving as much of the Spanish colonial forms of social structure and organization (and their own advantageous places within them) as possible. By the turn of the century, the city's wealthy thus had a number of reasons for aligning themselves with the Augustinian community. By creating a resemblance between the practices of the family and those of the Augustinian order, the families reinforced their claims to being as sacred, as powerful, and as worthy of fidelity, and to having the same unassailable moral standards and intentions, as the Santo Niño's home institution.

Initially, the Spanish influences apparent in the performances were of particular value in this respect, since they secured the orthodox status of the ritual and thus reaffirmed the families' commitments to the orthodox and colonial elements of the church. By 1984, however, the evaluation of the Spanish influences visible in the troupe choreography had changed. Currently influenced more by the nationalist ideology of the contemporary era, the ties between elite families and the basilica community were no longer recognized specifically in

terms of Spanish-derived symbols. However, the *sinulog* troupe ritual
of 1984 and 1985 remained a symbol of solidarity between the city's
prominent families and the local representatives of the Augustinian
order, since it was a practice that had been mutually supported by the
local church and local families for generations.

In addition to this expression of family religious identity, the *sinulog*
also reinforced values concerning other aspects of families' social
identities. It reaffirmed the class distinctions that had expanded in the
1860s and intensified during the 1890s, when, as a result of the 1880s
crisis in the world market for sugar, the new wealth of the city had
become concentrated in fewer and fewer hands.[41] The troupe *sinulog*
ritual served two such social class functions for the elite in Cebu City.
It reinforced a separation of the Cebu elite from the city's lower
classes, and it helped to align the elite of Cebu City with the elite
families of other regions.

Just as the *sinulog* dancing of the *tinderas* was sometimes considered
to be beneath the dignity of its customers, so, too, taking part in the
performance of the troupe *sinulog* was considered to be inappropriate
for members of its elite sponsors. As one distinguished Cebuana who
came from one of the most prominent local families recalled, when
"the boys from the *barrio*" would come around at fiesta time to her
home during her childhood, her young male relatives would want to
get costumes and join in the dancing (just as, when the troupes performed at the basilica, adults would want to join in as well). The
youths were not allowed to do so, however. They would be made to
watch and listen as their own names were called out by the *barrio* children during the performance.

My informant in this case was a middle-aged woman who described
herself as a *camarera*—a "lady in waiting" or "keeper of the wardrobe"
for the Santo Niño.[42] She held a graduate degree in linguistics and
maintained a small private practice giving voice lessons as well. Her
home, in what used to be the city's neighborhood of the aristocracy,
was the house of her childhood, which had been bombed five times,
she said, by the Japanese during World War II, but had survived.
Displayed in her entrance hall was a collection of ivory figurines, religious images that were the family heirlooms. Learning to take care
of these treasures, she recalled, had been one introduction to the religious practices that had become an important focus in her life.

A feudal hierarchy of attendance was a familiar model for this well-
to-do conservative, in which she found her own place, as a lady in
waiting, quite literally at the foot of the Santo Niño image. She was
currently one of the select few in the community who were allowed to
participate in the pivotal *hubo* ceremony, the ritual changing of the

Santo Niño image's clothing that marked the beginning and the ending of the fiesta celebration. Experience had taught her that every station in society had its corresponding religious practices. For the *barrio* children, there was the *sinulog*; for her and for her fellow *camareras*, there was the care of the heirlooms, the overseeing of religious treasures.

The relationship established between sponsoring families and troupe performers was one of patronage similar to that of the *tinderas* and their customers, but the status gap between the two parties was much wider. The customer and the *tindera* together faced the Santo Niño, aligned in opposition to the image as one actively performed the dancing while the other passively sponsored it. The families sponsoring the troupe *sinulog*, in contrast, considered themselves part of the audience, aligned with the Santo Niño in this respect. They expected the troupe to stand before them and entertain them. The troupe choreography reflected this change in the patron's alignment, presenting movement symbols designed not only to move the Santo Niño, but to entertain the patrons as well.

Along with reinforcing class distinctions between the elite families and those of the *barrio*, the troupe *sinulog* was also a means by which elites expressed their rapport with powerful factions of other regions. By 1900, when Cebu was second only to Manila in trade and transport, its mestizo elite, which by then was composed of about seventy-five families, had been firmly established for over a century and was gaining increasing recognition in Manila and abroad as it developed more and more entrepreneurial links to both interisland and foreign commercial houses.[43] The value that all sectors of the city's elite placed on external recognition during this period is evidenced in a 1903 quote from Cebu journalist Antolin Frias, which reads, "The [prominent families] stood out more by the height through which their wealth had ranked them, and as such, they were honoured with respect and admiration by their own and by foreigners."[44]

During this period of the city's history, its elite was actively engaged in developing networks with outside influences, which gave guest-host interactions an increased significance in social life. The troupe performance could serve as an important symbol of prestige, offered as a gift of entertainment for important guests, and its role in the 1965 celebrations illustrated that this social function had been maintained over the decades. This social function of the dancing could become as or more important than its ritual significance.

Pitang, for example, reported an episode in which her troupe had arrived late at a home where they had been requested to stage a private performance for a family and its visitors after a mass had been celebrated at the home. This was another prominent family whose members had been longtime patrons of the troupe. Pitang, however, had run several hours behind schedule—not an uncommon occurrence at fiesta time—because another household, located in the newer, affluent district of Beverly Hills on the city's eastern edge, had requested the troupe's services and was providing their transportation. When she and her dancers finally did arrive at the home, the priest and some of the guests had already departed, and the hostess was furious. She greeted Pitang by asking her if the Beverly Hills house had paid her more than she herself was going to, and if that was why Pitang liked the other house better. The hostess then warned Pitang that if she and her troupe were ever late again they would have "a real fight" on their hands.

The emphasis the hostess placed on promptness was unusual, since people in Cebu City typically tended to joke about their "Filipino time" relaxedness, and a few hours' difference in keeping appointments was not generally cause for great concern. After a few moments the hostess calmed down, and had the *sinulog* performed anyway—its value was not entirely dependent upon her guests' having seen it. However, the use of the performance as an entertainment for her visitors and as a means of upholding the family's reputation had clearly been a significant factor in her decision to sponsor it in the first place.

It was, in fact, the influence of Cebu City's distinctive urban social structure and its place within larger social structures that had generated and maintained the distinctive "troupe" organization of the ritual *sinulog*. The needs of the provincial urban society allowed the *sinulog* performers to develop private practices of sorts, in which they moved from sponsor to sponsor throughout the city on fiesta days.

The religious dance dramas of other areas, in contrast, were typically far more elaborate community events in which an entire *barrio* or village would perform. The structure of these performance casts could even be seen to present a mirror of the social hierarchy in which people lived their daily lives. The principle figures in the drama would be played by the leading citizens of the community, with the minor roles being handled by members of lower status.[45]

In Cebu City, however, class divisions turned the ritual into a performance that assigned different statuses to the performers and the audience, respectively. It was thus similar in its social organization to other secular dramatic phenomena, such as the theatrical *zarzuela* and *comedia* troupes that also came into being at this time, but whose circuits of performance were much larger, sometimes involving several islands.[46]

The Symbolism of a Social History

The layered and segmented symbolism of the troupe *sinulog* represented a history of social life in Cebu City that was, in large part, a history oriented by families and their religious and political commitments. The troupe *sinulog* was a tribute to the genius of the Diola family's devotion, as well as a sign of the city's and the region's social hierarchies. The interplay of influences produced some ambiguity in the choreography. On the whole, however, the clashing movement symbols had been adeptly employed to create an articulate and elaborate substitution for the more spontaneous, volatile variant of the ritual that had been lost to history. In any case, the stylistic impulse of the earlier collective practice had been preserved: the intent to use warrior movement patterns as the basis for a collective, public act of religious devotion.

The troupe *sinulog* initially had been organized as a strictly amateur expression of religious devotion, designed by Iklot to acculturate children to orthodox Catholicism by providing them with a localized but basically Hispanic means of experiencing religious feeling. However, in the affluent and externally dependent developing urban environment, the theatrical *sinulog* also evolved into a service offered to the influential families of the city, who were eager to demonstrate, for both the local community and foreigners, the richness of their links to orthodox Roman Catholicism. The fairly small, close-knit circle of elite families, living in close proximity to one another, sponsored performances both during the fiesta and occasionally on the birthdays of some younger-family members to celebrate the ties within their own private households as well as to honor their guests.

The troupe *sinulog* of 1984 and 1985 thus existed as a sort of intersection where the warrior and the saint, the local and the foreigner, the Christian and the infidel, the families of the poor and the rich, the colonial and the nationalist all assembled and confronted one another. In its complicated and sometimes contradictory meanings, this theatrical form of the *sinulog* ritual appeared as an elaborate example of what E. V. Daniel (1984:5–7, 297–301), in his study of Tamil culture, has called a "fluid sign." Within it, diverse, contrasting, and even antithetical substances met, intermingled, and struck a fragile balance with one another. Yet, unlike the fluid signs of Tamil culture, whose diverse compositions were formed from a single cultural scheme, the elements of which had been designed for interaction, the troupe *sinulog* symbolism mediated among cultural traditions that had never been intended for mutual exposure. The choreography, in this respect, symbolized most strikingly the cultural flexibility of its performers, who moved adeptly between fundamentally different styles of conduct and social action. However, the performance expressed as well the brute and accidental aspects of culture contact, the unforeseen absurdities resulting from the confrontation of different symbolic traditions, and the sometimes dissonant and disengaged nature of the formative stages of both compromise and collaboration.

Despite the tenacity of many generations of drummers and sponsors, the appreciation of the troupe *sinulog* ritual by performers and audiences alike by 1984 appeared to be diminishing markedly. Pitang, for example, remarked that in the old days the costumes were simpler, but the dancers were better. Even though she recruited new members on the basis of their aptitude for dance, she noted that her children now lacked the initiative and concentration to perform the different steps with the same degree of attention to form and style that had been used in previous generations. The dancers playing the *moro* parts forgot to adopt the crouching *hupohupo* posture, and the flaws noted earlier in the videotaped performance seemed impossible to cure. The overall spirit of dedication and faith that Pitang said used to bring the dancers together was disappearing.

A similar deterioration was apparent in the audiences. During one private showing I attended, for example, the family member who sat next to me ignored the dancing completely and talked to me continuously about the history of the Philippines right through the entire ritual. When the performance was over, the hostess commented that, while many used to come to her home to watch the dancers, now few appeared. She spoke at length of the perpetual vow her own family had taken to sponsor the performance, as though the vow were an explanation for what would otherwise have been an embarrassing event. Family loyalty and a deference for the wishes of ancestors appeared to be the one value associated with the ritual that remained meaningful for her. Her cousin described the troupe *sinulog* as a mix of pagan and Christian influence, being mainly pagan (a word he pronounced with his mouth wrinkling in distaste). For him, the dance reflected the tolerance of the Spanish friars, who used whatever native practices they found to bring the people around to Christianity.

From the vantage point of both the audience and the performers, the troupe *sinulog*'s independent activities were literally and figuratively no longer "where the action was" in Cebu City society. This ritual from the turn of the century had been increasingly upstaged by the promotional programs instituted in the 1980s. The *sinulog* that was now drawing the attention and participation of thousands of residents, the *sinulog* that was now putting Cebu City on the map as a tourist destination, was no longer simply a family affair. It had out-grown this form of social organization. More powerful forces had appropriated the dancing as a symbol of their own interests, leaving in their wake this now antiquated practice that, in spite of its choreographic complexity, seemed to be on the road to becoming an empty symbol of days gone by.

Chapter 11
The Parade *Sinulog*

People were everywhere: on rooftops, under awnings, perched on railings, peering from windows, standing by the roadside under umbrellas that shielded them from the sun's dense heat. I waited amongst the crowd on a dusty sidewalk of General Maxilom Avenue in the slim late-morning shadow of a two-story wooden storefront. Everyone had already been around for hours. There was a settled-in feeling to the crowd. They reminded me of baseball fans seated in a common bleacher section at around the sixth inning of play. No one really had a comfortable spot in the makeshift spectators' areas that stretched along the broad thoroughfare. No one was about to leave, however, for the parade was just a few hours into its course, just coming into view along this section of its six-mile route (Figure 11.1).

The parade stretched on down the avenue as far as the eye could see, pouring forth in a flood of color, music, and movement. Two immense human chains composed of five thousand army cadets stood with linked wrists along both sides of the roadway, separating the crowd from the performers. Floats and *higantes* (giant figures) appeared amidst the parade's contingents. However, dancing groups were its highlight. Miles of gaily bobbing faces, lightly stepping feet, and cheerful-looking figures passed by. Men and women, boys and girls, all moved in lively unison—a manner locally described as *alegre*—to the famous "*sinulog* rhythm," a forceful, unsyncopated four-beat cadence played in four-quarter time, occasionally accompanied by the sweet, light chimes of portable vibraphones.

The parade appeared as a huge swatch of rainbow, now green, now pink, now yellow, now white as the various contingents passed by. Each group waved decorative symbols, tracing scallops, circles, and arches in the air with them. A patch of flowered hoops cavorted gaily

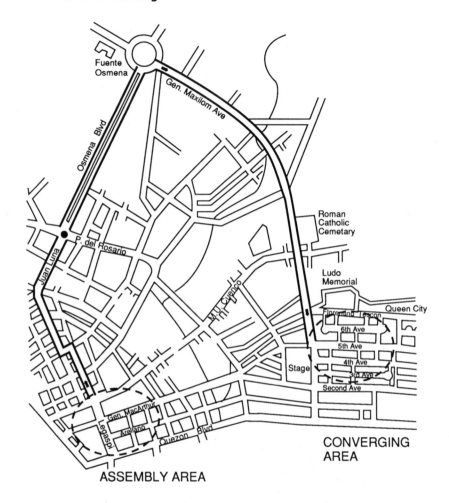

↑ SINULOG '85
    PARADE ROUTE

Figure 11.1. Map of 1985 *sinulog* parade route.

to and fro above the heads of fifty middle-aged women, who were
dressed as lowland peasants from the nineteenth century. A large collection of handkerchiefs danced about in a similar fashion above the
heads of another group of female performers, dressed in straight red
skirts and white, unfitted, *kimona*-style blouses, distinguishing them
as native Visayan women from some unidentifiable era. A field of

orange- and blue-plumed spears bobbed by, carried by a contingent of several dozen young, head-banded boys, dressed in multicolored, pastel miniskirts and unbuttoned white vests—references to a "pagan" prehistoric time. Eventually, a small fleet of Santo Niño images appeared along the trail, swung high in the air by young women dressed in bright red-and-yellow-print tunics, who formed and reformed marching columns that blended in and out of one another. Then a forest of bamboo came bobbing along, borne by would-be warriors from pre-Christian times, dressed in the vests and knee-length trousers of the *moro* tradition. The bamboo poles enclosed a cluster of a hundred shiny purple and yellow fans, fluttering about the heads and shoulders of more young women representing Muslim maidens from the Southern Islands.

Every dancing group had some sort of hand-held article, which the members waved around in unison in various ways. The key question for a passing observer soon became, "What will they choose to manipulate next?" Every group handled something different, the choices ranging from brass pots, to spears, to flower baskets, to candles. Whatever the item, every dance was designed around it. The parade choreography revolved around acts of gesturing.

On and on the dancers came, an enormous mass of humanity. The collective style was characteristically "Cebuano"—group after group reduplicated the buoyant "Cebuano-style" stepping as they marched along. Again and again, short dances erupted out of the flow of the parade, as each contingent, one after another, reached a designated stopping point on the route where it could pause and perform its own version of a *sinulog* dance. Although it took many hours to unfold, the parade was nevertheless a single, continuous, six-mile-long process whose organizing pattern was a resilient, repetitious phrase.

Hours passed, the sun beat down upon the crowd. Mild applause occasionally burst forth when a certain group staged a particularly entertaining maneuver. Two columns would become four, or six, or eight. Lines would change into circles, from which an arch of spears would be constructed. For the most part, people were content to contemplate the ongoing stream of changing forms without any noticeable reactions until the parade finally unwound completely, passing everyone by for another year.

As it ended, in the late afternoon, its spell lifted. The mesmerized and patient crowd stirred gently into action of its own. The better part of the day had been spent, and it was time to find a way back home.

It is difficult to give a general description of the parade *sinulogs*, since novelty was a prized characteristic of this form. Each contin-

gent's dance was different. Yet, like the *tindera's* improvisational varieties, certain commonalities of style did emerge. The dances, for
example, all were done on the move. They emerged out of marching,
signaled by drum cues, and, at their close, receded back into the
steady stream of the parade. Moreover, they were all quite brief, two
to three minutes long at most. They were long enough only to evoke
settings, mainly through costume design and material symbols. They
"raised a curtain," in a sense, on worlds within which some famous
action had taken place: pre-Christian festivals, Magellan and Lapulapu's duel, López de Legaspi's arrival in Cebu. These events themselves, however, were left to the imagination; there was no time for
the choreography to unfold them. Instead of a plot, a series of group
figures traced out abstract symmetrical designs that melted into one
another.

Like the troupe *sinulog*, collective statements superseded individual
ones in the parade dancing. The parade dancers' resilient steps were
patterned in unison. Like the *tindera* ritual, the parade dances simply
unwound, in a timeless interval. They had no climax. The energy
level of the dancers was, like the *tinderas'*, not noticeably higher than
that of the activity that normally went on in the context of the performance. In this case, it was about equal to that of a group of pedestrians crossing a busy city street.

The parade gestures, however, bore little resemblance to those of
the *tinderas* in other respects. The hand-held material symbols used
in the parade were moved through the air as if they rode on miniature freeways, progressing through relatively large areas of space
around the torso and above the head. The parade dancers' range of
arm movement was greater than that of the *tinderas'* gestures, and it
was more clearly formed into abstract spatial figures. Yet the *tinderas'*
movements, while they may not have been as visually compelling as
those of the parade dancers, had a coordinative complexity that the
more mechanical parade movements lacked. That is to say, *tinderas*,
in their *natural* performances, had moved, not only with their limbs,
but also from the center of their physical being, and these movement
processes were adeptly synchronized. There was thus never any
doubt as to where their gestures were coming *from*. With the parade
gestures, the action was different. While the material symbols were
held out to the farthest distance possible in the space available to the
dancer, what or who they were held out from was left uncharacter-
ized. The limb movement of the parade dancing in most cases was not
visibly related to the body's core. The gestures might please a viewer's
eye, but they clearly did not mediate for the performer's heart, an
interpretation that choreographer after choreographer corroborated

for me. This gestural movement style of the parade dancing was highly effective for producing the colorful, impersonal designs that were the main statement of the parade choreography. An overall decorative character for the parade resulted from this partial and fragmenting use of the dancers' bodies.

The parade *sinulog* seemed familiar. This 1985 practice was, indeed, a tourist-oriented form, a contemporary, popular, and promoted form. It was not ancient or sacred. The dances were not "exotically" spiritual, as the *tindera* ritual was, or historically distinctive as the troupe ritual was. The parade form of Cebu City's *sinulog*, in contrast, epitomized a kind of "contrived" activity that was more typically associated with the inhabitants of a border-zone culture, who now appeared, in this extravagant dance spectacle, mainly to be making a bid for an increased market share of the global tourist industry. This was, after all, the performance that had drawn a crowd of visitors estimated to be over a million strong, the performance that had filled the hotels and sold out the ferry boats and plane flights. This was the *sinulog* that was to be exported to Makati, the high-rise financial district of Manila, where the winners of Cebu City's dance competition would stage a street parade for the benefit of office workers in the nation's capital. This was the dance that was actually marketed abroad by sales representatives and on videotapes.

This was, in sum, a product of modern institutions that had international connections. The parade *sinulog* was monitored by helicopters with television cameras and evaluated by parade contest judges equipped with the latest computer technology. The 25,000 volunteers who danced and played in the 1985 parade represented over a hundred different schools, government agencies, commercial businesses, and civic and religious organizations. Of course it seemed familiar. The dancing was intended to meet me, and other foreigners, on our own terms.

My reaction to the parade dance style was not unique. Other foreign observers came away with a similar sense of familiarity. The American who directed the Cebu office of the United States Information Service, a man of Laotian descent, remarked that "Hollywood" influences were clearly apparent to him in the parade. He attributed their presence to the fact that the parade was being staged for an outside audience.

The parade dancing was familiar, however, not simply because it was aimed at outsiders like myself. It seemed familiar because the insider-outsider distinction was blurred almost to transparency in this context. The characters orchestrating this spectacle were professional people, city-dwellers of the late twentieth century. They were journalists and historians, businessmen and college dance teachers, all knowingly engaged in a transnational enterprise. Involved in this endeavor, they became people who were literally "just like me," even though I was a foreigner in their city. In this parade context, they sought, as did I, to move through existing boundaries and to claim their status as insiders in the outside world, able to cope with life from whatever "side" appeared most feasible.

The sense of familiarity vis-à-vis the parade, however, soon revealed itself to be partly an illusion. These seemingly typical products of tourist or commercial art, these suggestive portrayals of "local flavor" in the choreography, were not inspired by empty materialism and single-minded economic gain, as a recreational tourist encountering them might have assumed. Nor was "tourist art" a standard interpretation of the *sinulog* spectacle, although the struggle with what parade officials cast as the negative force of commercialism was seen as one that could be overcome only with a concerted effort. On the contrary, the symbolic content of the parade *sinulog* dances was recognized by participants and organizers alike as being rich, subtle, sharply defined, and elaborate, when it was at its best. Only failed efforts were deemed as belonging to a degenerate, "cheap and phony" commercial category. These were growing fewer and farther between by 1985. The purpose and value of the extravaganza, which at an outsider's first impression seemed limited to some transparent neocolonial socioeconomic considerations, definitely had more than a single, outsider-oriented dimension.

To the parade organizers and to many participants, the 1985 parade *sinulog* forms consciously represented the recognition and denial of the claim that Cebuanos were "people with no culture." The very idea of culture had been central to the development of the parade and its choreography. In 1985, the parade *sinulogs* represented, more vividly than either of the older *sinulog* forms, what it meant for the contemporary society to "have culture." The dancing was evidence that Cebuano culture was alive and well. Through a complicated but conventional series of reinterpretations, the parade dances reconstructed an authenticated local identity, and they asserted, with varying degrees of persuasiveness, the genuineness of this distinctive regional image to locals, to nationals, and to the world at large. The parade *sinulog* dancing was thus a deliberate reinvention of tradition, done not to reenter the past but to reclaim its unique integrity for contemporary purposes.[1] This reclamation project, so to speak, manifested a cultural predicament borne—and born—by the inhabitants of a border zone. It was a culture of symbols both found and made.

The Development Projects

While the history of the parade *sinulog* dancing was relatively brief (having begun in 1980), it was complicated. Manipulation was a central theme in its creation, just as it was in its choreography. The project had been handed from one promotional agent to another, and had become a pawn in a game of regional and national politics whose players changed frequently. The distant but cordial relationship the parade maintained with the Santo Niño fiesta, for example, was very different in 1985 from the integral and supportive one it had originally been designed to have in the first *Sinulog* Program of 1980. The gestural symbolism of the choreography aptly expressed the various twists and turns that had been taken in the parade's history.

1980: *Sinulog sa Sugbo*

The initial development scheme that led to a parade of *sinulog* dancing was called *Sinulog sa Sugbo*. It was begun under the combined sponsorship of the Central Visayas office of the national Ministry of Youth and Sports Development (MYSD) and the Cofradia del Santo Niño. The stated objective of this promotion was the enhancement of a "cultural awareness" and "Cebuano identity" through the revival of the *sinulog* ritual.[2] From the initial phases of the development on, the notion of "culture" figured prominently in the rhetoric of the *sinulog* promotion. In the early phases of the promotion, the idea was used to legitimize the initial appropriation by a government ministry of what had heretofore been a religious and largely unregulated devotional practice.

The first *sinulog* promotion program stressed the accurate revival of the traditional *sinulog* dance as performed by both the *tinderas* and the *sinulog* troupes. Teachers from various college physical education departments, who cooperated on a voluntary basis with the MYSD, met with both types of ritual *sinulog* performers—*tinderas* and troupe members—to study the *sinulog* dancing. They then went back to their students and set their interpretation of *sinulog* movement on them. The main activities of this promotion included a High Mass, attended by all participants, and two *sinulog* dance parades, all to be performed by students during the fiesta day for the Santo Niño.

This original promotional effort was instigated largely according to the designs of one man, the project director, who was the head of the Central Visayas Regional Office of the MYSD at that time. The director was a wealthy man with a large family and household staff who lived in a spacious, modern home in a southern suburb of the city, where he entertained my husband and me at a dinner party on one occasion. In many ways, the director typified a successful Cebu City culture bearer. His leadership of the program brought to bear a certain blend of influences on the *sinulog*, which transformed it from a local and provincial phenomenon into a "Filipino" and "regional" event.

The director's identity was forged from a wide variety of allegiances. Some were local; he was considering making a bid in 1985 to be mayor of the suburb where he lived. Some were international; his manner toward me warmed markedly, for example, when he learned toward the close of his dinner party that I, like he, had a Masonic affiliation, and particularly when he learned that my father was a Mason of high rank. Upon discovering this small fact about my background, he immediately pulled out one of his silken, elegantly printed business cards and pointed to the Masonic emblem embossed in its upper right-hand corner. My hand was then grasped and shaken again, as if he were meeting me for the first time, and I was assured, in what I took to be more heartfelt tones than I'd heard him use before, that he would be happy to give me any further assistance I might require in my research. Our common membership in this international organization established for him a shared cultural ground of sorts, which put our relationship on a more familiar footing than our shared interest in "Cebuano culture" had been able to do all evening.

The director made no claims to being a native son of Cebu. He was a recent arrival to the area, having come from Leyte Island to the east. He was an active reinventor of tradition and had, in fact, made something of a side career out of generating "culturally relevant" practices such as the *Sinulog sa Sugbo* program. Aside from the *sinulog* promotion, he had also developed the *Bahugbahug sa Mactan*, an elaborate restaging of Magellan's final battle at the very spot on Mactan Island where Magellan was supposed to have come ashore. These programs, the director candidly admitted, were designed to promote activities supportive of the Marcos regime. They had a largely diversionary effect, keeping the youth involved in progovernment activities as opposed to protest movements. While the programs were intended to be recreational and noncommercial, they were by no means apolitical in their design and implementation.

In this respect, the director was an active player in the game of national politics. Pictures on his living room walls, hung over large, newly acquired saltwater aquaria, displayed him shaking hands with Marcos and other national leaders. He had been involved in a variety of political occupations, from directing customs at the International Mactan Airport and the ports of Surigao, Bislig, and Butuan, on

Mindanao Island, to membership in the Presidential Security Guard. The director was no stranger to the darker side of Filipino power struggles. As an example of his faith in the miraculous power of the Santo Niño, he used the story of an assassination attempt on his own life, which was staged in Zamboanga.[3] The Santo Niño, he said, had saved him, since he had been off in Cebu for the *sinulog* festival at the time of the attack. His deputy had been killed instead. The recreational activities he promoted, like the *sinulog* program, were only one facet of a political career in which the stakes were obviously very high.

The irony of the director's role as premier revivalist of the Cebuano *sinulog*, when he himself was a Leyteño, was a fact not lost on him or his associates. He reported that he was often kidded by other city inhabitants about his outsider status. He saw himself, however, as acting in the national good, regenerating an appreciation for regional diversity among everyone involved in the events he developed. "It is true I am a Leyteño," he stated, "but foremost I am a Filipino." All Filipino Christians, the director argued, should be taking part in the *sinulog* program, because it was, in his view, the genuinely Filipino version of venerating the Santo Niño de Cebu.

The director saw in *sinulog* dancing a ritual practice comparable to the more famous ritual practices of other places, such as the *Ati-atihan* festival of Aklan[4] and the fiesta processions of Daan Bantayan.[5] Yet, he noted, while these other ritual events, and the cities in which they took place, enjoyed widespread fame and recognition, Cebu City's distinctive ritual practice was on the verge of extinction. In this respect, it appeared to be a prime target for rejuvenation. The director's motives for reviving the *sinulog* were thus overtly oppositional—his stated objective was to instill a sense of local history and culture in the participants that would reinforce contrasts between Cebu and other places in the archipelago.

The initial transformation of the *sinulog* was thus anything but a commercial tourist attraction. Even though the director emphasized that the restaging was intended to produce a genuinely religious experience, its inspiration was also political, and political at a national as well as regional and local level. The program was designed to help ensure the stability of the nation's current administration, as well as to start Cebu City on its way to earning a place for itself alongside other cities in the Philippines famous for their religious customs and practices. The director had skillfully used the Marcos administration's oppositional rhetoric, which played off fears of both global and national homogenization, to effectively mask the diversionary effect that was also motivating the national government's development strategy for the *sinulog* revival.[6]

The director's desire to gain national recognition for Cebu via the development of a legitimate symbol of regional ethnic uniqueness had a distinct effect on the transformation of the *sinulog* choreographic tradition. The political objectives of the program prompted a heightened attention to the details of choreographic design of the *tindera* and troupe *sinulog* dances that might otherwise have been deemed irrelevant or overly specific in a more strictly commercial development program. Given the political motivations for the program, however, the accuracy of the revived renditions of the *sinulog* was particularly critical to the maintenance of the director's own public authority. An obviously altered *sinulog* performance would have opened the director and his office up to charges of blatant propagandism. To make good on the "cultural enhancement" claim, therefore, the program had to pay close attention to the *sinulog* practices already in place.

This highly conservative development strategy was to have a profound and lasting effect on the entire *sinulog* tradition. When the promotion did become commercialized in later years—a transformation of which the director himself was outspokenly critical—the reconstruction of an "authentic" tradition had already been set in place. This was to enrich the symbolism of the parade *sinulogs* and ensure some physical continuity with respect to the older forms.

The Reconstruction of Authenticity

The new set of choreographers chosen in 1980 for the task of "reviving" the ritual *sinulog* were college and university dance instructors. Their goal was to learn the dancing of the ritual *sinulog* forms and teach it to the new revival performers, their own students. However, this effort to construct an accurate and authentic rendition of the ritual dancing had some additional effects as well. In order for the teachers to create a rendition they could verify as authentic, they had to develop some way of understanding and recognizing the movement. They had to place the ritual dances in a conceptual framework of some kind, literally to come to terms with it. In short, the dance instructors had to translate the ritual *sinulog* practices into a movement vocabulary domain that was comprehensible to them. This interpretive process itself served to produce some changes in the *sinulog* choreography.

Many of the teachers recruited to revive the *sinulog* had been exposed through their own often extensive training in folk dance to methods of dance description and characterization widely used in Philippine folk dance ethnography. Developed in large part by the pioneer dance ethnographer, Francisca Reyes Aquino, this method was clearly suited to the recording of Filipino social dances. The Aquino method emphasized detailed and precise observation of limb positions in relation to the body and in relation to space. For example, a typical description, done for the entrance section of the *binasuan* (drinking glass) dance of Pangasinan, Philippines, reads as follows:

> Starting with R [right] foot, take eight waltz steps forward to center of room or stage. Hold glasses in front, elbows close to waist. Move R hand up to chest level and down at waist or hip level alternately and L hand down at hip or waist level and up to chest level alternately, that means that when the R hand goes up to chest level, the L hand goes down to hip level on one count and reverse movement on the next count and so on for eight measures.[7]

The focus of attention in the Aquino method of description is given to noting "basic steps" and actions, phrases that were to come up often in my interviews with the parade choreographers. The specific folk music used is also an important consideration. Costumes and props, as well, are given careful attention in the recording of different dances in this method of dance documentation.[8]

The *tindera* style presented certain difficulties when viewed from within the categories of this descriptive system. No "basic" steps, as conventionally defined, were apparent in the vague foot-stepping style of *tindera* dancing. No set folk music existed. In its place was merely a widely varying resilient rhythmic mode. Finally, no clear set of gestural designs was featured as a standard element of the *tindera sinulog* dance form. One clear feature that did emerge, however, was the use of a hand prop, the candle. As to the rest, it was up to the observers to fill in the "blanks" left by the *tindera* style of *sinulog* dancing.

In working out a teachable rendition of the *tinderas'* performance, the instructors developed a reversible sagittal pathway (stepping forward and backward) as a pattern for a basic *tindera sinulog* step.[9] Spatial standards for the arm gestures were also assigned, which stipulated that they be waved along the front end of the rising forward sagittal plane diameter.[10] This repeatable step and gesture pattern became the standard stylized version of the "authentic" *tindera sinulog*. It was used thereafter by parade choreographers who wished to use authentic movement in designing parade *sinulog* performances. It was also acknowledged by dance specialist parade contest judges as the authentic representation of *sinulog* dance, as performed both by the *tinderas* and supposedly by the Santo Niño devotees of former times. The form developed a popular recognition as well, such that, when I interviewed a journalist involved in the parade development in 1984, he demonstrated this same step and gesture pattern as the "authentic" ritual *sinulog* dance.

The dance instructors, during this process of reinterpretation, modified and edited out some of the recurrent movement themes of the _tindera sinulog_ form noted in Chapters 6 and 8. They did not choose, for example, to focus on the gaze of the dancers, held in relation to a distant object, as a central feature of the performance. Neither did they focus on the relationship created between the hand and the body's central core. The significance of the candle—one main link between the old form and the new—was destined to change dramatically. Where the candle once had mediated a relationship between the Santo Niño and the dancer's inner emotional state, it now came into a new role as a kind of movement marker, carried about in order to reveal spatial trace forms at a far reach from the dancer's torso.

The theatrical _sinulog_ was more amenable to the choreographers' descriptive approach. Focus, again, was directed toward the use of hand props—the swords and shields. These did become popular, often-used symbols of the parade dances. Even when the dance movement itself was changed beyond recognition in parade renditions of the _sinulog_ and the performers represented kinds of characters entirely different from those represented in the troupe _sinulog_, swords and shields were still often carried as symbols of cultural authenticity.

The theatrical _sinulog_ also offered an established rhythmic accompaniment, the drumming cadences, which were tape-recorded and taught to the drum corps of some of the participating schools' marching bands. One of these drum rhythms became the single most well-known symbol of the dancing.[11] I never encountered a _sinulog_ participant, performer or spectator, who failed to mention the rhythm as a means of identifying the dancing of the parade _sinulog_.

As for the movement of the dance itself, the theatrical form also featured several varieties of clearly defined basic steps. The choreographers appropriated these for their own dance performances, pulling them out of the context of the traditional dance format—the sequence of collective dance figures of the theatrical _sinulog_ performance. These steps and the rhythmic cadences, like the _tindera_ movement fragments, became "authentic" movement symbols of the theatrical _sinulog_.

The movement behaviors extracted from the descriptive learning process of the dance instructors thus symbolized not only the _sinulog_ tradition, but also Filipino folk dance tradition and its ethnographic method, as well as the new performance context. The instructors, in effect, had constructed an abstract spatial cast around the nebulous _tindera_ performance and created a "space mold" of the dance style. Likewise, they succeeded in condensing the theatrical _sinulog_ into a

Figure 11.2. A parade contingent dressed in "Visayan style" and using authenticated gestures and props.

series of basic steps and a drum rhythm. The two sets of steps and the rhythm combined relatively easily into a movement vocabulary that could be used to represent the "authentic" rendition of what now could be conceived of as an "earlier" tradition, the ritual devotional *sinulog*.

In the dance instructors' process of reinterpretation, changes made in the *sinulog* performance were articulated in specific detail. The *tindera* form and the theatrical *sinulog* form were themselves merged into the new "revival" form, the first "parade" form of the *sinulog*. A conventional view of what the revived representation of the theatrical and *tindera sinulogs* must entail was brought about as a result of these reinterpretations of the ritual performances. The new vocabulary of basic steps and gestures made reference in a very specific, though not always completely imitative, way to the dancing of the past (Figure 11.2). The new practice connected itself to the older forms with precise characteristics that all could recognize. A spatial/gestural code of sorts had been created, which brought to mind each or every older form. The dance instructors thus forged a new tradition inspired by the older ones, and in so doing laid the groundwork for the development of a genuinely symbolic or rule-governed dance practice.[12]

Issue of Authenticity

This short chapter in the history of the *sinulog* development project consciously centered around the issue of "authenticity." Could the *sinulog* redesigned by the new parade instructors be called authentic? If authenticity were defined in terms of a perfect restoration of the older forms and their traditional significance, then no, they could not. That was indeed the sort of authenticity the director had had in mind as an ideal goal: the authenticity of symbols found in The Past, not made anew. In the new context he had created, however, the achievement of that sort of authenticity was impossible. The students and teachers, motivated by what they called a "spirit of cooperation" with the MYSD, had different reasons for performing the *sinulog* than had the earlier devotee participants. The new participants could not restore to the performance the significance it had lost with the passing of the drum-accompanied collective tradition. A bona fide restoration would have required a spiritual revolution, perhaps a millenarian movement, not a largely academic effort aimed at preserving the status quo.

Were these new forms, then, by definition inauthentic? Again, the answer must be no, for they were not forgeries or fakes. There was no intent to distort the performances or to create inferior substitutes for them. If authenticity is defined as the recognition of something that represents itself as reliable, trustworthy, and accepted—the standard definition of the term—then the new *sinulogs* were definitely authentic. They were "made up" symbols, to be sure, but they were made with careful reference to the traditional source material by the city's most well-trained in-house authorities. They were, in fact, the first *authenticated* forms of the tradition, the first to be assessed with regard to agreed-upon standards of validity. Henceforth, whenever a representation of the dance might be created, an informed community of local observers could evaluate it critically and form a consensus as to whether or not it was a "valid" rendition. As one parade choreographer, a Muslim from Mindanao, remarked to me, "These Cebuanos are very particular about their *sinulog*." That discriminating attitude, and the newly justified attribution of cultural depth to the *sinulog* dance style itself, was made possible by the efforts of the reinterpreters of the original traditions—the dance instructors. They complicated the *sinulog* practice through their astute reinterpretation of the ritual forms, while at the same time setting themselves up as the new authorities of the *sinulog* tradition.

The *Sinulog* Project

The following year, 1981, the MYSD, having successfully developed the revival program, turned over the *sinulog* promotion project to the Cebu City Mayor's Office. A major change in orientation occurred at this point that was to dramatically alter the significance and choreography of the *sinulog* dance in the years ahead. When the mayor and city government took charge of the promotion, the focus was shifted from the dancing of the *sinulog* alone to the Feast of the Santo Niño in its entirety. The model for this new development project was that of the "old-fashioned carnival," a phrase that appeared on the cover of the next year's *Sinulog* program.

While the dancing was still the regnant symbol of this new program, and the predominant activity around which all others revolved, it was no longer the sum and substance of the promotional event. A trade fair, as well as photo and art exhibits, a film festival that featured Tagalog films, a cockfight, a pop music festival, and a variety show, with an all-night disco following were instituted as well. The name of the promotion was also changed, from "*Sinulog sa Sugbo*" to "*Sinulog '81*." The old name had stressed tradition by using both the Cebuano language and the old Visayan name of the city, Sugbo. The new name reflected instead the more businesslike, up-to-date attitudes held by the new organizers.

The new leadership of the *sinulog* project decided to stress what were termed the "cultural highlights" associated with the fiesta over spiritual and religious ones. In so doing, they created a situation less unsuitable for generating commercial profits.[13] Again, the notion of "culture" played a pivotal role in the rhetoric of this new development project. In this phase of the development, culture gave a veneer of prestige to the process of secularization, fending off claims that the performance was now motivated by what could otherwise be seen as more base political and economic interests.

A new and larger parade was instituted in 1981 that presented the history of Cebu City from precontact times up to the present, using a series of floats that depicted the planting of the Cross of Magellan, the battle of Mactan, the Santo Niño in a pantheon of Cebuano gods, the arrival of López de Legaspi, the construction of the basilica, and, finally, Cebu in the present. The parade route, which the previous year had merely circled the basilica, was now enlarged to run right through the center of town along Osmeña Boulevard, a main artery.

What had started out as a small-scale attempt at a religious revival had now turned into a historical and folkloric review, promoting large-scale community involvement and tourism.

The intention of the new *sinulog* parade, as was made evident in the topics chosen for its various sections, was to have the past gloriously presented to a crowd of spectators. This was not a program designed to bring to life a dying ritual. Having a past took precedence over being a past, as the original revival format gave way to a spectacle plan.[14] The new emphases of the *sinulog* project changed the meaning of the celebration in general and of the dancing in particular. It was at this point that the external appearance of the dancing gained importance and its internal experience took on a relatively minor role.

While the motivations for staging the *sinulog* were now no longer hostile to commercial interests, this new promotion of the *sinulog* nevertheless strove to preserve the value on historical accuracy and authenticity emphasized by the earlier promotion. Many of the same individuals who had created the first *Sinulog sa Sugbo* project remained active in the planning and restaging of *Sinulog '81*. New research committees were formed to investigate the types of costumes worn during different historical periods now represented in the 1981 parade.

To further encourage participation, a contest was instituted among participating parade *sinulog* entries, with a top prize of 10,000 pesos awarded to the winners. The number of contingents more than quadrupled, from eight in 1980 to thirty-seven in 1981. The entries now represented government divisions, civic clubs, trade groups, commercial establishments, labor unions, veterans' organizations, shipping companies, professional organizations, the media, and even the Boy Scouts. In short, the development of the new contest parade reoriented the symbolism of the *sinulog* completely. What was represented was not simply the religious spirit of Cebu, but every facet of the city's character. The collective "self" of the city and of Cebu Province as a whole was put on display. As the 1981 program stated, the project celebrated the "oneness" of the Cebuanos as a community and as a people. Yet the unity that was sought was actually expressed through diversity, through an eclectic collection of contingents. The sole unifying factor in the new production was the idea that everyone was "doing the same dance," the *sinulog*.

The Evolution of the Guidelines

Ironically, the major force inspiring this increased show of unity was also one of the more divisive innovations of the *sinulog* project: the contest. The contest situation was seen by some as the beginning of the end of any authentic connection to the older *sinulog* traditions, since choreographers were now faced with a new motivation, one judged by many to be antithetical to the spirit of cooperation that had inspired the earlier development.

Conforming to a pattern typical of competitive dance environments, the new key features of the *sinulog* performances became their decorative aspects, as well as any innovative or novel elements they might introduce. Choreographers began experimenting with new costumes and material symbols and new group figures. These drew some applause from the crowds but criticism from more deeply invested observers, such as the MYSD director, who judged these performances "commercialized" and "Western-oriented." [15]

However, if the contest stimulated controversial and dramatic changes in the social meaning and choreography of the dances, it also reinforced and provided further articulation for the standards of the new authenticated tradition forged in the *Sinulog sa Sugbo* training program. In connection with the competition, a set of standards entitled the "Parade Guidelines" were drawn up and distributed throughout the community to all participating organizations. Over the years, these evaluative criteria were to change subtly as the nature of the spectacle changed. Throughout their evolution, however, the guidelines set out the criteria by which the *sinulog* dancing would be judged, revealing as they did so the values of the project organizers and the sectors of the city they represented that pertained to the *sinulog* performance. Specifically, the guidelines articulated a problematic and unstable but persevering validation of the ideas of uniqueness, authentication, and especially regional integrity that had inspired the revival project.

In 1981 the criteria for evaluating the dancing was divided into five categories, each weighted according to its importance for the overall presentation: number of participants (15 percent of the score), performance (40 percent), costume (15 percent), originality (15 percent), and overall impact (15 percent). As the categories indicated, quantity as well as quality counted for something in the parade *sinulogs*. Large groups were given a 15 percent advantage over smaller ones. However, the most important category, "performance," focused on the execution of the choreography itself, the precision timing and coordination demonstrated by the groups. This criterion encouraged renditions with a high degree of synchrony apparent in the corps' unison movements. Initially, such an appearance was the guidelines' most valued quality in the parade *sinulogs*, over and above "authenticity."

The issue of authenticity was addressed in all the other categories—"costume," "originality," and "impact." According to one of the original organizers, the "costume" category was evaluated by contest judges in terms of both apparent attractiveness and "authenticity." That is to say, the costume design had to match the historical period referenced by the performance and use indigenous materials, if possible. The "impact" category was a catch-all criterion that could include overall positive or negative impressions of the authenticity of the performance.

The category of "originality," oddly enough, was the one that most directly addressed the issue of authenticity. As defined in the *Sinulog '81* program, "originality" was equated with "relevance to *sinulog*"— relevance to the traditional ritual forms of the dance. That is to say, the choreography's originality was evaluated according to how creatively it made use of the authenticated movement vocabulary that represented the older *sinulog* forms. In this way, originality was conceived of within a context of adherence to official standards.

In 1982, the project gained stature. Imelda Marcos, as Minister of Human Settlements, was added to the list of Honorary Chairpersons, as were the Minister of National Defense, Juan Ponce Enrile, the Minister of Transportation, José Dans, and the Minister of Education and Culture, Onofre D. Corpuz. In the previous year, only the ministers of tourism, public information, and trade had been named to the list, along with the archbishop of Cebu and a chairman of Philippine Airlines, Roman Cruz, Jr. The program also acquired corporate backing in 1982 through what was to become the Sinulog Foundation of future years, which included such sponsors as Air France, Cebu Plaza Hotel, City Savings Bank, and the Ministry of Finance, among a number of others. The schedule of activities drawn up for the first project, however, remained basically unchanged, and the criteria for the performances remained unchanged as well.

In 1983, however, for reasons never made clear by the city leadership, the project's original standards for historical and cultural awareness were abandoned. An "anything goes" attitude, as some organizers described it, was adopted instead. Corporate sponsors entered parade floats carrying groups of male transvestites, giants representing American movie figures such as the extraterrestrial character E.T., and dance groups wearing Las Vegas-like showgirl costumes appeared as well. The new, nontraditional models for this celebration were drawn from abroad—Rio and New Orleans—as well as from within the Visayas. In particular, the *Ati-atihan* festival of Aklan on the island of Panay, which had a longstanding reputation for producing a "Mardi Gras" effect, was used as a source of inspiration for *Sinulog '83* (Figure 11.3).

Figure 11.3. A parade contingent dressed in "Mardi Gras" or "*Ati-atihan*" style.

The promotion that had begun as a "cultural" celebration had, in three years' time, been transformed into a Mardi Gras for commercial interests. As the influence of the major sponsors and their emphasis on commercialism grew, the importance of historical and cultural authenticity decreased. The *sinulog* dances of 1983 became associated with secular activities of tourism and of big business. As the motivation shifted from national political interests to local economic ones, the symbolism of the dancing abandoned the attempt to represent the notion of the "cultural past." Instead, images more typically attributed to the ahistorical borrowers of a port culture held sway. The parade was more entertaining than ever before—1983 was remembered by one resident who had worked on a film project about the *sinulog* as the best parade ever. However, the new expressions of the celebration also generated controversy. The Augustinian religious community, which had already insisted on a clear separation of what it had defined as separate "religious" and "cultural" activities in 1982, completely divorced itself from the celebration of 1983. Parade officials from later years, looking back, agreed that a line had somehow been crossed, presenting an unacceptable and unwanted image of the city and its regional culture.

In 1984 and especially 1985, the project organizers reverted back to the original standards of historical and cultural accuracy. In 1984, the guidelines reflected the enhanced awareness of the desired identity that it was hoped would be represented in the parade. The criteria were enlarged to include a sixth category, "relevance to the *sinulog*," which was specifically concerned with the issue of authenticity. The "relevance" category was given 20 percent of the contest score, which was taken from the 40 percent previously allotted to "performance." Both the subject of the performance and the choreography itself were evaluated in terms of their relevance to the older *sinulog* tradition. The "originality" category was also reduced to only 10 percent of the total score, from 15 percent, while "impact" was increased to 20 percent. The identity of the city as a place where authentic practices were valued was thus reasserted in this reorganization of the guideline criteria.

The parade entry requirements were also made more strict. Only groups of a certain size, between 30 and 150 participants, could participate. Guidelines required them to wear costumes depicting the traditional *sinulog* during some historical era that had to "conform to the tenets of morality and decency." Individuals or groups without registration numbers were not allowed inside the parade route. It was at this point that military cadets were brought in to line the entire route and to prevent spectators from joining in the parade. The dancing was not to be associated with spontaneous merrymaking, but rather with orderly performances that were to be watched from a distance.

The heightened positive value on representing authenticity was also expressed through explicit denials of any imitative aspects of the *sinulog* celebration—a return and reaffirmation of the original rhetoric of opposition voiced during the initial revival phase. The *sinulog* project was emphatically declared not to be a copy of any other festival, particularly the *Ati-atihan* festival of Aklan, its most powerful rival in the tourist trade. The overall chairman of the *sinulog* project in 1985, for example, stated emphatically at a preparatory ceremony for the parade that the *sinulog* was "not the *Ati-atihan*." He denounced attempts to transfer customs from Aklan's celebration to Cebu's, practices such as encouraging spectators to join in the dancing and the blackening of spectators' faces with charcoal or grease, which had been instigated informally during the parade in previous years.

These remarks and others of similar content were picked up by reporters and published in the daily papers, as were editorials and letters supporting the chairman's views. For example, one article appearing shortly before the 1985 fiesta in the local paper, *The Freeman*, complained about past attempts to present dancers from Aklan and *Ati-atihan*-style dancing in the *Sinulog '85* parade. The article stated:

> We Cebuanos can not be proud of this presentation being not our own traditional way of celebrating the feast day of our beloved patron of Cebu, Señor Santo Niño. Everybody knows that we only copied it from the Antiqueños or the people of Aklan and does not originally belong to us. (Labrada 1985:5)

Manuel Satorre, a columnist for the local *Sun Star Daily* newspaper and a veteran parade organizer, commented that some of the parade participants had been "overenthusiastic . . . bringing to Cebu what they got from the *Ati-atihan* in Aklan" (1985:4). Similar remarks appeared in other local commentaries as well.[16] The idea that the celebration was "authentically Cebuano" because it was not a copy of some other people's practice gained widespread support in public discourse. Whatever might have been borrowed was deemed out of place and was put into opposition with what was accepted as locally original. The parade had become an opportunity for the assertion of an ethnic discreteness.

Ironically, in denying that the promotion was in any way imitative of borrowed models, a genuinely ancient characteristic of the city's culture was also denied. What was most artificial about the promotion at this point was this very idea, that imitativeness and borrowing were not central to the local lifestyle. However, the leadership and supportive public opinion were committed to the idea that "authentic" local culture could manifest in a region with clear boundaries, inside of which distinctive practices originated. This idea of regionally pure culture was publicly imposed on the *sinulog* promotion.

The tightening of the guidelines produced the desired effect. The 1985 parade, and the entire *Sinulog '85* festival, was acclaimed by spectators and participants alike to be the most colorful, best organized, and generally the most successful *sinulog* event ever put on by the City Government.[17] Cebu City Mayor Ronald Duterte was quoted as saying, "This is the best coordinated, and prepared *Sinulog* the city has ever witnessed in years," while former mayor Florentino S. Solon was reported to have said that he felt "overjoyed at the progress attained by the project."[18] The Augustinian community reassociated itself with the event, staging its own "mini-*Sinulog*" contest and parade. The rector of the basilica, Fr. Ambrosio Galindez, contributed a "message" statement to the *Sinulog '85* souvenir program that began, "It is with greatest pleasure that I join the citizens of Cebu in the *Sinulog* Festival Celebration."

The floats, giants, and dancers, with few exceptions, portrayed what were deemed "relevant" historical and prehistoric events that used accurate presentations of folk costumes and authenticated dancing of Cebu (however, a *Ghostbusters* giant, who was greeted with much popular approval, was allowed entry in the parade nevertheless). The experiences of previous years were put to use, and the *Sinulog '85* festival achieved a clarity of form and a sustained momentum that was both satisfying and exhilarating to the organizers. The Cebuano identity asserted in this parade was an identity the organizers actively stood up for and vigorously asserted to the world at large. It affirmed uniqueness, connection to antiquity, and authenticity. It maintained a nationalist aspect to the extent that the theme chosen for the parade by its *barangay* (neighborhood) contingents was a "national prayer for peace." In sum, it traded the status of the culturally marginal border zone, perceived as a harbor for phony copies, for that of the culturally rich "region," a land that could be defended from cultural trespassers. The years of experimentation had culminated in a vibrant and enormously popular product that carried positive meanings of various kinds for a host of political, religious, and economic factions alike.

Chapter 12
The Symbolism of Desired Recognition

There was a writer working for the Ministry of Public Affairs in 1985 who had observed and reported on the *sinulog* performances at close range for several years, and whose insights into the *sinulog* project were among the most reflective and articulate I was to encounter. She went by the nickname "Lena" to her friends. I was introduced to her shortly after my arrival in the city because we shared an interest in the anthropological study of ritual. Lena had done a master's thesis on folk rituals of the family life cycle in a community on a neighboring island where her extended family was located.

Lena was another of the city's successful and particularly well-informed culture bearers, especially with respect to the promotional *sinulog* and the creation of its public image. She was not a "native" of the city, although she now divided her residence between a place in Cebu City and another home outside of town to the south, a situation she assessed for me with the remark, "Expensive, huh?" Married to a poet, mother of two, she was also connected to an international network of public relations professionals and had participated in an international conference held in Singapore during my residence in the city.

One afternoon, shortly after the 1985 *sinulog* celebration, while sitting at her desk in the large air-conditioned office of the ministry's downtown Cebu City office, Lena and I had a discussion about the large-scale social effect of the parade. She remarked that although the festival had created a certain threat from the beginning, since, in her words, "the profane appeared to dominate the sacred," nevertheless, a certain unity within the community was also gained from the spectacle. Cebu City, she remarked, seemed to have condensed into a more compact whole because of the *sinulog*. As she said the word "compact," her hands made visible a vague, voluminous form that they proceeded to squish, in a short, rapid series of tense pushes, into a smaller, more clearly spherical shape.

Lena's gesture described the city as a world influenced by outside pressures, a world where tension increased as opposing external forces simultaneously encountered it and sought to contain it and control it, to make it smaller than it would naturally be. Yet this seemingly hostile and constricting process effected a "product-ive" (appearance-rendering) result. The outcome of the action was the emergence of a more articulately defined visual form, an entity whose identity was more easily recognizable.

The movement process Lena represented depicted a major expressive theme, if not *the* major theme, of the parade *sinulog* symbolism: its embodiment of a number of different tensions that were being exerted on a receptive though unstable entity, the regnant symbol of the city's volatile and fluctuating "culture." These tensions originated from an array of different sources, as evidenced in different public discourses. They included the tensions between "the past" and "the present," between "big government" and "big business," and, finally, between the identity of "Cebuano society" and that of its individual members.

Past versus Present

Most centrally, the new dances embodied the tension between a popularly valorized "cultural past" and a tacitly influential contemporary socioeconomic and sociopolitical "present." As already mentioned, the choreography of the parade dances was expected to make reference in an articulate way to what were publicly conceptualized mainly as older and even ancient *sinulog* dance traditions, although it did not simply duplicate them. At the same time, however, the choreography symbolized a contemporary significance for the *sinulog*: its role as an enhancing accompaniment to the religious celebration.

The *sinulog* revival having been abandoned in the revised program of events in favor of the more spectacular "cultural" display performance, the parade *sinulog*, by 1985, had been officially separated from the religious activities of the fiesta. The masses, novenas, and religious processions that were the time-honored highlights, the core events of the occasion, were organized, sponsored, and affiliated with different authorities in the community, specifically the Augustinian clergy. In essence, the parade *sinulog* by 1985 had come to serve as a decorative frame, of sorts, for the central rituals of the religious fiesta.

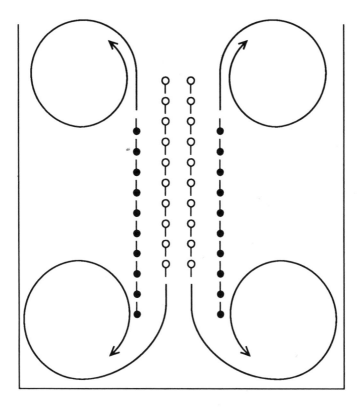

Figure 12.1. A floor pattern used in a parade *sinulog* featuring multiple spiraling pathways.

In this regard, the preference for increasingly complicated symmetrical curvilinear forms, which were used in creating group figures for the parade contingents, expressed aptly this new decorative role of the *sinulogs* (Figures 12.1–12.5).

Abstract curvilinear forms employed in the parade choreography bore a marked resemblance to the floral patterns that typically served as borders around the stone relief figures of Philippine churches, or around the frescoes of interior church walls, or on the pedestals of

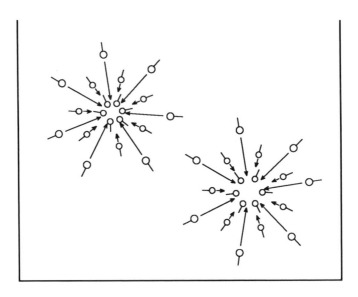

Figure 12.2a

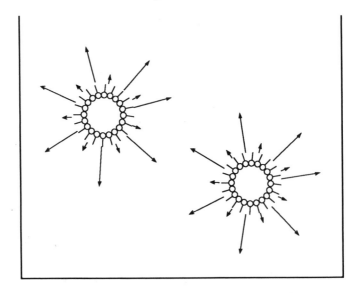

Figure 12.2b

Figure 12.2 a–b. A floor pattern used in a parade *sinulog* that features inwardly (Figure 12.2a) and outwardly (Figure 12.2b) radiating circular forms.

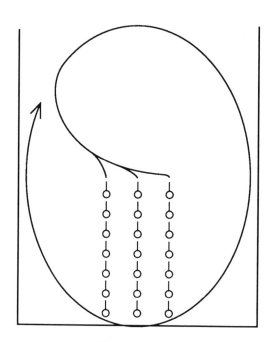

Figure 12.3a

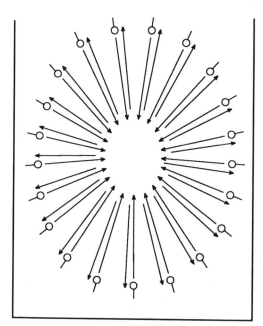

Figure 12.3b

Figure 12.3 a–b. A floor pattern used in a parade *sinulog* that features both spiraling (Figure 12.3a) and radiating (Figure 12.3b) pathways.

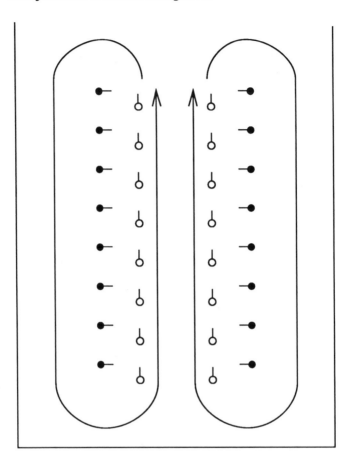

Figure 12.4. A floor pattern used in a parade *sinulog* that features gender-linked choreography: men (•) remain standing, facing inward while women (○) circle the outside columns.

statues of various saints, known as *santos* (Figure 12.6).[1] The choreography, in other words, tended to reproduce designs in the traditional "incipient baroque" style.[2] In this regard, the parade *sinulog* choreography effectively symbolized on different levels both its origins and its present status. It included authenticated steps and gestures, "re-presenting" the "past" dance traditions. It also depicted its contemporary role as an appealing frame for the religious celebration. These two statements were simultaneously possible because they were

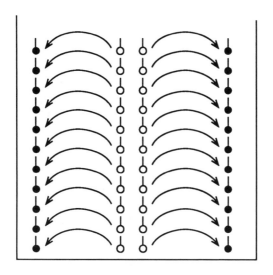

Figure 12.5a

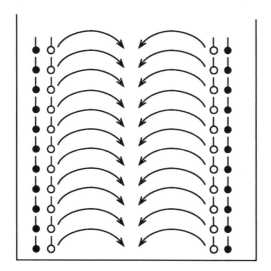

Figure 12.5b

Figure 12.5 a–b. A floor pattern used in a parade *sinulog* that features multiple semicircular pathways that radiate outward (Figure 12.5a) and inward (Figure 12.5b). ● = male dancers; ○ = female dancers.

Figure 12.6. A bas-relief of the Santo Niño located over the main entrance of the basilica shows characteristic "incipient baroque" curvilinear decorative designs.

conveyed through different symbolic channels made visible in the choreography. "Cultural pastness" was represented through patterns of personal conduct—the movement symbolism of individual bodies. Contemporary "framehood" was represented through patterns of collective movement—the movement symbolism of the collective space.

The National versus the Commercial

Another tension symbolized in the parade *sinulog* choreography was the tension between nationalism and commercialism, between big government and big business. Unlike the symbolism of past and present, these two influences did not work in confluence on the dance style. They asserted, through the choreography, opposing identities that created an ironic inversion of reference in the performance symbolism.

The symbolism of the parade dances was paradoxical in this respect: while national policies and programs had inspired the development of the parade choreography to a large extent, the nation itself, the Philippines, was not represented as such in the choreography. Instead, the "Filipino-ness" of the performance was visible only in the "Cebuano-ness" of the dancing. "The nation," in effect, had symbolically appropriated the image of "Cebuano-ness" to represent itself. The more "Cebuano" the performance became, the more regionally "authentic" its steps and gestures, the more "Filipino" it became as well. Recognition of the regional tradition was thus designed to lead toward an appreciation of inclusive "Filipino-hood"—at least, this was the stated intent of the MYSD director when he instigated the program. The authenticated steps and gestures represented the national government and its policies at least as specifically as they represented Cebuano culture. The symbolism actually worked to conflate the two conceptions.

Commercial interests, on the other hand, inspired the more decorative, ahistorical, and popular aspects of the performances. They produced choreographic statements that were deemed Westernized and tourist-oriented. Unlike the national influence, which became increasingly invisible in the choreography as its potency increased, commercial symbolism worked in the reverse. Its potency could be measured by the heightened visibility of its expressions.

In both cases, however, invisibility and credibility worked together. The less visible the national influence on the *sinulog* program was in the performance, the more credibility the dancing achieved. The more visible the commercial symbolism, the more it was condemned by the authorities. Again, a paradox was created. Expressions of commercialism were interpreted as culturally inauthentic, having no relevance to the authenticated cultural identity asserted in the dances, which was itself largely a construct of national programs. The closer the dances moved toward representing authenticated "regional" (actually nationally oriented) culture, the more displaced they became from the de facto economic scene. On the other hand, the closer the choreography moved toward representing local commercial interests, which were themselves, in many cases, part and parcel of transnational enterprises, the farther they moved from the locally authorized "cultural" renditions of the *sinulog*. Either way, the standards of authenticity served to mask the more geographically dispersed forces actually driving the spectacle, highlighting in their place the symbolism of a locality in isolation.[3] A sort of "through the looking glass" effect resulted from the reflection of the two enormous influences of nationalism and commercialism against each other in the choreography.

Society versus the Individual

The problem of striking a balance between the opposing forces of big business and big government was left to the talents of the parade choreographers, whose efforts in part embodied a third tension manifest in the parade *sinulog* symbolism, the tension between individual and collective catalysts for the parade *sinulogs*. The symbolism of the parade *sinulogs* did not represent only the large-scale interactions of national, civic, private, and Roman Catholic institutions mentioned above. While the portrayal of a regional identity was publicly asserted as the most important message of the parade performances, the dances were also, as were all the *sinulog* forms, the works and the statements of individuals.

The personal motivations of the parade participants were as varied and complex as the responses the parade evoked among different elements of the city's society. In this respect, a multitude of nested identities were symbolized and asserted in the parade *sinulog* forms in addition to their paradoxical "cultural" statements.

The Choreographers

The choreographers, like the *tinderas*, were a varied lot of individuals who, although they generally shared a common background as dance educators and physical education instructors, brought a wealth of varied experiences to their work. One of the more well-informed members of this group, for example, was a college dance instructor, Misud, who proved to be another atypically typical city resident. Misud's identity was divided between a number of occupational and regional affiliations. He described himself as half Cebuano and half Higaonon.[4] He was not from Cebu, but from Cagayan de Oro City on Mindanao Island. His knowledge of Philippine dance traditions extended beyond Cebu Island to the whole of the Visayas and Northern Mindanao. He saw the dance practices of these areas as all belonging to a related tradition, of which he was one culture bearer. He was not a devotee of the Santo Niño, or a Roman Catholic at all, but described himself as a Muslim.

Misud looked with some humor on his own role as a parade *sinulog* choreographer, noting the contradiction between his religious commitments and his professional responsibility as a dance instructor. His friends in the Muslim community, he said, disapproved of his choreographing for the *sinulog* project, but he laughed that off, preferring to participate in the "spirit of cooperation" mentioned by other college instructors. The conflict of interests was not a serious one, in his view. Both Protestants and Muslims were performing in his *sinulog* dance, along with Roman Catholics, so he did not see himself as a particularly unusual or contradictory figure in this respect.

Misud's group of parade dancers was no exception. Many of the *sinulog* contingents, especially those of the colleges and universities participating in the projects, were composed not only of local Catholics but of students from other islands and provinces. These performers were not necessarily Santo Niño devotees themselves. Choreographers reported that newcomers to the island were usually as eager to be a part of the parade as were longtime residents. One dance instructor reported that students coming from other islands and other provinces would often go to considerable expense to finance their own costumes for a performance and pay to have color photographs taken of their contingents, which they proudly took home to their family residences. The ideal "Cebuano" identity asserted in the parade was in fact asserted by a diverse collection of participants, among them people like Misud, who made no claim to being "pure" natives or even permanent locals.

In spite of his semi-alien status, however, Misud was well-versed in the values of the Cebuano *sinulog* dance tradition. He had studied dance in Cebu City in one of the leading university departments with a prominent choreographer who had been experimenting with *sinulog* revivals for over a decade. Again, Misud was fairly typical in this respect. Several of the younger choreographers participating in the 1985 parade had similar backgrounds. They had been students of one or another of the original trainers and had gone on to find positions as dance instructors themselves. Misud acknowledged the influence of his teacher, against whom he was now competing in the parade contests. He had enjoyed success in the parade contest—his first attempt at entering a group in the 1985 parade had won a prestigious fourth place in the competition.

As a student, Misud had participated in Cebuano ritual dance demonstrations since 1974 and was familiar with the authenticated basic steps and rhythms drawn from the *tindera* and troupe practices. He attributed his recent success in the parade to the way he had modified what he described as the "real" *sinulog* movements, which, he said, were so repetitious that they were boring to watch. Misud introduced Manobo steps[5] into his choreography. These, he believed, preserved the traditional and authentic flavor of the performance while adding new movement as well.

The introduction of elements from other regional dance traditions was a common though somewhat controversial strategy among parade choreographers. While Manobo steps were not specifically employed by other choreographers, a more general "Muslim style" of movement and costume, which was copied or derived from the folk dances of Mindanao and the Sulu Archipelago, was frequently introduced into parade *sinulog* choreography. This Muslim style was considered to have a more sophisticated look, featuring a more highly orchestrated use of the body, with hands, head, and hips moving in pronounced isolation, often at juxtaposing, slanting pathways to one another (Figure 12.7). Muslim-style costumes were also employed to depict the elaborate and distinctive metal-working traditions of the Islamic sultanates, as well as the indigenous sarong and jacket styles of that region.

The relevance of this appealing style, however, to the local *sinulog* rituals was problematic. The Muslim style was clearly borrowed from across a border—what had historically been a provincial border, and what in the present day was a regional border as well. A few pretexts for employing the style were available. One choreographer in 1985, for example, justified the use of such "foreign" influences by staging a parade *sinulog* that represented the arrival of a group of pilgrims from Mindanao who had come to the fiesta to make an offering to the Santo Niño. She acknowledged a boundary between two regions, and, in so doing, legitimized the crossing of it. However, most choreographers who employed the Muslim-style movements and costume did so without such recognition, blurring the boundaries of the Cebuano region with those of the southern islands in the process. They were willing to incur the resulting criticism of the judges for the sake of increasing the visual appeal of the dancing. Misud's *sinulog* dances, although they were not completely "real" in their modified presentation of the basic steps, were within the bounds of credibility. The choreography avoided "overmodification" (his term), which would have resulted in dances of poor quality (*banga*).

Misud's prizewinning routine was composed of a dozen different group figures, which were his own creations. In his view, the *sinulog* choreography was two-thirds "tradition," meaning the steps, theme, and costumes, and one-third the choreographer's own work, meaning the modification of the steps and the group figure design. Again, Misud was no exception in this respect. The choreographers tended to see the parade dances as a blend of personal talent, which catered to audience appeal, and official doctrine. The main challenge in designing a performance centered around balancing the representation of both essential aspects. Those who solved this problem effectively went on to do relatively well in the competitions.

When I spoke with the choreographer who had won first place in the competition in 1985, for example, his assessment of the parade

Figure 12.7. Parade contingent dressed in "Muslim style" and using "Muslim-style" gestures.

contest challenge was stated in similar terms. Rene Rosales, like Misud, was an instructor at a local college. His 1985 first-place parade group had not dressed in "Cebuano-style" costumes. The women had worn purple tunics that fastened over one shoulder (not a traditional costume in any area of the Philippines), and the men had worn yellow vests and red knee-length trousers, a version of the Muslim style of dress. The material symbols used for the dance were long bamboo poles for the men and large, multicolored fans for the women— again, not items that were on the list of authentic material symbols. Rosales's choreography employed a number of elaborately complex group figures. One formation, for example, created multiple groups of dancers, each group stationed in three concentric circles. The gestures of these circles were made at different levels: above the heads in the inner circle, mid-level at the next, and at a still lower level by the outermost. The combined effect resembled the coordinated actions of sea anemones flexing and extending their needles underwater. Rosales also choreographed a figure where the bamboo poles handled by the male dancers were used as a kind of throne for one of the lead female dancers, who was seated on a pole and carried about while holding above her head a miniature Santo Niño.

When I had watched Rosales's choreography, I had found no traces of the *tindera* dancing recognizable within the movement, and traces of the troupe *sinulog* seemed limited to the use of a single drum rhythm and the use of a variation of one of the basic steps. His innovative choreography had apparently overwhelmed the sanctioned, traditional designs.

However, Rosales assured me that, yes, his winning *sinulog* choreography was in keeping with the standards of historical accuracy, because he had used the "basic steps" of the *tindera* dancing—the authenticated forms—as well as those of the theatrical *sinulog* dancing to move into and out of the group figures he had designed. He had also choreographed a section where the women closed their fans and gestured with them as though they were candles in the *tindera* style, meaning that they used the standard spatial form of extending the props to a forward, high position and made small circles in the air with them there. His choice of material symbols, he admitted, was not really appropriate. In this respect, he had succumbed to the Muslim style for audience appeal. However, he had endeavored to use the articles, at least part of the time, in the way that was recognized as the traditional *sinulog* manner. The props were also in keeping with the motif he had chosen, which depicted the arrival of the Santo Niño to the Philippines, which was at that time, he reminded me, considered the territory of Muslim sultanates. Using this historical view, Rosales had found his own solution to the problem of regional purity. Having included these relevant features in his performance, he, like Misud, had felt free to create his own dance, designing his own group figures in an original sequence that won for him and his group the top prize of eleven thousand pesos.[6]

While Rosales believed that the motivation for entering into the parade by the prizewinning groups—those that were not "overmodified" or entirely commercialized—was typically the traditional one of wanting to praise the Santo Niño, he also remarked that the choreography of these routines depended more on the choreographer's own ideas than on the "authentic" steps. His approach was strikingly similar to the *tinderas'* in this respect. He set his *sinulog* on his students according to his own personal image of the performance, just as the *tinderas* danced according to their own designs. The goal for the choreographers, however, was no longer to create a genuinely sacred act, but instead to create a scene that would be, in Rosales's words, "nice to look at." The choreographers' personal contributions to the performances thus tended to support the more commercial influences acting on the parade *sinulog*, even though they could also be working from basically religious inspirations. Their respect for the official steps and gestures, however, showed the influence of basically sociopolitical interests on their work.

The importance of the standardized reinterpretation of the older *sinulog* forms stands out in the context of these examples of the choreographers' processes. One consequence of the establishment of the symbolic code was that it freed the choreographers to develop the spatial aspects of their routines that were recognized as being unrelated to the standards of authenticity. The choreographers, because they were able to incorporate the recognized movements, managed to achieve two very different effects at once. They displayed the authenticated traditional *sinulog* and also did something that sprang mainly from their own imaginations, as they were the first to acknowledge. The clearly defined set of movements, the *sinulog* "vocabulary," made clear what aspects of the dance were outside the bounds of the tradition and so were wide open to interpretation. In this way, a choreographer could develop a performance that looked completely different from the older forms, yet was about the older forms. In effect, the *sinulog* code had allowed the choreographers to have their traditional cake and eat it, too. The tension between individual and society evident in the parade *sinulogs* was, in this respect, made workable by the standardized reinterpretations. The authenticated code allowed at least two channels of meaning to become visible and distinct in the choreography: one of individualistic action and another of collective, conventional formation.

By 1985, choreographers had had several years of experience organizing parade exhibitions. The choreography had evolved into intricate and spatially complex dance performances, with the winning performances staging elaborately costumed depictions of how the *sinulog* dancing might have happened in other times and other circumstances of Cebuano history. Signature dance styles were beginning to emerge, such that choreographers and the groups they worked with were starting to achieve recognition for their own style of sinulog performance. Rosales, for example, was just beginning to develop a reputation for his unusual group formations and choice of hand-held symbols. Another choreographer was becoming known for his careful preservation of some of the basic steps and formations. Within the parade contest context, the choreographers reclaimed the "tradition" of the dance and reinvented it, reforming its symbolism dramatically so as to reflect their own ability as well as the authenticated *sinulog* movement vocabulary.

The Participants

Another expression of the tension between individual and collective interests that was symbolized in the parade *sinulog* choreography involved the dancers themselves. The dancing afforded a huge display of membership, by means of which the various smaller worlds of Cebu City—the organizations and institutions that constituted its public life—made their presence in the community visible. An ironic theme asserted itself in the choreography in this respect. While the predominant motivation for individuals participating in the performances was to express their solidarity within these various collective organizations, the major statement made by the choreography was not one of synthetic unity, but one of pluralized individuality.

The motivation for participating in the spectacle, which was given again and again by the dancers, choreographers, and friends of performers to whom I spoke, was one of loyalty to their particular contingent or organization. Their intention was to personally identify themselves with and represent these smaller worlds, institutions, and subcultures that existed within and around the city. Sometimes this loyalty was forced, as in the case of office workers who were obliged to dance in the parade as a requirement for keeping their jobs. Sometimes the loyalty was reinforced, as in the case of physical education students who were told they would be guaranteed a top grade in their class if they participated. Much of the time, however, the loyalty was genuinely personal, as with members of some religious organizations, who paid individually to hire a choreographer for their group and financed the other costs of the performance as well.

For the winning parade groups, which were mainly those of colleges and universities, the desire to compete against other groups and demonstrate the superiority of their own *sinulog* rendition was of central importance to the dancers. Misud, for example, somewhat hesitantly confessed that he had acknowledged this competitive and exclusive drive in his own parade dance group. He told them on the eve of the competition, "I hope you win," even though he believed that, as their authority figure, he shouldn't have encouraged competitive instincts. The dancers, however, unashamedly viewed the parade as an opportunity to improve the reputation of their schools or community groups by taking prizes in the parade competition. Two top choreographers, in fact, admitted that the interest in competition was so prevalent in their school's parade *sinulog* dancers that they actually ceased having groups participate in the celebration because of it.

The social experience of group solidarity was particularly evident during the 1985 "awards rites," which were held in front of the City Hall/Municipio building several days after the parade. The top twenty-five dance groups were awarded trophies on this occasion. In spite of the fact that, from the parade organizers' perspective, this celebration was yet another opportunity to experience the "oneness" of the Cebuano community, the atmosphere generated by the participants during this award ceremony was anything but unified. As each winning group's name was called, its members would burst out in applause for themselves, while the rest of the assembled groups waited to hear their own names announced. The top three groups' responses were especially raucous, the shouts accompanied by drum beating and bell ringing, as the students jumped up and down, waving their group's symbols and crying out cheers of victory. Not once during the presentations did the assembled gathering of schools respond as one body to an announced winner. The crowd repeatedly revealed instead its own divisions and the importance of its members' small group loyalties.

Yet, in spite of the importance these organizations held for the dancers, the various schools, businesses, and neighborhoods to which the individuals owed their participation in the parade were not themselves depicted or symbolized in any way in the parade *sinulog* choreography. That is to say, it was only by virtue of the *bodies* presented in the *sinulog* parade and not by the dancing that these collective entities were represented. The *sinulog* group representing San Miguel Corporation, for example, did not form huge initials ("SMC") in their group figures or perform actions that in any way symbolized that company or its products. Invisibility and credibility again worked together. Modern institutions were not part of the authentic image of the city's culture, even though they were the substance of its composition. The actual connection made by the *sinulog* parade choreography to the sponsoring organizations was simply the presentation of the organization's membership in the parade.

Instead of in some way depicting the distinctive character of the organizations with which the parade dancers identified themselves, the parade choreography symbolized the opposite: the movements of a single person dancing for the Santo Niño. That is to say, the authenticated basic steps and gestures precluded to a great extent the possibility of developing group sculptures and figures that might have represented the synthetic and distinctive characters of the sponsoring organizations. The representation of the traditional *sinulog* necessitated choreographic techniques that preserved the essential discreteness of each and every participant, while at the same time creating a semblance of unity, a highly personalized form of unity: unison timing of gestures and steps. To add to the nonsynthetic effect, the fragmenting and mechanistic gestural style of the dances, noted in Chapter 11 as contrasting with the *tindera* gesturing style, created literally a dance of isolated members—arms waving and feet moving. This patterning reinforced a symbolism of discrete individuals, as opposed to collective structures. On more than one level, the symbolism of the parade *sinulogs* was a symbolism of the one made many, and only in a tacit sense the symbolism of the many made one.

It was thus an image of Cebu City as a place composed of a huge following of resilient, minor members that was asserted with enormous magnitude by the parade *sinulog* choreography. What this membership was *in*, however, was left largely unrepresented by the dancing. National and corporate symbolism was virtually invisible in this global bid for ethnic recognition. Only the banners carried by each dance group indicated these entities. Instead, images of innovative and traditionally aesthetic designs—frames constituted by a diverse collection of cooperative and innovative "little guys" (hands and their props)—were put on display by the sponsors. By 1985, abstract gestural formalism was well on its way to becoming the new dominant symbolism of the city's public culture.

It might be argued that this promotional *sinulog* was the least "real" or culturally valid version of the *sinulog* dance tradition, the thought voiced by Misud in his assessment of his own choreography. This assertion supports a stronger, more insidious argument of cultural derangement made perhaps most eloquently by writer Ian Buruma. Buruma (1989:94) has said of the Philippines in particular, "With nothing but borrowed language, borrowed ideas, borrowed points of view, theatre becomes a way of life. Fantasy is the last recourse of the dispossessed."

The tremendous success of the parade *sinulog* form did indeed suggest that "theatre" was becoming a central concern, if not a "way" of local life in this lowland urban Philippine community. The *sinulog* parade was definitely a major avenue of meaning for Cebu City. Moreover, there was no denying the fact that the images represented by the parade dances were fantastic. In spite of its amiable form, the parade *sinulog*'s reason for being was, in the end, to appear as something that it could never fully be, an ideal, purely original, and wholly continuous cultural practice emerging cleanly from what might mythically be called a "Land of Cebuano-ness." Having first sought to achieve this cultural effect through the manipulation of already exist-ing local artifacts—the rediscovered elements of the local *sinulog* ritual practices—the *sinulog* promotion evolved into a largely creative phenomenon whose symbols were not simply found in established lo-cal practices, but made up by the parade choreographers. It moved in this respect from the realm of fact to that of fiction and became more and more a product of inventive contemporary make-believe. To follow the argument given above, the success of the parade could be seen ironically as the unwitting representation of dispossession, of the abandonment of a sensitivity to local actualities.

However, while the parade *sinulog*, and the culture it represented, were without doubt imaginary and fantastic, they were by no means unreal or even unrealistic. The tens of thousands of bodies that pro-duced the spectacle and the hundreds of thousands who attended it made real its ironic symbolism, literally "realizing" it in the process of witnessing and performing it. What the parade performance re-flected more vividly than any state of dispossession was the real value of the imaginary in this urban neocolonial culture. It represented the value of the imagination of reality—that is to say, the value of the locality's imagination in an era when both marginal and regional eth-nic identities were being challenged and appropriated by national and corporate forces.[7] The *sinulog* parade represented a line of local de-fense as well as global offense in the game of what Fredric Jameson, following Ernest Mandel, has termed "late capitalism."[8]

It was most likely due to its involvement in the serious play of trans-national identity-making that the *sinulog* promotion did not manifest many of the stereotypes that smaller-scale "culture-brokering" efforts of this kind are popularly noted to entail. The promotion did not abandon entirely the *sinulog* dance style, for example, or disconnect the parade choreography completely from the "traditional" *sinulog* forms. On the other hand, the promotion was not a rigid and static reproduction of "tradition"—a parading of the museumized "pure" renditions gleaned from a seemingly frozen past. While the parade guidelines did constrain, they did not stifle the creative work of the parade's individual choreographers. Moreover, the parade did not ca-ter only to Western influences at the expense of its local audiences, nor was it completely enslaved to local customs for the sake of na-tional interests. Neither did it ignore or succumb fully to commercial-izing forces, or to the rivalries of the constituent competing groups. The parade choreography mediated among all of these various influ-ences, acting as a kind of crosstalk, a symbolic interface relevant to all contemporary influences.[9]

In sum, the parade *sinulog* choreography had a variety of meanings that resonated at different levels of magnitude. It had meaning for many onlookers, including most of the *tinderas*, mainly as a beautiful moment. It was as well a tribute to an older ritual. It attracted attention from foreign elements and so meant financial gain for the commercial community indirectly. And it proved to the active participants, whether the choreographers, the dancers, the judges, or the cadets that formed the human chain along the route, that the city's residents valued a resilient spirit of cooperation among themselves, and between themselves and others, and that they could produce that social movement together on a huge scale despite divisive, subversive, and oppressive influences. While the parade *sinulog* was the youngest of the three dance forms practiced in Cebu City, it also spoke to a relatively ancient and originative theme: the city's status as a point of contact for external and internal forces. The decorative frames symbolized in its choreography aptly represented not only the new role of the *sinulog* in the fiesta, but also the city's most fundamental character as a peripheral and marginal locus of human activity—as a place on an edge.

The parade *sinulog* was in many ways an ironic symbol, a paradoxical symbol of desired ethnic recognition that could never be fully understood or interpreted because its image presented conflicting realities. Perhaps the greatest irony of all was the choreography's ultimate assertion of a cultural "region-hood," the successful expression of which was achieved via a choreographic form depicting exactly that which was being denied: the frame or border. Yet the irony of the parade *sinulog* also conveyed the juxtaposition of the contradictory tensions operating in its world. And, in any case, as the choreography made clear, a border could indeed be seen as a sort of region unto itself.

Chapter 13
The Resilience of the *Sinulog*

To return, in conclusion, to the central question of this study, the question of the enduring and dynamic significance of the *sinulog* movement experiences in their urban, transnational, Philippine context, two ways of answering present themselves. There is a semiotic answer, which addresses the symbolic capabilities inherent in the *sinulogs* and their contemporary interrelationship, which produced a complex reality, a resonant polysemic meaningfulness. There is also an answer that focuses on the historical processes influencing the success of the revival, development, and evolution of the *sinulogs*. There is as well an ethnographic question and answer to address: the significance of the *sinulog* as a means of access to understanding the "Culture" and the cultural predicament of the city and its inhabitants.

Contemporary Significance

As the previous chapters have illustrated, the differences in design, performance, and interpretation among the various *sinulog* dances of Cebu City were many and varied. Different forms of symbolism were operating in each of the performance processes. The *sinulogs* presented everything from narrative dance dramas to quasi-trance states and abstract, geometrical designs. The dance events represented everyone from sick children, to civic organizations, to the central figures of local history, to multinational corporations. In their choreography and its symbolic effects, the three *sinulog* variants of Cebu City could hardly have been more different from one another in terms of how they mediated various kinds of information, for whom, and to whom.

The *tindera sinulog* was essentially *mediational*. Of fundamental importance to the choreographic process of the dancing was the awareness that the *tindera* was virtually nothing other than a connecting link in a process of prayer. She was not a shaman, whose movement might reveal some privileged access to extraordinary supernatural powers. The dance characterized the *tindera* simply as a substitute,[1] an empathetic stand-in who acted on behalf of a customer and faced the Santo Niño. The role of the carrier, as opposed to that of the catalyst or instigator, was the primary role assumed by the dancer. The dance thus signified most essentially an effort toward almost completely unqualified continuity, an attempt simply to become or constitute a bridge for an apparent gap that existed between two other subjects, one human, one divine.

The troupe *sinulog*, in contrast, was primarily *depictive*, or iconic in a diagrammatic fashion.[2] Its choreography literally mapped out via dancing bodies the structure of a complex world in action, which was set out before the Santo Niño and before its relatively privileged sponsors. As an exhibitionary statement about the various movement realms associated with *moro* conflict and orthodox Hispanic Roman Catholic worship, the troupe *sinulog* choreography did not seek, as the *tindera* practice did, to represent processually the act of connecting its sponsors and their divine patron. Instead, the choreography attempted to create a likeness between itself and certain collective conventional forms of social action. Its movement symbolism was thus oriented toward the projection of visions and events, not the unfolding of ongoing, inherently unfinishable processes.

The parade *sinulog*, for its part, while also depictive of the "older" ritual *sinulogs*, was at the same time fundamentally *referential* or indexical[3] in terms of its symbolic effect. That is to say, the parade choreography made visible through the organization of its participating contingents an enormous city roster of sorts. The dancing groups catalogued the existence of a growing web of institutions, which were literally behind the parade scenes and which were giving more and more incoming residents a stake in the city's future and a place in its society. The parade *sinulog* idealized the ritual *sinulog* forms. At the same time, however, it also provided through its own processual movement a spectacular vision of integration that attempted to transcend symbolically the fragmented reality of the developing urban situation in which it was located.

In spite of these fundamental differences in choreographic appearance, effect, and symbolism, there also existed among the *sinulog* practices common bonds of meaning. They were bonds so influential that the *sinulogs*, whether they were discussed by observers or performers, were typically referred to as a single dance phenomenon. People did not generally pause to qualify remarks as being relevant to one of the variants in particular, indicating, for example, that a certain statement had been made with specific reference to the *tindera* rituals alone. Nor did they generally deem it necessary to indicate that a certain opinion or description was relevant to "all" the different *sinulog* variants, as opposed to only the ritual or only the secular forms. The choreographic differences, noteworthy as they may have seemed to a foreign observer like myself, were not frequently invoked as "differences that *made* a difference," to use Gregory Bateson's words.[4] They did not often come up as distinctive features carrying information about the meaning of "*sinulog* practice" in the city. Whenever I began an interview regarding a *sinulog*, whenever I came across the mention of the *sinulog* in a text, or whenever the subject was brought up in informal conversation, I never encountered any awareness of ambiguity in what had come to seem to me, after my many observation processes of the three practices, a relatively unspecific use of the term "*sinulog*." Likewise, no one ever asked me, "Now which *sinulog* do you mean?" when I would begin to ask them to describe "*sinulog* dancing" or discuss "its" meaning. The question did not arise, I assumed, because there was, in fact, only one referent of the term "*sinulog*," in spite of my own observations of the choreographic variants.

The generic use of the term, however, did not seem to indicate that a single *sinulog* dance practice had gained prestige over the others as the favored referent. Different people used the term to refer specifically to each of the three forms without qualification, so that it was I who was often obliged to be the one to ask, "Now which *sinulog* do you mean?" I found myself resisting asking this question because it usually created slightly awkward, silent moments. Occasionally people would answer by making a distinction between a "*sinulog*" (the parade dancing) and a "*sinu'ug*" form (the *tindera* and individual devotee dancing). However, for the most part, the term "*sinulog*" was used in what was evidently to me alone an ambiguous manner. Even people who, I was certain, knew of all three dance forms in detail—physical education teachers, theatrical troupe leaders, and *tinderas*—generally did not attempt to discriminate between the three forms of *sinulog* in their own references to them. The *tinderas* would, if drawn out, articulate differences between the style of their own dancing and that of the parade contingents, but nevertheless spoke of the parade dancing as a different version of the same *sinulog* that they practiced themselves. One of the younger *tinderas*, for example, a thirty-five-year-old mother of seven who had been selling regularly at the basilica for only about a year, noted that while the *sinulog* parade was a form of entertaining people (*paghatag ug kalingawan*), its difference from the *tindera* dancing was mainly a matter of costuming. The dancing, this *tindera* believed, could still be considered an act of thanksgiving, particularly since it was only done during the fiesta weekend. Another middle-aged *tindera*, who had been selling for about three years, noted that all *sinulog* movements depended on who was doing the dancing. Among the array of examples she cited were her own style, the style of the *tinderas* at a church on Mactan Island, and the fiesta parade dances, which she noted used many more varied movements than she herself did. The parade *sinulog* was thus included as one variant of a single dance practice.

These repeated conversational experiences made it clear that the three *sinulog* practices had achieved by 1984 and 1985 a certain degree of confluence in the discourse of the city's inhabitants. The dancing of the *tinderas*, the troupes, and the parade contingents appeared to be participating in some sort of public conceptual merger, represented verbally by a single generic "*sinulog*." The basis for this confluence appeared to stem both from common stylistic characteristics inherent in the choreographic details of all three practices, and from certain contextual circumstances influencing the perception and interpretation of all the variants together.

Stylistic Confluences

In regard to the choreographic style, every variant of *sinulog* dancing presented two key stylistic features, both of which were multivocal symbols of local movement habits. These, as previously noted, were resilient phrasing of whole-body weight shifts and a predominantly manipulative gestural process. While both features appeared in every variant, their emphasis and definition were different from practice to practice. However, in all of the forms the relative tacitness of the resilient phrasing, or, to turn the argument around, the relative salience of the gestural movement, formed a common choreographic ground for all the variants.

The significance of resilient phrasing has already been noted in Chapter 4 and elsewhere as a general movement symbol of temporal organization in many domains of Cebu City's public life—linguistic, political, social, and aesthetic. In every *sinulog* variant, however, the presence of resilient phrasing was found to be a tacit feature of the dancing. That is to say, it was not the result of intention or training. Choreographers usually did not speak of teaching resilient stepping to their students, nor did the theatrical troupes or the *tinderas* practice making their steps resilient, even though the *tinderas* did recognize the *kiay* (sway) style of stepping in their dancing as having a positive value. In general, resilience appeared in the movement style as a matter of course, as a character that "went without saying." While it was more pervasive throughout the dancers' bodies in the _tindera_ practice than it was in either the theatrical or parade _sinulog_s, resilience was nevertheless a distinctive feature in all three variants. Its role in each of the three forms was similar. In every case it mobilized the weight support system.

The manipulation of material symbols also appeared in each _sinulog_ practice as a common choreographic feature. In contrast to the tacit character of resilient weight shifting, however, manipulation was a recognized focus of skill development in every case. Moreover, in every variant, manipulation of hand-held symbols was meant to attract the attention of observers specifically to what was being held in hand, diverting the focus from the dancers' persons to the moving objects on their periphery. The material symbols could have been used to reinforce and magnify the presence of their users. When a symphony conductor uses a baton in leading an orchestral performance, for example, the baton becomes an extension of the conductor's body. However, in the _sinulog_ forms, the articles held in hand served as miniature companions to the body, not as limb extensions. They were available as mediators or sources of distraction for the performers as the performers addressed themselves to various observers.

The three _sinulog_ forms all exhibited this trait of being dances of salient material symbols.[5] The hand-held props symbolized a go-between relationship of sorts in every _sinulog_ variant. In the case of the _tindera_ dancing, the "go-between-ness" was most elaborate. The candle was used as a go-between for a dancer who was herself acting mainly as a go-between (the _tindera_) and whose focus of attention was as well a divine go-between—the Santo Niño, Son of God. In the case of the troupe and parade _sinulog_ dances, the material symbols also served as go-betweens mediating the relationship between the dancers and their respective audiences.

These two common stylistic characteristics, resilience and manipulation, complemented one another, creating in every _sinulog_ variant an activity that had a salient theme of manipulating an object and a supportive, tacit resilient energy baseline. Resilient phrasing linked the dancing to the "natural" patterns of healthy life. The general concern with the manipulation of material symbols located all of the performances within a social arena in which animating or realizing a social relationship of manipulating others to deal with still more distantly removed others was a central issue. These two features gave all of the _sinulog_ variants a basic common experiential ground, of sorts, as being to this limited extent the same kind of body movement processes.

Contextual Confluences

Aside from the common details of movement style, however, other sources of commonality were also present in the local *sinulog* context of Cebu City. Most notably, every *sinulog* related its practitioners to the Santo Niño de Cebu. The entry of this most important local figure onto a scene in which a *sinulog* was performed catapulted the significance of the dances, regardless of their choreography, into a special realm, a realm where the most precious icon of Cebuano identity was located. By virtue of this connection alone, the *sinulogs* achieved a prestige unapproached by other local folk dance forms, a prestige that was a reflection of the tremendous influence attributed to the Santo Niño in the city.

The most basic differences in choreographic style among the three *sinulogs* could be understood as being little more than a reflection of the relation each practice established with the Santo Niño de Cebu. That is, when the effect on the Santo Niño alone was most significant, as with the *tindera sinulog*, for example, the dancing exhibited formal characteristics most centrally concerned with internal dynamics of the body's torso or core. When the performance was least concerned with the Santo Niño and most oriented toward a human audience, as with the parade forms, the dancing exhibited formal characteristics most centrally concerned with external effects accomplished by gestural movements. In sum, even though all the *sinulog* performances exhibited both features of resilience and manipulation, resilient weight shifting was the more dominant theme in the ritual practices, while material symbol manipulation became the dominant theme in the more secular or "cultural" parade *sinulog* form. Differences in the relative importance of human and divine reactions created the more noticeable differences in movement style.

In any case, the connection to the Santo Niño, be it weak, as in the parade dances, or strong, as in the ritual forms, created an aura of importance and virtually unquestionable legitimacy about the *sinulog* that dominated its understanding in the city. The Santo Niño de Cebu was thus a main source of confluence for the three *sinulog* variants.

By 1985, the three *sinulog* forms were also generating among themselves new relationships that complicated the contemporary *sinulog* reality in the city. That is to say, the dances were taken as signs of one another, signs that bound them more closely together, even as they served to clarify distinctions among them and among different factions of the residents of the city.

Not all comparisons were contrastive. Consuelo, the *tindera*, for example, reported that the identification of her dancing with that of the *sinulog* parade had increased the appeal of her own performances. More people were now interested in having her dance the *sinulog* when they bought candles than before the promotion had begun. More often, however, comparative observations of the *sinulog* variants tended to be critical. The elaborate group performances of the parade *sinulog*, for example, tended to generate attitudes of disapproval among some members of the city's long-time elite as well as among some of the city's intelligentsia. As a result, the ritual *sinulog* dances gained new meaning and new importance as a "real ritual" for these residents. Troupe members, for example, in 1985 referred to themselves as the "original" *sinulog* performers, the bearers of the authentic ritual tradition. The relationships of comparison most often resulted in increased prestige for the ritual *sinulog* practices, which would have been unimaginable save for the *sinulog* parade development.

In sum, the generic *sinulog* situation in Cebu City was not the result of a simple merging of the older two ritual *sinulog* practices into a newer form—the parade officials' objective in their idealistic *sinulog* synthesis project. Instead, a tension existed between the parade form and the independent courses followed by the ritual practices. This more complex relationship between the older *sinulogs* and the new parade *sinulog* formed the ground from which the notion of "a" contemporary Cebuano *sinulog* emerged. This contemporary Cebu City *sinulog* reality had, as far as I could gather, no actual individual referent in performance. It was a largely conceptual entity that no choreography represented to perfection, and on which no two culture bearers agreed completely. "The" *sinulog* dancing of Cebu City was composed of features of both style and meaning that all three forms possessed in common, as well as being a product of the tensions that their differences, when viewed as interrelationships, created.

Historical Significance

The story of the *sinulog* dancing of Cebu City, when viewed from a historical perspective, is basically a story of revival—a twisted revival, perhaps, but a revival nonetheless. Changes and upheavals of the developing urban society dating back roughly to independence had created a set of constraints and pressures less and less relevant to the ritual *sinulog* performances, which themselves reflected values originating in the nineteenth century and long prior to that time. By 1985, the *habitus* that had inspired and perpetuated the improvised devotee *sinulog* had all but given way to a social scene in which public life was determined less and less by the tacit logics of longstanding daily practices and more and more by conscious choices calculated with respect to increasingly rapid processes of social change. The feeble character and appearance of the *tindera sinulog* body movement style, and the low level of energy and attention exerted by troupe *sinulog* participants, were evidence of the degree to which the style of the ritual performances, by 1985, was becoming exhausted. The performances, particularly the troupe *sinulog*, had achieved a state that anthropologist Stanley Tambiah has defined as "ossified." They were antiquated practices, whose public meaning within the city was in the process of steadily atrophying.[6]

The festival promotion accomplished a spectacularly successful reversal of this process of ossification, infusing meaning into the "traditional" *sinulog* forms that achieved recognition and participation on a massive scale. This government-backed revival was anything but pure. What was revived was not actually the religious practice of the ritual *sinulog* itself, which would have required the restoration of the socioreligious contexts in which the ritual had developed over the centuries. The promotions instead achieved a more limited, though undeniably "revivalesque" effect. That is to say, they effectively revived specifically the *performative* aspect of the ritual *sinulog*. They regenerated a popular interest in the "happening" of the dancing in and of itself, apart from its spiritual and devotional effects. What is most striking about this spectacularly successful revival process is the unlikely historical moment in which it occurred.

Tambiah's model of the cycle of ossification and revivalism, which is conceived of as an unceasing dynamic of oscillation inherent in all ritual, argues that successful popular revivals typically emerge in times of reform, in the dawnings of new eras.[7] Rituals, which necessarily reflect the epistemological and ontological assumptions of their age of origination, inevitably become dated and "ossify" as succeeding generations find the truth and knowledge claims asserted by them increasingly irrelevant to the changes and upheavals of history. Revivalism, then, typically occurs when charismatic leaders first emerge and attempt to coin new doctrinal concepts, often at the same time infusing purified meaning into traditional forms as a means of demonstrating their own commitment to reform. The *sinulog* revival of Cebu City, however, emerged in what was generally perceived to be the closing stage of an increasingly hopeless, desperately conservative period in the nation's history. It appeared toward the end of what many considered to be the country's most disastrous downward spiral of economic and political life, which was usually spoken of as having begun in 1972 with the imposition of martial law. The *sinulog* project was not undertaken in some spirit of reform generated by a recent radical change in leadership or power relations on any level, local, regional, or national. It would be more accurate to characterize it as having been instigated in a spirit of rescue.

The twisted revival of the ritual practice began as one attempt by a badly degenerating national regime to retain its fast-slipping grasp on a troublesome sector of one Filipino society: the college students of Cebu City. Subsequently, the *sinulog* project was transformed into a public relations campaign designed to help keep the city's regional, national, and international reputation afloat during a traumatic, depressed, and uncertain period of its history. In spite of this bleak historical context, or perhaps because of it—because of the pervasive need the times generated to believe in the *possibility* of a new era dawning even when its actual occurrence remained gravely uncertain—a successful, though "impure," revival of the *sinulog* performance process occurred. The dances were transformed from ossified rituals into engaging, immensely popular public culture.

The transformation of *sinulog* dancing in Cebu City was, in this respect, to some extent a reflection of tensions in the urban community's local life. However, the revival was more than a mere reflection. Once its success had been established, it became as well an active agent within the city, a force that influenced the course of sociocultural change. The parade choreography introduced new attitudes toward local realities and asserted new images of local identity. By 1985, these assertions already were beginning to fundamentally change the representation and understanding of several key aspects of the city's self-image.

The Manipulation of the Santo Niño

The most striking example of a changing local identity inspired by contemporary *sinulog* practice directly involved the Santo Niño de Cebu image and its duplicates. By 1985, Santo Niño images had become a popular choice of material symbol for use in the parade *sinulog* choreography.[8] The choice of the Santo Niño image as a hand-held movement symbol lent additional prestige and religious flavor to performances by increasing their resemblance to the traditional religious procession of the Santo Niño de Cebu. The use of the Santo Niño images in the parade *sinulogs*, however, was anything but traditional. The innovations in parade choreography, in fact, radically altered the images' cultural "standing" by involving them in the *sinulog* dancing in this way, as hand props. They graphically depicted a virtual upsetting of the Santo Niño's longtime hold over the city's identity.

As was noted in Chapter 5, the carriage of the Santo Niño in the time-honored processional style of the religious fiesta was performed yearly in Cebu City in a manner consistent with the established character of the Santo Niño de Cebu as a centralizing force in the city. The Niño inspired movement in others, but was meant to remain unmoved itself, and even its orthodox processional ritual minimized the movement possibilities of the image. The manner in which miniature Santo Niño images were handled in the *sinulog* parade, however, was entirely different from this traditional carriage of the Santo Niño image in the solemn fiesta procession. The parade choreography did not employ a carriage style for the images that stressed a ponderous, rigidly controlled form of transportation. In the parade, Santo Niño miniatures were used like the brass pots, flower baskets, and handkerchiefs that also served as material symbols. Their bearers manipulated them with equally buoyant, spatially decorative movements, for the purpose of gestural enhancement (Figure 13.1).

The *sinulog* troupe choreographer, Pitang Diola, was the first to bring to my attention this profound change of attitude apparent in the new style of relating to the Santo Niño. She herself was critical of the treatment of the Santo Niño in the *sinulog* parade choreography. Demonstrating her own rendition of the parade dancers, she defined their behavior as unfocused, uncontrolled, impulsive tossing actions that transported the images around in the space, "here and there" (*itsaitsa*) in a careless manner. She contrasted this behavior to the gesturing done in the troupe ritual, which occurred *in front of* a Santo Niño image that had been placed down somewhere with candles lighted around it. The idea of *sinulog* dancers gesturing *with* a Santo Niño image instead of *for* one was distasteful and even shocking to her. The use of the miniature Santo Niño images made a statement that went directly against the grain of the *sinulog* ritual tradition as she had practiced it.

The parade *sinulog* performances, by choosing to manipulate images of the Santo Niño itself, waving images to and fro in a carefree, high-spirited manner, abolished the fundamental symbolic opposition between motionless divinity and mobile devotee that had played such a crucial role in stabilizing Cebu City's identity and making the city into something other than a mercantile transit point. The new use of the Santo Niño images destabilized what had heretofore been the single most stable element in the *sinulog* ritual performances and relegated the image to a subordinate role. No longer cast as a center inspiring pilgrimage, the age-old apparent magnetism of the Niño image was symbolically obliterated in this new parade style of image manipulation.

The spectators and performers engaged in the parade *sinulog* performances thus constructed and bore witness to a new, less "center-

Figure 13.1. Parade dancer manipulating a Santo Niño in the *"itsaitsa"* style.

ing" role for the Santo Niño in Cebu City. The dancing reinforced both physically and mentally the attitude that the Niño was available for manipulation and that it was the object, not the magnetic source, of inspiration for "cultural" movement.

Through innovations like the manipulation of the Santo Niño miniatures, the changing *sinulog* choreography allowed parade participants to apprehend the changes that had taken place and were taking place in their society in terms of vivid and meaningful symbols. The choreography also served as a means of persuasion. It encouraged participants to empathize and go along with the various institutions governing the city by involving them in an aesthetic, recreational practice that restructured their thoughts and feelings about the organizations via familiar and pleasurable forms. My anthropologist friend, Elizabeth, had once remarked that she and all her extended family looked forward to the yearly *sinulog* parade as an enjoyable occasion. They perceived the parade as a time to join in, in whatever manner might be allowed, a beautiful celebration. People participating in the *sinulog* intellectually and physically "went along with" the values and attitudes represented in the choreography. They watched, cheered, and danced with the various contingents, getting themselves "in sync" with one after another over the course of the huge spectacle.

In this respect, the new parade forms achieved the status of something similar to what James Peacock, in his landmark study of Javanese popular theatre, has described as a "rite of modernization."[9] They provided one means of defining the movements of Cebu City's complex society from one set of patterns of thinking about itself to another—a distinctly cultural movement. The dances articulated the modern awareness of the city as a network not simply of families, but of institutions, which were immensely influential, if not easily visible. They also defined the city as a regional center not only for religious pilgrimage, but for visitors with a variety of secular interests, tourism prominent among them. Finally, they represented Cebuanos as a people who, as Filipino citizens, were concerned with their collective identity and who, aside from performing authentic rituals, valued the preservation of authenticated cultural forms.

Ethnographic Significance

In one of the landmark works establishing the legitimacy of interpretive ethnographic inquiry, Clifford Geertz (1973:453) argued, "Societies, like lives, contain their own interpretations. One has only to learn how to gain access to them." Gaining access to the depictions, the images, the indicators, the accounts, the arguments—in sum, to all the various interpretative expressions of an "other" people—invariably involves the study of symbolism. However, no single form of symbolism, as the open-ended quotation indicates, necessarily has more to offer ethnographic inquiry than any other. Each facet of social life, from mythology to subsistence practices, provides some possibility of insight into cultural phenomena. Virtually no moment of social existence is completely without some ongoing process of representation or utterly beyond some subsequent process of culturally relevant interpretation. In the effort to "gain access" to cultural insights, the interpretive ethnographer is not bound to start anywhere or in any way in particular.

In my attempt to start with choreographic phenomena to perform an ethnographic process, I sought to interpret Cebu City through its most intangible and immaterial (some would say its most inconsequential) symbolic forms, in the symbolism evident in the physical behavior and personal conduct of its inhabitants. To borrow Lévi-

Strauss's famous structural categories, I sought it in both the relatively "raw" behavior of everyday pedestrian life and in the relatively "cooked" behavior of choreographed, more explicitly "symbolic" public action. The exoticism and "otherness" of the city became accessible to me through these physical movements. "Readable" social dramas in miniature occurred every time passing strangers had to organize their collective process of doing something as universally ordinary as crossing a street. Likewise, in the choreographic choices of the *sinulog* practices, a mix of interpretations regarding the city's cultural predicament were also inscribed and expressed.

That Cebu City was in fact a locus of culture, in spite of the aura of cultural uncertainty that arose from its geo-economic marginality, was never a question for me, given my particular points of choreographic access. As a student of performance stepping into this culture, learning to identify and execute the movements of everyday practice immediately attuned me to distinctive values implicit in the city's activity profile. The culture of the city—its enduring patterns of learned collective experience—leapt out at me every time I waved hello, said good-bye, picked up a spoon, caught a ride, made an agreement, or heard an announcement. Observing carefully and attempting to *assume* completely the tiny, nondescript moments of bodily conduct (appreciating the design and construction of rising quickness in a consenting eyebrow raise, for example) there could be no doubt that the culture of the local scene was one in which the patterning of balance, timing, cooperation, attention giving, power grabbing, freedom finding, and numerous other kinds of social processes had been as deftly and distinctively crafted here as they were any place in the world. The jeepney drivers navigating Colon Street, the market vegetable vendors seeking shelter from the midday sun, the stevedores loading and unloading produce at the pier, all of the characters that inhabited this port throughout their daily lives bore its habits of action, which were both as old as the city's steeply sloping hills in some cases and as new as its postmodern tourist hotels in others.

However, as I also was to learn through my choreographic projects, what was at issue in Cebu City was the "productivity" (in the sense of being rendered visible) of culture, or more precisely the disturbing, seductive capacity for disappearance attributed to the more conventional signs of that phenomenon. As was noted in Chapter 4, in this developing neocolonial environment, the materialistic and objective aspects of social life were growing more and more problematic in terms of their capacity to bear resemblance to anything noted as being distinctively local in design—a concern that was itself a product of the neocolonial situation. Unlike the behavior I was performing and observing, material constructs in the city were a source of cultural anxiety. The more prestigious and outstanding edifices drew most purely on resources and technologies that were globally prevalent. To the more materially minded observer, and certainly to many of those who supported the *sinulog* parade development, Cebu City in 1984 and 1985 appeared to be on its way to becoming another colorless example of the "global village" syndrome. Its local culture seemed to be in danger of disappearing forever.

It was thus partly in its opposition to the city's material realm that the choreography of each *sinulog* variant became ethnographically meaningful. The *sinulog* choreography was a point of access for understanding the articulation of local "othernesses" in the contemporary urban context. The choreography made what were judged to be the disappearing aspects of local social life—forms of local symbolism possessing a relatively high degree of temporal continuity—visible and productive.

This ethnography of the *sinulog* is thus, in the end, a story of the emergent relationships that choreographic phenomena can maintain both with culture and with various cultural predicaments—that is to say, with the social strategies of communities constantly negotiating among radically different cultural traditions in postmodern contexts. Working as a student of choreography with the performers, choreographers, and other participants involved with the *sinulog* performances, it was evident to me that in Cebu City these relationships were not mechanical, automatic, or completely dominated by any established power structure. They did not present some transparent reference to the locality, be it the *habitus* of the *tinderas,* evolved from antiquity, or an institution of the contemporary moment sponsoring a parade *sinulog* contingent. These choreographic relationships worked imaginatively via a physical symbolism and practice that had to effect a poignancy and immediate sense of relevance in its practitioners if it was to survive. They were thus relationships that were never absolutely constrained by established "powers" or by the idiosyncrasies of individual practitioners, even though they were relationships that entailed both of these. They were not predictable relationships. To comprehend them, it was necessary to move with them as they were in the process of unfolding.

Decisions were revealed in the *sinulog* choreographic forms, bodily experiences that were *rendered* and made to acquire both formal constraints and social values. Choices were made in the genesis and practice of these choreographic practices that attuned them to the moment-to-moment realities of the city, to the actuality of being alive in that place, and to an especially vivid experience of that actuality.

What was preserved, what was erased, what was put in, what was left out, what was modified, qualified, distorted, or developed—these were choices evident in the *sinulog* choreographic practices that gained meaning as they were set against the location where they were created and employed. They were decisions that revealed what, in the face of a changing and uncertain cultural environment, was worth being included in the visible record of the city's identity. They were also decisions that revealed, sometimes more through the creation of absences than the creation of presences, perceptions of the changing forces that governed local social life.

Choreographic forms, when interpreted in this light, as one crystallization or precipitate of a people's habits of life and philosophies of action, become one point of access to cultural phenomena such as Geertz envisioned. They become interpretive acts that represent the dynamics of culture and of cultural interaction and transformation. Cultural phenomena, as far as they can be defined in universal terms, are, if nothing else, learned and thus vulnerable phenomena. Cultural phenomena must find various means of being borne through time, of remaining present in the face of social change. Choreographic activity, through its own decision-making processes of physical rendering, serves in a distinctive way this cultural need: the need to be remembered—the need to be rendered animate in an immediate sense. Choreographic phenomena, in this respect, always represent on some level the recent findings of culture bearers, findings about the world they physically inhabit, findings about the society they embody, findings about what it means to be a living, breathing human being in their particular place, in their particular historical moment. These were the findings made available to me in my "ethnographic waltz" with the *sinulog*s of Cebu City. They are the findings of a form of symbolism that should always be of central value to the discipline of ethnography: the uniquely human act of dancing.

Notes

Chapter 1. Ethnography and Choreography

1. The notion of a "cultural predicament," used here in place of the standard notion of culture, was developed by James Clifford (1988) in order to recognize the general and profound impact of "modernity," in his terms, on small- and large-scale societies all over the world. The "predicament" of culture in the contemporary multinational world system arises from the constant movements *between* radically different cultural frameworks, as was the case in Cebu City. This perpetual displacement of social frames of reference (which is directly related in Clifford's view to the merger of local and global economic institutions) results in a perception of loss vis-à-vis "pure" cultural traditions, and in social situations where the "exotic" becomes uncannily nearby and accessible, while at the same time "global village" homogenization appears increasingly prevalent as well. Cultural identities become negotiable, and a public sense of an endangered culture related to the destruction of some mythic source of ancient culture becomes increasingly prevalent. All of these conditions manifested in the case of the *sinulog* civic promotional project of Cebu City. Clifford argues that a realistic study of "cultures" must recognize their contemporary predicament: their attunement to processes of both homogenization and inventive differentiation. The present study attempts to maintain Clifford's orientation.

The phrase "choreographic phenomena" is used here and throughout the text to identify a range of symbolic body movement processes somewhat broader than the term "choreography" generally denotes. "Choreographic phenomena" include movement processes, such as ritual body movement practices, and folk dance traditions that, although they are not the work of an individual choreographer, nevertheless are composed of patterned, symbolic (whether it be latent or explicitly recognized) body movement experiences that are generally recognized as "dance" behavior or "dance-like" behavior.

2. The "powerful reasons" here alluded to are both philosophical and methodological in kind, and a study of their own would be needed to address them comprehensively. Very briefly, as several scholars writing on dance already have noted (see, for example, Cowan 1990; Novack 1988, 1990; Foster 1986; Hanna 1979, 1983, 1988; and Hackney 1988, to name only a few),

also sounds like Stuart Hall

"thick" as opposed to "shallow" interpretations of choreographic phenomena, when attempted from within Euro-American philosophical, linguistic, and socio-political paradigms, have encountered and must bear, oppose, or transcend a number of trivializing, denigrating, and, above all, naturalizing or essentializing cultural biases regarding the possible meaning(s) dance practices might conceivably acquire or mediate. Foster (1986:xiii–xxi), in particular, adopting a theoretical orientation combining elements of the work of both Barthes and Foucault, has addressed the problematic predominance of the notion of the "natural" as a constraining interpretive frame for American dance practices, viewing both the relatively oppressed role of dance artists in American society and the devaluation of choreography as an inferior form of symbolic expression as consequences, in part, of this essentializing interpretive stance. Foster argues that the popular understanding of dance practices as "natural" forms of activity tends to cast choreographic phenomena as an outlet mainly for intuitive or unconscious feelings, which are then seen to be expressed in transparent and obvious ways, requiring little or no interpretive effort (1986:xiv–xv).

This restrictive orientation toward interpreting and analyzing choreographic phenomena can itself be understood as an outgrowth or carryover of deeply rooted negative attitudes toward bodily experiences in general and toward the notion of "the body" itself, with which choreographic phenomena are typically closely associated. This notion of "the body" in Western thought generally connotes mortality and instinctive, vulgar animality. In all the bodily systems, in the neuromuscular system that orchestrates the act of dance, voluntary and involuntary processes work simultaneously. Both voluntary and involuntary processes exert an influence on the act of performance, which is constrained by mechanical and biological conditions as certainly as it is liberated by the creativity of human intelligence. "The body" thus serves as a frustrating reminder that its corresponding element in the Western human being, "the mind" is not free of physical and mechanical laws. (See Todd 1937, Hall 1959, Scheflen 1982, and Murphy 1987 for discussions of "the body" from a variety of perspectives—kinesiology, nonverbal communication, behavioral psychology, and cultural anthropology—as a problematized, anxiety-ridden concept in Euro-American worldviews. See also Hackney 1988, and especially Novack 1988, 1990, for statements concerning the constraining impact of this stigmatized notion of "the body" on dance research and education. Also see de Certeau 1984 for a discussion of the biases against the notion of "the individual" in the social sciences—a concept closely associated with and imposed on the analysis of choreographic phenomena via the concept of "the body.") Sexist biases toward the art of dance, which may themselves be considered one particular manifestation of essentially body-oriented prejudices, have also discounted and inhibited the serious study and interpretation of choreographic phenomena. (See Hanna 1988: 119–49 for a discussion of the constraining effects of sexist biases against dance in Western cultures.)

Recent works in cultural anthropology studying "the self" as a social construct—work built in part on the pioneering efforts of such nonverbal behavior researchers as E. Goffman and Ray Birdwhistell—have gone some distance toward calling into question this prevailing "anti-body/individual" orientation. (See especially Singer 1980 and Rosaldo 1980 in this regard. Bourdieu 1977; Douglas 1973; Foucault 1978, 1979; and Scarry 1985 have also contributed landmark studies toward developing a "de-naturalized" theory of the body as historically and socially constituted.) Nevertheless, a general prejudice against work that aims "merely" to account for patterns of bodily-hence-"natural" conduct remains. This situation makes the articulation and analysis of cultural salience in choreographic symbolism particularly problematic for contemporary Euro-American readerships.

In addition to the various philosophical biases inscribed within Euro-American interpretive paradigms, there is the related methodological problem of representing choreographic phenomena in textual form, through written language. All views of human action that are represented in language, from the most literal and seemingly transparent to the most figurative—are "linguicentric" views, which carry cultural baggage of their own sort. To give only a very basic example of the problems of distortion and interference inherent in cross-linguistic, cross-cultural representation of choreographic practices, compare the terms that refer to "lower limb" in English and in Cebuano (one dialect of the Visayan language spoken throughout the Central Philippines). In English, the term "leg" refers to this general area of the body. In Cebuano, the term *tiil* is used to refer to the same area. The two terms appear to be simple equivalents at first glance. *Tiil*, however, actually translates as either "lower limb" or "foot." In English, "leg" also has a more narrow, although somewhat archaic, meaning, referring specifically to the calf area, the columnar tissue mass between knee and foot. The Cebuano *tiil* generalizes the distal end of the limb, so that the more generic reference to the lower limb is made in terms of that distal end. The English "leg," in contrast, generalizes from the muscular aspect of the less proximal long bone. The prototypical element for "lower limb" in Cebuano thus differs from that in English, creating two markedly different images of what "lower limbness" amounts to in each language. Describing the mental and physical experience of doing a Cebuano dance step can thus easily be distorted if English labels for body parts are used without qualification.

However, difficulty may also arise among observers from the same culture in describing even the most obvious aspects of a performance process, aspects that may seem transparent and straightforward to the naive observer. The following conversation between Franz and Franziska Boas about a Kwakiutl dance, for example, illustrates the awareness of the descriptivist tradition in ethnographic inquiry to this issue:

Franziska Boas:	I am impressed with the lightness of the feet even with the difficult bending of the knees. . . .
Franz Boas:	Lightness!
Franziska:	Even in dancing on the plank.
Franz:	Very complicated.
Franziska:	In most Indian dances there is a stamping of the foot which I miss completely among Kwakiutl. Even Blackfeet have the stamp. That is more significant, this lightness, than the cramped position in a canoe.
Franz:	Don't you think the Pueblo are light?
Franziska:	They stamp, the body goes down with a push. Such a different relationship to the earth. (Boas 1944:19)

Franz Boas's exclamation, "Lightness!," reveals the problematic nature of describing the quality of even a familiar movement, such as a stamp. What exactly is meant by the term "lightness" in the above discussion? Does this term refer to a dynamic quality, a kind of energy apparent in the movement process? Does it mean that the foot's contact with the ground is controlled? Does it mean that only the edges of the body move and not the center of gravity? As Franz Boas's responses indicate, there is no way of knowing what exactly Franziska means by this term or to what it might be compared.

There are no easy solutions to the problem of representing choreographic phenomena legitimately and without distortion in linguistic textual form, just as there are no easy alternatives for Western readers to the philosophical paradigms problematizing "the body" and its practices. There is no escape from the historical and cultural baggage that inevitably accompanies a linguistic representation of the bodily experiences of another culture. There can be no absolutely objective and completely unproblematic description of an "other" culture's dances. To attempt a pure representation of such phenomena would involve either redefining or annotating every term used in the description or inventing a new vocabulary set and perhaps a new set of syntactic operations. In sum, it would require a new language altogether, something that would be practically impossible and that would inhibit readership significantly, if not absolutely.

It is the position of this study that a linguistic account of choreographic experiences, such as is here attempted, must acknowledge the ever-present potential for distortion, but at the same time must use the full resources of the language conscientiously and creatively in order to represent these experiences as vividly and accurately as the language will allow. Ideally, the very act of careful descriptive interpretation, when successful, can serve to override whatever negative cultural biases might be at work, inhibiting the reader's interpretive process. Linguistic systems and the ideological frameworks they include must be recognized as deeply compromised instruments of communication, insofar as the field of cross-cultural dance research is concerned. However, they remain nonetheless widely accessible modes of representation and analysis that the discipline cannot yet do without.

3. Fredric Jameson (1983, 1984), in fact, has gone so far as to suggest that the quintessential aesthetic expressions of contemporary U.S. society are precisely those in which the well-informed, spatially relevant movement of the bodily self (i.e., dancing) becomes a mental and physical impossibility. Choreography thus appears to be inherently meaningless and inappropriate as an art form in this historical moment. This culturally dominant "postmodern" expressive mode is directly linked, in Jameson's view, to the emergence of multinational capitalism (1984:55, 78). In the society of consumer-oriented "late capitalism," Jameson argues, social space becomes transformed into "postmodern hyperspace," in which the capacity of the individual human body to locate itself and organize its activity in relation to the now overbuilt environment is lost (1984:83–84). As a result, the individual subject disappears, the privileged space of art is radically antianthropomorphized, the human body is fetishized, and, through technology, the human being is immobilized and its movement capabilities are replaced by transportation machinery. For a particularly vivid description of the cultural predicament of

the moving body in postmodern experience, see Jameson's description of the
Bonaventura hotel (1984:80–84).

4. To speak briefly to the contemporary marginality of research on dance
within the discipline of cultural anthropology, it should be noted (as Anya P.
Royce most notably has done in *The Anthropology of Dance*, 1980) that the cultural significance of choreographic phenomena was once recognized and
taken seriously by leading figures at the centers of the discipline, both in
Europe and in the United States. From the work of Lewis Henry Morgan,
Edward B. Tylor, and Sir James Frazer through to Franz Boas, Radcliffe-
Brown, Evans-Pritchard, Gregory Bateson, and Margaret Mead, anthropologists of earlier research generations, to paraphrase Stanley J. Tambiah (1979:
113), once paid surprisingly close attention to choreographic traditions. That
Tambiah should characterize this interest in choreographic phenomena as
surprising reveals a change in orientation that occurred within the discipline,
roughly concurrently with the ascendency of what may be seen as a third
generation of cultural anthropologists in the United States. Nevertheless, to
follow Paul Spencer's summary account (1985:1–46), anthropologists have
long acknowledged, and continue to acknowledge in a general way, choreographic phenomena as a noteworthy sign of culture in several respects. The
emotional, often cathartic experiences afforded by dance practices, the educational role of dance traditions in the transmission of cultural sentiments and
values, the importance of dance practices as organs of social control, these
have all served as legitimate topics of anthropological inquiry. Yet, as the discipline of cultural anthropology has expanded and developed, the tendency,
as Royce has noted (1980:38), has been to regard dance more and more as
an artistic mystery, to enjoy it as an entertaining artifact of culture, but to
ignore it as a topic of serious research. Dance practices, instead of remaining
in the mainstreams of research on cultural phenomena, have instead become,
in Spencer's words, "an obscure rather than a challenging phenomenon, . . .
too big to miss—and yet we still somehow miss it" (1985:ix). As Jane K.
Cowan, following Adrienne Kaeppler (1978a), has most recently expressed
the situation, a "legacy of inattention" to dance has evolved and continues
within the field of ethnographic inquiry (1990:5).

The general tendency to "naturalize," discount, and dismiss bodily/choreo-
graphic phenomena, noted by Foster with respect to contemporary American
concert dance (see note 2 above), has appeared in the discipline of anthropology as well, with similar consequences. To quote Novack (1990:7), "many
cultural observers and researchers ignore the body and its trappings, seeing
them as irrelevant trappings for the mind." Even cultural observers, including such nonmarginal anthropologists as Mary Douglas, for example, who
currently do pay attention to movement and the body, tend to do so, Novack
argues, only in order to see the "mind" that lies behind them.

The present study follows Novack's orientation in its attempt to return
bodily experience *as a form of consciousness and understanding* to a central place
within the discipline of ethnographic inquiry, recognizing that to deny the
interpretive potential of bodily/choreographic phenomena is to deprive ethnography of understanding an activity that may be as central to the human
experience of another culture as it is marginal to that of mainstream U.S.
society.

5. Stoller has called for an anthropology of "radical empiricism" that would

refocus ethnographic writing on evocative descriptions (as opposed to universal explanations) toward the end of creating vivid and novel insights into the heterogeneity of cultural experience. See Stoller (1989:54–55, 142–56.)

6. See, for example, Cynthia Novack's discussion of the myth of the mind/body dissociation in U.S. popular culture (1988).

7. To compare the movement analyst's observatory experience to that of a deaf person, see the detailed observations of Oliver Sacks in his account of the congenitally deaf, *Seeing Voices: A Journey into the World of the Deaf* (1989).

8. The phrase "ways of operating" and the claim for their general obscurity in social science research are both asserted by Michel de Certeau (1984:xi) in his attempt to find a means of discussing the human experience of the relatively dominated members of contemporary societies, the "consumers." The present study, with its performative and choreographic approach and focus, closely aligns itself with de Certeau's "practice" orientation. It may be seen as one way of taking seriously his call to examine carefully and bring into the foreground of analysis some of the routine physical practices of the members of a complex society, in this case a Philippine coastal urban society. As in de Certeau's approach, the objective of such an inquiry is to make explicit the models of action developed and actively employed by social subjects who might otherwise be represented only as passive, thoughtless postindustrial pawns, trapped into systems of production whose rules and structures apparently leave them no place or means to act creatively or intelligently, or in ways that would lead to the fulfillment of their own individual desires and interests. In paying attention to such features of everyday practice as the unremarkable daily uses of space, the ways of frequenting or dwelling in public places, the physical culture of subsistence practices (cooking, eating, resting, walking, sleeping, etc.)—in short, all of the aspects of life a student of choreography is *also* drawn to observe and value as sources of inspiration and insight into human experience—an appreciation may be gained of otherwise hidden, desirous, and enjoyable dimensions of these members' cultural predicament. The full range of meaning implicit in more extraordinary forms of symbolic action, such as dance practices, may be better understood as well. In this regard, de Certeau's interest in "practiced" life is not fundamentally different from a choreographic interest; hence his ideas and insights have been particularly influential in this study and will appear as organizing concepts in several chapters.

9. This notion of "at-one-ment" was suggested by E. V. Daniel with reference to the category of "firstness" in semeiotic theory in a lecture given at the University of Washington in 1986. Daniel (1984:233–87) has observed that certain kinds of South Asian ritual experiences may be designed around what semeiotic theory would describe as a "degenerative" process of signification, whereby participants move through stages of awareness that progress from experiences of "thirdness" (mediation, continuity, interpretation, regularity, destiny) to those of "firstness" (emotion, miraculousness, aliveness). The notion of achieving "at-one-ment" through an ethnographic or choreographic experience suggests a similar sort of degenerate progression: a learning process that moves from a largely conceptual, object-oriented, self-removed, and relatively superficial understanding of some given form of social action and social grouping to a practiced, intersubjective (following Dumont 1978), and more profoundly humane and masterly awareness of that same phenomenon.

10. To speak briefly to the specific derivation of the interpretive method used in this study, the general orientation assumed here follows most closely the pragmatic semiotic approaches to ethnographic inquiry developed by E. V. Daniel (1984) and Michelle Z. Rosaldo (1980). The methodology of this study is also consistent with the intersubjective approach developed by Jean-Paul Dumont (1978) and with the process- and performance-oriented work of such symbolic anthropologists as Victor Turner, Roy Rappaport, Simon Ottenberg, James Fernandez, James Peacock, Edward Schieffelin, Stephen Feld, and Judith Hanna. To elaborate briefly, Daniel's approach, which is itself derived from the interpretive ethnography of Clifford Geertz following Max Weber (see Geertz 1973:3–32), is to view the object of ethnographic inquiry, "culture," as a complex pattern of signs, a creative and inherently communicative phenomenon. Culture manifests when public and private aspects of human experience become "mutually immanent" (Daniel 1984:13) or simultaneously present and active in moments of social action. Culture, according to this view, is constructed through interaction. It is a product that the ethnographer and those he works with create together, as the accounts given in the chapters to follow will exemplify. Rosaldo's approach also focuses ethnographic inquiry on the study of symbols (mainly linguistic symbols) in relation to social action and locates cultural phenomena in subjective, emotional, and physical experience, as personal in some cases as the awareness of the movements of one's own heart. Both Rosaldo's and Daniel's approaches place special emphasis on attending to the dynamism inherent in cultural signification. Both envision an ethnographic process focused on the analysis of symbolic movements, which construct culturally distinctive notions of the self in social life. In this respect, these approaches are especially supportive of and compatible with a study such as this one, which seeks to identify relationships between bodily/choreographic action and cultural meanings. Viewed from these perspectives, choreographic practices ("dance traditions") may be conceived of as the public crystallizations of phrases of bodily movement symbolism that, for various reasons, gain prestige in communities and achieve the status of performing arts or ritual acts. Even a movement symbol as subtle as the scoop of a person's arm may be seen to represent a complex of bodily relationships, each of which may carry information about the performer, about the performance, about the design of the choreography, or about some aspect of the performance context. Choreographic phenomena thus present both mental and physical patterns that may signify the dynamic reality of social life and make visible both collective and individual and public and private experiences of that reality. By identifying the preferences that create the style of a choreographic practice, it is possible to articulate a value system, a system of "significant moves," the close observation and interpretation of which may reveal key attitudes toward, and models of coping with, a given way of life. In sum, as Allen (1988) has said of the coca-chewing practices of the *runakuna* people of highland Peru, the study of choreographic phenomena may provide one inroad toward understanding the kind of hold life can have on a group of human beings. As such, the study of choreographic phenomena is centrally relevant to studies of culture that adopt a pragmatic semiotic perspective.

11. As Baudrillard has noted (1990:34), the original literal meaning of the verb "to produce" was not "to fabricate" but "to render visible" or "to make appear."

Chapter 3. Views from the Swimming Pool

1. San Carlos University is one of the oldest, largest, and most prestigious Catholic universities in the Central Philippines. It is administrated by priests from the order of the Society of the Divine Word. The institution, however, traces its origins to a Jesuit school, the Seminario de San Carlos, founded in 1595. See Mojares (1983:73) for a more detailed discussion of the history of San Carlos University; see also Fenner (1985:43–45, 160–65).

2. Michel Foucault defines the notion of the "gaze" as an act of seeing, an act of selective perception that has a direct bearing on thought and action. See Foucault (1963, 1975); see also Stoller (1989:37–39, 56–68) for extended discussion and application of the Foucaultian gaze.

3. See Rafael (1988:1–23, especially pages 15–17), for a more detailed analysis of this process and its significance for social scientists specializing in Philippine studies.

4. As quoted in Mojares (1983:80).

5. See Mojares (1983) and Cullinane (1982:251–96; 1989) for extensive accounts of the history and protohistory of Cebu City, including the origin and development of its mestizo community. See also Fenner (1985:45–49, 144–75) for an account of the emergence and development of the entrepreneurial mestizo group.

6. A significant exception to the pattern was the Cebuano Studies Center—the richest reservoir of local information and a prime mover in the localization process. The director, Resil B. Mojares, came from a Cebuano family originally from the southern part of the island.

7. See Keyes (1977:259–338) for a more extensive discussion of the "temple city."

8. See, for example, Renato Rosaldo's arguments concerning the informal disciplinary evaluation of cultures (1988:77–87).

9. The Philippines in 1984 had seventy-three provinces, combined into twelve regions plus the National Capitol Region; Cebu City is the capital of Cebu Province and the regional center of Region VII, Central Visayas. The region includes Bohol, Siquihor, and Negros Oriental provinces. According to *Philippines 1980: Population, Land Area, and Density, 1970, 1975, and 1980* (1981), Cebu City had a population of 490,281. However, even if only its two largest suburbs of Mandaue City (population 110,590), and Lapulapu City (population 98,723) were taken into account, the urban settlement population approached 600,000. Mojares (1981) estimated that the population of the Metro Cebu area was around 800,000. The next largest urban settlement in the province was Toledo, with a population of only 91,668—a little more than one-tenth the size of Metro Cebu, which, according to a 1987 Visayas Human Development Agency, Inc. (VIHDA) study, eventually included the six municipalities of Compostela, Liloan, Consolacion, Talisay, Minglanilla, and Naga in addition to Mandaue City to the northeast and the city of Lapulapu on the island of Mactan to the east (the provincial government of Cebu, however, in its Five-Year Integrated Development Plan put out in 1976, included Danao City, 33 kilometers from Cebu City, and Cordova municipality, 19 kilometers from the city, in their definition of Metro Cebu, giving it a population of 844,449 as early as 1975). Likewise, if growth were measured in terms of population density increase, Cebu City proper was growing at a

rate of around 30 percent over a ten year-period, from 1970 to 1980. Mandaue and Lapulapu cities were growing at even faster rates for the same period, roughly 90 percent and 40 percent, respectively, and their growth rates were on the rise. The density of the province, in contrast, was changing at a rate of only about 30 percent over the same span, about three fifths the rate of the average of the main urban settlements composing Metro Cebu, about 50 percent over ten years. Metropolitan Manila, or the National Capital Region, was also growing denser at a rate of around 50 percent over a decade, in contrast to the nation, which was growing denser at only around 30 percent for the same period of time. Both the relatively large population and the relatively rapid growth pattern are typical of "primate" cities. See Keyes (1977:259–337) and Ginsburg (1955:455–57).

10. According to *Philippines 1980: Population, Land Area, and Density 1970, 1975, and 1980*, Cebu City proper grew from 347,116 in 1970 to 490,281 in 1980, a 40 percent increase over ten years (National Economic and Development Authority 1981).

11. The estimate of 40 percent is taken from survey research conducted by VIDHA in 1985 and published in 1987: *A Study of Urban Poor Dwellers, Their Attitudes and Responses to Government Initiated Development Programs: The Case of Four Selected Communities in Cebu City* (Visayas Human Development Agency, 1987). The study estimated that 232,520 people were living in slum settlements, with population in these areas increasing at a rate of 15 percent a year, based on 1975 survey information.

12. The *Cebu Labor Situationer: Base to Societal Change* (Visayas Human Development Agency, 1983:84), in a socio-economic profile of Cebu, included a report based on data from the Ministry of Labor and Employment Services (MOLE) stating that the average earnings for 96 percent of the urban households in Cebu Province were 23 pesos a day, or 690 pesos a month. The National Census and Statistics Office was quoted as reporting that the average minimum monthly rate a worker should receive in order to support the average family of six should be around 1,755.14 pesos a month (1983:70). The poverty line figure was quoted as 1,999 pesos a month (1983:84). The same publication calculated the inflation rate for 1982 to be 15 percent a year. In October 1984, however, *The Far Eastern Economic Review* estimated an inflation rate of 60 percent for the nation for the year ahead (Sacerdoti 1984:84).

13. See William Henry Scott (1968:41, 42); Karl Hutterer (1973); Rosa Tenazas and Karl Hutterer (1968); and Otley Beyer (1947) for discussions of the pre-Hispanic trade network in which Cebu City participated. Bruce Fenner (1985:14–19), summarizing these earlier writings, notes that Ming blue and white ceramics excavated in the city provide the best evidence of Cebu City's trade with China at least a century before Spanish arrival. In exchange for porcelain imports, Cebu City traded gold brought from other islands in the archipelago, as well as pigs, wine, fruits, and cotton. In addition to Chinese trade, archaeological evidence indicates that a porcelain trade with Sukhotai and Sawankalok, in Thailand, as well as areas of Vietnam was also in existence. There is also evidence of a spice, silk, and religious imagery trade with the Moluccas. As Fenner summarizes, "When the Spanish arrived in Cebu they found a prosperous port with a long-standing tradition of commercial relations with other parts of Asia" (1985:30). He estimates

the city's population at contact at around 2,000, citing Canute Van de Meer (1967:319).

14. Land area for the city was measured at 281 square kilometers, according to *Philippines 1980: Population, Land Area, and Density, 1970, 1975, and 1980* (National Economic and Development Authority 1981).

15. The city of Davao had a population of 610,375 in 1980, still one-tenth the size of Metro Manila's; however, Davao's land area of 2,211 square kilometers made it nearly four times as large as Manila, and ten times as large as Cebu City. While Davao was comparable to Cebu City in population, it was also much less dense. However, it was growing denser even more rapidly than Cebu City, at a rate of 55 percent between 1970 and 1980. See *Philippines 1980: Population, Land Area, and Density, 1970, 1975, and 1980* (National Economic and Development Authority 1981).

16. *The Cebu Labor Situationer* reported that the exports for Cebu had totaled nearly U.S. $183 million and that imports were valued at over U.S. $60 million during the first two quarters of 1983 (Visayas Human Development Agency, 1983:46). It also estimated that Cebu Island held 61 percent of the nation's reserves in copper and gold and 96 percent of the nation's cement raw materials reserves. In addition, 98 percent of the nation's limestone reserves were located on the island. In 1982, the mining industry was the single most lucrative industry in the province, with a gross domestic product in constant pesos valued at 873 million. Copper exports from the province for the first two quarters of 1983 were valued at over U.S. $100 million (1983:80). However, according to the *The Cebu Labor Situationer* (citing the Region 7 National Census and Statistics Office), mining employed less than 2 percent of the province's work force (1983: table 8 and figure 2-B, pages unnumbered).

17. *The Cebu Labor Situationer* (Visayas Human Development Agency, 1983: 380) estimated that 72 percent of the Cebu port trade was made up of copper, coconut oil, copra products, lumber, and dolomite, using the term "traditional" to describe these products. All other crop production was included in the remaining 28 percent of the trade. Mangoes, for example, were the province's largest fruit crop (National Census and Statistics Office 1985). In 1985, 9,992,376 kilograms of mangoes were produced in Cebu Province, the largest production figure for all fruit crops listed. Mangoes, however, were reported as only a U.S. $500,000 export trade, ranking far behind rattan and buri furniture, which together amounted to a U.S. $24 million export trade total. *The Cebu Labor Situationer* (citing the Region 7 National Census and Statistics Office as its source) estimated that 58 percent of Cebu's work force (estimated at 1,149,675, or 55 percent of the total population) was employed in agriculture, fishing and forestry occupations (1983:83x, table 8, figure 2-B). The *1980 Census of Agriculture* reported that 149,486 farms were operating in Cebu province, run by 541,701 workers, with a total population of 748,746 (the province's population in 1980 was 2,091,692 according to the Philippines 1980 census). The *1980 Census of Fisheries* (NEDA and the National Census and Statistics Office 1981) reported that 32,847 households (total population, 185,036) with a work force of 70,231 were engaged in municipal fishing, with less than half of the workers (29,405) working on a full-time basis. An additional 1,427 workers were employed in commercial fishing.

18. See *The Cebu Labor Situationer* (Visayas Human Development Agency,

1983:73–84) and Mojares (1983:32 and 119) for analyses of the neocolonial and colonial status, respectively, of Cebu City.

Chapter 4. The Looks of the City

1. This coexistence of radically different technologies was not a recent development in Cebu. It had been the case for decades. See, for example, William D. Boyce's 1914 remarks about the manner in which "the old and the new are blended in a bewildering fashion" in Cebu City, as quoted in Mojares (1983:119).

2. See the Paul S. Leitz translation of *The Muñoz Text of Alcina's History of the Bisayan Islands (1668)* (1960, 4:6).

3. Mojares (1983:10) notes that a makeshift fort was constructed by López de Legaspi in 1565, less than two weeks after the Spanish arrival in Cebu. A stone fort, which was named San Pedro, was built on the site sometime in 1600 (Mojares 1983:14), and rebuilt, still on the triangular plan, in 1835 (see *Cebu Commercial Guide 1972–1973* 1973).

4. The galleon trade that linked the Philippines to China, Mexico, and Europe during the seventeenth, eighteenth, and nineteenth centuries did not directly involve Cebu City, except from 1594 to 1604, when a limited trade in beeswax, cotton cloth, and local fruits was allowed. Until 1860, Manila was designated as the only international port of call in the archipelago, and Cebu's role in the galleon trade was limited to supplying Manila with one product, *lampotes*, a kind of cotton gauze. By the mid-eighteenth century, as Fenner states, the Cebuanos were "a commercially anonymous group" (1985:42). See Mojares (1983) and Fenner (1985:32–63) for more detailed accounts of the influence of the galleon trade on Cebu City.

5. See Fenner (1985:22–30) for an account of Visayan society and the status of Cebu at Spanish contact. Fenner notes that "pre-Hispanic Cebuano society possessed a well-defined religious and social structure" (1985:30). See Mojares 1983 for a discussion of López de Legaspi's implementation in Cebu City of the Royal Ordinances of 1573, which served as the model for Spanish colonial urbanization worldwide, and for a description and interpretation of the physical layout of the gridiron pattern adopted throughout the Spanish empire.

6. Fenner (1985:32–33) notes that López de Legaspi originally intended to make the port of Cebu the capital of a far-reaching colonial empire. However, Portugese blockades and food shortages forced him to abandon the location. See Mojares (1983:10) for a discussion of López de Legaspi's initial efforts toward establishing a capital city at Cebu.

7. See Mojares (1983:10–46) for a history of the ethnic planning and growth of Cebu City. See also Cullinane (1982:256) for an account of the initial settlement plan of the city.

8. Sergio Osmeña, for example, one of the most prominent figures in Cebuano political history, was a most active member on the city's urban renewal committee in 1905, which was formed after two devastating fires had destroyed much of the city. Cullinane (1989:345–46) argues that Osmeña used the road-building project as an opportunity to impress key American officials with whom he was serving. Among them was William Cameron Forbes, who became one of Osmeña's most influential supporters before and during Os-

meña's years as Speaker of the Philippine Assembly (1907–22). The extent to which street planning during the American era reflected the interests of government officials, as opposed to those of individual citizens, is indicated in an unsigned article published in the periodical, *Engineering News*, on May 11, 1916 (75 [19]:882–83; found in the National Archives Record Group 350, series 5, 1898–1915, file 2055–25), in which the author describes the process of replanning Cebu City's streets as "remarkable, not from a technical standpoint, but as an example of what appears to be high-handed juggling of private property." Modernization of the city center's streets was not done via a deed adjustment process that allowed for due judicial process, but instead via a re-registration of deeds through an appointed committee, which reassigned individual lots in almost any manner that would ensure their fitting into the blocks provided in the new street plan.

9. Cebu Island is 139 miles long and has an area of 1707 square miles. See Wernstedt and Spencer (1978:28).

10. See Wernstedt and Spencer (1978:16–60) for a summary of precipitation patterns.

11. Cebu's average rainfall was 64 inches a year, giving it a "moist subhumid" climate, if rated in terms of the Thornthwaite system, while most places in the Philippines received between 80 and 200 inches a year. See Wernstedt and Spencer (1978:610) for exact figures. Fenner (1985:12) notes that of the 420 streams on the island, only six carry water throughout the entire year.

12. Cogon grass covered over 47 percent of the island in the 1960s and would have covered even more by the 1980s; see Wernstedt and Spencer (1978:103). Wernstedt and Spencer (1978:78) also cited Cebu as one of the most seriously eroded islands in the archipelago, noting that on 30 percent of the land surface, all topsoil had been completely removed. Fenner (1985:11, 130) notes that deforestation occurred shortly after the port of Cebu City was opened to international trade, as a result of both increased timber trade and agricultural cultivation. Prior to deforestation, the island's Central Cordillera range was covered with *molave, narra,* and *ipil* forest.

13. A *Five-Year Integrated Development Plan of Cebu*, put out in 1976 by the Office of the Governor, Provincial Government of Cebu, quoted the Bureau of Soils survey of the province, stating that the island's soil was composed of different varieties of well-drained, residual clays developed from shale rocks that were ideally suited for the planting of coconut, corn, and *palay* (1976:11 and table 1, 170). The *1980 Census of Agriculture* (National Census and Statistics Office 1985) reported that 119,993 farms in the province produced a total of over 3,675,000 kilos of corn, making it the fourth largest crop in the province, behind mango, vegetable, and tuber or root or bulb crops. The *Plan of Cebu* estimated that around 84 percent of the population of the province ate corn (1976:19), causing a shortage such that roughly two-thirds of the corn eaten in the province was actually imported (1976:176, table 7).

14. See H. Mendoza 1985 for an account of the experiences and letters of U.S. school teachers living in the Philippines during the early twentieth century.

15. The aphorism is cited as printed in the August 20, 1984, issue of the popular periodical, *Bagong Kusog*.

16. For the full version of this myth, see *The Filipino Nation* (Haskins 1982, 3:179).

17. See Leitz (1960, 3:232–45).

18. See Leitz (1960, 3:240).

19. See Leitz (1960, 3:197).

20. As discussed above (note 8), much of the street plan in Cebu City had been redesigned after the devastating fires of 1905. See Cullinane (1989: 345–46).

21. The *Port of Cebu: Handbook and Directory of Cebu Philippine Islands*, for example, published in Cebu City by the Cebu Chamber of Commerce in 1928, asked, in a series of what were intended to be impressive rhetorical questions about the city's distinctive identity, "Did you know that Cebu is the Possessor of the oldest Street of the Philippine Islands?" (1928:43). The fact reappeared frequently in more recent commercial publications. See, for example, Lourdes S. Mercado (1965:3).

22. See, for example, Mojares's discussion of the importance of air circulation engineering in Cebuano architecture (1983:46, 66–70).

23. See Ness (1990) for a discussion of relationships between guests and hosts in Cebuano society in fiesta contexts. Portions of this chapter have been reprinted with the permission of the publisher from the article, "The Latent Meaning of a Dance: The Cebuano Sinulog as a Model of Social Interaction" (in *Communication and Culture; Language, Performance, Technology, and Media. Selected Proceedings from the Sixth International Conference on Culture and Communication, Temple University, 1986*, ed. Sari Thomas and William A. Evans, pp. 128–33 [Norwood, N.J.: Ablex Publishing Corporation, 1990]).

24. Ian Buruma (1989:95) also makes note of this negative "spineless" self-image.

25. See data in *Philippines 1980: Population, Land Area, and Density, 1970, 1975, and 1980* (National Economic and Development Authority 1981).

26. See *Philippines 1980: Population, Land Area, and Density, 1970, 1975, and 1980* (National Economic and Development Authority 1981).

27. See *A Study of Urban Poor Dwellers, Their Attitudes and Responses to Government Initiated Development Programs; The Case of Four Selected Communities in Cebu City* (Visayas Human Development Agency, 1987).

28. See Leonardo N. Mercado (1976:187) and Lynn C. Bostrom (1968: 399–413).

29. The term "resilient phrasing" is taken from the technical jargon of Laban Movement Analysis (LMA). It is used here in to refer to a specific case of the same general kind of phrasing pattern to which it refers within LMA body movement theory.

Chapter 5. The Niño

1. See Elwood (1971:154–63) and Elwood and Magdamo (1971).

2. See, for example, Rosa Tenazas (1965:4) quoting L. Nemec's *The Infant of Prague* (1958:8).

3. The properties of miniature here cited are identified and exemplified by Gaston Bachelard (1969:148–82). Claude Lévi-Strauss (1966:22–25) also notes the capacity of miniatures to condense and simplify the quality of the objects they represent, and to facilitate and enhance the comprehension of a complex object in so doing.

4. The hand position symbolized the Trinity, the two raised fingers sig-

nifying the Father and Son, the thumb connecting with the bent fingers and thus encircling the extended fingers symbolizing the unifying spirit of the Holy Ghost. However, the hand posture also has been reinterpreted by local devotees as symbolizing a prophecy that in the year 2000 the world will end.

5. The comment was made in a newspaper article authored by Quijano de Manila—Juaquin's pen name (journal unknown, 1965 [collected from the files of the Cebuano Studies Center, University of San Carlos, Cebu City, Philippines]).

6. Tenazas (1965:79–80) reports that the image's numerous albs are donated yearly by devotees and are removed and replaced every year, becoming relics that are distributed throughout the island. The layers may number as many as eighteen, and occasionally so many are donated that the image cannot wear them all. Extras are pinned to the underside of the cape.

7. Tenazas (1965:80) reports that evidence documenting the tradition of offering gifts and treasures to the Santo Niño dates back to 1736, with the *Libro Endon Seasientan Las Limosnas.* Among the more famous treasures are the *Toissone* ("Fleece") of pure gold studded with square-cut emeralds, garnets, rubies, and diamonds, said to be a gift from Charles III of Spain, and the twenty-two-carat gold crown studded with forty-four good-sized diamonds, donated by the former First Lady of the Philippines, Mrs. Leonila Garcia, on the occasion of the fourth centenary of the Santo Niño's discovery, celebrated in 1965.

8. See Tenazas (1965:6). The Santo Niño de Cebu, however, is believed to have been made in Flanders in the sixteenth century and exported to Seville. Older images of the Christ Child are found in Italy, where the Bambino Gesu is the oldest, dated approximately to 1480. The image that inspired the enormously successful cult of the Infant of Prague, with which the devotion to the Santo Niño of Cebu is often associated, is believed to be of sixteenth-century Andalusian origin (Tenazas 1965:6–27).

9. See Tenazas (1965:7).

10. For a comparative discussion of the devotion in all of these areas, see Tenazas (1965:7–17).

11. See the translation of Antonio Pigafetta's *Primo Viaggio Interno al Mundo* in *The Philippine Islands, 1493–1898,* edited by Emma Blair and James Robertson (1903–1909, 23:155–57, 159) for a translation, and Tenazas (1965:21–22).

12. See Tenazas (1965:25). See also Pigafetta's account in Blair and Robertson (1903–1909, 23:167) and the translation of Pedro Chirino's *Relacion de las Islas Filipines* in Blair and Robertson (vol. 12, especially 12:181). See also Blair and Robertson (1903–1909, 2:120, 216).

13. See Tenazas (1965:29); see also various early accounts translated in Blair and Robertson (1903–1909, 2:120 and 23:169).

14. See Tenazas (1965:34); see also various early accounts in Blair and Robertson (1903–1909, 23:13a; 36:208; and 12:192, note 47).

15. See Tenazas (1965:17, 37–38).

16. See Tenazas (1965:17).

17. Cebu City was first named Villa del San Miguel by López de Legaspi in 1565. In 1571, it was renamed El Santísimo Nombre de Jesus by López de Legaspi after the image of the Holy Child. See Mojares (1983:11); see also Tenazas (1965:26–27, 29) and Fenner (1985:32).

18. Lévi-Strauss (1966:23–24) notes the inherent capacity of miniatures to stimulate creative reflection in their observers by reducing the scale and hence the complexity of their objects. The Niño idol, as described here, can also be seen as a trace or mark of what Derrida (1973:129–60) has termed "differance." The symbol is a sign of a missing, nonexistent, or "protoexistent," object—an object that, as the sign itself makes evident, has no possibility of achieving real presence or actuality, yet continues to inspire efforts toward its own comprehension, recognition, and, ultimately, its own realization. It is a sign that thus beckons its interpreters to interrogate the limits of their familiar systems of thought, particularly their notions of presence, absence, and being—their ontological axioms.

19. Kerima Polotan took over the publication of *Focus Philippines* during the period of martial law and later became Imelda Marcos's official biographer. Her perspective should be considered with this political alignment in mind.

20. See Mojares (1981:21) quoting the chronicler Pedro Chirino.

21. According to Phelan (1959:74), *cofradia* organizations originated as medieval Spanish institutions whose religious function was the practice of piety and the performance of works of charity. In the Philippines, they were used as instruments to consolidate Christianization, the members visiting the sick and the dying to urge them to receive the sacraments as well as attending funerals in order to discourage ritual drinking. According to Rafael (1988: 185–86), *cofradias* were one common alternative to the development of a native clergy; most such organizations, Rafael reports, emerged in the early seventeenth century and were supported particularly by the Jesuits (see also Tenazas, 1965:81). The Cofradia del Santo Niño was the first of such organizations in the Philippines and was supported by the Augustinians (see *Constitutions and By-Laws of the Cofradia del Santo Niño De Cebu* [National Level] ca. 1984:1–13). By 1984, the Cofradia del Santo Niño de Cebu had developed a reputation for fanaticism and religious conservatism.

22. Tenazas (1965:91) confirms the observations given here, indicating that the makeup of the devotee population has been fairly consistent, at least over the past several decades.

23. See Victor Turner (1974:45, 207–8), for a discussion of antistructure and its relationship to dominant symbols and to pilgrimages.

24. A basilica is an especially prestigious Roman Catholic church. It is accorded the same privileges as the seven main churches in Rome and is directly under the supervision of the Vatican. The Basilica del Santo Niño de Cebu was referred to in tourist literature in 1985 as "the only basilica in Asia." It was elevated to basilica status by Holy See on the occasion of the fourth centenary of the Christianization of the Philippines in 1965.

25. The fiesta is set for the second Sunday after Epiphany, which falls on the third weekend in January.

26. See Tenazas (1965:86).

27. Tenazas (1965:82–83) credits a specific Augustinian prior, the Very Reverend Restituto Suarez, with the instigation of this service. The perpetual novena, begun in October 1958, was first propagated among students of the Colegio del Santo Niño—the Augustinian school. Within weeks, the services were tripled to accommodate public interest, and within the year they were being broadcast over three radio stations. Two years later, novena pamphlet printings exceeded 35,000 copies.

28. The concluding prayer, for example, read as follows:

O miraculous Santo Niño!*
prostrate before Your sacred Image,*
we beseech You*
to cast a merciful look*
on our troubled hearts.*
Let your tender love,*
so inclined to pity,*
be softened at our prayers,*
and grant us that grace*
for which we ardently implore You.*
Take from us*
all unbearable affliction and despair.*
For Your sacred infancy's sake*
hear our prayers*
and send us consolation and aid*
that we may praise You,*
with the Father and the Holy Spirit, forever and ever. Amen.

The phrasing of the text is printed as given in *Perpetual Novena to Santo Niño de Cebu* (1960).

29. See Lorenzo Cesar (1966:1, 3–14).

30. On *tautau* images, see Kathleen Adams (1987). See also Toby A. Volkman (1990:97–101).

31. I was informed by two different sources that the authentic Santo Niño image had, in fact, been returned to the Vatican. However, I was unable to confirm these rumors. The conviction that the image in Cebu City was, in fact, the authentic one, was still widespread.

32. See Tenazas quoting Dean Worcester (1965:83).

33. See Manuel Enriquez de la Calzada (1965:82–84) for a longer version of this myth, in which the caretaker, himself a homeless foundling, attempted to rob the San Augustin church, but, when he had reached his distant hide-out, he opened the bag of coins only to find the Santo Niño image inside the bag instead. The guilty man repented, returning the image to the church, and resumed his job. He was later seen to be picking out numerous *amor seco* burrs from the Child's dress, cautioning the image not to wander in the fields alone at night any more. See also Tenazas (1965: 64–65) for a shortened version of the same legend.

34. See Tenazas (1965:64–65) for detailed accounts of the legends.

35. See Tenazas (1965:64–65) for a detailed version of the fish-buying myth.

36. See de la Calzada (1965:47–49).

37. The Cross of Magellan, or a wooden duplicate that was believed to be the original, for many years stood exposed inside the octahedral kiosk shrine mentioned in Chapter 4. By 1984, however, a wooden case had been built to enclose what was still believed to be the original cross.

38. See de la Calzada (1965:79–81).

39. See de la Calzada (1965:70–73).

40. See de la Calzada (1965:41–42).

41. See de la Calzada (1965:32–33).

42. See de la Calzada (1965:27–28).

43. See Tenazas (1965:64–65).

44. For variations, see Mojares (1981:29, 30).

45. Claude Lévi-Strauss (1963:229) has argued that the function of myth is to provide logical models capable of representing the overcoming or resolution of a society's most disturbing inherent conceptual contradictions.

46. See Tenazas (1965:2).

47. Accounts of the finding of the image report that it was discovered inside what appeared to be its original pine box, which was itself enclosed inside yet another crate that was tied up with a cord. The box was found inside a large, well-built house that contained several boxes and what might be interpreted as ritual paraphernalia. Whether the house was a storage facility or a religious house or both is impossible to determine completely from the accounts. See Tenazas (1965:25); see also various early accounts in Blair and Robertson (1903–1909, 2:120, 216; 12:181; and 23:167) and Mojares (1981:9–12).

48. See de la Calzada (1965).

49. See de la Calzada (1965:95–96); see also Mojares (1981:26–27) for renditions of the myth. Cullinane (1982:251–96) also cites the story of "Juan Diong," placing it in the context of elite-peasant relations as they existed during the early part of the nineteenth century. In Cullinane's account, the conflict actually occurred between Don Blas, a Chinese mestizo member of the elite (not a Spaniard), and the peasants led by Juan Diong, with the mediating role being played by the Augustinian Fr. Julian Bermejo (1982:259). Cullinane (1982:262) interprets the episode as an example of the mestizo-Augustinian rivalry, noting that Juan Diong's conflict was actually not with the Spaniards on the island (although in Enriquez de la Calzada's recording of the folk version of the story, it is), but with the "enterprising mestizos" of the city's Parian district. Cullinane suggests (1982:262), in fact, that an alliance may actually have been formed between the Spaniards and Juan Diong's following, and that the legendary uprising was actually staged in order to keep the mestizo community from penetrating into the Augustinian-controlled territory southeast of the city. In any event, the folk version highlights the Santo Niño's role as an intermediary between the peasant Juan Diong and the Spanish segment of the local society and further highlights the contrast between Spanish and native factions by recasting the landholders as Spaniards as well. Given the difference between historical and folk versions, the legend would seem to indicate how strongly the Niño was valued as a cross-cultural (versus a cross-societal) symbol.

50. For a comprehensive reference of Philippine folk religious beliefs and practices, with a concentration in Visayan beliefs and practices, see Francisco Demetrio (1970).

51. See Richard Arens (1958:16).

52. For a detailed description of the different classes of supernatural beings in the pre-Hispanic Philippine spirit world, see Mateo C. Natividad (1979). Natividad (1979:82–84, 102), argues that saints obviously represented the new influence of Catholicism and were essentially new additions to the indigenous conceptual universe. Nevertheless, they closely matched indigenous concepts of the lesser deities who were pure spirits—as opposed to human spirits—of the skyworld, and who were worshipped in a similar manner. Stephen K. Hislop (1971:147) also presents a sketch of the pre-Hispanic folk spirit world, conceived by the contemporary missionary John

A. Rich, which illustrates the importance of lesser spirits of nature, of misfortune, and of dead ancestors as intermediaries between humans and the supreme deity. According to Magellan's chronicler, Pigafetta, the deity was named "Abba." Abba was considered unapproachable by humans, who were not worthy to worship the deity directly. According to Hislop, this supreme being was also referred to as *Laon* in the western Visayas and by the terms *Bathala, Badhala, Badla*, and *Bahala* in Luzon. The name *Laon* is taken from Pedro Chirino's account (Blair and Robertson 1903–1909, 12:169–321) and is used also by Fenner (1985:30) to refer to the Cebuano supreme deity.

On the nature of the pre-Hispanic Philippine Supreme Being, see also Leonardo N. Mercado (1974:172). See also F. Lande Jocano, who presents a listing of Bisayan divinities and their universe, as well as those of Luzon and Mindanao, in his "Notes on Philippine Divinities" (1968). Jocano makes an argument similar to Hislop's concerning the unapproachable nature of the supreme god in *Folk Christianity: A Preliminary Study of Conversion and Patterning of Christian Experience in the Philippines* (1981:22–23), in *Growing up in a Philippine Barrio* (1969:105), and in "Filipino Catholicism: A Case Study in Religious Change" (1967). In the latter article (1967:48), as well as in "Conversion and the Patterning of Christian Experience in Malitbog, Central Panay, Philippines" (1965:101–2), Jocano focuses specifically on the resemblance between the worship of the saints and that of *engkantu* spirits, which, he states, occurs "in many rural areas."

For sixteenth- and seventeenth-century Spanish accounts of indigenous Philippine religious beliefs and practices, see accounts of Diego Aduarte, *Historia de la Provincia del Santo Rosario de la orden de Predicadores, 1640* (in Blair and Roberston 1903–1909, vols. 30, 31, 32, and especially 30:285–98). See also Pedro Chirino, *Relacion de las Islas Filipinas, 1602–1604*, (in Blair and Roberston 1903–1909, 12:169–321, especially 12:179–84, 262–75 [on idolatry], and 12:302–8 [on funerals]; also 12:60–68). See Fransisco Colin, *Native Races and Their Customs 1690–1691*, (in Blair and Roberston 1903–1909, 40:37–98, especially 69–82); Miguel de Loarca, *Relacion de las Yslas Filipinas, 1582–1583* (in Blair and Roberston 1903–1909, 5:34–187, especially 121–41, 153–71, and 171–75 [on gods and *anitos*]); Antonio Pigafetta, *Primo Viaggio Interno al Mondo, 1519–1522* (in Blair and Roberston 1903–1909, 33:135–75); Juan de Plasencia, *Costumbre de los Tagalos, 1588–1591* (in Blair and Roberston 1903–1909, 7:173–96, especially 185–96); and Paul S. Leitz, trans., *The Muñoz Text of Alcina's History of the Bisayan Islands (1668)* (1960).

53. Hislop (1971:154), for example, writes: "The rural Filipinos in general believe the Christian *santos* are either the same, or in the same class as, the *anitos* of pagan belief. This is a serious problem for the Catholic Church. From the very beginnings of Christianity in the Islands, the same images through which the *anitos* were worshiped were then used to worship the *santos* of the Church." Hislop (1971:150) summarizes Filipino primitive religion as consisting mainly of the worship of ancestors and *anito* spirits. John L. Phelan (1959:54, and 184, note 1) indicates that the use of wooden spirit images in pre-Hispanic times was widespread. See also P. Francisco de Santa Inés, *Crónica de la Provincia de San Gregorio Magno de Religiosos Descalzados de N. S. P. San Fransisco en Islas Filipinas, China, Japón, etc.* (1892 [first published Manila in 1676] 2:177 ff.), for a graphic description of pre-Hispanic iconoclastic activity. See also Tomás Ortiz, *Práctica del ministerio que siguen los religiosos del orden de N. S. Augustín en Filipinas*, as translated in Rafael (1988:111–12);

Natividad (1979:103, 105n); Jocano (1975:217–18); and Laura Benedict (1916:1–308, especially 193). Fenner (1985:30) notes that in Cebu, images representing *diwata* were made of bone, tooth, or gold.

On the meaning and worship of *nono* spirits in pre-Hispanic Tagalog culture, see Rafael (1988:114–15). On the special curing powers of *anito* spirits, see Frank Lynch (1984:197–207). Hislop (1971:144, note 4) reports that, according to R. A. Kern, the word *anito* is of Malayan origin and has spread eastward of Polynesia from the Philippines. Throughout the Philippines the term has acquired the general meaning, "spirit." According to Hislop, who cites as his source the chronicles of Pedro Chirino recounting the Santo Niño's discovery in the Visayan Islands the term *diwata*, itself of Indian origin, was the equivalent of *anito* and was used to refer to any god, especially to an image of a god. Rafael (1988:188) equates the *anito* with the *nono* spirits.

54. Lynch (1984:204) has advanced this argument.

55. The biblical references are taken from D. M. Estabaya, "The Story of the Santo Niño," printed in the Philippine periodical *Post* (1965:1).

56. For an example of a Juan Pusong story, see *Cebuano Folktales*, ed. Erlinda K. Alburo (1977, 2:22–25).

57. See Nagasura T. Madale (1984).

58. In Sulawesi, Indonesia, for example, a similar trickster character, named Dodong, appears. See Kathleen Adams (1988).

59. See Margaret Mead's "Introduction" to Gregory Bateson and Margaret Mead's *Balinese Character: A Photographic Analysis* (1942:1–48).

60. For a more extended version of the myth, see Tenazas (1965:56–57); see also Mojares (1981:15, 27).

61. See Natividad (1979:87); see also Donn V. Hart (1966:68).

62. See Natividad (1979:91–92). See also Lieban (1962:306–12); Demetrio (1968:136–43; 1970); Jocano (1967:48); and Rafael (1988:111–14).

63. The alignment of the Santo Niño spirit with *ingkanto* spirits, though obvious, was by no means absolute. A most striking difference, as Demetrio notes (1968:143), is that interaction and enchantment between *ingkanto* and mortal is always based on romantic emotions, whereas with the Niño, child/parent feelings of affection create the mortal/divinity bond.

64. For an analysis of indigenous attitudes toward earthworld spirits during the early phases of Spanish contact, see Rafael (1988:114–15, and 189–91).

65. See Mojares (1981:28).

66. The English translation given was taken from the basilica novena booklets; a more literal translation for the last four lines in verse one and the second verse might read:

Now as then
You set alight our souls
Our one who keeps us from sinking
Strengthening these hearts
Their sailing ship docked here
To conquer our land
But you decided
To join with them
In order that you be king of
Your Chosen Ones

67. See Sales as translated by Fe Susan Go in "An Annotated Translation of the 1935 History of Cebu" (1976).

68. In this respect, the localization of the Santo Niño de Cebu paralleled that of Tagalog localization and translation of Spanish missionary texts described by Rafael (1988; see especially pp.110–35).

69. The Virgin of Guadalupe developed a Mexico-wide cult that, like the Santo Niño devotion in the Philippines, appealed to *criollos*, or Spanish-Mexican inhabitants, and indigenous *indios* alike. The Virgin of Guadalupe was also a figure that fit easily with indigenous mythology, resembling in many respects the Aztec earth mother goddess, Tonantzin, who was worshiped at the very site, Tepeyac Hill, where the basilica for the Virgin of Guadalupe now stands, and who, like the Virgin of Guadalupe, was associated with the moon. The Virgin is represented in myth as having been the original sponsor of the indigenous *indios'* acceptance into Christendom, a topic of heated debate among the early Spanish missionaries in Mexico, who could not agree on whether or not the native populations were fully human and capable of conversion. The Virgin of Guadalupe, according to legend, was the first Catholic saint to appear miraculously before an Indian catechumen, Juan Diego, and to provide him with irrefutable miraculous evidence of his meeting with her. Like the Santo Niño, the Virgin of Guadalupe was characterized as fluent in both the native vernacular and Spanish. Also like the Santo Niño, the Virgin of Guadalupe was employed as a war symbol and as a symbol of independence used in opposition to Spanish colonial powers. See Turner (1974:98–155, especially 105–6, 151–53), for an analysis of the role played by Our Lady of Guadalupe in the Mexican Revolution. See also Eric Wolf (1958:34–39) for a discussion of the political, religious, and familial significance of the Virgin of Guadalupe in Mexican culture.

70. The Santo Niño's adoption by the Katipunan as a symbol of its cause in Cebu also reflects a general tendency among Katipunan groups to use religious imagery as an inspiration for their political efforts. Prayer was a critically important activity for Katipunan members everywhere, one that was believed to increase self-control and to heighten awareness. Religious images that inspired prayer played such an important role in the Katipunan that analogies were apparent in the characterization of images and in the characterization of the Katipunan as a whole—both were described as enlightening forces. For an analysis of the role of religious imagery in the Katipunan Society, as well as an analysis of the political significance of the *sinakulo* passion plays, see Reynaldo Ileto (1979).

71. See, for example, the accounts of devotees reported in de la Torre (1980:13–15).

72. My emphasis. See de la Torre (1980:13).

73. Fr. Ben J. Villote (1980:11).

74. The argument made here runs in accord with those of Mary Douglas (1979). In Douglas's view, as a social system provides less and less overt political control of behavior, pollution rituals become increasingly important as a means of stabilizing social conduct. See Douglas (1979:1–40) for an extended discussion of the relationship between pollution, social order, and religious experience.

The "chapel-like" function of images, and consequently the absence of a need for specialized sanctuary dwelling constructions, is also evident in Visayan communities outside Cebu City. Jean-Paul Dumont (1986), for example, has noted how, in the *barangay* of Gabayan on Siquijor Island, the religious significance of the community's chapel building is minimal, and praying rarely occurs there (1986:17, 18). Instead, praying occurs in private households before crucifixes or pictures and statuettes of the Virgin Mary and the saints. The practice of praying inside the household dwelling evidently dates to pre-Hispanic times and was noted by the chronicler Colin in the late seventeenth century (see Blair and Robertson 1903–1909, 40:74).

Chapter 6. The *Tindera Sinulog*

1. Lisa Quimat (1955).
2. The quality of timelessness evident in the *tindera sinulog* has also been noted in other Malay ritual forms, and most likely relates the Cebu City ritual to a widespread style of trance dance. See Clifford Geertz, for example, on Balinese ritual temporality (1973:360–412).
3. *Tindera*, a word of Spanish derivation, is glossed as "vendor"; the word form ending with "a" denotes a female vendor. The term was used to describe vendors of all kinds. However, only the candle-selling *tinderas* danced the *sinulog* at the basilica in Cebu City.
4. Quoted from the *Sinulog '85 Souvenir Program* (1985:10, 11).
5. See "The Sinulog in Philippine Culture," by Nick Joaquin (1981).
6. Mojares (1981:1), for example, conceded that there was no direct evidence to show that the *sinulog*—either the term or the dance itself—was present before 1521. However, he argued nonetheless that the *sinulog* obviously had pagan or pre-Hispanic origins, which could be assumed from accounts offered by Pigafetta, Colin, Alcina, and others, in addition to the evidence of ethnic minorities such as the Bagobos, Tirurays, and Kalingas, whose pagan dances have persisted into the present era. The accounts cited, however, provide no observations detailed enough to support any conclusion that the body movement performed today in the *sinulog* ritual was performed in a like manner before or at the time of Spanish contact.
7. See Pierre Bourdieu (1977:72–95).
8. The analytical orientation employed here parallels that of James Peacock in his 1968 study of the Javanese *ludruk* theatre performed in Surabaya, Java. Peacock focused on the relations the symbolic action of the *ludruk* maintained with what he termed "technical" actions of daily life—activities such as sowing seeds, fighting, or market bartering that directly addressed empirical economic, political, or social ends. In the comparison of "technical" and "symbolic" forms of action, Peacock was able to articulate contributions that *ludruk* symbolic action made to the lives of its participants. See especially 1968:234–36.
9. In this respect, the *sinulog* form of prayer may be distinguished from the type of "soul-oriented" praying that Dumont (1986:24) notes makes up much of the prayer activity of another Visayan community. Dumont has argued that praying in the barangay of Gabayan is often centered around the effort of facilitating the movement of souls toward heaven so that they will not return to earth to haunt the living. The *sinulog* form, however, was not used to facilitate such movement, but to move the Santo Niño to intercede

protectively on the devotee's behalf—the second major function of Visayan prayer noted by Dumont (1986:28).

Chapter 7. Customers and Performers

1. The Santo Niño image of San Nicolas is also considered to be miraculous and is sometimes referred as the Cebu Niño's "general" or "first officer." Before the Santo Niño de Cebu is carried through the streets on fiesta day, the San Nicolas Santo Niño is carried from its own chapel to the entrance to the basilica, where it is said to "stand guard" until the return of the Santo Niño de Cebu at the conclusion of the procession.

2. As Rafael (1988:122–32) has noted, the roles of the debtor and creditor were constantly employed in Spanish missionaries' orthodox communications about the relationship Filipino converts should maintain with God in all His manifestations. The debtor-creditor relationship, having already occupied a central place in local forms of social organization, was one that natives felt constrained to attend to. However, the native strategy of dealing with the incalculable debt incurred to the Catholic God(s) was to defer full payment in favor of token gestures of indebtedness, which could appease Celestial Authority without fully surrendering to it. The perpetual vows made by Santo Niño devotees to perform the *sinulog* on a regular basis, be it yearly or monthly or weekly or according to some other temporal rhythm, conform closely to the pattern of rapport Rafael defines for Tagalog converts during the early years of the Spanish regime.

3. See Dumont (1986:20–21) for a discussion of the typical gender-based division of labor that structures the act of praying in lowland Visayan communities. Fenner (1985:30), citing both Pedro Chirino and Pigafetta, also notes that in Cebuano society the general preference for elderly women to assume the role of religious practicioner or *bailan* goes back to pre-Hispanic times.

4. For more detailed information on the social organization of the basilica candle vendors' selling situation, see Ness (1985:71–84).

5. For a discussion of the classification of folk Catholic practices, see Lynch (1984).

6. The phrase here is quoted as a reference to James Scott's work, *Weapons of the Weak: Everyday Forms of Peasant Resistance* (1986). Scott identifies various forms of everyday resistance that Malay peasants in a village in Kedah, Malaysia, have adopted to cope with the class conflicts that have arisen as a consequence of the development of their local rice economy. The strategies of the Cebu City *tinderas,* such as those described in this passage, may be considered microexamples of coping mechanisms basically analogous to similar interrelationships among relatively advantaged and relatively disadvantaged members of the developing society studied.

7. *Jai alai* is a form of handball, of Basque derivation. It was a popular professional sport for betting in urban areas of the Philippines large enough to support the construction and maintenance of a club and court, as was true in both Cebu City and in Manila.

8. Vincenta used the Visayan terms *siyagit, bungol,* and *hunghung* for "shout," "deaf," and "whisper" respectively.

Chapter 8. Latent Symbolism in the *Tindera Sinulog*

1. See Bourdieu (1977:79).
2. See, for example, Victor Turner's analysis of the Mukanda circumcision ritual of the Ndembu (1967:151–279), Audrey Richards' study, *Chisungu* (1956), and A. van Gennep's definitive work, *The Rites of Passage* (1960).
3. The highlighted use of distal body parts to initiate movement is a feature of many Asian dance styles. As Colin McPhee (1970:292) has noted, Cambodian, Javanese, and Balinese dancers all use their hands in brilliant, crystallized gestures that add the final significant accent to the body in motion. Hands never relax, are never vague, casual, or forgotten.

In the *wayang wong* of Javanese dance, action that indicates the entrance of any character onto the stage is an arm gesture initiated by the wrist/hand. The action involves the manipulation of long streamers, which hang from the sashes of the dancers to below their knees and which are manipulated so that they float forward and backward. These gestures can be a conventional symbol with the specific meaning, "I am now entering into the action of the story." They are also used, however, simply to fill in much of the incidental action or "stage business" occurring in a classical dance drama. This distally initiated arm patterning, which has been noted to put the stress on the lower arms and hands, is associated with the *alus*, or refined style of movement that was cultivated in the *kratons*, or ruling places of Java. See Mirriam J. Morrison (1977); see also Faubion Bowers (1956, chapter 3); see also Soedarsono's "Classical Javanese Dance: History and Characterization" (1976) for a discussion of the restrained female step style in *wayang wong* dance drama.

Balinese court dances also highlight distally initiated hand gestures that lead the arms into elaborately segmented movement phrases. McPhee (1970: 306) notes that the hands are considered the "flowers" of Balinese dancing, embellishing all movement. See also Spies and Zoete (1973), for an analysis of Balinese aesthetics in relation to dance. See also Bowers (1956:232–33) for further description of the walking and gesturing style of Balinese court dance. For illustrations of Balinese dance gesturing, see Bandem and deBoer (1981). See also Daniel (1981); and *Trance and Dance in Bali*, by Margaret Mead (1952).

Classical dances of Thailand and Burma show similar initiation patterning. Burma's Zat Pwe tradition has, in fact, been described as "a series of gesticulations" (Bowers 1956:119). Likewise, the Khmer classical dance tradition, which, like the Balinese, Burmese, and some Thai forms, is a translation of Indian traditions, emphasizes hand and wrist action. In Khmer forms, a great portion of the symbolic content of a dance is concentrated in the *kbach*, the gestural symbolism of the hands derived from Indian *mudras*, or hand gestures. The role of the wrist as an initiator of action is particularly important in these dance traditions. A stylistic emphasis is also placed on the subdued and stabilizing use of the weight center, which has been referred to as "the master control point," and the foreshortened step style. For a detailed description of Khmer dance gesturing technique, as well as a comparison of Khmer dancing in relation to other Southeast Asian dance traditions, see Chan Moly Sam, *Khmer Court Dance: A Comprehensive Study of Movements, Gestures and Postures as Applied Techniques* (1987).

Aside from the Hindu/Buddhist-derived classical traditions of Southeast Asia, ritual dances of women in some areas of insular Southeast Asia also feature distal initiation patterning similar to those of the *tinderas*. Claire Holt's description of the *ma'gellu'* dance of the Toraja of highland Sulawesi, for example, notes that "the play of the hands consisted of light rhythmic flaps from the wrist" (1939:72). The *ma'gellu'* dance is part of the *maro* ceremony that concludes the death rites for a person of high rank, and is done by girls to prevent illness and to mark the final liberation of the diseased person's soul. Holt's description of Torajan children imitating the *ma'gellu'*, in fact, could almost pass for a description of the *tindera sinulog*, so similar is the movement process depicted: "Without the aid of any instrument or voice, they started to move in a soft lilting step, as if treading on something. The girls kept their elbows close to the waist and put forward or extended sideways their forearms, gently flapping from the wrist the little hands with outstretched fingers at every second beat. Despite the timidity and a certain helplessness of the little performers there was something solemn about their dance" (1939:46).

Similar patterning of initiation is seen as well in women's dances of East Asia. In Chinese dance, it is evident in the pervasive combined tradition of sleeve manipulation and foot restraining. *Hsiu*, or sleeve gesturing, is an ancient and dominant element in Chinese dance that has been described as a "rhythmic language" for the hand and fingers. The short, mincing steps used in walking have been a notable feature of Chinese women's dance since the tenth century, at least, when the custom of foot binding is believed to have been instituted (see Gloria B. Strauss 1975).

In Japan, the ideals of Zen Buddhism resulted in dance traditions where hand gestures were employed to communicate the bulk of any performance's emotional and dramatic content. Scholars have compared the *shosa* or *furi* gestures of the *kabuki* dance to the *pas* or "step" and "pose" in classical ballet. A carefully engineered floating step style of *noh* drama and *kabuki* dance emphasizes a diminished range of movement that transports a held center of weight. As *kabuki* analyst Hidesato Ashihara has noted, what the spectator is encouraged to see in a *kabuki* performance is "the upper half of the dancer's body, chiefly the motions of his hands, shoulders, head and face" (1980:95). On Zen influences in *noh* dance, see Carl Wolz, "The Spirit of Zen in Noh Dance" (1977).

Only in Korea is the initiation patterning of limb movement markedly different from that mentioned above. This lack of hand highlighting, in fact, has been noted by Christine J. Loken (1983:72–80) as one of the most distinctive features of the Korean dance style.

This style of distal initiation, typical of women's dances throughout Asia, is by no means a human universal. Melanesian dances, for example, such as those of the Trobriand Islanders, the Andaman Islanders, and the dances of the Maring on Papua New Guinea, exhibit initiation styles that are purely core-initiated and integrate the entire bodily system into unified repetitive actions that radiate outward from the weight center. Different, though equally contrasting, are numerous dance styles of Africa, both sub-Saharan and North African, in which movement is initiated purely in the core of the body but engages the limbs in complex, segmented movement sequences. In European dance styles, particularly women's dancing, as illustrated in many ballet techniques and in folk dance styles, initiation style tends to use the whole limb as a unit. For examples of Trobriand Island dancing, both male and female, see Jerry Leach's film, *Trobriand Cricket: An Ingenious Response to Colonialism* (1976). For descriptions of the Andaman Islanders dancing, see

Radcliffe-Brown (1948:246–53). For examples of the Maring body move-ment initiation style as evident in their dance, see Alison Jablonko's film, *Maring in Motion* (1968). For analysis of the Maring movement style, see Jablonko's "Dance and Daily Activities among the Maring People of New Guinea: A Cinematographic Analysis of Body Movement Style" (1968). For examples of a variety of women's dance styles, see Alan Lomax and Forrestine Paulay's film, *Dance and Human History* (1974).

Obviously, the intention here is not to claim that all Asian movement, or all Asian dance movement, is distally initiated or that no dance movement else-where in the world is. It is simply to say that the style of highlighted wrist-led gesturing and near-reach foot stepping is a distinctive feature of the women's dance styles of the area and of a broadly Asian movement aesthetic.

4. "Participatory" in this context is meant to specify that people actually wanted to play the game themselves, versus watching other players. In my observation, cockfighting and *jai alai* were more popular spectator sports.

5. The discussion of the *tindera sinulog* as a model of the local guest-host relationship presented here is also discussed at length in Ness (1987). Portions of this chapter have been reprinted with the permission of the publisher from the article, "The Latent Meaning of a Dance: The Cebuano Sinulog as a Model of Social Interaction" (in *Communication and Culture; Language, Perfor-mance, Technology, and Media. Selected Proceedings from the Sixth International Conference on Culture and Communication, Temple University, 1986*, ed. Sari Thomas and William A. Evans, pp. 128–33. [Norwood, N.J.: Ablex Publish-ing Corporation, 1990]).

6. For an analysis of the role of *utang* concepts in Filipino social life, see Hollensteiner (1973). See also Ness (1990).

Rafael (1988:122–32) goes so far as to argue for a fundamental structural relation between the concepts of "inside" (*loob*) and "debt" (*utang*) in Tagalog culture, claiming that for early converts to Christianity it was nothing other than the experience of indebtedness that constituted an understanding or awareness of an interior domain. The whole notion of a personal inside, fol-lowing Rafael, becomes founded not on the perception of the body as a con-tainer with impermeable boundaries that separate and distinguish external and interior domains, but on the dynamics of any individual's source of mo-tivation, which appears internal insofar as it appears indebted. The notion of an individual's insides, then, appears to correspond to indigenous architec-tural forms, whose interior domains were also defined, not by solid protecting walls, but by distinctive tasks and other habits of action associated with being "inside."

7. The missionary Alcina (see Leitz's translation, 1962, 4:71), for example, made special note of the importance of slave-master relations in Visayan social structure. Fenner (1985:22–28), also notes that the social role of the debt peon was well-established in Cebuano political structure at the time of Spanish contact.

8. Judith Lynne Hanna (1979:91), for example, has argued that Uba-kala dance "seems to be a pervasive metonym . . . as specialized cultural motion. . . . The processes of reproduction and recreation in the human-supernatural cyclical pattern of reincarnation merge and the ancestors con-tinue their existence in the dancers' bodies." Hanna found Ubakala dance to be the embodiment of fundamental regenerative social processes. T. Polhe-mus as well, aligning himself with Douglas and with Marcel Mauss, called for

a Durkheimian structural analysis of bodily symbolism in all its forms, including dance, that would recognize the body as an image of socially constructed reality (1975:15). Philip Rawson, in his analysis of body symbolism in Tantra ecstacy cults, concluded that the body portrayed a "womb of its own world" (1975:275). In Tantric practice, humans embodied their universe (1975: 271–90). Adrienne Kaeppler, in an ethnoscientific structuralist analysis of Tongan dance (1978b:261–75, especially 274), found that the dance embodied unstated general principles by which Tongans ordered a variety of different social domains, aesthetic and nonaesthetic. In each of the cases cited, the body was seen to symbolize fundamental and pervasive principles of social life.

9. The *sinulog* in this respect is considered here to be a case in point supporting Suzanne Langer's early theory of nondiscursive symbolism, in which the value of symbolic forms other than those of linguistic propositional discourse could be defined as the thoughtful and articulate expression of otherwise unknowable, unnameable emotional experience, which is represented through skilled, transformative reconstruction. See Langer (1959:75–93).

Chapter 9. The Troupe *Sinulog*

1. This gender-linked split of a symbolic action into collective or publicly oriented and individual, privately oriented versions is seen in symbol systems around the world, most notably with regard to language. Recognizably feminine versions of symbolic forms, such as "women's talk," tend to address individual, private needs and remain relatively "pure" in performance style in cases of contact with foreign influences, but become stigmatized as well. Male versions, in contrast, are addressed to public concerns and, as a result, are more likely to become "corrupted" by external influences, which allow them to maintain and even increase their prestige within the community. Such was the case with the masculine and feminine versions of the *sinulog* ritual. For a discussion of the association of gender-linked symbolism with public and private spheres of relevance, see Michelle Rosaldo (1974:17–42).

2. This mode of representation is technically defined in semiotic terms as a mixed sign—an iconic-symbolic form. It establishes a meaningful relationship, in this case an iconic relationship of likeness, between the Niño and the dancer/soldier in terms of principles or rules of design. The abstract principle of unchanged upper limb asymmetry, as opposed to any more concrete likeness in specific pose or gesture of the arms, maintains the connection between divine image and human performer. Symbolic-iconic connections of this kind were seen by Charles Peirce as the intermediate stage in the transformation of an iconic relation into a fully symbolic one—one in which the principle itself, and not the resemblance created, became the meaningful element of the relationship. See Peirce (1932:2.292–2.302).

3. This idea is noted and exemplified in John Lansing's film, *The Three Worlds of Bali* (1981).

4. Edward Hall (1966:101–2, 113) has identified this sort of "microcultural" action—the actual instances when social uses of space construct organized forms—as "proxemic" patterning. In Hall's terms, this case of proxemic organization, which deals specifically with the constructs generated by individual movements, as opposed to the construction of buildings or fixtures of

some kind, would fall under the category of "informal" proxemic patterning, although it is a kind of informal patterning different from the distance patterning that Hall has documented, and that is most well known.

5. See, for example, *The Augustinian Monastery of Santo Niño de Cebu*, a tourist's pamphlet published in Cebu City, Philippines, ca. 1966, which describes the basilica stonework as having an "incipient baroque" style.

6. For an example of this dance style, see Robert Garfias's film, *Music and Dance of the Yakan Peoples of Basilan Island, the Philippines* (1969b).

7. For illustrations of northern and southern island war dances that adopt this spiraling pattern, see R. Garfias's films, *Music and Dances of the Hill People of the Northern Philippines, parts 1 and 2* (1969a), and *Music and Dance of the Yakan Peoples of Basilan Island, the Philippines* (1969b).

8. Athletics in general, and particularly baseball and track and field, played a significant role in U.S. colonization strategies throughout the U.S. occupation of the Philippines, and were recognized by colonial authorities as having made key contributions to both the spread of the English language throughout the archipelago and the increased physical size and improved health of the Filipino people (see E. Young Wead ca. 1913; see also the *17th Annual Report of the Director of Education*, 1917:35).

Exercises and calisthenics were a part of the primary public school curriculum at least as early as 1913, and physical education courses were instituted on a required basis for both primary and secondary schools by 1921, thus being well in place by Pitang Diola's time. Instruction in physical education was systematized throughout the archipelago through the use of a teacher's manual on physical education first published by the Bureau of Education in 1921. The courses were specifically designed not to emphasize specialty competitive sports such as baseball and track and field, but instead to include activities such as marching, calisthenics, dancing, impromptu games, and "group atheletics" such as pickaback relay and volleyball, in which it was believed the average pupil could "make a creditable showing." (See the *12th Annual Report of the Director of Education*, 1912:24; see also the the twentieth and twenty-first annual reports, 1920:34 and 1921:40, respectively).

By 1923, phonographic and orchestral accompaniment were included to stimulate physical education activities, and playground demonstrations, which involved simple gymnastic events of the kind used in Pitang Diola's choreography, were popular as periodic showpieces for the physical education programs (*23rd Annual Report of the Director of Education*, 1923:19).

There is no evidence to indicate that Pitang duplicated exactly any of the acrobatic movements that may have been used in physical education courses of the U.S. colonial era, and she made no mention in my interviews with her of physical education activities as being a model for her designing of the "tumbling" section. However, the similarity of this section to playground demonstrations and physical education group games would appear to indicate that these activities did exercise some indirect influence on her choreographic process.

9. Assessments of the musical forms of the *sinulog* ritual were made with the assistance of the St. Lawrence University music faculty in 1989–90, whose help I gratefully acknowledge. Aside from its Hispanic influences, it should also be noted that the underlying pentatonic structure of some of the *kantas* could also be interpreted as reminiscent of Philippine tribal music as described by Maquiso (1968:92–110). For transcriptions of *kanta* lyrics, see Ness (1987).

10. The Casa Gorordo, which by 1984 had become a museum maintained by the Ramon Aboitiz Foundation, was a nineteenth-century residence built by the family of Bishop Juan Gorordo, the first Filipino Bishop of Cebu, who served in that capacity from 1910 to 1932 (Mojares 1983:82). The Casa Gorordo was located in the city's Parian district, a sixteenth-century ghetto of Chinese merchants that became the residential district of the city's wealthiest families in the nineteenth century and that, by the 1980s, had degenerated into a heterogeneous "inner-city" area. For a detailed history of the Casa Gorordo and its urban setting, see Mojares (1983).

Chapter 10. Historical Development of the Troupe *Sinulog*

1. This masculine form of *sinulog* was practiced throughout the Visayas for saints other than the Santo Niño. Libertad Fajardo (1979:100–102), for example, has described a *sinulog* folk dance done in Iloilo that was performed by men as an act of devotion for the image of San Martin on his feast day every November 10, featuring warlike dance movement and the use of spears. Fajardo reported that the *sinulog* was done to "depict an imaginary combat to drive the evil spirits away" (1979:100), and was performed to drum accompaniment. It involved no set group formations or set step and gesture sequences.

Male improvisational war dancing has also been documented by Francisca Reyes Aquino (1983:94–95), who described a similar *sinurog* performed in Antique during weddings or religious processions. Again the function of this warlike dancing was to drive away evil spirits. Boys carried spears or daggers and were accompanied by fast, forceful drumming. Again, the dancers had no set steps or group figures that they performed in unison. In this respect, the male form of *sinulog* once performed in Cebu City for the Santo Niño was most likely one manifestation of a widespread tradition of devotional practice.

2. From a typescript by Leonard (ca. 1922).

3. The descendants of Iklot with whom I spoke were uncertain as to the date of Iklot's vow-taking and his age relative to the present generation of performers. They did not remember his full name or the date of his death. They did identify him positively as the great-grandfather of the current troupe leader, Espilita Diola. However, they had no recollection of any descendants from the generation directly following his. Tenazas (1965:86, n.15), who knew and interviewed the man my own informants claimed to be the grandson of Iklot, Buenaventura or "Turang" Diola, reported a slightly different geneology. Turang, in this text, attributed the start of the troupe *sinulog* to his own father, whose name Tenazas did not report in her publication, indicating that Iklot was only two generations removed from the troupe leader of 1984. This version was corroborated by a former member of Turang's troupe who also claimed that the troupe dancing had started in 1905. I was unable to obtain any other evidence concerning the actual starting date of the theatrical form. In any case, Tenazas indicates that Turang was born sometime between 1884 and 1893, which would have meant his father could have made the vow twenty years or more before that time, although he probably made it around the time of Turang's early childhood—the 1890s. The songs sung in the ritual also indicated that the dancing was originally choreo-

graphed in the late nineteenth century, and definitely no earlier than the 1860s.

4. Duplicating innovative fiesta practices of neighboring *barrios* and cities is a characteristic pattern of Philippine popular culture. As mentioned earlier, the Santo Niño devotion of such cities as Tacloban and Kalibo was modeled after that of Cebu City. A new event introduced into the fiesta of one community, if successful, would quickly be picked up and imitated by other communities, spreading rapidly throughout a region in this manner. The *sinulog* dance parade and contest instituted in 1981 in Cebu City, for example, was borrowed from a neighboring town, Carmen, which had borrowed it from a town on a neighboring island. By 1985 contests were being held all over the island in neighboring towns and *barrios*.

5. Mendoza, in *The Comedia (Moro-moro) Rediscovered* (1976), has described dance drama forms known as *comedias* that were popular in the nineteenth century and earlier throughout the archipelago, which staged narrative performances similar to that of the *estocada* segment of the Cebu sinulog. Mendoza (1976:79) relates that the *comedia* was closely related to the *sinulog*, as described by Aquino and Fajardo. In the town of Cuyo, for example, a *sinulog* was performed at least as early as the 1910s (during the 350th Christianization anniversary), and involved dancing with both shields and swords.

On nearby Bohol Island, Juan I. Balane (1954) has reported that dance dramas of this kind were performed in the town of Jagna during the fiest day of San Vincente Ferrer, the patron saint of Jagna. Balane, however, gives no date of origin for these performances, although he indicates that they had had a long-established history in Jagna by 1937. In Iligan, the capital of Lanao del Norte on the northern part of Mindanao, as well as in Tanjay, a town in the mountains near Dumaguete on the island of Negros, dance drama versions known as "*sinulogs*" were established traditions by 1984 (see Steven P. Fernandez 1983).

6. See Balane (1954); Fernandez (1983); Mendoza (1976); Aquino (1983); Fajardo (1979).

7. It should be noted that the actual floor patterns of the choreography performed by *Los Seizes*, as documented by Deborah Poole (1990:113) and Lynn Matluck Brooks (1988:123−32), were and are markedly different from those of the Cebu City troupe *sinulog*. Both authors report that only two columns were used in the *Los Seizes* choreography, not three. Group figures were also more complicated, featuring squares, circles, diagonally crossing lines, and indented rectangular patterning. However, the basic step pattern used by the Seville choristers described by Brooks (1988:123) was a waltz pattern performed in the baroque style that closely resembles the *sayaw* step pattern. In addition, the segmented character of the troupe *sinulog* performance, with its flexible ordering of various short figures, resembles the basic compositional format of the *Los Seizes* choreographic tradition (Poole 1990:114).

8. For a discussion of religious dancing in Europe, see E. Louis Backman (1952).

9. See Backman (1952:101, 77−85, 158−59); see also Lynn Matluck Brooks (1988:1−9, 91−122).

10. See Backman (1952:78); see also Poole (1990:110, 112) and Brooks (1988:5, 91).

11. See Backman (1952:160).

12. See Brooks (1988:115−22); see also Poole (1990:112). Iklot's reported

intent was preserved by his descendants, although broadened somewhat. The theatrical *sinulog* was still performed only on special days in 1984 and 1985: to honor the Santo Niño celebration, or sometimes San Roque's day, or on the birthday of a child in a sponsoring family.

13. See Backman (1952:86); see also Brooks (1988:115–22).

14. The chorister dance could also have been inspired by a similar form practiced in Toledo, which was also reported by Backman (1952:85) to have had such a performance. Chorister dancing was brought to Latin America as well, appearing in Peru, among other locations (see Poole 1990). It is possible that the Cebu City form was copied from an American rendition of the devotion. No sources, however, have been found to confirm such a geographic diffusion.

15. See Rafael (1988:13).

16. See Fenner (1985:80–99), for an account of Cebu City's growth in the 1840s and 1850s. Fenner notes that the sudden expansion of sugar cultivation that began on the island during the 1840s was one major change directly stimulated by Manila's becoming a world port. See also Cullinane (1982:268).

17. See Fenner (1985:106–43) for an account of the economic ramifications of the opening of the port of Cebu City to world trade. Fenner (1985:108) notes that between 1868 and 1883 Cebu City's export trade doubled in value. See also Mojares (1983:17); and Cullinane (1982:254, 271).

18. See Cullinane (1982:252).

19. See Fenner (1985:109–11), and Cullinane (1982:271).

20. See Fenner (1985:144–75) for an account of the diversification and increased complexity in social structure that occurred in Cebu City from 1860 to 1896. See also Cullinane (1989:23) in reference to the emergence of the middle sector in Cebu City.

21. See Mojares (1983:21). It should be noted, however, that, along with the increase in foreign goods, the opening of Cebu City to world trade also served to reestablish the city as an emporium for Visayan products. As Fenner notes (1985:107), sugar and tobacco from Bohol Island, rice from Panay Island, and coffee, wax, mother-of-pearl, and abaca from Mindanao Island, were all traded through the port of Cebu by the end of the 1860s.

22. For an analysis of the increasing importance of education in Philippine politics, see Cullinane (1989:35–50). Fenner (1985:160–74), however, notes that, while the interest in acquiring an education grew significantly in Cebu City from the 1860s on, the city was never a center for intellectual activity to the same extent as was Manila. Cullinane notes (1989:88) that the provincial elite of the Philippines, which included those of Cebu City, maintained their interest in Spanish culture even after the end of the Spanish colonial era. The provincial elite remained aloof to both the rebellion against Spain and the formation of the Republic. In Cebu City, in particular, Cullinane reports that established urban aristocrats and provincial elites had "found life under Spain somewhat satisfying" (1989:297). In 1896, they had supported Spain against the independence movement. In 1898, they had not supported the rebellion staged in their own city, and in 1899 they surrendered to the U.S. gunboat arriving in their harbor without firing a shot (Cullinane 1989:297–301).

Cebu's aristocracy conserved much of their European colonial lifestyle during the American era, collaborating with the new colonial power without making any real commitment to it. Cullinane (1989:223) also notes that

American officials in Cebu City adopted Spanish as a lingua franca with the local elite and used Spanish culture as a common ground for establishing rapport with local officials. The Cebu elite, for their part, maintained polite but distant relations with U.S. officers (1989:327). The popularity of an Hispanic ritual during the early years of American rule was thus by no means out of keeping with prevailing attitudes.

23. For a discussion of the growth of the Spanish community in Cebu City during the latter half of the nineteenth century, see Fenner (1985:149–58); see also Mojares (1983:20).

24. Fenner (1985:150–51) also notes that, while the Spanish community in Cebu City mixed with other ethnic groups, they nevertheless occupied a higher position in the city's society than did either the Cebuano or the Chinese factions.

25. Fenner (1985:159) states that the cultural orientation of the wealthy urban principalia of Cebu City was centered on the acquisition of European luxury goods. See also Mojares (1983:70), who gives details of the types of acquisitions purchased by wealthy Cebu City families of this era.

26. See, for example, Concepcion G. Briones (1983:79–81).

27. The ritual process described in Chapter 9 represented the troupe that was organized by Iklot's own descendants, the Diola family, who had preserved the largest collection of his choreographic forms. This was the most well-known troupe in the city, and the other troupe's renditions of the ritual that I observed presented reduced versions of this troupe's performance, using one or two segments and their drum cadences.

28. Again, the discrepancy over the generation link, the son/grandson status, should be noted. See note 3 above.

29. Cacoy Cañete maintained that the *sinulog* ritual was once actually used as a vehicle for the covert training and practice of martial artists during the Spanish colonial era, when the practice was outlawed. Senior members of the present-day Diola troupe, however, denied that the dancing was ever used toward such an end, even though *arnis* experts did belong to the adult troupe. With the membership of the troupe being limited to small boys prior to 1965, and with the probable origin of the troupe being around the turn of the century, it seems unlikely that the troupe *sinulog* ever served as a covert *arnis* training forum. It is possible, however, that individual male *sinulog* dancers appearing to improvise with drum accompaniment at the basilica may have been practicing their *arnis* skills covertly while dancing for the Santo Niño de Cebu.

30. See, for example, references in notes 1, 5, and 6 above, particularly Balane (1954) and Fernandez (1983).

31. These included chromatic alterations to melodies structured on diatonic scales in addition to the pentatonic chants. Pitang's singing style was markedly different from the Cebuano type of singing described by Maquiso (1968:103) as *pinaloray*—a common style of hymn singing that featured slurring or scooping of the melodic tones and was possibly a survival of ancient pre-Hispanic practice. Pitang's tonal placements were unslurred and deliberate, reflecting more clearly nonindigenous practices in singing style.

32. The basilica was later to reconsider repeatedly its position vis-à-vis the performance, rejecting and reaccepting its connection with the dancing as the changing social context continued to redefine its significance. The vacillations eventually rested on a return to longstanding arrangements. In 1985, a mini-

fiesta parade was organized by the basilica in which *sinulog* troupes were invited to join along with a few other selected dance groups. This parade was modeled after the 1965 reenactment of Magellan's arrival in Cebu. By inviting the troupes into the celebration, the church recognized once again that this *sinulog* was related to the church's own orthodox traditions.

33. While the support of conservative elite families was undoubtedly essential to the survival of the troupe *sinulog* ritual, the performance, nevertheless, should not be construed simply as a symbol of the most conservative elements of the urban aristocracy. What Cullinane refers to as "middle-sector" families were also regular patrons of the troupe rituals. Members of the Aliño family, for example, who were patrons of the troupe, were not only of middle-sector status, but were also aligned in the early part of the twentieth century with the more progressive, anti-Catholic faction in the society led for a time by Vicente Sotto (Cullinane, personal communication, July 1989). The cross-cutting influence of the Santo Niño image was apparent with respect to the diverse sponsorship the troupe enjoyed over the decades.

34. For an account of the post-1860 development of sugar haciendas on Cebu Island, see Fenner (1985:106–43). Fenner notes (1985:143) that, as a result of the hacienda expansion, "by the end of the Spanish period Cebu City had become more closely linked economically with the countryside than at any other time in its history." See also Cullinane (1982:272–73).

35. See Briones (1983:73–79) for descriptions of these practices in Cebuano society.

36. See Colin, *Native Races and Their Customs 1690–1691*, in Blair and Robertson (1903–1909, 40:74). See also Fenner (1985:30). Dumont (1986) has also noted that elsewhere in the Visayas, on the island of Siquijor, praying to images still takes place more often in the family home than it does in local chapels. Dumont notes that praying is conducted not in terms of individuals, but as family discourse, as contracts that bind supernatural forces to an entire household (1986:29). In this respect, the "family-style" troupe *sinulog* fit into a traditionally Visayan pattern of worship. While the *tindera sinulog* usually was oriented around the household, its practice was not observed within a given household setting, but at the basilica, and it involved a vendor who was not a member of the household.

37. Cullinane (1982:254–55) reports that the Augustinians were first granted land in the area of Banilad, north of the city, by López de Legaspi. This area contained some of the best agricultural land on the island. The Augustinian holdings expanded over the centuries until by the beginning of the nineteenth century they had two large estates consisting of more than nine thousand hectares—the largest monastic estate in the area. During the nineteenth century, the land was developed for cultivation of sugar, mainly for export, and some rice for local consumption. Aside from these holdings, the Augustinians also held property in the old Spanish city itself. Cullinane (1982:261) reports that by the 1820s the Augustinians held more than one-fourth of the lots in the city proper, much of the best urban property.

38. For an account of the conflict between the Parian parish and the Augustinians, see Cullinane (1982:251–96).

39. See Cullinane (1982:269–71).

40. See Cullinane (1982:272); see also Fenner (1985:80–143).

41. See Fenner (1985:134–43); see also Mojares (1983:21).

42. *Camarera* has been used variably in the literature on Cebuano religious

practices. Briones (1983:83) defines it as a group of elite women in the nine-teenth century that was devoted to the care and maintenance of the Santo Niño image but had been disbanded as its members passed away. Tenazas (1965) uses the term as did the informant mentioned here, as a group that had continuous membership. In either case, the term was defined as "lady in waiting," and the services performed by the group centered around the care of religious imagery.

43. The estimated size of the elite family core in Cebu City is given in Cullinane (1982:276). Cullinane (1989:29–30) notes that the interaction be-tween provincial and urban elites operated more horizontally than vertically and that, in Cebu province in particular, interaction between urban elite families and provincial ones was underscored by mutual commercial and ad-ministrative interests. Cullinane (1982:271) also notes that "symbiotic rela-tionships" were quickly established between Cebuano mestizo and Spanish merchants, who collected sugar and hemp from the Visayas and Mindanao, and foreign business houses, who handled the international export shipping. Spanish and Chinese mestizos from Manila were also developing connections with the city, as members of prominent Manila families immigrated to the city, mainly to fill posts in the bureaucracy (Cullinane 1982:277).

44. Given as cited in Cullinane (1982:276).

45. See, for example, Mojares's study of theatrical productions in Vallado-lid, Carcar (1985).

46. As regards the *zarzuela* and *comedia* troupes frequenting Cebu City, see Cullinane (1982:279); see also Mojares (1983:77).

Chapter 11. The Parade *Sinulog*

1. In this respect, the *sinulog* promotion indicated that Cebu City had en-tered what Arjun Appadurai (1990:4) has termed a "post-nostalgic" phase. The notion of "the past" was not dealt with as something over and done with, as a simple memory, but rather as something that was to have a significant impact on the city's future, as well as being made to appear as an idealized moment of the present.

2. These quotes are taken from a private communication prepared for me by the project director in 1985.

3. Zamboanga is a city on the southwestern tip of Mindanao Island (see Figure 4.1).

4. Aklan is an area on the northwestern side of the island of Panay, the social center of which is the town of Kalibo, where the *Ati-atihan* festival is held.

5. Daan Bantayan is a town on the northern tip of Cebu Island.

6. The contrasting notions of "oppositional" and "diversionary" are taken from William Kelly's analysis of the noh festival of Kurokawa, Japan (1990: 66–68). As Kelly notes, both orientations tend to mark the focus of attention—in this case the parade *sinulog*—as contrived and self-consciously traditional. The project's critics definitely evaluated the director's efforts in this light. However, as Kelly also notes, this stigmatization may not be the only outcome, and may not lead to the failure or diminution of the event itself. In the case of the *sinulog*, where numerous other motivations aside from MYSD's were

present and operating among participants, the ultimate evaluation and significance of the spectacle became more complicated.

7. See Aquino (1983, 4:1).

8. See Aquino (1983; 1946).

9. In the instructors' observations, the *tinderas* showed a general preference for backward and forward foot stepping. My own observations did not confirm this preference.

10. Again, my own observations did not confirm this impression. However, no single other spatial orientation appeared as any more characteristic than the sagittal orientation adopted by the choreographers.

11. Musical notation: ♩ ♩ ♫ ♩

12. The notion of "genuinely symbolic" is taken from C. S. Peirce's definition of the symbolic mode of representation, one that does not rely on imitation or spatio-temporal contiguity alone, but relies on rule-governed relationships in order for a semiotic process to continue. See Peirce (1932: 2.292–2.302).

13. The quoted phrases here are taken from an anonymous document, "Comparison: *Sinulog sa Sugbo* 1980 and the *Sinulog* Project ('81 & '82)" developed ca. 1982 and found in the files of The Sinulog Foundation, Cebu City, Philippines.

14. See William Kelly (1990:65–66) for an elaboration of the contrast between "having a past" and "being a past," as it is manifest in instances of public culture.

15. Personal communication from the director, March 25, 1985.

16. Jaunito V. Jabat's article, "Sootisfaction" in his regular column, "Have Bat, Will Strike" in the local Cebu City paper, *The Freeman* (January 21, 1985, 4), is one example.

17. The unsigned article "Pageantry and Color" appearing in *The Sun Star Daily* (January 21, 1985, 3[54]: 3), for example, reported, "It was bigger and better this year—and more well-organized. That was the consensus of observers and critics."

18. Both quotes appeared in Espinoza (1985:13).

Chapter 12. The Symbolism of Desired Recognition

1. For more illustrations see, Fernando Zobel de Ayala (1963).

2. This label appears in descriptions of the bas-reliefs of the Basilica Minore del Santo Niño. See *The Augustinian Monastery of Santo Niño de Cebu* (ca. 1966:21).

3. Creating the illusion of local control and regional integrity by diminishing the representation of translocal and transnational influences is a process Arjun Appadurai (1990:16) has termed "production fetishism." The locality becomes a fetish disguising the larger forces driving it. The authenticated symbolism of the *sinulog* choreography can be seen as one manifestation of this process.

4. The Higaonon are an ethnic group living along the narrow coastal strip of northern Mindanao Island.

5. "Manobo" is a general name for some of the highland swidden farming peoples surrounding the Davao Gulf of Mindanao Island, the majority of whom are Islamic.

6. In 1985, 11,000 pesos was the rough equivalent of U.S. $600.

7. Appadurai argues with respect to global cultural processes that imagined and imaginary phenomena have become critically important to social practice as forms of "negotiation between sites of agency" ('individuals') and globally defined fields of possibility" (1990:5). Moreover, Appadurai claims that "imagined worlds" may be constructed by personal agents that "are able to contest and subvert the imagined worlds of the official mind and of the entrepreneurial mentality that surround them" (1990:7). The *sinulog* promotion case study generally supports these arguments. The social work of the promotion was certainly directed toward generating the constructed landscapes of various imaginations, personal, entrepreneurial, and, on several levels, official. However, the *sinulog* case study also shows that the dynamic of resistance made visible in such instances of public culture might not manifest itself simply as one of the personal against the official/entreprenurial, as Appadurai suggests. The imagined worlds of personal agents made visible in the *sinulog* parade choreography, in contrast, reveal personal agents mediating between the efforts of entreprenural and official interests that appear to undermine one another. In addition, the main manifestation of contesting interests was made apparent with respect to the play of sub-civic, contingent loyalties.

8. "Late capitalism" refers in Mandel's scheme to a third stage or period of capitalism that follows that of imperialism and is characterized by multinational capital. In "late capitalism," an ideology of consumerism eliminates all enclaves of precapitalist organization, penetrating even to the realm of the unconscious in its subjects via its control over an ever more influential global media and advertising industry. Jameson associates the "late capitalist" period with the emergence of postmodernism in art and architecture (1984:77–78). The parade *sinulog* choreography also may be interpreted in part as a postmodern expression of a multinational capitalist system, exhibiting such defining characteristics of the postmodern as obsessive nostalgia, depthlessness, and particularly the representation of fragmented subjects.

9. The notion of "crosstalk" is taken from Kelly (1990:65–81), who uses it with reference to his analysis of the noh festival of Kurokawa, a small village in northern Japan. As a prominent heritage spectacle, Kelly argues that the Kurokawa noh festival is a production of "public culture" that is capable of transposing, transmitting, or interrogating various cultural registers or spheres vis-à-vis one another. In the case of the Kurokawa noh festival, the spheres included those of a national culture of the state, a mass culture of the media, a metropolitan culture of greater Tokyo, and subordinate regional cultures—a set of registers, in other words, basically similar to some of those transposed by the *sinulog* project.

Chapter 13. The Resilience of the *Sinulog*

1. The term "substitute," used here to identify the representational nature of the *tindera sinulog*, has a specific technical definition in semiotic theory, developed in the unpublished work of Phil Huston (1988), that is instructive for clarifying the precise character of the movement symbolism inherent in the *tindera* choreography. Expanding from the trichotomy of "image, diagram, and metaphor" given by Peirce (1932:2.277; henceforth all references

to the *Collected Papers* will refer simply to volume and paragraph number) for iconic signs, an analogous trichotomy can be constructed for symbolic signs, generating three categories of signs that may be termed "substitute," "metonym," and "allusion."

The symbolic trichotomy of substitute, metonym, and allusion follows the same logic employed by Peirce at the iconic level of identifying "modes of being" (2.276) vis-à-vis the representamen (agent of signification)/object valency. A "mode of being" can be understood in terms of its character of existence or "secondness" (defined roughly as "elseness"), which, Huston argues, becomes the definitive aspect generating the sign trichotomy. That is to say, the distinction between the three types, "image," "diagram," and "metaphor," may be conceptualized in terms of the degree to which the representamen differentiates itself from that which it represents (i.e., its object). In the first case, with the example of the "image," the representamen signifies its object in an undifferentiated, "monadic," unreflexive, totally self-evident, unintentional way. The image operates sheerly by inherent qualities of identity that overwhelm whatever interpretive agent participates in the relation. The nature of an image is such that until an interpretive agent is formed, which implicitly recognizes a representamen-object relation, no other recognition of the difference between the two would be imaginable. An example would be a cloud appearing accidentally in the exact form of an elephant. The representamen-object relation of the image can be considered one of "degenerate secondness" in the sense that no evidence of difference is present in the representamen to mark the "elseness" of it as an agent of signification for what it signifies. In contrast, the "diagram," or second category of iconic sign, preserves and makes apparent differences between the representamen and its object even while constructing a relationship of likeness or resemblance to the object. A diagram (2.277, 2.282) also constructs a relationship of similarity to its object, but by exhibiting relationships between the parts of its own representative agent that are analogous or identical to the part-to-part relations of the object it represents. The diagram, unlike the image, exhibits a "dyadic" relation of "elseness" to its object that Huston argues may be considered "genuine secondness" in that the essential difference between the representamen and the object is recognizable as inherent in the actuality of the representamen itself and is not a characteristic imposed upon it by some subsequent interpretive agent or mind. An example of a diagram would be a blueprint made of paper and ink whose contrastive ink-to-paper relations (i.e., line drawings) depict the internal structure of the various parts of the Statue of Liberty. In addition to the "degenerate secondness" and "genuine secondness" classes of representamen-object relations, Huston has proposed a third class of "pseudo" representamen-object relations, to which the "metaphor" iconic type belongs. At the "pseudo" level (which may also be typed as that of "degenerate thirdness"), the representamen-object relation makes evident the "elseness" of the representamen in relation to the object as not only actual but intentional and "constructional," meaning that the logic of the design of the signifying agent itself—as it has been rendered so as to represent its object while at the same time meant to be "other" than its object—is evident in the representamen-object relation (2.277).

To return to the case of the *tindera* as a substitute, symbolic signs may be distinguished from iconic signs by virtue of their achieving a relation of representation, not by means of likeness or resemblance (as is the case with iconic signs), but by means of the consistent, habitual employment of some rule of sign recognition (2.292–2.302). This rule may be entirely arbitrary, as is the case with most linguistic signs. However, it may involve the habitual recognition of nonarbitrary relations as well (hence symbolic relations are possible in nonlinguistic semiotic processes whenever "tradition," "custom," or some conventional, time-honored practice of recognition is employed to interpret the semiotic process at issue). While the nature of the signification process is thus different at the symbolic level from that operating at the iconic level, symbolic signs, like iconic signs, do involve representamen-object relations as well. The same trichotomy used to understand representamen-object relations at the iconic level, therefore, can be equally instructive at the symbolic level.

According to Huston's 1988 extended classification scheme, then, a substitute would be the term for the initial or, more strictly speaking, "degenerate second" form of symbol, which occupies the same position at the symbolic level occupied by the image sign form at the iconic level. As a degenerate second symbol, a substitute is the sort of symbol that accomplishes representation (in this case, the *tindera* representing a devotee customer) without evidencing any significant distinction between the representamen (the *tindera*) and its object (the devotee). That is to say, a substitute replaces its object via a rule, or habit, or customary act of recognition, yet without qualifying itself as anything other than a replacement, as a "blank" sign of sorts. The absence of interest in the *tinderas'* capacity to develop *sinulogs* that would highlight their own virtuosity as performers, an orientation to performance that itself maintained for lack of other concerns the common values on "natural" body movement patterns as the main influence on the choreographic style of the practice, was intrinsically related to the substitutional nature of the *tindera sinulog*. The dance was a vehicle of specifically undifferentiating customer representation.

2. As mentioned in note 1, the term "iconic" here is used as defined by C. S. Peirce (2.275) to identify a type of representation that effects a relationship of similarity or likeness between its signifying agent or "representamen" (in this case the choreography of the troupe *sinulog*), and its object, or that which it represents (in this case the realms of conflict and worship represented in these *comedia*- and *Los Seizes*-derived practices). In Peirce's semiotic theory, "iconic" signs (also called "hypoicons") are contrasted with "indexical" signs (see 2.283–2.291), which effect representation via relationships of shared existence or spatio-temporal continuity, and "symbolic" signs, which effect representation via relationships of rule recognition, which may be arbitrarily formulated (see 2.230, 2.274–2.302).

The term "diagrammatic" (see note 1) specifies that the troupe *sinulog* choreography achieved an iconic relationship of likeness to the various movement realms it represented, not by accident or self-evident qualities of identity, but via the construction and "re-placement" in an identical manner of key distinctive features or "parts" of these realms, such as linearity, "solemnity," and spiraling three-dimensionality. These key features were made visible or reconstructed through the coordinated use of the individual parts or members of the troupe *sinulog*—its array of human bodies in movement.

3. The term "indexical" is used here as defined by C. S. Peirce (2.283–2.291; see notes 1 and 2 above). Indexical signs effect a relationship of shared existence or spatio-temporal contiguity between the signifying agent, or re-

presentamen, and its object. The parade *sinulog* may be further specified as a "genuine" as opposed to "degenerate" index (2.283), given that it was composed of nothing other than the individuals themselves who in part constituted the larger organizations represented. In this regard, each of the *sinulog* practices achieved a fundamentally different form of semiosis via its choreographic process with the troupe practice being basically iconic, the parade practice basically indexical, and the *tindera* practice basically symbolic.

4. See Bateson (1972:453).

5. Of the three forms, the troupe *sinulog* was the least extreme in this regard. The articles in the troupe *sinulog* were sometimes used as weapons, which magnified the movement capabilities of the dancers, particularly in the improvised duel scene between the characters of Magellan and Lapulapu. In this scene, the figures of the performers themselves emerged as the masters of their instruments. However, even in the troupe *sinulog*, the predominant use of the material symbols was not as weapons but as instruments of display. As instruments of display, the swords and shields of the troupe *sinulog* dancers performed the same function as did the material symbols of the other *sinulog* forms, diverting the attention of the audience away from the dance of the performers and maintaining the attention on the dance of the hand-held symbols.

6. See S. J. Tambiah (1979:113–69, especially 165).

7. See Tambiah (1979:165).

8. In 1987, for example, Ethel Soliven Timbol in the "Pacesetters" column of the *Manila Bulletin* described the parade *sinulog* as a dance in which "pretty maidens . . . swing images of the little king high in the air" (January 23, 1987, 36). The Santo Niño image was thus used as the archetypal material symbol for parade dancing.

9. For extended discussions of the nature of rites of modernization, see James Peacock (1968:6–10, 239–56).

References

Adams, Kathleen
1987 "Image and Identity: Reconceptualizations of Torajan Carvings in the Context of Change." Paper delivered in a session entitled *Myth and Reality in Asian Dance, Drama, and Imagery*, held at the Association for Asian Studies meetings in Boston, Mass.
1988 "Carving a New Identity: Ethnic and Artistic Change in Tana Toraja, Indonesia." Ph.D. diss., University of Washington, Seattle.
1991 "Touristic Pilgrimages, Identity and Nation-Building in Indonesia." Paper presented in a session entitled *Tourism and Pilgrimage: Case Studies from Asia*, held at the Association for Asian Studies meetings in New Orleans, La.
Alburo, Erlinda K., ed.
1977 *Cebuano Folktales*. 2 Vols. Cebu City: San Carlos Publications.
Allen, Catherine J.
1988 *The Hold Life Has: Coca and Cultural Identity in an Andean Community*. Washington, D.C.: Smithsonian Institution Press.
Appadurai, Arjun
1990 "Disjuncture and Difference in the Global Cultural Economy." *Public Culture* 2 (2): 1–24.
Aquino, Francisca Reyes
1946 *Filipino National Dances*. Manila: Silver Burdett Co.
1983 *Philippine Folk Dances*. 6 vols. Manila: Francisca Reyes Aquino.
Arens, Richard
1958 "Social Scientists Point the Way to Religious Acculturation and Accommodation." *Philippine Sociological Review* 6: 14–18.
Ashihara, Hidesato
1980 *The Japanese Dance*. New York: Arno Press.
The Augustinian Monastery of Santo Niño de Cebu
ca. 1966 Pamphlet. Cebu City, Philippines: n.p.
Bachelard, Gaston
1969 [1958] *The Poetics of Space*. Boston: Beacon Press.
Backman, E. Louis
1952 *Religious Dances in the Christian Church and in Popular Medicine*. Trans. E. Classen. London: George Allen and Unwin.

Balane, Juan I.
1954   "The Fiestas of the Coastal Towns of Southern Bohol: An Evaluation of Their Socio-Educational Significance." Master's thesis, University of San Carlos.

Bandem, I Made, and Fredik Eugene deBoer
1981   *Kaja and Kelod: Balinese Dance in Transition.* Kuala Lumpur: Oxford University Press.

Barthes, Roland
1972   *Mythologies.* Trans. Annette Lavers. New York: Hill and Wang.
1974   *S/Z.* Trans. Richard Miller. New York: Hill and Wang.
1975   *The Pleasure of the Text.* Trans. Richard Miller. New York: Hill and Wang.
1977   *Barthes by Barthes.* Trans. Richard Howard. New York: Hill and Wang.
1978   *Elements of Semiology.* Trans. Annette Lavers and Colin Smith. New York: Hill and Wang.
1978   *Image, Music, Text.* Trans. Stephen Heath. New York: Hill and Wang.

Bateson, Gregory
1972   *Steps to an Ecology of Mind: A Revolutionary Approach to Man's Understanding Himself.* New York: Ballantine Books.

Bateson, Gregory, and Margaret Mead
1942   *Balinese Character: A Photographic Analysis.* New York: New York Academy of Sciences.

Baudrillard, Jean
1990 [1979]   *Seduction.* New York: St. Martin's Press.

Belo, Jane, ed.
1970   *Traditional Balinese Culture.* New York: Columbia University Press.

Benedict, Laura
1916   "A Study of Bagobo Ceremonial." *Annals of the New York Academy of Sciences* 25:1–308.

Benthal, J., and T. Polhemus, eds.
1975   *The Body as a Medium of Expression.* New York: E. P. Dutton and Co.

Beyer, Otley
1947   "Outline Review of Philippine Archaeology by Islands and Provinces." *The Philippine Journal of Science* 77 (3, 4): 205–374.

Birdwhistell, Ray
1970   *Kinesics and Context: Essays on Body Motion Communication.* Philadelphia: University of Pennsylvania Press.

Blair, Emma, and James Robertson, eds. and trans.
1903–1909   *The Philippine Islands, 1493–1898.* 55 vols. Cleveland, Ohio: A. H. Clark and Co.

Boas, Franz
1944   "Dance and Music in the Life of the Northwest Coast Indians of North America." In *The Function of Dance in Human Society*, ed. Franziska Boas, 5–19. New York: Dance Horizons.

Bostrom, Lynn C.
1968   "Filipino Bahala Na and American Fatalism." *Silliman Journal* 15 (3): 399–413.

Bourdieu, Pierre
1977   *Outline of a Theory of Practice.* Trans. Richard Nice. Cambridge: Cambridge University Press.

Bowers, Faubion
1956 *Theatre in the East: A Survey of Asian Dance and Drama.* London: Thomas Nelson and Sons.
Briones, Concepcion G.
1983 *Life in Old Parian.* Cebu City: Cebuano Studies Center, University of San Carlos.
Brooks, Lynn Matluck
1988 *The Dances of the Processions of Seville in Spain's Golden Age.* Kassel: Edition Reichenberger.
Bulatao, J.
1965 "The Santo Nino of Cebu." *Catholic Digest,* April 4, 1965, 28–38. [Volume unknown; issue found in the files of the Cebuano Studies Center, University of San Carlos, Cebu City, Philippines.]
Buruma, Ian
1989 *God's Dust: A Modern Asian Journey.* New York: Farrar, Straus, Giroux.
Cebu Commercial Guide 1972–1973
1973 Cebu City, Philippines: E. Johansson.
Cesar, Lorenzo
1966 "The Santo Nino of Tacloban in History, Legend and Devotion of the People." *Leyte-Samar Studies* 1:1–14.
Clifford, James
1988 *The Predicament of Culture; Twentieth-Century Ethnography, Literature, and Art.* Cambridge, Mass.: Harvard University Press.
"Comparison: *Sinulog sa Sugbo* 1980 and the *Sinulog* Project ('81 & '82)"
ca. 1982 Unsigned typescript found in the files of The Sinulog Foundation, Cebu City, Philippines.
Constitutions and By-Laws of the Cofradia Del Santo Niño de Cebu (National Level)
ca. 1965 Unsigned pamphlet. Cebu City, Philippines: Cebu Star Press.
Cowan, Jane K.
1990 *Dance and the Body Politic in Northern Greece.* Princeton: Princeton University Press.
Cullinane, Michael
1982 "The Changing Nature of the Cebu Urban Elite in the 19th Century." In *Philippine Social History: Global Trade and Local Transformations,* ed. A. W. McCoy and E. C. de Jesus, 251–96. Manila: Ateneo de Manila Press.
1989 "*Illustrado* Politics: The Response of the Filipino Educated Elite to American Colonial Rule, 1898–1907." Ph.D. diss., University of Michigan.
Daniel, Ana
1981 *Bali Behind the Mask.* New York: Alfred A. Knopf.
Daniel, E. V.
1984 *Fluid Signs: Being a Person the Tamil Way.* Berkeley: University of California Press.
de Ayala, Fernando Zobel
1963 *Philippine Religious Imagery.* Manila: Ateneo de Manila Press.
de Certeau, Michel
1984 *The Practice of Everyday Life.* Trans. Steven F. Rendall. Berkeley: University of California Press.

de Kleen, Tyra
  1970 *Mudras: The Ritual Hand-Poses of the Buddha Priests and the Shiva Priests of Bali.* New York: University Books.
de la Calzada, Manuel Enriquez
  1965 *Legends of Santo Niño de Cebu.* Cebu City, Philippines: Manuel Enriquez de la Calzada and Martin Abellana.
de la Torre, Visitacion R.
  1980 "Five Men Who Dote on the Child." *Philippine Panorama,* January 27, 1980 , 13–15.
Demetrio, Francisco
  1968 "The Engkanto Belief: An Essay in Interpretation." *Philippine Sociological Review* 16 : 136–43.
  1970 *Dictionary of Philippine Folk Beliefs and Customs.* 4 vols. Cagayan de Oro City, Philippines: Xavier University.
Derrida, Jacques
  1973 "Differance." In *On Speech and Phenomena and Other Essays on Husserl's Theory of Signs,* 129–60. Evanston, Ill.: Northwestern University Press.
de Ribadeneira, Marcelo, O.F.M.,
  1970 *Historia del archipelago y otros reynos.* Manila: Historical Conservation Society.
de Santa Inés, P. Francisco
  1892 [1676] *Crónica de la Provincia de San Gregorio Magno de Religiosos Descalzados de N. S. P. San Fransisco en Islas Filipinas, China, Japón, etc.* Vol. 2. Manila: Chofre.
Director of Education
  1912 *12th Annual Report of the Director of Education.* Manila: Bureau of Printing. Found in Central Classified Files, Record Group 350, Bureau of Insular Affairs, U.S. National Archives.
  1917 *17th Annual Report of the Director of Education.* Manila: Bureau of Printing. Found in Central Classified Files, Record Group 350, Bureau of Insular Affairs, U.S. National Archives.
  1920 *20th Annual Report of the Director of Education.* Manila: Bureau of Printing. Found in Central Classified Files, Record Group 350, Bureau of Insular Affairs, U.S. National Archives.
  1921 *21st Annual Report of the Director of Education.* Manila: Bureau of Printing. Found in Central Classified Files, Record Group 350, Bureau of Insular Affairs, U.S. National Archives.
  1923 *23rd Annual Report of the Director of Education.* Manila: Bureau of Printing. Found in Central Classified Files, Record Group 350, Bureau of Insular Affairs, U.S. National Archives.
Douglas, Mary
  1973 *Natural Symbols.* New York: Penguin Books.
  1979 [1966] *Purity and Danger: An Analysis of the Concepts of Pollution and Taboo.* London: Routledge and Kegan Paul.
Dumont, Jean-Paul
  1978 *The Headman and I: Ambiguity and Ambivalence in the Fieldworking Experience.* Austin: University of Texas Press.
  1986 "Praying in the Barangay: The Indigenization of Christianity in a Visayan Community." Paper presented at the conference on Indigenization of Christianity in Southeast Asia, Cebu City, Philippines, September, 1986.

Elwood, Douglas
    1971   "Popular Filipino Concepts of Christ." *Silliman Journal* 18 (2): 154–63.
Elwood, D., and P. Magdamo
    1971   *Christ in Philippine Context.* Quezon City, Philippines: New Day Publishers.
Espinoza, Fred C.
    1985   "1 M turn out for Sinulog." *The Sun Star Daily* 3 (54): 1, 13. January 21, 1985.
Estabaya, D. M.
    1965   "The Story of the Santo Niño." *Post,* 1–5. [Issue unknown, document found in the files of the Cebuano Studies Center, Univesity of San Carlos, Cebu City, Philippines.]
Fajardo, Libertad
    1979   *Visayan Folk Dances.* Vol. 1. Manila: n.p.
Falar, Jaime
    1965   "The Big Event 410 Years Ago Today." *The Freeman,* April 25, 1965. [Issue found in the files of the Cebuano Studies Center, University of San Carlos, Cebu City, Philippines.]
Feld, Stephen
    1982   *Sound and Sentiment.* Philadelphia: University of Pennsylvania Press.
Fenner, Bruce L.
    1985   *Cebu under the Spanish Flag, 1521–1896: An Economic-Social History.* Cebu City, Philippines: San Carlos Publications.
Fernandez, James
    1977   "The Performance of Ritual Metaphors." In *The Social Use of Metaphor,* ed. J. David Sapir and J. Christopher Crocker, 101–31. Philadelphia: University of Pennsylvania Press.
Fernandez, Steven P.
    1983   *The San Miguel Fiesta: Rituals of Iligan City: A Study of Form, Function and Value.* Ed. Luis Lacar and Gabino T. Puno. Cagayan de Oro City, Philippines: Coordination Center for Research and Development, Mindanao State University/Iligan Institute of Technology.
Foster, Susan Leigh
    1986   *Reading Dancing: Bodies and Subjects in Contemporary American Dance.* Berkeley: University of California Press.
Foucault, Michel
    1963   *Naissance de la clinique: Une archéaologie du regard medicale.* Paris: Presses Universitaires de France.
    1973 [1966]   *The Order of Things: An Archaeology of the Human Sciences.* New York: Vintage Books.
    1975   *The Birth of the Clinic.* New York: Random House.
    1978   *The History of Sexuality.* Vol. 1, *An Introduction.* New York: Random House.
    1979   *Discipline and Punish: The Birth of the Prison.* Trans. Alan Sheridan. New York: Random House.
Garfias, Robert
    1969a   *Music and Dances of the Hill People of the Northern Philippines, Parts 1 and 2.* Ethnic Music and Dance Series. Robert Garfias and Harold Schultz, film-makers. Produced and distributed by the University of Washington Press, Seattle, Wash. Videotape.
    1969b   *Music and Dance of the Yakan Peoples of Basilan Island, the Philippines.*

Ethnic Music and Dance Series. Robert Garfias and Harold Schultz, film-makers. Produced and distributed by the University of Washington Press, Seattle, Wash. Videotape.

Geertz, Clifford
1973 *The Interpretation of Cultures.* New York: Basic Books.

Ginsburg, Norton S.
1955 "The Great City in South-East Asia." *American Journal of Sociology* 60:455–62.

Go, Fe Susan
1976 "An Annotated Translation of the 1935 History of Cebu." Master's thesis, University of San Carlos.

Goffman, E.
1956 *The Presentation of Self in Everyday Life.* Edinburgh: University of Edinburgh Social Research Centre.

Hackney, Peggy
1988 "Moving Wisdom: The Role of the Body in Learning." *Context* 18: 26–29.

Hall, Edward T.
1959 *The Silent Language.* Garden City, N. Y.: Doubleday and Co.
1966 *The Hidden Dimension.* Garden City, N. Y.: Doubleday and Co.

Hanna, Judith Lynne
1979 *To Dance is Human: A Theory of Nonverbal Communication.* Austin: University of Texas Press.
1983 *The Performer-Audience Connection: Emotion to Metaphor in Dance and Society.* Austin: University of Texas Press.
1988 *Dance, Sex and Gender: Signs of Identity, Dominance, Defiance, and Desire.* Chicago: University of Chicago Press.

Hart, Donn V.
1966 "The Filipino Villager and His Spirits." *Solidarity* 1 (4): 65–71.

Haskins, Jim, ed.
1982 *The Filipino Nation.* Danbury, Conn.: Grolier International. 3 vols: vol. 1, *A Concise History of the Philippines* by Helen R. Tubangui, Leslie E. Bauzon, Marcelino A. Foronda, Jr., and Luz U. Ausejo; vol. 2, *The Philippines: Lands and Peoples, a Cultural Geography* by Eric S. Casino; vol. 3, *Philippine Art and Literature* by Felipe M. de Leon, Jr.

Hislop, Stephen K.
1971 "Anitism: A Survey of Religious Beliefs Native to the Philippines." *Asian Studies* 9 (2): 144–56.

Hollensteiner, Mary R.
1973 "Reciprocity in the Lowland Philippines." In *Four Readings on Philippine Values.* Manila: Ateneo de Manila University Press, IPC Papers no. 2.

Holt, Claire
1939 *Dance Quest in Celebes.* Paris: Les Archives International de la Danse.

Holt, Claire, and Gregory Bateson
1970 "Form and Function of the Dance in Bali." In *Traditional Balinese Culture,* ed. Jane Belo, 322–30. New York: Columbia University Press.

Huston, Phil
1988 The Papers of Phil Huston. [Unpublished notes in the author's possession, Department of Dance, University of California–Riverside, Riverside, Calif.]

Hutterer, Karl
1973 *An Archaeological Picture of a Pre-Spanish Cebuano Community.* Cebu City, Philippines: San Carlos Publications.

Ileto, Reynaldo
1979 *Pasyon and Revolution: Popular Movements in the Philippines, 1840– 1910.* Quezon City, Philippines: Ateneo de Manila University Press.

Jabat, Jaunito, V.
1985 "Sootisfaction." *The Freeman,* January 21, 1985, 4.

Jablonko, Alison
1968 "Dance and Daily Activities among the Maring People of New Guinea: A Cinematographic Analysis of Body Movement Style." Ph.D. diss., Columbia University.
1968 *Maring in Motion.* University of Washington Extension Media Services. 16mm film.

Jameson, Fredric
1983 "Postmodernism and Consumer Society." In *The Anti-Aesthetic: Essays on Postmodern Culture,* ed. Hal Foster. Port Townsend, Wash.: Bay Press.
1984 "Postmodernism, or the Cultural Logic of Late Capitalism." *New Left Review* 146:53–92.

Joaquin, Nick
1981 "The Sinulog in Philippine Culture." Press materials available from Cebu City Ministry of Public Information, Region 7. Photocopy.

Jocano, F. Lande
1965 "Conversion and the Patterning of Christian Experience in Malitbog, Central Panay, Philippines." *Philippine Sociological Review* 13: 96–119.
1967 "Filipino Catholicism: A Case Study in Religious Change." *Asian Studies* 5 (1): 42–64.
1968 "Notes on Philippine Divinities." *Asian Studies* 6 (2): 169–82.
1969 *Growing up in a Philippine Barrio.* New York: Holt, Rinehart and Winston.
1975 *Philippine Prehistory.* Manila: Community Publishers.
1981 *Folk Christianity: A Preliminary Study of Conversion and Patterning of Christian Experience in the Philippines.* Quezon City, Philippines: Trinity Research Institute.

Kaeppler, Adrienne
1978a "Dance in Anthropological Perspective." *Annual Review of Anthropology* 7:31–49.
1978b "Melody, Drone, and Decoration: Underlying Structures and Surface Manifestations in Tongan Art and Society." In *Art and Society,* ed. M. Greenhalgh and V. Megaw, 261–75. London: Duckworth.

Kelly, William
1990 "Japanese No-Noh: The Crosstalk of Public Culture in a Rural Festivity." *Public Culture* 2 (2): 65–81.

Keyes, Charles F.
1977 *The Golden Peninsula: Culture and Adaptation in Mainland Southeast Asia.* New York: Macmillan Publishing Co.

Korean National Commission for UNESCO
1983 *Korean Dance, Theatre and Cinema.* Korea: Si-sayong-o-sa Publishers.

Labrada, Ben
  1985 "Ati-atihan is not for Cebuanos." *The Freeman*, January 9, 1985, 5, 10. [Issue is incorrectly dated 1984.]
Langer, Suzanne K.
  1959 [1942] *Philosophy in a New Key: A Study in the Symbolism of Reason, Rite, and Art.* New York: New American Library.
Lansing, John
  1981 *The Three Worlds of Bali.* Odyssey Series. Watertown, Mass.: Documentary Educational Resources. Videotape.
Leach, Jerry
  1976 *Trobriand Cricket: An Ingenious Response to Colonialism.* Gary Kildea, film-maker. Produced by the Office of Information, Government of Papua New Guinea. Distributed by University of California Extension Media Center, Berkeley, Cal. Videotape.
Leitz, Paul S., trans.
  1960 *The Muñoz Text of Alcina's History of the Bisayan Islands (1668).* 4 vols. Chicago: Department of Anthropology, University of Chicago.
Leonard, Irving A.
  ca. 1922 The Papers of Irving Albert Leonard. Michigan Historical Collections, Bentley Library, University of Michigan, Ann Arbor. Typescript.
Lévi-Strauss, Claude
  1963 *Structural Anthropology.* New York: Basic Books.
  1966 *The Savage Mind.* Chicago: University of Chicago Press.
Lieban, Richard
  1962 "The Dangerous Ingkantos: Illness and Social Control in a Philippine Community." *American Anthropologist* 64:306–12.
Loken, Christine J.
  1983 "Moving in the Korean Way." In *Korean Dance, Theatre, and Cinema*, 72–80. Korea: Korean Commission for UNESCO, International Communication Foundation.
Lomax, Alan, and Forrestine Paulay
  1974 *Dance and Human History.* Movement Style and Culture Series no. 1. Produced by Alan Lomax. Distributed by University of California Extension Media Center, Berkeley, Cal. Videotape.
Lynch, Frank
  1984 "Folk Catholicism in the Philippines." In *Philippine Society and the Individual: Selected Essays of Frank Lynch, 1949–1976*, ed. Aram A. Yengoyan and Perla Q. Makil, 197–207. Michigan Papers on South and Southeast Asia no. 24. Ann Arbor: University of Michigan Center for South and Southeast Asian Studies.
Madale, Nagasura T.
  1984 "Pilandok Tales." Paper presented to the Fifth Philippine Folklore Congress, Cebu City, Philippines, Nov. 9–11, 1984.
Maquiso, Elena G.
  1968 "Characteristics of Indigenous Filipino Music." *Silliman Journal* 15 (1): 92–110.
McPhee, Colin
  1970 "Dance in Bali." In *Traditional Balinese Culture*, ed. Jane Belo, 290–321. New York: Columbia University Press.

Mead, Margaret
  1942 "Introduction." In *Balinese Character: A Photographic Analysis*, by Gregory Bateson and Margaret Mead, 1–48. New York: New York Academy of Sciences.
  1952 *Trance and Dance in Bali.* New York: New York University. 16mm film.
Mendoza, Felicidad M.
  1976 *The Comedia (Moro-moro) Rediscovered.* Manila: Society of St. Paul.
Mendoza, Helen
  1985 Untitled paper presented at the First National Philippine Studies Conference, Quezon City, Philippines, February 11, 1985.
Mercado, Leonardo N.
  1976 *Elements of Filipino Philosophy.* Tacloban City, Philippines: Divine Word University Publications.
Mercado, Lourdes S.
  1965 *Cebu Through the Centuries.* Cebu City, Philippines: Cebu Star Press.
Mojares, Resil B.
  1981 The Feast of the Child: A Popular Guide to the Santo Nino Festival in Cebu. [Manuscript on file at the Cebuano Studies Center, Cebu City, Philippines.]
  1983 *Casa Gorordo in Cebu: Urban Residence in a Philippine Province 1860–1920.* Cebu City: Ramon Aboitiz Foundation.
  1985 *Theatre in Society, Society in Theatre: Social History of a Cebuano Village, 1840–1940.* Quezon City, Philippines: Ateneo de Manila University Press.
Morrison, Mirriam J.
  1977 "Women's Dance and Tradition in Jogjakarta." In *Asian and Pacific Dance: Selected Papers from the 1974 CORD-SEM Conference*, ed. A. Kaeppler, J. Van Zile, and C. Wolz. Dance Research Annual 8. New York: Committee on Research in Dance.
Murphy, Robert F.
  1987 *The Body Silent.* New York: Henry Holt and Co.
National Census and Statistics Office
  1985 *1980 Census of Agriculture*, vols. 1, 3. Manila: National Census and Statistics Office.
National Economic and Development Authority
  1981 *Philippines 1980: Population, Land Area, and Density, 1970, 1975, and 1980.* Manila: National Economic and Development Authority, National Census and Statistics Office, Republic of the Philippines.
Natividad, Mateo C.
  1979 "An Ethnology of Ingkantos: Filipino Folk Catholicism." Master's thesis, Northern Illinois University.
Nemec, L.
  1958 *The Infant of Prague.* New York: Benziger Brothers.
Ness, Sally A.
  1985 "The Tinderas of Opon and Cebu: Exploring Relationships between Dance Style and Social Organization." *Philippine Quarterly of Culture and Society* 13:71–84.
  1987 "The *Sinulog* Dancing of Cebu City, Philippines; a Semeiotic Analysis." Ph.D. diss., University of Washington.

1990 "The Latent Meaning of a Dance: The Cebuano Sinulog as a Model of Social Interaction." In *Communication and Culture: Language, Performance, Technology, and Media. Selected Proceedings from the Sixth International Conference on Culture and Communication, Temple University, 1986*, ed. Sari Thomas and William A. Evans, 128–133. Communication and Information Science, vol. 4, series ed. Melvin J. Voigt. Norwood, N.J.: Ablex Publishing Corporation.

Novack, Cynthia J.
1988 "Looking at Movement as Culture; Contact Improvisation as Culture." *The Drama Review* T120: 102–19.
1990 *Sharing the Dance; Contact Improvisation and American Culture.* Madison: University of Wisconsin Press.

Office of the Governor, Provincial Government of Cebu
1976 *Five-Year Integrated Development Plan of Cebu.* Cebu City, Philippines: Office of the Governor.

Ortiz, Tomás
1731 *Práctica del ministerio que siguen los religiosos del orden de N. S. Augustín en Filipinas.* Manila: Convento de Nuestra Senora de los Angeles.

Ottenberg, Simon
1982 "Illusion, Communication, and Psychology in West African Masquerades." *Ethos* 10 (2): 149–85.

"Pageantry and Color"
1985 Unsigned article published in *The Sun Star Daily* 3 (54): 3. January 21, 1985.

Peacock, James
1968 *Rites of Modernization: Symbolic and Social Aspects of Indonesian Proletarian Drama.* Chicago: University of Chicago Press.

Peirce, Charles S.
1932 *The Collected Papers of Charles Sanders Peirce.* Ed. C. Hartshorne and P. Weiss, vols. 1–6. Cambridge, Mass: Harvard University Press.

Perpetual Novena to Santo Nino de Cebu
1960 Pamphlet. Cebu City, Philippines: Augustinian Fathers.

Phelan, John
1959 *The Hispanization of the Philippines: Spanish Aims and Filipino Responses 1565–1700.* Madison: University of Wisconsin Press.

Polhemus, T.
1975 "Social Bodies." In *The Body as a Medium of Expression*, ed. J. Benthal and T. Polhemus, 13–35. New York: E. P. Dutton and Co.

Polotan, Kerima
1974 "A Very Personal Basilica." *Focus Philippines*, January 19, 1974, 55.

Poole, Deborah A.
1990 "Accommodation and Resistance in Andean Ritual Dance." *The Drama Review* 34 (2): 98–126.

Port of Cebu: Handbook and Directory of Cebu Philippine Islands
1928 Cebu City, Philippines: Cebu Chamber of Commerce.

Quimat, Lisa
1955 "Devotion to the Child Jesus." *Southern Star*, January 16, 1955, Women's Page. [Issue found in the files of the Cebuano Studies Center, University of San Carlos, Cebu City, Philippines.]

Radcliffe-Brown, A. R.
1948 *The Andaman Islanders.* Glencoe, Ill.: Free Press.

Rafael, Vicente L.
1988   *Contracting Colonialism: Translation and Christian Conversion in Tagalog Society under Early Spanish Rule.* Ithaca, N.Y.: Cornell University Press.

Rappaport, Roy
1979   *The Obvious Aspects of Ritual: Ecology, Meaning and Ritual.* Berkeley: University of California Press.

Rawson, Philip
1975   "The Body in Tantra." In *The Body as a Medium of Expression,* ed. J. Benthal and T. Polhemus, 271–90. New York: E. P. Dutton and Co.

Richards, Audrey
1956   *Chisungu.* London: Faber and Faber.

Rosaldo, Michelle Z.
1974   "Woman, Culture, and Society: A Theoretical Overview." In *Woman, Culture, and Society,* 17–42. Stanford, Cal.: Stanford University Press.
1980   *Knowledge and Passion: Ilongot Notions of Self and Social Life.* Cambridge: Cambridge University Press.

Rosaldo, Renato
1988   "Ideology, Place, and People without Culture." *Cultural Anthropology* 3 (1): 77–87.

Royce, Anya Peterson
1980 [1977]   *The Anthropology of Dance.* Bloomington: Indiana University Press.

Sacerdoti, Guy
1984   "No Will, No Way." *Far Eastern Economic Review* 126 (40): 84, 86. October 10, 1984.

Sacks, Oliver
1989   *Seeing Voices: A Journey into the World of the Deaf.* Berkeley: University of California Press.

Sam, Chan Moly
1987   *Khmer Court Dance: A Comprehensive Study of Movements, Gestures and Postures as Applied Techniques.* Ed. Diana Schnitt. Newington, Conn.: Khmer Studies Institute.

Satorre, Manuel
1985   "Manuel Satorre." *The Sun Star Daily,* 3 (55): 4, January 22, 1985.

Scarry, Elaine
1985   *The Body in Pain: The Making and Unmaking of the World.* Oxford: Oxford University Press.

Scheflen, Albert E.
1982   "Preface: Comments on the Significance of Interaction Rhythms." In *Interaction Rhythms: Periodicity in Communicative Behavior,* ed. Martha Davis. New York: Human Sciences Press.

Schieffelin, Edward
1976   *The Sorrow of the Lonely and the Burning of the Dancers.* New York: St. Martin's Press.

Scott, James C.
1986   *Weapons of the Weak: Everyday Forms of Peasant Resistance.* New Haven, Conn.: Yale University Press.

Scott, William Henry
1968   *A Critical Study of the Prehistoric Source Materials for the Study of Philippine History.* Manila: University of Santo Tomas Press.

Singer, Milton
  1980 "Signs of the Self: An Exploration in Semiotic Anthropology." *American Anthropologist* 82 (3): 485–507.
Sinulog '85 Souvenir Program
  1985 Cebu City, Philippines: Our Press, Inc.
Soedarsono
  1976 "Classical Javanese Dance: History and Characterization." In *Dance in Africa, Asia, and the Pacific: Selected Readings*, ed. J.Van Zile, 27–35. New York: MSS Information Corporation.
Spencer, Paul
  1985 "Introduction: Interpretations of the Dance in Anthropology." In *Society and the Dance: The Social Anthropology of Process and Performance*, ed. Paul Spencer, 1–46. Cambridge: Cambridge University Press.
Spies, Walter, and Beryl de Zoete
  1973 [1938] *Dance and Drama in Bali*. London: Faber and Faber.
Stoller, Paul
  1989 *The Taste of Ethnographic Things: The Senses in Anthropology*. Philadelphia: University of Pennsylvania Press.
Strauss, Gloria B.
  1975 "The Art of the Sleeve in Chinese Dance." *Dance Perspectives* 16 (63): 1–47.
Tambiah, Stanley J.
  1979 "A Performative Approach to Ritual." *Proceedings of the British Academy* 65:113–69.
Tenazas, Rosa C. P.
  1965 *The Santo Niño of Cebu*. Manila: Catholic Trade School.
Tenazas, Rosa, and Karl Hutterer
  1968 "Preliminary Report on the Salvage Excavation Project in Cebu City." In *Dr. H. Otley Beyer, Dean of Philippine Anthropology: A Commemorative Issue*, ed. Rudolf Rahmann and Gertrude R. Ang. Cebu City, Philippines: University of San Carlos.
Timbol, Ethel Soliven
  1987 "Pacesetters." *Manila Bulletin*, January 23, 1987, 36.
Todd, Mabel E.
  1937 *The Thinking Body: A Study of the Balancing Forces of Dynamic Man*. New York: Dance Horizons.
Turner, Victor
  1967 *The Forest of Symbols*. Ithaca, N.Y.: Cornell University Press.
  1969 *The Ritual Process: Structure and Anti-Structure*. Chicago: Aldine.
  1974 *Dramas, Fields, and Metaphors: Symbolic Action in Human Society*. Ithaca, N.Y.: Cornell University Press.
  1977 "Variations on a Theme of Liminality." In *Secular Ritual*, ed. Sally F. Moore and Barbara G. Myerhoff. Amsterdam: Van Gorcum.
Van de Meer, Canute
  1967 "Population Patterns on the Island of Cebu, the Philippines 1500–1900." *Annals of the Association of American Geographers* 57 (2): 315–38.
van Gennep, Arnold
  1960 *The Rites of Passage*. London: Routledge & Kegan Paul.
Villote, Ben, J., Fr.
  1980 "Lest We Forget Our Spiritual Encounter with the Grown-up Christ,

The Sto. Niño is a Flashback to Jesus' Life." *Philippine Panorama*, January 27, 1980, 11.

Visayas Human Development Agency
  1983 *The Cebu Labor Situationer: Base to Societal Change.* Cebu City, Philippines: Visayas Human Development Agency.
  1987 *A Study of Urban Poor Dwellers, Their Attitudes and Responses to Government Initiated Development Programs: The Case of Four Selected Communities in Cebu City.* Cebu City, Philippines: Visayas Human Development Agency.

Volkman, Toby A.
  1990 "Visions and Revisions: Toraja Culture and the Tourist Gaze." *American Ethnologist* 17 (1): 91–110.

Wead, E. Young
  ca. 1913 "The Training of a People; What the United States Has Done for Education in the Philippines." N.p. [Found in File 3725–50, Record Group 350, Bureau of Insular Affairs, U.S. National Archives.]

Wernstedt, Frederick L., and J. E. Spencer
  1978 *The Philippine Island World: A Physical, Cultural, and Regional Geography.* Berkeley: University of California Press.

Wolf, Eric
  1958 "The Virgin of Guadalupe: Mexican National Symbol." *Journal of American Folklore* 71:34–39.

Wolz, Carl
  1977 "The Spirit of Zen in Noh Dance." In *Asian and Pacific Dance: Selected Papers from the 1974 CORD-SEM Conference*, ed. A. Kaeppler, J. Van Zile, and C. Wolz, 55–64. Dance Research Annual 8. New York: Committee on Research in Dance.

Index

Adams, Kathleen, 250, 253
agipo myth, 76, 78
Alcina, J., 33, 40, 255, 259
anito spirits, 74, 252
Appadurai, Arjun, 267–69
Aquino, Corazon (Cory), 21
Aquino, Francisca Reyes, 186–87, 262–63, 268
arnis, 13–15, 112, 155; as used in troupe *sinulog*, 162–63, 265; initiation in, 121; repetition in, 52
Ati-atihan, 24, 185, 194, 196–97, 267
atonement, at-one-ment, 11–12, 240
Augustinian Order, 42, 62, 165, 169–71, 195, 197, 200; Augustinian priests in Cebuano mythology, 69; Augustinian school, 249; landholdings of, 266
authenticity: of culture, 27, 230; of parade *sinulog*, 186–91, 193–98, 207, 212–13, 215; of *tindera sinulog*, 89–90, 129–31, 155, 187; of troupe *sinulog*, 188

Bachelard, Gaston, 247
bahala na, 51
Bahugbahug sa Mactan, 184
Barthes, Roland, 236
Basilica Minore del Santo Niño, 24, 27, 44, 46, 64–66, 155, 166, 249–50, 268
Bateson, Gregory, 129, 221, 239, 253, 272
Baudrillard, Jean, 241
Benitez, Consuelo, 79–83, 89, 94, 98, 102, 115–16, 224
Boas, Franz, 12, 239; and Franziska Boas, 237–38
body, 5; as a culture bearer, 7; as a figure

of expression, 12; as a fluid entity, 40; as a microcosm, 129, 260; body's weight center in *tindera sinulog* dancing, 114–15; fragmentation of the body in parade *sinulog*, 181, 206, 216; "having a body," 6; ideas of the body in Western thought, 236–38; of Santo Niño, 60; use of the body in troupe *sinulog*, 220
Bohol Island, 263–64
bounce: in Cebuano dance, 139; in *tindera sinulog*, 114–15, 117–18, 130; *kiat* bouncing, 114, 120. *See also* Resilience
Bourdieu, Pierre, 91, 118, 236–37, 255, 257
Bulatao, J., 72
Buruma, Ian, 216, 247

camarera, 61, 171–72, 266–67
Cañete, Cacoy, 13–15, 52, 65, 163, 265
Casa Gorordo, 153, 262; Gorordo family, 168
Catholicism: conversion to in the Philippines, 71, 256; folk, 76, 99, 106, 133, 147, 251–52, 256; Roman, 27, 64, 81, 85, 96, 174, 208–9; Roman Catholic Church, 73, 100, 106, 167, 249; Roman Catholic universities, 242; Spanish, 158–59, 220
Cebu City: as a primate city, 28; as a temple city, 27, 242; basketball in, 124; Cebu Reclamation Project, 38; chess games in Cebu City, 51; endings, 51–52; heat, 39–40; Jesuits, 42; music, 49–50; port facilities, 30–31; puns used in, 54; Recollects, 42; surfaces of, 43–47; sun's effect on, 39–40; urban planning, 36–38, 42, 246; values re-

Cebu City (*continued*)
lated to skin, 44–45; values related to temporality, 49–55; values related to water, 36, 40–41

Cebu Island: erosion on, 39; rain patterns on, 39

Cebuano, Cebuano-ness, 207, 216; Cebuanos, 230, 265; community, 215; culture, 25, 182–84; dance, 54–55, 179; greetings, 41; identity, 55, 78, 89, 130, 183, 197–98, 200, 209; language, 26, 55, 80, 83, 125, 145, 152, 237; region, 210; singing, 265; society, 256; style, 87, 90, 139, 179, 211; Studies Center, 242, 248

Chinese, 26–27, 36, 65; faith of, 42; mestizo elite on Cebu, 170, 251, 265, 267; trade in Cebu, 243

"chopping hands" dance, 7–10

choreography: as a spatial occurrence, 12–15; choreographers of parade *sinulog*, 208–14; choreographic experience, 12; choreographic figures, 3–7, 12; choreographic inquiry, 7; choreographic phenomena, 2–4, 232–33, 235–41; choreographic tradition/style of *sinulog*, 186, 222–24; in parade *sinulog*, 181, 186–98, 200, 204, 206–18, 220, 227–30; in *tindera sinulog*, 97, 101, 106, 109, 118, 127, 186, 220; in troupe *sinulog*, 132–53, 158, 166–67, 172, 174, 186, 220; performing choreographed movement, 1–17

Cofradia del Santo Niño, 65, 183, 249

Colon Street, 42, 231

comedia, 158–59, 263, 267, 271

commercial crops of Cebu, 30, 244; success in late nineteenth-century Cebu, 160

commercialism: in the parade *sinulog*, 182, 185–86, 192–93, 195, 206–8, 213, 217–18; in the *tindera sinulog*, 89, 102, 104, 106

communitas, 66

contest, of parade *sinulog*, 192–98, 209, 263

crosstalk, 217, 269

Cullinane, Michael, 161, 242, 245, 247, 251, 264, 266–67

culture, 10, 12, 16, 25, 31, 38, 161–62, 182–83, 191, 200, 217–19, 231, 241;

cultural dispossession, 216–17; cultural field, 3; cultural phenomena, 25, 79, 195–98, 200, 206–8, 218, 224, 227, 229–33, 239; cultural predicament, 2, 182, 219, 231–33, 235, 238, 240; cultural transformation, 5; cultural understanding, 2; culture bearers, 2, 3, 5, 7, 24, 91, 99, 102, 106, 163, 199, 233; culture bearing, 3, 31; culture brokering, 217; culture contact, 175; culture shock, 6; "cultured," 29; "high" culture, 25, 27; "local" culture, 27, 197; "low" culture, 26; "other" cultures (*see* Other), "no culture," 25–26, 182; physical culture, 240; popular culture, 240, 263; public culture, 216–17

Daan Bantayan, 185, 267

dance, 1–3, 5, 89, 141, 235, 239, 241; as a human act, 233; as imaginary reservoir, 10; as microcosm, 129; *binasuan* (drinking glass), 187; Cebuano style of, 54–55; dancers in parade *sinulog*, 214–16; Philippine folk, 186–88; stigmatized aspects of, 2; versus sport, 7–8; war dancing in *sinulog*, 155, 158; women's dances of Asia, 257–59

Daniel, E. V., 174, 240–41

Davao, 28, 30, 244

de Certeau, Michel, 236, 240

Demetrio, Francisco, 251–53

Derrida, Jacques, 63, 249

Diola: Buenaventura "Turang," 162–64, 168, 262; Espilita "Pitang," 163–68, 172–73, 175, 228, 261–62, 265; family, 167, 174, 265; Iklot, 157–63, 168, 174, 262–65

diwata, 74, 253

Douglas, Mary, 129, 236, 239, 254, 259

Dumont, Jean-Paul, 240–41, 255–56, 266

duplication, 43, 47–55

elevación, 134–41, 146–47, 153, 158

Elwood, Douglas, 58, 247

Enrile, Juan Ponce, 194

estocada, 134, 145–51, 153, 158, 163, 166

ethnography, 232–33; as an act of performance, 10–12; dance ethnography, 186–87; ethnographic experience,

240; ethnographic inquiry, 7, 230, 237–39, 241; ethnographic inter-action, 3; ethnographic method, 12; ethnographic mode, 19; ethnographic voice, 241; interpretive ethnography, 241

Europeanization, 160–61, 168

Evans, Bill, 3

exotic, 2–3, 5, 42, 51, 235; exoticism, 231

Fajardo, Libertad, 262–63

Falar, Jaime, 68

Fenner, Bruce J., 242–43, 245–46, 248, 252–53, 256, 259, 264–66

fieldwork, 10, 22–23, 25

fiesta: customs of, 45, 65, 124, 153; endings of, 51, 60; for Santo Niño de Cebu, 66–67, 89, 104, 155–56, 159, 171, 172, 183, 200, 227–28, 249; functions of in nineteenth century, 169

figure, figurative expression, 10; figuring out, 6; of action, 3; of choreography, 2–7, 12; of Los Seizes, 263; of performers in troupe *sinulog*, 272; of Santo Niño, 76, 82; of thought, 3; plastic figure of mind, 6; spatial figures in *sinulog*, 126–33, 136–39, 146–51, 180, 193, 201–6, 210–11, 215

Forbes, William Cameron, 245

formal movement: in *tindera sinulog*, 114–15, 120; in troupe *sinulog*, 143, 165

Fort San Pedro, 36, 42, 245

Foster, Susan Leigh, 235–36, 239

Foucault, Michel, 23, 236, 242

Frias, Antolin, 172

Geertz, Clifford, 116, 230, 233, 241, 255

gesture, 4, 7, 9, 15, 51, 200; in Southeast Asian dance, 257–58; of Santo Niño, 60; use of in parade *sinulog*, 179–81, 189–90, 211–13, 215–16; use of in *tindera sinulog*, 87, 111, 115, 120–21, 126, 155; use of in troupe *sinulog*, 140–43, 147

Gonzales, Rosa, 19, 44–46, 65, 68, 80–81, 108–9

Graham, Martha, 5

guests: in Cebuano society, 45; guest-host relationships, 127–29, 172–73, 259. *See also* Host/hostessing behavior guidelines of parade *sinulog*, 192–98

habitus, 10, 91, 118–19, 225, 232

Hackney, Peggy, 235–36

halad, 92, 130

Hall, Edward T., 236, 260–61

Hanna, Judith Lynne, 235–36, 241, 259

hierarchy, in troupe *sinulog*, 144, 171, 173–74

Hislop, Stephen K., 251–53

host/hostessing behavior of *tinderas*, 101, 127–29; hosting of troupe *sinulog*, 169, 173

hubo, 60, 65, 171–72

Humabon (Cebuano leader), 62, 70, 73, 139, 141

Huston, Phil, 269–71

"I," as a cultural construct, 3–7

Iklot. *See* Diola

Ileto, Reynaldo, 254

Iloilo City, 47, 262

imagination, 4, 6, 217, 269

improvisation: in Cebu City, 31; in *sinulog*, 2, 156; in *tindera sinulog*, 95–96; in troupe *sinulog*, 163

Infant of Prague, 62–63, 248

ingkantos (engkantu) spirits, 252–53

initiation, 51; in Asian dance, 257–59; in *tindera sinulog*, 119–22

Jameson, Fredric, 217, 238–39, 269

jeepneys: drivers' devotional practices, 80; movement, 42; ornamentation, 44; space inside, 47; strikes, 21

Jocano, F. Lande, 252–53

Juan Dyong, 73–74, 251

Juan Pusong, 75, 253

kantas, 152–53, 158, 164–65, 261

Katipunan, 78, 254

Kelly, William, 267–69

kiaykiay, 115, 222

Langer, Suzanne, 260

Laon, 74, 252

Lapulapu, 62, 139, 141, 145, 148, 151, 161, 166–67, 180, 272

Leonard, Irving A., 155–56, 262

Lévi-Strauss, Claude, 71, 230–31, 247, 249, 251
Leyte Island, 67, 184
localization, 25; of the Santo Niño, 71–79, 254
López de Legaspi, Miguel, 41–42, 62, 65, 68, 72, 76, 90, 180, 191, 245, 248, 266
Los Seizes, 158–59, 263–64, 271
Luzon Island, 79
Lynch, Frank, 253, 256

Mactan Island, 28, 62, 100, 184, 191, 222, 242; Mactan Export Processing Zone, 28; Virgen sa Regle, image of, 67
Magellan, Ferdinand, 42, 62, 72, 78, 90, 139, 141, 144–45, 148, 151, 161, 166–67, 180, 184, 266, 272; Magellan's Cross, 42, 69, 79, 191, 250
Malay: cosmology, 75; rituals, 255
Mandel, Ernst, 217, 269
Manila, 20, 22, 28–30, 36, 47, 67, 70, 80, 111, 160, 172, 181, 243–45, 256, 264, 267
manipulation: in *arnis*, 15; in parade *sinulog*, 179, 183; in *sinulog* style, 222–24; in *tindera sinulog*, 119, 122–26, 130; in troupe *sinulog*, 138; of Santo Niño, 227–30
Manobo steps, in *sinulog*, 209, 268
Marcos, Ferdinand, 21, 184; regime of, 20, 184–85
Marcos, Imelda, 194, 249
marginal: culture, 198, 218, 231; situation of *tinderas*, 97, 102, 107; vantage point of dancing, 3
Mead, Margaret, 239, 253
meaning: in choreography, 1–17; in *tindera sinulog* movement, 117–19; of *sinulog* practices, 220–25; of troupe *sinulog* for Cebuano families, 167–74
memory, 4, 14; dance as a form of, 7–10; re-membering, 5, 6
Mercado, Leonardo, 247, 252
Mercado, Lourdes S., 247
Mindanao Island, 26, 28, 30, 110–11, 158, 185, 190, 208, 210, 263–64, 267–68
miniature, 47, 223, 231, 247, 249; Santo Niño as, 59–62, 85, 228–29

Ministry of Youth and Sports Development (MYSD), 183–86, 190–91, 193, 207, 267
Misud, 208–12, 214, 216
mixmix, 26–27, 81–82
Mojares, Resil B., 84, 169, 242, 247–49, 251, 253, 255, 262, 264–67
movement, 1, 4, 241; daily patterns of in Cebu City, 42–57, 231; in Santo Niño, 64; "movement world," 41–55, 150–51; of parade *sinulog*, 180, 186–91, 194, 206, 213–14, 220; of *tindera sinulog*, 87, 94–96; of troupe *sinulog*, 138, 150; phrasing, 7; symbolism, 241; symbols of parade *sinulog*, 227–30; symbols of *tindera sinulog*, 91, 96, 101, 117–31, 269–70; symbols of troupe *sinulog*, 172
Muslim, 208–9; elements of parade *sinulog*, 179, 210–11

nationalism: in troupe *sinulog*, 133, 144, 165, 167–68, 170; in parade *sinulog*, 198, 206–8; nationalist sentiments, 23
Natividad, Mateo C., 251, 253
"natural": interpretations of dance, 236–37, 239; movement in collective ritual *sinulog*, 155–56, 162; movement in *sinulog* tradition, 223; movement in *tindera sinulog*, 114–15, 155, 180, 271; movement in troupe *sinulog*, 132
Negros Island, 24
neocolonial, 2, 29–30, 217, 231
nono spirits, 74, 253
Novack, Cynthia, 235–36, 239–40
novena, 112–13, 169, 200; for Santo Niño, 66–67, 77, 249–50, 253–54

Osmeña family, 168, 245
"ossified" status of *sinulog*, 226
"other": culture(s), 2–3, 7, 32, 238; people, 230; othering in Santo Niño, 64, 76; otherness in manipulation, 124; otherness in physical movement, 231

pagampo, 92, 130
pagtukod sa espada, 134, 144, 153, 158
panaad, 92–94
Panay Island, 24, 47, 67, 194, 264, 267

Parian district of Cebu City, 36, 170, 251, 262
paso segment of *sinulog*, 134–41, 146, 153, 158
Peacock, James, 230, 241, 255, 272
Peirce, Charles S., 260, 268–72
performance, in parade guidelines, 193, 196; performative aspect of *sinulog*, 226; performers' orientation, 16, 241; performers' view of *tindera sinulog*, 101–16; performing choreography (*see* Choreography); performing ethnography, 10–12
peripheral spatial tension, 118, 126–31
Phelan, John, 249, 252
Philippines, the, 1, 3, 8, 15, 30, 54, 86, 110, 175, 207, 212, 216, 237, 242, 248–49, 256; aesthetic traditions, 138–39; American teachers, 39; churches, 201; cities, 185; devotion of the Holy Child, 62–63, 77, 254; galleon trade, 245; hawking styles, 53; nationalist imagery, 144; politics, 264; quadracentennial of Christianity, 165–67; rainfall, 246; rebellion, 161; religious centers, 67; religious conversion, 72; spirits, 253; worship of saints, 74; war dances, 145, 261–62
Pigafetta, Antonio, 62, 248, 252, 255–56
pilgrims: in parade *sinulog*, 210; to Santo Niño, 66, 89, 94, 228
Pina, 99–100, 105, 113
Pit Señor, 146, 152, 168
plurality, 43, 47–55
Polotan, Kerima, 65, 249
postcultural, 29, 31
postmodern, 29, 91, 231–33, 238, 269
posture, 4–5, of Santo Niño, 60, 248; posturing in *tindera sinulog*, 96; posturing in troupe *sinulog*, 134–36, 140, 147
prayer: as a *kargo*, 113; as "loosening," 113–14; for Santo Niño, 66–68, 81–85, 249; in Cebuano family homes, 169; in Katipunan, 254; in *tindera sinulog*, 92, 97, 102, 115–16, 220; in Visayan communities, 255–56, 266; of *elevación*, 134, 139–40, 152
Presidential Security Guard, 185
production fetishism, 268; "produce," 241; "product-ive," 200; productivity,

231; products of choreography, 13; unproductive activity, 2
proxemics, 260–61

Radcliffe-Brown, A. R., 239, 259
Rafael, Vincente, 159, 242, 249, 252–54, 256, 259, 264
Ramos, Fidel, 21
rapport, symbolism of, 12–15
reduplication, 55, 179
resilience, 2, 219; in Cebuano dance, 54; in Cebuano language, 53–55; in parade *sinulog* choreography, 180, 216, 218; in *sinulog* style, 222–24; in *tindera sinulog* dancing, 87, 90, 115, 119, 130; in troupe *sinulog* choreography, 144; resilient phrasing in movement, 247
revival, of *sinulog*, 183–86, 189, 192, 196, 219, 225–27
ritual, cycles of oscillation and renewal, 226–27; process in the *tindera sinulog*, 89–90, 92–97, 100, 225; process in the troupe *sinulog*, 132, 225, 228; rite of modernization, 230; women's dance rituals of Asia, 257–58
Rizal, José, 41
Rosaldo, Elizabeth, 23–24, 26, 229
Rosaldo, Michelle, 236, 241, 260
Rosaldo, Renato, 29, 242
Rosales, Rene, 211–14
Royce, Anya P., 239

Sacks, Oliver, 240
saints, 59, 251, 262; "saint-centered" devotion, 74–75, 79; *santos*, 204, 252
Sales, Felix, 67, 78
San Carlos University, 23, 45, 242
San Nicolas, 36, 99
Santo Niño: de Cebu, 1, 9, 25, 27, 57, 58–85, 87, 91–96, 100, 104, 109, 115, 117–18, 127, 129–31, 155, 224, 247, 256, 265; Church (*see* Basilica Minore del Santo Niño); Hymn, 77–78, 253–54; manipulation of in parade *sinulog*, 227–30, 272; of Tacloban, 67; of San Nicolas, 99, 256
satanes, 118
Satorre, Manuel, 197
sayaw, 134, 141–44, 151, 153, 158, 165, 263
Schick, Pam, 12

Scott, James, 256
Scott, William Henry, 243
self: as a social construct, 5–7, 56–57, 98, 192; self-carriage, 134; self-conduct, 7, 10; self-image, 227, 247; self-removal, 240; self-sacrifice, 165
semiotic, 219, 260, 268–72; firstness, secondness, and thirdness in semiotic theory, 240, 270
sigue principle, 125–26, 138
sinakulo, 79, 254
Sinulog Foundation, 194
Spain, 27, 29, 31, 71, 78–79, 158–59, 161–62, 248, 264–65
Spencer, Paul, 239
"spineless" behavior, 46, 247
Stoller, Paul, 3, 239–40, 242
Sugbo (Cebu), 33, 40; *Sinulog sa*, 183–86, 191–92
suki relationships, 105
Sulu Archipelago, 210
surfaces: of basilica in *tindera sinulog* dancing, 97; of Cebu City, 43–47; of the Santo Niño, 60–62
symbolism, 2, 230, 237; different forms of, in *sinulog*, 219–25; dominant symbols, 58, 85; iconic, 84, 220, 260, 271–72; in parade *sinulog*, 177, 180, 183, 186, 190, 192, 200–218; in *tindera sinulog*, 90, 95, 101, 106–7, 267; in troupe *sinulog*, 133–37, 157, 162, 167, 171–72, 174–75; indexical, 220, 271–72; latent, in *tindera sinulog*, 118, 121; movement symbolism in choreographic phenomena, 241, 260; multivocal (polysemic), 55, 118, 121–22, 219, 222; of antiquity, 90; of candles in *tindera sinulog*, 95; of death, 19; of rapport, 12–15; of Santo Niño, 60–61, 64, 79–85, 227–30; symbolic action, 4, 120, 231, 260; symbolic mode of representation, 268, 270–72

Tacloban City, 67, 263
Tambiah, Stanley, 226, 239, 272
tautau, 67, 250
Tenazas, Rosa, 243, 247–51, 253, 262, 267
tinampilan, 134, 144–45, 148, 153, 158
tourism, as a factor in *sinulog* dancing, 24, 181–82, 185, 195, 230
tumbling, 134, 151–53, 261
Turner, Victor, 58, 66, 249, 254, 257

United States, 2–3, 8, 13, 28, 31, 239; walking behavior in, 45–46, 121

Vargas, Eloisa, 83
Ver, Fabian, 21
Virgin of Guadalupe, in Mexico, 78, 254
Visayan: Christians in *sinulog*, 166; elements of parade *sinulog*, 178, 191; language, 26, 77–78, 83, 139, 141, 152, 237, 256; religious beliefs, 251, 254–55, 266; society, 245, 259, 264
Visayas, 21, 26, 74, 158, 208, 253, 262, 266–67

"ways of operating," 10, 240
Western, 32, 76, 217, 236, 238; dance, 3; Westerner(s), 23–24, 29, 98; Westernized, 99, 207; Western-oriented, 193; Western-style, 26, 138

Zamboanga, 185, 267

LIBRARY, UNIVERSITY OF CHESTER

University of Pennsylvania Press
SERIES IN CONTEMPORARY ETHNOGRAPHY

Dan Rose and Paul Stoller, General Editors

Camille Bacon-Smith. *Enterprising Women: Television Fandom and the Creation of Popular Myth.* 1991
John D. Dorst. *The Written Suburb: An American Site, An Ethnographic Dilemma.* 1989
Douglas E. Foley. *Learning Capitalist Culture: Deep in the Heart of Tejas.* 1990
Kirin Narayan. *Storytellers, Saints, and Scoundrels: Folk Narrative in Hindu Religious Teaching.* 1989
Sally Ann Ness. *Body, Movement, and Culture: Kinesthetic and Visual Symbolism in a Philippine Community.* 1992
Dan Rose. *Patterns of American Culture: Ethnography and Estrangement.* 1989
Paul Stoller. *The Taste of Ethnographic Things: The Senses in Anthropology.* 1989
Edith Turner, with William Blodgett, Singleton Kahona, and Fideli Benwa. *Experiencing Ritual: A New Interpretation of African Healing.* 1992
Jim Wafer. *The Taste of Blood: Spirit Possession in Brazilian Candomblé.* 1991

This book was set in Baskerville and Eras typefaces. Baskerville was designed by John Baskerville at his private press in Birmingham, England, in the eighteenth century. The first typeface to depart from oldstyle typeface design, Baskerville has more variation between thick and thin strokes. In an effort to insure that the thick and thin strokes of his typeface reproduced well on paper, John Baskerville developed the first wove paper, the surface of which was much smoother than the laid paper of the time. The development of wove paper was partly responsible for the introduction of typefaces classified as modern, which have even more contrast between thick and thin strokes.

Eras was designed in 1969 by Studio Hollenstein in Paris for the Wagner Typefoundry. A contemporary script-like version of a sans-serif typeface, the letters of Eras have a monotone stroke and are slightly inclined.

Printed on acid-free paper.